CHINESE LA

廖莲

Related Titles Published by The Chinese University Press

Business Chinese
《商業漢語》
By Jiaying Howard and Tsengtseng Chang 莊稼嬰、張增增 合著 (2005)

Gateway to Chinese Language
《漢語入門》
By Jing Heng Sheng Ma 馬盛靜恆 著 (2005)

Business Chinese: An Advanced Reader
《商貿漢語高級讀本》
By Songren Cui 崔頌人 著 (2004)

Talk Mandarin Today
《今日學說普通話》
By Hong Xiao 肖紅 著 (2003)

Zhongda Chinese-English Dictionary
《中大漢英詞典》
Edited by Liang Derun and Zheng Jiande 梁德潤、鄭建德 主編 (2003)

Kung Fu (Elementary Putonghua Text)
《功夫》
Edited by John C. Jamieson and Tao Lin
簡慕善、林濤 主編 (2002)

A Student Handbook for Chinese Function Words
《漢語虛詞學習手冊》
By Jiaying Howard 莊稼嬰 著 (2002)

A Learners' Handbook of Modern Chinese Written Expression
《現代漢語書面語學習手冊》
By Yu Feng 馮禹 著 (2000)

Chinese-English Dictionary
《漢英小字典》
Edited by Chik Hon Man and Ng Lam Sim Yuk
植漢民、吳林嬋玉 合編
(1994 second edition)

A Practical Chinese Grammar
By Samuel Hung-nin Cheung,
in collaboration with Sze-yun Liu and Li-lin Shih (1994)

Fifty Patterns of Modern Chinese
By Dezhi Han (1993)

漢語與文化讀本
Chinese Language and Culture
An Intermediate Reader

黃偉嘉、敖群 合著

By Weijia Huang and Qun Ao

The Chinese University Press

Chinese Language and Culture: An Intermediate Reader
  By Weijia Huang and Qun Ao

© **The Chinese University of Hong Kong**, 2002

All rights reserved. No part of this publication may
be reproduced or transmitted in any form or by any
means, electronic or mechanical, including photocopying,
recording, or any information storage and retrieval
system, without permission in writing from
The Chinese University of Hong Kong.

ISBN: 978–962–996–006–3

First edition	2002
Second printing	2004
Third printing	2007
Fourth printing	2008
Fifth printing	2010

THE CHINESE UNIVERSITY PRESS
The Chinese University of Hong Kong
SHATIN, N.T., HONG KONG
Fax: +852 2603 6692
   +852 2603 7355
E-mail: cup@cuhk.edu.hk
Web-site: www.chineseupress.com

Printed in Hong Kong

目 錄
Contents

重印版序言
Preface to the Second Printing vii

序
Preface xi

詞類簡稱表
Abbreviations of Parts of Speech xvii

1. 中文難不難？
   Is Chinese Difficult to Learn? 1

2. 漢字介紹
   Introduction to Chinese Characters 19

3. 長城
   The Great Wall 39

4. 中國的名稱
   How Names for China and the Chinese Have Changed 57

5. 婚姻介紹
   Matchmaking 75

6. 麻煩的同音字
   The Trouble with Homophones 91

7. 在中國上大學
   Going to College in China 109

8. 計劃生育和人權
   Birth Control and Human Rights 127

9. 繁體字和簡體字
   Complex Characters and Simplified Characters 147

10. 一字多義的問題
    Words with More Than One Meaning 167

11. 中國年和壓歲錢
    Chinese New Year and New Year Money 185

12. 中國的情人節
    Chinese Valentine's Day 205
13. 婦女能頂半邊天
    "Women Can Hold Up Half the Sky" 225
14. 家家有老人
    Every Family Has Its Elderly Members 243
15. 節日的食品
    Special Foods for Festivals and Holidays 263
16. 到中國旅遊
    Touring Around China 285
17. 神話故事
    Myths and Folklore 307
18. 成語的來源
    The Origins of Chinese Proverbs 325
19. 顏色的含義
    The Implications of Colors 343
20. 吃虧是福、難得糊塗
    "To Suffer Losses Is Good" and "Ignorance Is Bliss" 365
21. 中國人信仰的宗教
    Religious Beliefs in China 387
22. 長江三峽
    The Three Gorges of the Yangtze River 405

詞彙索引
Vocabulary Index 425

語法和詞語註釋索引
Grammar and Terms Index 463

主要參考書目
References 469

重印版序言

《漢語與文化讀本》2002年11月出版，現在要重印了。重印前我們做了一些修訂，主要是改正了錯別字。個別難解和容易誤解的詞語、幾處解釋得不夠明確的語法詞語註釋以及意思不夠清晰的英譯語句，我們也都加以改寫、訂正。

《漢語與文化讀本》能夠在這麼短的時間內重印和修訂，要感謝許多使用這本教材的老師，並且感謝他們把在使用中發現的錯誤及時地告訴給我們。特別是俄克拉何馬大學的桂明超老師，他從使用這本教材開始，每隔一段時間就把發現的問題以及修改的建議整理好寄給我們，一直到最後一課。哈佛大學的李冬梅老師，她在批改學生作業時，從學生的錯誤中發現了課本中幾個需要改進的地方，也都及時地告訴了我們。

哈佛大學的黃蕭惠媛老師用《漢語與文化讀本》教有中文背景的學生；馮禹老師用它來教暑期班沒有中文背景的學生。兩位老師不僅給了我們很多很好的建議，而且在學期末組織老師學生與我們座談，幫助我們瞭解教材使用的情況和老師學生對教材的意見。黃蕭惠媛老師、紐約州水牛城大學的呂雪虹老師以及其他使用本書的老師，還為本書做了大量的各種類型的練習。

我們很慶幸能得到這麼多學識淵博、治學嚴謹的老師的幫助；我們很欽佩他們這種認真的態度和無私的精神，在這裏我們向各位老師表示真摯的謝忱！我們還要感謝熱心推薦這本教材的紐約大學的何文潮老師和呂雪虹老師，感謝許多正在使用和即將使用這本書的老師。

這本書出版一年多了，我們從與老師學生的座談中、從學生的評價表裏得知，學生們非常喜歡這種以講解"漢語與文化"為主的教材。他們覺得這樣的課文很有用處，也很有意思。他們說在學習漢語的同時學到了許多真實的中國文化知識，而這些文化知識又進一步促動了他們學習語言的興趣。老師們說，因為課文有意思，學生有興趣，所以在教學中學生主動性高，參與性強，課堂活潑。老師們還說，由於課文的長度和難度、語法點和生詞量，都是嚴格地隨著教學進度逐步增加，沒有忽長忽短、忽難忽易、忽多忽少的現象，所以學生在學習的過程中沒有緊張和畏懼的心理，學生是在一種不知不覺的狀態中進步的。

我們很高興，因為這樣的教學效果正是我們當初編寫教材時所企盼的，而這種利用語言與文化的互動作用來激發學生學中文的興趣也正是本書編寫的宗旨。

如果要問我們自己對這本教材有什麼不滿意的話，那就是這裏面的一些文章讀起來似乎不是那麼地流暢舒適。

在編寫《漢語與文化讀本》的前後，我們撰寫了八十多篇用於教學的文章，這本書裏面只收了其中的四十四篇。當初寫的時候，我們只注意詞語的規範和語句的通順流暢。可是後來在編排成課本時，因為既要保障課文由短到長的平緩延伸，又要考慮課文難度的循序漸進；不僅要顧及每一課詞語和語法均勻合適，還要不斷地重覆學過的詞語句式，所以把寫好的文章翻來覆去地刪減增加，挖空填補，甚至按照詞匯和語法的需求重新寫過。經過多次修改之後就成了今天這種離痕斑斑的課文。然而我們也很高興，因為她們雖然不算是一篇篇流暢的散文，卻是一課課合適的課文。

《漢語與文化讀本》出版的時間不長，已經有很多學校在使用了，而且還有很多學校正準備使用。我們期待在不斷擴大的使用中得到更多的批評和指正，使《漢語與文化讀本》得到更進一步地完善。

作者 謹識
2004年5月15號於波士頓

Preface to the Second Printing

Chinese Language and Culture was first published in November 2002, and it is now ready to have a second printing. In this second printing, we have made some revisions, such as: correcting typographical errors, refining a few explanatory notes on grammar and vocabulary, polishing certain English translations, and getting rid of a few difficult and ambiguous phrases.

Reprinting *Chinese Language and Culture* in such a short period of time since its first publication cannot be made possible without the help of many of our friends and colleagues, who have used this textbook and generously provided us with their feedback and suggestions. In particular, we wish to thank Professor Mingchao Gui of the University of Oklahoma. He shared with us his recommendations and raised his queries regularly from the first lesson through the last. We also want to thank Professor Dongmei Li of Harvard University for having pointed out several problems in the text, which she didn't realize until reading the mistakes made in her students' homework.

Professors H.-Y. Emily Huang and Yu Feng of Harvard University used *Chinese Language and Culture* for both heritage learners and non-heritage learners. They provided us with their valuable suggestions. In addition, they also held a forum on using this textbook at the end of the semester, which gave us a good opportunity to collect students' feedback directly. Professor H.-Y. Emily Huang, Professor Xuehong Lu of the State University of New York at Buffalo as well as other teachers have developed various types of exercises to complement the use of this textbook in class.

We are delighted to have the help from such erudite and wonderful friends and colleagues. We admire their earnest and unselfish attitude towards this book. We would like to take this opportunity to express our profound gratitude to them for their help and encouragement. In addition, our gratitude also goes to Professor Wenchao He of New York University and Professor Xuehong Lu for endorsing this book. We are also grateful to those who have used or will be using this book in their classes.

From students' evaluations and teachers' discussions on *Chinese Language and Culture*, we have learnt that students very much appreciate our approach, namely integrating cultural insights into language texts. They feel that the texts are very interesting to read and very meaningful. They are happy to be introduced to Chinese culture through the studying of the texts, which in turn makes the learning of the language more fun. Several teachers have observed that the texts have motivated their students to become very actively involved in classroom activities. Teachers have also noted that, the gradual increase in the level of language complexity, in the length of the texts, and in the number of new words do help students to develop and improve their language proficiency naturally. They need not worry about having too many new words in one lesson or too many new or overly difficult grammar concepts introduced in a time.

We are particularly delighted to see this result, because it is exactly our goal of writing this textbook: to motivate Chinese language students to integrate their study of the language with that of Chinese culture.

We had written more than eighty essays, but only forty-four were included in the textbook. At the beginning, we only emphasized if the grammar of the writing and the use of vocabularies conformed to the standard, and if the texts were easy to read. Later, we made some rigorous adjustments and even rewrote some texts or paragraphs in order to make sure that the complexity of this book is increased in a gradual and systematic manner. Although some of the texts might not be as easy to read as we would like them to be, they are nonetheless appropriate and user-friendly.

As of today, *Chinese Language and Culture* has been adopted at many universities, colleges and schools. We have made our best effort to make this edition as accurate as possible; we also realize that there is always room for improvement. We sincerely invite suggestions and feedback from users on any aspect of this textbook.

The Authors
May 15, 2004
Boston

序

　　這是一本以講解基礎漢語知識和中國文化知識為主旨的中級漢語教材。教材的內容涵蓋了學生在學習中級漢語時可能會遇到的有關語言文字、民俗節慶、社會現象、詩詞成語、故事傳說、宗教思想、山川地理等各方面的知識。

　　全書分為二十二課，有四十四篇課文。

　　課文的順序主要是按照它的難易程度及其所涉及的詞語是否常用來排列的，同時也考慮到課文內容與實際教學上的聯繫以及學生的學習興趣，所以，我們把〈中文難不難〉和〈漢字介紹〉放在第一學期的開始；把〈中國年和壓歲錢〉和〈中國情人節〉排在接近於中國新年和西方情人節的時間；而把〈到中國旅遊〉和〈長江三峽〉排在後一個學期。

　　為了讓學生能夠在一個相對穩定的語言環境中，把相近的詞語和相關的內容聯繫起來學習，我們把內容有關聯的課文，每兩篇作為一個單元排列在一起。

　　為了避免課文忽長忽短，我們根據排列好的課文順序，對課文進行了縮減和增加。這樣保證課文的長度從第一課的四百字均勻地擴展到第二十二課的八百字；生詞量基本上也是從第一課的三十字逐漸地增加到最後一課的五十字。

　　每一課的課文後面都附有相應的閱讀課文。閱讀課文不但在內容上與主課文有關係，而且盡可能地重複出現主課文中講解過的語法及詞語。

　　在語法和詞語註釋的編排上，我們從《現代漢語八百詞》、《現代漢語虛詞例釋》、《現代漢語虛詞用法小詞典》等詞書中，挑出適合中級水平的語法和詞語，然後依照難易程度把它們均勻地放進文章中，同時刪掉原先文章裏一些不合適的語法和詞語。這樣做的結果，使得我們幾乎對所有的文章又做了一次大幅度的改寫。語法和詞語的註釋以及作業練習是依據最後改定的課文編寫的。

　　作業練習的形式多樣化，作業練習的例句儘量做到簡單而有趣味性，同時注意與課文內容相聯繫。

　　為了便於學生學習，我們在每一課的前面，用中英文列出本課的學習大綱，並且將課文後面的語法和詞語註釋的例句全都做了英文翻譯。同時，為了幫助學生理解課文，我們在很多課文後面加上相關的附錄，例如：〈漢字部首簡表〉、〈容易寫錯的字〉、〈家庭親屬稱謂簡表〉等等。

　　為了照顧使用不同字體的學生，課文及閱讀文章均採用繁簡對照的形式。每一課語法註釋和作業練習所列舉的例句，也都是繁簡對照。至於語法註釋和作業練習中的各類標題，因其涉及的詞彙不多而重複出現的頻率較高，所以只列出繁體字一種。

本書的課文除了哈佛大學和布蘭黛斯大學，明德暑校也曾經試用過。

　　本書的編寫得到哈佛燕京學社社長杜維明教授的大力支持，本書的出版得到哈佛燕京學社的資助，在此表示我們真摯的謝意！

　　我們非常感謝布蘭黛斯大學文學院副院長Elaine Wang女士和布蘭黛斯大學研究生章文女士。布蘭黛斯大學在本書編撰和試用中提供了很多幫助，章文女士協助我們做了很多英文翻譯工作。

　　我們衷心地感謝香港中文大學出版社社長陸國燊老師和本書編輯曾誦詩老師。從我們萌發編寫本書的念頭到本書的最後付梓出版，他們自始至終指導我們，並且熱心地幫助我們，特別是曾誦詩老師為此書的編輯出版做了大量的工作，花費了許多心血。

　　英國的梅凱蘭女士為全書的英文做了詳盡的修訂，我們在此表示真摯的感謝。

　　在本書的編寫過程中，哈佛大學中文部何寶璋主任給予了我們支持；哈佛同事馮禹和李愛民兩位老師給了我們很大的幫助；李金玉、徐蘭婷、白瑞戈、胡文澤、賈志杰、史耀華、劉憲民等諸位老師也都曾經幫助過我們；王學東老師細心地審閱了全稿，提出了許多寶貴的建議，在這裏一併表示我們深深的謝忱！我們還要感謝一直在鼓勵我們的吳素美、鄧立立、陳珮嘉、戴曉雪、齊燕榮等許多老師。

　　最後要說的是，編寫這本以語言知識和文化知識為主旨的中級漢語教材，對我們來說是一次嘗試。我們盡力想做好，但由於水平所限，錯誤及遺漏在所難免，這裏真切地希望老師和同學們多多指正。

作者 謹識

2001年秋於哈佛大學中文部

Preface

This textbook is designed for an intermediate level Chinese course in which students not only develop proficiency in the Chinese language but also gain some knowledge of Chinese culture. The contents of the book cover a wide variety of topics, including Chinese language structures and characters, Chinese customs, proverbs, holidays, social phenomena, religions, poetry, geography, as well as Chinese folklore.

The textbook consists of twenty-two lessons, each of which contains a core text and a reading text. The lessons are arranged according to their level of difficulty. The lessons titled "Is Chinese Difficult to Learn?" and "Introduction to Chinese Characters" are presented at the beginning of the first semester; "Chinese New Year and New Year Money" and "Chinese Valentine's Day" are best taught around the actual time of the Chinese New Year and Valentine's Day; "Touring Around China" and "The Three Gorges of the Yangtze River" are presented at the end of the second semester when students are ready for summer vacation. The textbook is designed to stimulate students' interest. The topics of the lessons presented encourage students to participate in discussions on subjects related to Chinese culture and to their own lives.

The textbook units are also grouped according to related topics. Each unit consists of two lessons; thus the students' knowledge of the Chinese language is reinforced by texts on related topics, with the appropriate grammatical patterns and vocabulary. Furthermore, each lesson ends with a reading text in which students comprehend the new passage by applying the grammatical patterns and vocabulary that have been explained previously. This coherent language environment serves as a framework for students who are developing their Chinese proficiency in an expanding context.

In order to control the level of language complexity and the number of new words introduced, we have reviewed all the texts thoroughly so that the length of the texts and the number of new words increase gradually. For instance, the reading in the first lesson is approximately 400 characters long with 30 new words, whereas the reading in the last lesson is 800 characters long with 50 new words. The lessons are therefore sufficiently challenging to develop students' linguistic ability but not too far beyond their current level of language competence.

In addition, we have selected some appropriate grammatical patterns and expressions from well-known books, such as *800 Words in Modern Chinese* (by Shushuang Lu, 1996), *Function Words in Modern Chinese* (compiled by Peking University, 1982), and *Dictionary of the Function Word Usage in Modern Chinese* (by Ziqiang Wang, 1982). These patterns and expressions are all explained in English and are evenly distributed throughout the lessons. They are also illustrated in Chinese sample sentences, all with English translations.

A variety of exercises follow the explanations of grammatical patterns and expressions in each lesson. These exercises are written in a simple and humorous style to maintain the students' interest.

Each lesson begins with a study outline in Chinese and English to give students a general idea of what they will be learning in that lesson. In some lessons appendices are provided to give students additional information for reference, such as "Chart of Chinese Radicals," "Commonly Mistaken Characters," and "Chart of Family and Relative Titles," etc.

Both complex characters and simplified characters are given in the core texts, the reading texts, the vocabulary lists, the sample sentences as well as the exercises to facilitate the comprehension of students who are familiar with only one of the writing systems.

We want to express our sincere thanks to the Chinese Program at Harvard University, Brandeis University, and the Middlebury Chinese Summer School, where this textbook has been field-tested and received many valuable comments and suggestions. We are very grateful to Professor Weiming Tu, the Director of Harvard-Yenching Institute and Dean Elaine Wang, the Associate Dean of Arts and Sciences at Brandeis University, who funded part of our work, to Dr. Baozhang He, the Director of the Chinese Program at Harvard University, who gave us support in writing this textbook, and to Wen Zhang, a graduate student at Brandeis University, who made a great contribution to the English translation of examples in the grammar notes.

We would like to express out gratitude to Dr. Steven Luk, the Director of The Chinese University Press, Esther Tsang, the editor with The Chinese University Press for their great patience and support, and Ms Caroline Mason for her help in revising the English of this book. We also wish to thank Dr. Yu Feng and Dr.

Aimin Li, who gave us enthusiastic encouragement and help, as well as Jinyu Li, Lanting Xu, Craig Butler, Dr. Wenze Hu, Zhijie Jia, Dr. Yaohua Shi, and Dr. Xianmin Liu. In particular, we are greatly indebted to Xuedong Wang, who proofread the entire textbook and gave us valuable comments and suggestions. Finally, we would like to express our heartfelt thanks to Dr. Sue-mei Wu, Li-li Deng, Pei-Chia Chen, Xiaoxue Dai, Yanrong Qi, who has helped us in many ways.

It is a new experience for us to integrate cultural insights into a language text rather than to separate cultural content from the text. We would welcome comments or criticisms from teachers and students alike. Their views will be very valuable in helping us correct any errors or omissions in future editions of this book.

The Authors
Chinese Program, Harvard University
Fall 2001

詞類簡稱表
Abbreviations of Parts of Speech

n.	noun	名詞	名词	míngcí
pn.	pronoun	代詞	代词	dàicí
v.	verb	動詞	动词	dòngcí
aux.	auxiliary verb	助動詞	助动词	zhùdòngcí
adj.	adjective	形容詞	形容词	xíngróngcí
num.	numeral	數詞	数词	shùcí
m.	measure word	量詞	量词	liàngcí
adv.	adverb	副詞	副词	fùcí
prep.	preposition	介詞	介词	jiècí
conj.	conjunction	連詞	连词	liáncí
par.	particle	助詞	助词	zhùcí
int.	interjection	嘆詞	叹词	tàncí

1

中文難不難?
Is Chinese Difficult to Learn?

學習大綱

通過學習本課,學生應該能夠:

1. 掌握這些句型和詞語的意思和用法:"因為……(所以)"、"用……V"、"不但……而且/也/還"、"其實"、"從"、"差不多"、"雖然……但是/可是"。
2. 認識和運用課文以及閱讀文章內的生詞。
3. 了解在學習中文的過程中要特別注意哪些方面。

Study Outline

After studying this chapter, students should:

1. Have a good command of the meaning and usage of these sentence patterns and terms: "yīnwèi ... (suǒyǐ)" (because ...[therefore]), "yòng ...V" (use/using/with ... V), "bùdàn ... érqiě/yě/hái" (not only ... but also), "qíshí" (in fact; actually), "cóng" (from), "chàbuduō" (almost), "suīrán ... dànshì/kěshì" (although ...[but]).
2. Be familiar with the meaning and usage of the vocabulary introduced in the text and the reading.
3. Be aware of the special areas to which attention should be paid in learning Chinese.

課文

　　學中文難不難？難，也不難。為甚麼這樣說呢？因為學任何一種語言都難，都要學聽、說、讀、寫，都要學發音、學語法，都要記單詞。

　　有人說：漢字不是用字母拼寫的，漢字不但難認而且難唸。其實這也不一定。因為有許多漢字，我們可以從偏旁上看出它的意思，也可以從偏旁上讀出它的聲音，所以有時候你會覺得很容易。

　　學中文一定要先學漢語拼音，漢語拼音是用字母拼寫的，所以不難學。學漢語拼音可以幫助你練習發音。發音的時候要特別注意聲調，中文裏面同樣的字音，聲調不同，意思就不一樣。有些字的聲調，在句子裏和別的字一起讀的時候還會有變化。

　　學了漢語拼音以後，不但可以幫助你練習發音，還可以幫助你查字典，現在的中文字典差不多都是用拼音排列的。有一些人很喜歡用電腦做中文作業，電腦的中文軟件也有很多是用拼音輸入的。

　　漢字雖然有五萬六千多個，但是一般常用的字只有三千五百個。我們學會了這三千五百個字，差不多就可以看懂一般的報紙和書了，也可以寫一些簡單的文章了。

1. 中文难不难

课文

　　学中文难不难？难，也不难。为什么这样说呢？因为学任何一种语言都难，都要学听、说、读、写，都要学发音、学语法，都要记单词。

　　有人说：汉字不是用字母拼写的，汉字不但难认而且难念。其实这也不一定。因为有许多汉字，我们可以从偏旁上看出它的意思，也可以从偏旁上读出它的声音，所以有时候你会觉得很容易。

　　学中文一定要先学汉语拼音，汉语拼音是用字母拼写的，所以不难学。学汉语拼音可以帮助你练习发音。发音的时候要特别注意声调，中文里面同样的字音，声调不同，意思就不一样。有些字的声调，在句子里和别的字一起读的时候还会有变化。

　　学了汉语拼音以后，不但可以帮助你练习发音，还可以帮助你查字典，现在的中文字典差不多都是用拼音排列的。有一些人很喜欢用电脑做中文作业，电脑的中文软件也有很多是用拼音输入的。

　　汉字虽然有五万六千多个，但是一般常用的字只有三千五百个。我们学会了这三千五百个字，差不多就可以看懂一般的报纸和书了，也可以写一些简单的文章了。

生詞

因為……(所以)	因为……(所以)	yīnwèi ... (suǒyǐ)	conj.	because ... (therefore)
任何	任何	rènhé	adv.	any/every no MW required
種	种	zhǒng	m.	kind
發音	发音	fāyīn	n.	pronunciation
單詞	单词	dāncí	n.	word
不但……而且	不但……而且	bùdàn ... érqiě	conj.	not only ... but also
字母	字母	zìmǔ	n.	letters of an alphabet
拼寫	拼写	pīnxiě	v.	spell
其實	其实	qíshí	adv.	in fact; actually
從	从	cóng	prep.	from
偏旁	偏旁	piānpáng	n.	radicals (of characters)
它	它	tā	pn.	it
聲音	声音	shēngyīn	n.	sound
覺得	觉得	juéde	v.	feel; think
容易	容易	róngyì	adj.	easy
特別	特别	tèbié	adv.	especially
注意	注意	zhùyì	v.	pay attention to
同樣	同样	tóngyàng	adj.	same
字音	字音	zìyīn	n.	pronunciation of a character
變化	变化	biànhuà	n.	change
查字典	查字典	chá zìdiǎn		look up ... in the dictionary
排列	排列	páiliè	v.	put ... in order
電腦	电脑	diànnǎo	n.	computer

軟件	软件	ruǎn jiàn	n.	software
輸入	输入	shūrù	v.	input
雖然……但是	虽然……但是	suīrán ... dànshì	conj.	although ... (but)
萬	万	wàn	num.	ten thousand
差不多	差不多	chàbuduō	adv.	almost; about
一般	一般	yībān	adj.	usually; commonly
常用	常用	chángyòng	adj.	often used
報紙	报纸	bàozhǐ	n.	newspaper
簡單	简单	jiǎndān	adj.	simple
文章	文章	wénzhāng	n.	essay

語法和詞語註釋

一、因為……（所以） because ... (therefore)

The structure "因為……所以" connects two clauses of a cause and effect sentence. The first clause indicates the reason, and the second clause gives the result.

1. 因為許多漢字可以從偏旁上看出它的意思，所以有時候你會覺得不難。
   因为许多汉字可以从偏旁上看出它的意思，所以有时候你会觉得不难。
   Because the meanings of many Chinese characters can be made out from their radicals, sometimes you may feel they are not hard (to learn).

2. 因為你不做作業，所以考試考得不好。
   因为你不做作业，所以考试考得不好。
   You don't do your homework, therefore you haven't done well in the exams.

3. 因為我頭疼，所以我不想去上課了。
   因为我头疼，所以我不想去上课了。
   Because I have a headache, I don't want to go to class.

> Sometimes, the first clause gives the "result" and the second clause provides the "cause".

4. 為甚麼說中文難也不難？因為任何一種語言都很難。

   为什么说中文难也不难？因为任何一种语言都很难。

   Why do we say Chinese is difficult but also not difficult? Because any language is difficult (to learn).

5. 我昨天沒有去買書，因為我沒有錢了。

   我昨天没有去买书，因为我没有钱了。

   I didn't go to buy books yesterday, because I had no money left.

二、用……V　　use/using/with ... V

1. 漢字不是用字母拼寫的。

   汉字不是用字母拼写的。

   Chinese characters are not written alphabetically.

2. 很多人喜歡用電腦寫中文。

   很多人喜欢用电脑写中文。

   Many people like to use computers to write Chinese characters.

3. 我用媽媽的錢買衣服。

   我用妈妈的钱买衣服。

   I use my mom's money to buy clothes.

三、不但……而且/也/還　　not only ... but also

> "不但……而且/也/還" indicates further meaning beyond the preceding meaning. "而且/也/還" is used in the second clause that introduces a further statement.

1. 學漢語拼音不但可以幫助你練習發音，而且可以幫助你查字典。

   学汉语拼音不但可以帮助你练习发音，而且可以帮助你查字典。

   Learning Pinyin can not only help you practice pronunciation, it can also help you look up words in the dictionary.

2. 漢字不但難認而且難唸。
   汉字不但难认而且难念。
   Chinese characters are not only hard to recognize but also hard to read aloud.

3. 有的字不但可以從偏旁上看出它的意思，還可以從偏旁上讀出它的聲音。
   有的字不但可以从偏旁上看出它的意思，还可以从偏旁上读出它的声音。
   For some Chinese characters, you can not only make out the meaning from their components, you can also know how to pronounce them from these components.

四、其實   in fact; actually

1. 大家都説中文很難，其實中文一點兒都不難。
   大家都说中文很难，其实中文一点儿都不难。
   People say Chinese is very hard. In fact, Chinese is not hard at all.

2. 她好像很喜歡我，其實她喜歡另一個男同學。
   她好象很喜欢我，其实她喜欢另一个男同学。
   She seems to like me a lot, but actually she likes another boy in our class.

3. 有人説大學的學習很忙，其實我覺得一點兒都不忙。
   有人说大学的学习很忙，其实我觉得一点儿都不忙。
   Some people say you're very busy when you're at university, but actually I don't feel busy at all.

五、從   from

1. 從偏旁上看出它的意思。
   从偏旁上看出它的意思。
   Make out the meaning from the radicals.

2. 從考試成績可以知道他學習好不好。
   从考试成绩可以知道他学习好不好。
   From the exam grades, you can tell whether he's doing well in his studies.

3. 從書裏面可以找到答案。
   从书里面可以找到答案。
   You can find the answer in the book.

六、差不多　　almost

> This is followed by a verb, an adverb or a numeral + measure word.

1. 中文字典差不多都是用拼音排列的。
   中文字典差不多都是用拼音排列的。
   Most Chinese dictionaries are arranged in the alphabetical order of Pinyin.

2. 老師講的話我差不多都能聽懂。
   老师讲的话我差不多都能听懂。
   I can understand almost all that the teacher says.

3. 我們差不多一個星期聽寫一次漢字。
   我们差不多一个星期听写一次汉字。
   We have Chinese character dictation about once a week.

七、雖然……但是/可是　　although ... (but)

> "雖然……但是/可是" indicates the admission of a fact in the first clause, but it does not change the truth of the second clause. "雖然" can be put before or after the subject, but "但是/可是" should be put at the beginning of the second clause only.

1. 雖然漢字很多，但是常用字只有兩千五百個。
   虽然汉字很多，但是常用字只有两千五百个。
   Although there are many Chinese characters, only 2,500 of them are commonly used.

2. 雖然我學了三年中文，可是我看不懂中文書。
   虽然我学了三年中文，可是我看不懂中文书。
   Although I've been studying Chinese for three years, I can't read Chinese books.

3. 漢字雖然不是用字母拼寫的，但是我覺得不太難。

   汉字虽然不是用字母拼写的，但是我觉得不太难。

   Although Chinese characters are not written alphabetically, I don't feel they are difficult to learn.

練 習

一、用所給的詞語回答問題

1. A：為甚麼說中文比別的語言難？（因為……所以）

   为什么说中文比别的语言难？（因为……所以）

   B：_____。

2. A：你考試為甚麼沒有考好？（因為……所以）

   你考试为什么没有考好？（因为……所以）

   B：_____。

3. A：為甚麼他們覺得漢字很難？（不但……而且）

   为什么他们觉得汉字很难？（不但……而且）

   B：_____。

4. A：你的女朋友怎麼樣？（不但……而且）

   你的女朋友怎么样？（不但……而且）

   B：_____。

5. A：你怎麼知道這個字的意思呢？（從）

   你怎么知道这个字的意思呢？（从）

   B：_____。

6. A：你怎麼知道我的電話號碼？（從）

   你怎么知道我的电话号码？（从）

   B：_____。

7. A：你怎麼做你的中文作業？（用……V）
　　　你怎么做你的中文作业？（用……V）

　　B：＿＿＿＿＿＿＿＿＿＿＿＿＿＿＿＿＿＿＿＿＿＿＿＿＿＿＿＿。

8. A：你的電話壞了，你怎麼給父母打電話呢？（用……V）
　　　你的电话坏了，你怎么给父母打电话呢？（用……V）

　　B：＿＿＿＿＿＿＿＿＿＿＿＿＿＿＿＿＿＿＿＿＿＿＿＿＿＿＿＿。

9. A：漢字有五萬多個，人怎麼能記住五萬個漢字呢？（雖然……但是）
　　　汉字有五万多个，人怎么能记住五万个汉字呢？（虽然……但是）

　　B：＿＿＿＿＿＿＿＿＿＿＿＿＿＿＿＿＿＿＿＿＿＿＿＿＿＿＿＿。

10. A：你不是中國人，為甚麼要學中文？（雖然……但是）
　　　你不是中国人，为什么要学中文？（虽然……但是）

　　B：＿＿＿＿＿＿＿＿＿＿＿＿＿＿＿＿＿＿＿＿＿＿＿＿＿＿＿＿。

11. A：漢字是不是很難認？（其實）
　　　汉字是不是很难认？（其实）

　　B：＿＿＿＿＿＿＿＿＿＿＿＿＿＿＿＿＿＿＿＿＿＿＿＿＿＿＿＿。

12. A：你說你都聽懂了，為甚麼又寫錯了呢？（其實）
　　　你说你都听懂了，为什么又写错了呢？（其实）

　　B：＿＿＿＿＿＿＿＿＿＿＿＿＿＿＿＿＿＿＿＿＿＿＿＿＿＿＿＿。

13. A：現在的中文字典是用甚麼排列的？（差不多）
　　　现在的中文字典是用什么排列的？（差不多）

　　B：＿＿＿＿＿＿＿＿＿＿＿＿＿＿＿＿＿＿＿＿＿＿＿＿＿＿＿＿。

14. A：學中文的同學有中文名字嗎？（差不多）
　　　学中文的同学有中文名字吗？（差不多）

　　B：＿＿＿＿＿＿＿＿＿＿＿＿＿＿＿＿＿＿＿＿＿＿＿＿＿＿＿＿。

二、用所給的詞語改寫句子

1. 我生病了，沒有上學。(因為……所以)
   我生病了，没有上学。(因为……所以)
   _____。

2. 今年暑假我要工作，不能回臺灣。(因為……所以)
   今年暑假我要工作，不能回台湾。(因为……所以)
   _____。

3. 小李常常不來上課，每次考試都能考一個A。(雖然……但是)
   小李常常不来上课，每次考试都能考一个A。(虽然……但是)
   _____。

4. 我頭很疼，我還要做作業。(雖然……但是)
   我头很疼，我还要做作业。(虽然……但是)
   _____。

5. 漢字難寫又難記。(不但……而且)
   汉字难写又难记。(不但……而且)
   _____。

6. 中文課的作業很多，也很難。(不但……而且)
   中文课的作业很多，也很难。(不但……而且)
   _____。

三、用所給的詞語造句

1. 因為……所以
   因为……所以
   _____。

2. 雖然……但是
   虽然……但是
   _____。

3. 不但……而且
   不但……而且
   _____ 。

4. 差不多
   差不多
   _____ 。

5. 用……V
   用……V
   _____ 。

四、翻譯

1. People say that because Chinese characters are not written alphabetically, the Chinese language seems more difficult than other languages.

   _____
   _____ 。

2. Chinese tones are a major problem for Chinese language learners, because Chinese characters can be pronounced with more than one tone, and the differences in tone reflect differences in meaning.

   _____
   _____ 。

3. It is very important to learn Chinese Pinyin. Most Chinese dictionaries are arranged in the alphabetical order of Pinyin, and the input method of most Chinese language software also uses Pinyin.

   _____
   _____ 。

五、根據課文回答問題

1. 為甚麼說學任何一種語言都很難？
   为什么说学任何一种语言都很难？

   _____

   _____ 。

2. 為甚麼說有時候會覺得中文很容易學？
   为什么说有时候会觉得中文很容易学？

   _____

   _____ 。

3. 為甚麼要學漢語拼音？
   为什么要学汉语拼音？

   _____

   _____ 。

4. 為甚麼學發音要特別注意聲調？
   为什么学发音要特别注意声调？

   _____

   _____ 。

5. 學中文和學別的外語(法語、西班牙語、日語)有甚麼不同？
   学中文和学别的外语(法语、西班牙语、日语)有什么不同？

   _____

   _____ 。

閱讀

湯姆學中文

　　湯姆的女朋友叫趙小燕。趙小燕是從北京來的,她不但漂亮而且很聰明。因為湯姆要去北京見小燕的父母,所以湯姆想去學一點兒中文。

　　湯姆覺得中文不好學。他聽說中文和西方的語言完全不一樣。中國字不是用字母拼寫的,中文發音很難,寫起來也不容易。

　　湯姆知道學習任何一種語言都要學聽、說、讀、寫四個部分,但是他不想用很多時間去學中文。他去問趙小燕能不能只學習聽中文,不學說話,不學讀書,也不學寫字。

　　小燕說:"不可以。因為明年暑假你要去北京見我父母,那時候,他們會問你很多問題。比方說:他們會問你喜歡不喜歡我?愛不愛我?你只會聽,不會說,怎麼能回答他們的問題呢?"

　　湯姆說:"嘿!這不難。進了你們家門以後,我就不停地笑。你爸爸媽媽問我問題,我同意的都點頭,不同意的就搖頭。"

　　趙小燕說:"那不行,他們一定會問你為甚麼愛我?你為甚麼要和我結婚?你怎麼辦?"

　　湯姆:"啊!……"

阅 读

汤姆学中文

汤姆的女朋友叫赵小燕。赵小燕是从北京来的,她不但漂亮而且很聪明。因为汤姆要去北京见小燕的父母,所以汤姆想去学一点儿中文。

汤姆觉得中文不好学。他听说中文和西方的语言完全不一样。中国字不是用字母拼写的,中文发音很难,写起来也不容易。

汤姆知道学习任何一种语言都要学听、说、读、写四个部分,但是他不想用很多时间去学中文。他去问赵小燕能不能只学习听中文,不学说话,不学读书,也不学写字。

小燕说:"不可以。因为明年暑假你要去北京见我父母,那时候,他们会问你很多问题。比方说:他们会问你喜欢不喜欢我?爱不爱我?你只会听,不会说,怎么能回答他们的问题呢?"

汤姆说:"嘿!这不难。进了你们家门以后,我就不停地笑。你爸爸妈妈问我问题,我同意的都点头,不同意的就摇头。"

赵小燕说:"那不行,他们一定会问你为什么爱我?你为什么要和我结婚?你怎么办?"

汤姆:"啊!……"

生 詞

湯姆	汤姆	Tāngmu		name of a person: Tom
趙小燕	赵小燕	Zhào Xiǎoyàn		name of a person
燕	燕	yàn	n.	swallow
漂亮	漂亮	piàoliang	adj.	pretty
聰明	聪明	cōngming	adj.	intelligent; smart
父母	父母	fùmǔ	n.	parents
聽説	听说	tīng shuō		hear (of); be told (of)
西方	西方	xīfāng	n.	Western
完全	完全	wánquán	adv.	entirely; totally
部分	部分	bùfen	n.	part
比方說	比方说	bǐfāngshuō		suppose; for example
喜歡	喜欢	xǐhuān	v.	like
嘿	嘿	hēi	int.	hey
不停地	不停地	bùtíng de	adv.	ceaselessly; continuously
同意	同意	tóngyì	v.	agree
點頭	点头	diǎn tóu		nod
搖頭	摇头	yáo tóu		shake one's head
結婚	结婚	jiéhūn	v.	marry
怎麼辦	怎么办	zěnmebàn		What's to be done? What can one do?

問 題

1. 湯姆為甚麼要學中文？
   汤姆为什么要学中文？

2. 湯姆想怎樣學中文？
   汤姆想怎样学中文？
   _____
   _____。

3. 他的女朋友趙小燕是怎麼說的？
   他的女朋友赵小燕是怎么说的？
   _____
   _____。

4. 湯姆怎麼回答的？
   汤姆怎么回答的？
   _____
   _____。

5. 趙小燕為甚麼說不可以只學聽中文？
   赵小燕为什么说不可以只学听中文？
   _____
   _____。

漢字介紹
Introduction to Chinese Characters

學習大綱

通過學習本課，學生應該能夠：

1. 掌握這些句型和詞語的意思和用法："照着"、"作為"、"由……組成"、"百分之 X"、"A 跟 B 有關係"、"還是"、"如果／要是……那麼"。
2. 認識和運用課文以及閱讀文章內的生詞。
3. 簡單地了解漢字裏偏旁的含義及作用。
4. 了解正確書寫漢字的重要性。

Study Outline

After studying this chapter, students should:

1. Have a good command of the meaning and usage of these sentence patterns and terms: "**zhàozhe**" (according to; in accordance with), "**zuòwéi**" (be used as; be regarded as), "**yóu ... zǔchéng**" (be made of; consist of), "**bǎifēnzhī X**" (X percent), "**A gēn B yǒu guānxì**" (A is related to B; A has something to do with B), "**háishì**" (still), "**rúguǒ/yàoshì ... nàme**" (if ... then).
2. Be familiar with the meaning and usage of the vocabulary introduced in the text and the reading.
3. Understand the meaning and use of the parts of a Chinese character.
4. Understand the importance of writing Chinese characters correctly.

課文

　　最早的漢字是照着物體的形狀畫出來的,那時候的字就像是一幅幅的畫兒,例如:"山"像一座大山,"木"像一棵大樹,"水"就是流水的形狀。

　　後來,這些字作為漢字的偏旁又組成了許多新字。現在百分之八十的漢字,都是由表示意思的偏旁(形旁)和表示讀音的偏旁(聲旁)組成的。

　　我們常常可以從字的形旁上看出這個字跟甚麼有關係。比如說:黃河的"河"、眼淚的"淚"有"水"字旁,這些字都跟水有關係;抓人的"抓"、打電話的"打"有"手"字旁,它們跟手有關係。

　　雖然漢字現在的讀音和古代不完全一樣,但是有時候還是可以從字的聲旁上唸出它的讀音。例如:湖水的"湖"、糊塗的"糊"、燒煳的"煳"、蝴蝶的"蝴",這些有胡字旁的字都唸"胡(hú)"。

　　現在的字典差不多都是用拼音排列的,但是在字典的索引裏面,人們還是把偏旁相同的字排列在一起。偏旁在字典的索引裏叫做部首。如果你不知道一個字的讀音,那麼你可以到部首裏面去查。

课文

最早的汉字是照着物体的形状画出来的，那时候的字就像是一幅幅的画儿，例如："山"像一座大山，"木"像一棵大树，"水"就是流水的形状。

后来，这些字作为汉字的偏旁又组成了许多新字。现在百分之八十的汉字，都是由表示意思的偏旁（形旁）和表示读音的偏旁（声旁）组成的。

我们常常可以从字的形旁上看出这个字跟什么有关系。比如说：黄河的"河"、眼泪的"泪"有"水"字旁，这些字都跟水有关系；抓人的"抓"、打电话的"打"有"手"字旁，它们跟手有关系。

虽然汉字现在的读音和古代不完全一样，但是有时候还是可以从字的声旁上念出它的读音。例如：湖水的"湖"、糊涂的"糊"、烧煳的"煳"、蝴蝶的"蝴"，这些有胡字旁的字都念"胡 (hú)"。

现在的字典差不多都是用拼音排列的，但是在字典的索引里面，人们还是把偏旁相同的字排列在一起。偏旁在字典的索引里叫做部首。如果你不知道一个字的读音，那么你可以到部首里面去查。

生詞

介紹	介绍	jièshào	v./n.	introduce; introduction
照着	照着	zhàozhe	prep.	according to
物體	物体	wùtǐ	n.	object
形狀	形状	xíngzhuàng	n.	form; shape
畫	画	huà	v.	draw
像	像	xiàng	v.	be like
幅	幅	fú	m.	measure word for paintings
例如	例如	lìrú	v.	for example
樹	树	shù	n.	tree
流水	流水	liúshuǐ	n.	running water
作為	作为	zuòwéi	v.	(be) used as; (be) regarded as
組成	组成	zǔchéng	v.	form; be made of
百分之……	百分之……	bǎifēnzhī		… percent
由	由	yóu	prep.	from; by
表示	表示	biǎoshì	v.	express; indicate
形旁	形旁	xíngpáng	n.	semantic element of a character
聲旁	声旁	shēngpáng	n.	phonetic element of a character
跟	跟	gēn	prep.	with
關係	关系	guānxi	n.	relationship; link
黃河	黄河	Huánghé		the Yellow River
眼淚	眼泪	yǎnlèi	n.	tears
抓	抓	zhuā	v.	grab; seize; catch
古代	古代	gǔdài	n.	ancient times

湖	湖	hú	n.	lake
糊塗	糊涂	hútu	adj.	confused; bewildered
燒煳	烧煳	shāohú		be burnt
蝴蝶	蝴蝶	húdié	n.	butterfly
胡	胡	hú	n.	a family name
索引	索引	suǒyǐn	n.	index
叫做	叫做	jiàozuò	v.	to be addressed as
部首	部首	bùshǒu	n.	radicals (or other character components) used in dictionaries for indexing purposes

語法和詞語註釋

一、照着　　according to; in accordance with　　照着

1. 這些字是照着物體的形狀畫出來的。
   这些字是照着物体的形状画出来的。
   These characters are drawn according to the shapes of the objects (they refer to).

2. 小張照着書上的句子做練習。
   小张照着书上的句子做练习。
   Xiao Zhang does the exercises in accordance with the sentences in the book.

3. 照着舊衣服的樣子做一件新衣服。
   照着旧衣服的样子做一件新衣服。
   Make a new item of clothing according to the design of the old clothes.

二、作為　　be used as; be regarded as　　作为

1. 這些字後來作為漢字的偏旁又組成了許多新字。
   这些字后来作为汉字的偏旁又组成了许多新字。

Later these characters were used as parts of (other) Chinese characters and formed many new characters.

2. 我把中文作為我的第二外語。
   我把中文作为我的第二外语。
   I regard Chinese as my second language.

3. 我把跑步作為鍛煉身體的方法。
   我把跑步作为锻炼身体的方法。
   I use jogging as a way of working out.

三、由……組成　　be made of; consist of

"由……組成" introduces the components, sources or materials that the objects are made of.

1. 現在百分之八十的漢字都是由形旁和聲旁組成的。
   现在百分之八十的汉字都是由形旁和声旁组成的。
   Nowadays eighty percent of Chinese characters are composed of a semantic element and a phonetic element.

2. 水是由氧氣和氫氣組成的。
   水是由氧气和氢气组成的。
   Water is made up of oxygen and hydrogen.

3. 電腦是由硬件和軟件組成的。
   电脑是由硬件和软件组成的。
   A computer consists of both hardware and software.

四、百分之X　　X percent

1. 這一課百分之五十的字我都認識。
   这一课百分之五十的字我都认识。
   I know fifty percent of the characters in this lesson.

2. 我們班上百分之八十的同學都有中國名字。
   我们班上百分之八十的同学都有中国名字。

Eighty percent of students in our class have Chinese names.

3. 全世界百分之二十的人會說中文。
   全世界百分之二十的人会说中文。
   Twenty percent of people in the world speak Chinese.

五、A 跟 B 有關係　　A is related to B; A has something to do with B

1. 有水字旁的字跟水有關係。
   有水字旁的字跟水有关系。
   Characters with the "water" radical are related to water.

2. SAT的成績跟上大學有關係。
   SAT的成绩跟上大学有关系。
   SAT grades affect one's college entrance.

3. 中文課考得好不好跟拿獎學金有關係。
   中文课考得好不好跟拿奖学金有关系。
   Getting a scholarship is related to whether you do well in the Chinese exams.

六、還是　　still

"還是" indicates the situation or action will not be changed by the preceding condition.

1. 字典雖然用拼音排列，但是在索引裏還是把偏旁相同的字排列在一起。
   字典虽然用拼音排列，但是在索引里还是把偏旁相同的字排列在一起。
   Although a dictionary is arranged in Pinyin order, characters with the same structural parts are still put in the same category in the index.

2. 現在漢字讀音和古代不完全一樣，但是我們還是可以從字的聲旁上唸出它的讀音。
   现在汉字读音和古代不完全一样，但是我们还是可以从字的声旁上念出它的读音。
   The modern pronunciation of characters is not exactly the same as that of

ancient times, but we can still tell the pronunciation of the characters from their phonetic elements.

3. 今天老師講得很清楚，可是我還是有點兒不太懂。
今天老师讲得很清楚，可是我还是有点儿不太懂。
The professor gave a very clear explanation today, but I still can't quite understand it.

七、如果/要是……那麼　　if ... then

"如果/要是……那麼" connects the conditional clause in a sentence and the result or suggestion clause.

1. 如果你不知道這個字的讀音，那麼你可以到部首裏面去查。
如果你不知道这个字的读音，那么你可以到部首里面去查。
If you don't know how to pronounce this character, you can look it up in the radical index of the dictionary.

2. 如果明天下大雪，那麼我們還去上課嗎？
如果明天下大雪，那么我们还去上课吗？
If it snows heavily tomorrow, should we go to class?

3. 如果你不學中文，那麼你就不能唱中文的卡拉OK了。
如果你不学中文，那么你就不能唱中文的卡拉OK了。
If you don't learn Chinese, you can't sing Chinese karaoke.

練習

一、用所給的詞語回答問題

1. A：最早的漢字為甚麼像一幅畫？（照着）
最早的汉字为什么像一幅画？（照着）
B：_____。

2. A：為甚麼有的漢字可以從偏旁上看出它的意思？（由……組成）

为什么有的汉字可以从偏旁上看出它的意思？（由……组成）

B：＿＿＿＿＿＿＿＿＿＿＿＿＿＿＿＿＿＿＿＿＿＿＿＿＿＿＿＿＿＿。

3. A：SAT的成績為甚麼很重要？（A 跟 B 有關係）
　　SAT的成绩为什么很重要？（A 跟 B 有关系）

B：＿＿＿＿＿＿＿＿＿＿＿＿＿＿＿＿＿＿＿＿＿＿＿＿＿＿＿＿＿＿。

4. A：我不會拼音，怎麼去查字典？（如果……那麼）
　　我不会拼音，怎么去查字典？（如果……那么）

B：＿＿＿＿＿＿＿＿＿＿＿＿＿＿＿＿＿＿＿＿＿＿＿＿＿＿＿＿＿＿。

5. A：今天老師講得很清楚，你都懂了嗎？（還是）
　　今天老师讲得很清楚，你都懂了吗？（还是）

B：＿＿＿＿＿＿＿＿＿＿＿＿＿＿＿＿＿＿＿＿＿＿＿＿＿＿＿＿＿＿。

6. A：你為甚麼每天都跑步？（作為）
　　你为什么每天都跑步？（作为）

B：＿＿＿＿＿＿＿＿＿＿＿＿＿＿＿＿＿＿＿＿＿＿＿＿＿＿＿＿＿＿。

7. A：現在有多少字是由形旁和聲旁組成的？（百分之……）
　　现在有多少字是由形旁和声旁组成的？（百分之……）

B：＿＿＿＿＿＿＿＿＿＿＿＿＿＿＿＿＿＿＿＿＿＿＿＿＿＿＿＿＿＿。

二、用所給的詞語填空（一個詞語可以用多次）

如果……那麼、不但……而且、因為……所以、雖然……但是
如果……那么、不但……而且、因为……所以、虽然……但是
　　　　　　　Not only bAt also

1. ＿＿＿＿漢字是照着物體的形狀畫出來的，＿＿＿＿漢字就像是一幅一幅的畫兒。
　　_因为_ 汉字是照着物体的形状画出来的，_所以_ 汉字就像是一幅一幅的画儿。

2. 漢字不是用字母拼寫的，漢字＿＿＿＿難認，＿＿＿＿難唸。
　　汉字不是用字母拼写的，汉字 _不但_ 难认，_而且_ 难念。

3. _____生病了，_____沒有上學。
   _____生病了，_____没有上学。

4. 中文課的作業_____很少_____也很容易。
   中文课的作业_____很少_____也很容易。

5. 小李_____常常不來上課，_____他每次考試都能考一個A。
   小李_____常常不来上课，_____他每次考试都能考一个A。

6. 明天_____下大雪，_____我們就不去上課了。
   明天_____下大雪，_____我们就不去上课了。

三、用所給的詞語造句

1. 由……組成
   由……组成

   _____。

2. A跟B有關係
   A跟B有关系

   _____。

3. 如果……那麼
   如果……那么

   _____。

4. 照着
   照着

   _____。

5. 作為
   作为

   _____。

6. 還是
   还是

   _____。

7. 百分之……
   百分之……
   _____。

四、翻譯

1. These days, eighty percent of Chinese characters are made up of both a phonetic element and a semantic element.
   _____
   _____。

2. The pronunciation of modern Chinese characters is not exactly the same as that of the ancient ones, but we can still often tell the pronunciation from the character's phonetic element.
   _____
   _____。

3. We can usually tell what a character relates to from its semantic component.
   _____
   _____。

五、根據課文回答問題

1. 最早的漢字像甚麼？
   最早的汉字像什么？
   _____
   _____。

2. 現在百分之八十的漢字是由甚麼組成的？
   现在百分之八十的汉字是由什么组成的？
   _____
   _____。

3. 在漢字裏面，有水字旁的字跟甚麼有關係？
   在汉字里面，有水字旁的字跟什么有关系？
   _____
   _____。

4. 為甚麼漢字的偏旁可以幫助我們認字和發音？
   为什么汉字的偏旁可以帮助我们认字和发音？
   _____
   _____。

5. 字典的索引裏面把甚麼樣的字排列在一起？
   字典的索引里面把什么样的字排列在一起？
   _____
   _____。

6. 如果你不知道一個字的讀音，那麼你怎麼去查字典？
   如果你不知道一个字的读音，那么你怎么去查字典？
   _____
   _____。

閱讀

當心寫錯字

　　因為每一個漢字都是由點、橫、豎、撇、捺組成的，所以很多漢字看起來好像都一樣。現在百分之八十的漢字是由形旁和聲旁組成的，有的字有同樣的形旁，例如：河、湖、淚、湯；有的字有同樣的聲旁，例如：湖、糊、蝴、煳。

　　有人說寫漢字就像畫畫兒，多一劃、少一點兒沒關係。其實，他們說得不對。有的字如果你多寫一劃、少寫一點兒，那就會變成兩個不同的字。例如：大—太、今—令、日—目；有的字筆劃長一點兒、短一點兒，也會變成不一樣的字，例如：土—士、己—已、田—由—甲。

　　有些字的筆劃雖然一樣，但是偏旁位置不同，也就變成兩個不一樣的字。例如：陪—部、呆—杏；還有一些字，偏旁的位置離開了一點點兒：可—叮、入—八；有的歪了一點點兒：天—夭、干—千；也有的忘了彎鉤：干—于、平—乎，都會變成完全不一樣的字。

　　漢字的形體看起來差不多都一樣，所以，我們在寫字的時候要特別當心，不可以多寫一筆，也不可以少寫一劃；不可以隨便延長和縮短筆劃，也不可以隨便顛倒和調換漢字的偏旁位置。

阅读

当心写错字

因为每一个汉字都是由点、横、竖、撇、捺组成的,所以很多汉字看起来好像都一样。现在百分之八十的汉字是由形旁和声旁组成的,有的字有同样的形旁,例如:河、湖、泪、汤;有的字有同样的声旁,例如:湖、糊、蝴、煳。

有人说写汉字就像画画儿,多一划、少一点儿没关系。其实,他们说得不对。有的字如果你多写一划、少写一点儿,那就会变成两个不同的字。例如:大—太、今—令、日—目;有的字笔划长一点儿、短一点儿,也会变成不一样的字,例如:土—士、己—已、田—由—甲。

有些字的笔划虽然一样,但是偏旁位置不同,也就变成两个不一样的字。例如:陪—部、呆—杏;还有一些字,偏旁的位置离开了一点点儿:可—叮、入—八;有的歪了一点点儿:天—夭、干—千;也有的忘了弯钩:干—于、平—乎,都会变成完全不一样的字。

汉字的形体看起来差不多都一样,所以,我们在写字的时候要特别当心,不可以多写一笔,也不可以少写一划;不可以随便延长和缩短笔划,也不可以随便颠倒和调换汉字的偏旁位置。

生 詞

當心	当心	dāngxīn	v.	be careful
錯字	错字	cuòzì	n.	wrongly written characters
點	点	diǎn	n.	dot stroke in Chinese characters
橫	横	héng	n.	horizontal stroke in Chinese characters
豎	竖	shù	n.	vertical stroke in Chinese characters
撇	撇	piě	n.	left-falling stroke in Chinese
捺	捺	nà	n.	right-falling stroke in Chinese
好像	好像	hǎoxiàng	v.	seem (to be)
劃	划	huà	n.	strokes of a Chinese character
沒關係	没关系	méi guānxi		does not matter
變成	变成	biànchéng	v.	change into
令	令	lìng	v.	order
目	目	mù	n.	eye (classical)
筆劃	笔划	bǐhuà	n.	strokes of a Chinese character
士	士	shì	n.	scholar
田	田	tián	n.	field
甲	甲	jiǎ	n.	first; shell
位置	位置	wèizhi	n.	place; position
陪	陪	péi	v.	accompany
部	部	bù	n.	ministry
呆	呆	dāi	v.	stay
杏	杏	xìng	n.	apricot
叮	叮	dīng	v.	sting; bite

入	入	rù	v.	enter
歪	歪	wāi	v.	askew
夭	夭	yāo	v.	die young
彎鈎	弯钩	wān'gōu	n.	turn-hook
于	于	yú		classical Chinese particle
乎	乎	hū		classical Chinese particle
隨便	随便	suíbiàn	adj.	do as one pleases; casual(ly)
延長	延长	yáncháng	v.	extend; lengthen
顛倒	颠倒	diāndǎo	v.	reverse
調換	调换	diàohuàn	v.	exchange; swap

問題

1. 漢字是由甚麼組成的？
   汉字是由什么组成的？
   _____
   _____。

2. 為甚麼有人說寫漢字就像畫畫兒？
   为什么有人说写汉字就像画画儿？
   _____
   _____。

3. 有的字多一點，少一點，就會怎麼樣？
   有的字多一点，少一点，就会怎么样？
   _____
   _____。

4. 筆劃一樣偏旁位置不同的字是一個字嗎？
   笔划一样偏旁位置不同的字是一个字吗？

2. 漢字介紹

_____

_____ 。

5. 為甚麼寫漢字的時候要當心？
   为什么写汉字的时候要当心？

_____

_____ 。

附錄一

漢字偏旁部首簡表

部首	名稱	例字	例字	例字	例字
冫	兩點水 ice liǎngdiǎnshuǐ	冰 bīng ice	冷 lěng cold	寒 hán cold	凍 dòng freeze
氵	三點水 water sāndiǎnshuǐ	洗 xǐ wash	河 hé river	汗 hàn sweat	淚 lèi tear
雨	雨字頭 rain yǔzìtóu	雪 xuě snow	霧 wù fog	雷 léi thunder	霜 shuāng frost
艹	草字頭 grass cǎozìtóu	草 cǎo grass	花 huā flower	芳 fāng fragrant	蕊 ruǐ stamen
竹	竹字頭 bamboo zhúzìtóu	籃 lán basket	筆 bǐ pen	竿 gān pole	筷 kuài chopsticks
扌	提手旁 hand tíshǒupáng	打 dǎ hit	拉 lā pull	推 tuī push	抓 zhuā catch
衤	衣字旁 cloth yīzìpáng	被 bèi quilt	褲 kù pants	襪 wà socks	裙 qún skirt
口	口字旁 mouth kǒuzìpáng	唱 chàng sing	喝 hē drink	吃 chī eat	吹 chuī blow
言	言字旁 speech yánzìpáng	課 kè class	說 shuō say	講 jiǎng say	話 huà talk
心	心字旁 heart xīnzìpáng	想 xiǎng think, miss	忘 wàng forget	愁 chóu worry	怒 nù angry
疒	病字旁 sick bìngzìpáng	疼 téng pain	瘦 shòu thin	瘋 fēng crazy	疤 bā scar

附录一

汉字偏旁部首简表

部首	名称	例1	例2	例3	例4
冫	两点水 ice liǎngdiǎnshuǐ	冰 bīng ice	冷 lěng cold	寒 hán old	冻 dòng freeze
氵	三点水 water sāndiǎnshuǐ	洗 xǐ wash	河 hé river	汗 hàn sweat	泪 lèi tear
雨	雨字头 rain yǔzìtóu	雪 xuě snow	雾 wù fog	雷 léi thunder	霜 shuāng frost
艹	草字头 grass cǎozìtóu	草 cǎo grass	花 huā flower	芳 fāng fragrant	蕊 ruǐ stamen
竹	竹字头 bamboo zhúzìtóu	篮 lán basket	笔 bǐ pen	竿 gān pole	筷 kuài chopsticks
扌	提手旁 hand tíshǒupáng	打 dǎ hit	拉 lā pull	推 tuī push	抓 zhuā catch
衤	衣字旁 cloth yīzìpáng	被 bèi quilt	裤 kù pants	袜 wà socks	裙 qún skirt
口	口字旁 mouth kǒuzìpáng	唱 chàng sing	喝 hē drink	吃 chī eat	吹 chuī blow
讠	言字旁 speech yánzìpáng	课 kè class	说 shuō say	讲 jiǎng say	话 huà talk
心	心字旁 heart xīnzìpáng	想 xiǎng think, miss	忘 wàng forget	愁 chóu worry	怒 nù angry
疒	病字旁 sick bìngzìpáng	疼 téng pain	瘦 shòu thin	疯 fēng crazy	疤 bā scar

附錄二

容易寫錯的字

筆劃長短：日—曰、未—末、天—夫、午—牛、匕—七、汨—汩、
士—土—工、己—已—巳、田—由—甲—申

筆劃多少：大—太、日—白、今—令、目—自、王—玉、厂—广、
万—方、又—叉、勺—匀、衤—礻、住—往、免—兔、
刁—习、弋—戈、爪—瓜、夫—失、斤—斥、茶—荼、
侯—候、竞—竟、肓—盲、毫—毫、氐—氏、戊—戌

筆劃斜正：干—千、王—壬、人—入、子—孑、戍—戌、刀—刁、
叨—叼、佘—余、弈—奕、睢—睢、耽—眈、井—并

筆劃偏離：入—八、可—叮

有無彎鉤：干—于、平—乎

偏旁位置不同：太—犬、部—陪、杏—呆

偏旁不同：符—苻、冷—泠、梁—粱

3

長城
The Great Wall

學習大綱

通過學習本課，學生應該能夠：

1. 掌握這些句型和詞語的意思和用法："當……時候"、"為了"、"只要……就"、"不管……都"、"並且"、"連起來"。
2. 認識和運用課文以及閱讀文章內的生詞。
3. 了解中國建造長城的原因和經過。
4. 知道"孟姜女哭長城"的故事。
5. 簡單地了解"大運河"的歷史。

Study Outline

After studying this chapter, students should:

1. Have a good command of the meaning and usage of these sentence patterns and terms: "dāng ... shíhou" (when), "wèile" (for the purpose of; in order to), "zhǐyào ... jiù" (if only; as long as; provided that), "bùguǎn ... dōu" (no matter what/how/who), "bìngqiě" (and; moreover; furthermore), "lián qǐlái" (connect; link [together]).
2. Be familiar with the meaning and usage of the vocabulary introduced in the text and the reading.
3. Understand why and how the Great Wall in China was built.
4. Be familiar with the story of "Mengjiangnu crying at the foot of the Great Wall".
5. Know something of the history of the Grand Canal in China.

課文

　　長城很長，從東到西有一萬三千四百多里；長城的歷史也很長，從戰國時期到現在有兩千五百多年了。

　　戰國時期，中國分裂成許多小國家，這些小國家常常打仗。他們為了防止別的國家侵略，就在自己的邊界上修建了城牆。

　　秦始皇統一中國以後，為了阻擋北方少數民族的侵略，就把原來的一些城牆連起來，並且又修建了一些新城牆，這就是中國最早的長城。

　　人們只要說到長城，就一定會說到秦始皇，說秦始皇修長城害死了很多人。那時有一個民間故事，叫做"孟姜女哭長城"。

　　這個故事是說孟姜女的丈夫被抓去修長城，當孟姜女去給丈夫送冬天的衣服的時候，發現丈夫早已經累死了，並且被埋在長城的底下。她傷心地哭啊、哭啊！最後把長城哭倒了一大段。

　　秦朝以後，許多朝代也都修建過長城，現在我們看到的長城很多都是明朝修建的。當然，不管哪個朝代修建長城，累死的都是老百姓。

　　雖然過去修建長城害死了很多人，但是在今天，長城是中國人的驕傲。長城很有名、很偉大，不管哪個國家的人，只要去過中國就都知道中國的長城。

课文

长城很长，从东到西有一万三千四百多里；长城的历史也很长，从战国时期到现在有两千五百多年了。

战国时期，中国分裂成许多小国家，这些小国家常常打仗。他们为了防止别的国家侵略，就在自己的边界上修建了城墙。

秦始皇统一中国以后，为了阻挡北方少数民族的侵略，就把原来的一些城墙连起来，并且又修建了一些新城墙，这就是中国最早的长城。

人们只要说到长城，就一定会说到秦始皇，说秦始皇修长城害死了很多人。那时有一个民间故事，叫做"孟姜女哭长城"。

这个故事是说孟姜女的丈夫被抓去修长城，当孟姜女去给丈夫送冬天的衣服的时候，发现丈夫早已经累死了，并且被埋在长城的底下。她伤心地哭啊、哭啊！最后把长城哭倒了一大段。

秦朝以后，许多朝代也都修建过长城，现在我们看到的长城很多都是明朝修建的。当然，不管哪个朝代修建长城，累死的都是老百姓。

虽然过去修建长城害死了很多人，但是在今天，长城是中国人的骄傲。长城很有名、很伟大，不管哪个国家的人，只要去过中国就都知道中国的长城。

生詞

長城	长城	Chángchéng		the Great Wall
里	里	lǐ	n./m.	Chinese unit of length (=1/2 kilometer)
戰國時期	战国时期	Zhànguó shíqī		Warring States period (475–221 B.C.)
分裂	分裂	fēnliè	v.	split; divide
打仗	打仗	dǎ zhàng		go to war
防止	防止	fángzhǐ	v.	prevent; avoid
侵略	侵略	qīnlüè	v./n.	invade; invasion
邊界	边界	biān jiè	n.	boundary; border
修建	修建	xiū jiàn	v.	construct; build
城牆	城墙	chéngqiáng	n.	(city) wall
秦始皇	秦始皇	Qínshǐhuáng		the First Emperor of the Qin dynasty (259–210 B.C.)
統一	统一	tǒngyī	v.	unify
阻擋	阻挡	zǔdǎng	v.	stop; block
少數民族	少数民族	shǎoshù mínzú	n.	ethnic minority
連	连	lián	v.	connect; link
並且	并且	bìngqiě	conj.	and; furthermore
只要……就	只要……就	zhǐyào ... jiù	conj.	if only; as long as
害死	害死	hàisǐ	v.	kill; cause someone's death
民間故事	民间故事	mín jiān gùshi	n.	folktale
孟姜女	孟姜女	Mèng jiāngnǚ		name of a person
當……時候	当……时候	dāng ... shíhou	prep.	when
丈夫	丈夫	zhàngfu	n.	husband

3. 長城

累	累	lèi	v.	tire
埋	埋	mái	v.	bury
底下	底下	dǐxia		under
傷心	伤心	shāngxīn	adj.	sad; grieved
段	段	duàn	m.	section
秦朝	秦朝	Qíncháo		the Qin dynasty (221–207 B.C.)
明朝	明朝	Míngcháo		the Ming dynasty (1368–1644)
朝代	朝代	cháodài	n.	dynasty
有名	有名	yǒumíng	adj.	famous; well-known
不管……都	不管……都	bùguǎn ... dōu	conj.	no matter what
驕傲	骄傲	jiāo'ào	n.	pride

語法和詞語註釋

一、當……時候　　when

1. 當孟姜女去給丈夫送冬天的衣服的時候,發現丈夫早已經累死了。
   当孟姜女去给丈夫送冬天的衣服的时候,发现丈夫早已经累死了。
   When Mengjiangnü went to take her husband some winter clothes, she found he had died of exhaustion some time before.

2. 當我看到不認識的字的時候,就去查字典。
   当我看到不认识的字的时候,就去查字典。
   When I come across unknown characters, I look them up in the dictionary.

3. 當我醒來的時候,第一節課已經快下課了。
   当我醒来的时候,第一节课已经快下课了。
   When I woke up, the first class had almost finished.

二、為了　　for the purpose of; in order to

"為了" introduces the purpose or goal of an action. It can appear at the beginning of a sentence, but when it follows "是", it appears in the second part of the sentence.

1. 為了防止別的國家侵略，就在自己的邊界修建了城牆。
   为了防止别的国家侵略，就在自己的边界修建了城墙。
   In order to stop invasions from other countries, they built walls around their own borders.

2. 為了去中國看長城，我今年開始學中文了。
   为了去中国看长城，我今年开始学中文了。
   In order to go and see the Great Wall of China, I started learning Chinese this year.

3. 為了學好中文，我每天都練習寫漢字。
   为了学好中文，我每天都练习写汉字。
   In order to learn Chinese properly, I practice writing Chinese characters every day.

4. 我去中國是為了學中文。
   我去中国是为了学中文。
   The reason I went to China was to learn Chinese.

三、只要……就　　if only; as long as; provided that

"只要" introduces the necessary condition that brings about a result. It is used in conjunction with "就", which occurs after the subject (if there is one) in the second clause.

1. 人們只要說到長城，就一定會說到秦始皇。
   人们只要说到长城，就一定会说到秦始皇。
   Whenever people talk about the Great Wall, they will definitely mention Qinshihuang.

2. 我們只要學會三千五百字，就可以看簡單的報紙了。

   我们只要学会三千五百字，就可以看简单的报纸了。

   As long as we have learned 3,500 characters, we can read simple newspapers.

3. 只要每天來上課，你就可以得一個 A。

   只要每天来上课，你就可以得一个 A。

   As long as you come to class every day, you can get an A.

四、不管……都　　no matter what/how/who

"不管……都" indicates that no matter what happens, the result of a situation will not change. "無論" can replace "不管" here, but is mostly used in written Chinese, whereas "不管" usually occurs in the spoken language.

1. 不管哪個朝代修建長城，累死的都是老百姓。

   不管哪个朝代修建长城，累死的都是老百姓。

   No matter in which dynasty, it was the common people who died of exhaustion when building the Great Wall.

2. 不管學哪一種語言都很難。

   不管学哪一种语言都很难。

   No matter which language you learn, they are all difficult.

3. 不管在甚麼地方都可以看到中國人。

   不管在什么地方都可以看到中国人。

   No matter where you go, you can see Chinese people.

五、並且　　and; moreover; furthermore

"並且" indicates two actions occur in a sequence or introduce a progression meaning in second sentence.

1. 把原來的一些城牆連起來，並且又修建了一些新的城牆。

   把原来的一些城墙连起来，并且又修建了一些新的城墙。

   They linked together some of the original walls, and moreover, built some new walls.

2. 孟姜女發現丈夫早已經累死了，並且被埋在長城的底下。
   孟姜女发现丈夫早已经累死了，并且被埋在长城的底下。
   Mengjiangnü found her husband had died of exhaustion long before, and was buried under the Great Wall.

3. 漢字很難寫，並且也很難記。
   汉字很难写，并且也很难记。
   Chinese characters are hard to write and also hard to remember.

六、連起來　　connect; link (together)

1. 秦始皇把原來的一些城牆連起來。
   秦始皇把原来的一些城墙连起来。
   Qinshihuang linked together some of the original walls.

2. 有些字在句子裏和別的字連起來讀的時候，聲調會有變化。
   有些字在句子里和别的字连起来读的时候，声调会有变化。
   There are some characters which, when read together with other characters in a sentence, may change their tone.

3. 愛可以把兩個人的心連起來。
   爱可以把两个人的心连起来。
   Love can link the hearts of two people.

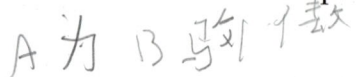

練習

一、用所給的詞語回答問題

1. A：甚麼時候孟姜女發現丈夫累死了？（當……時候）
     什么时候孟姜女发现丈夫累死了？（当……时候）
   B：_____。

2. A：你甚麼時候想家？（當……時候）
     你什么时候想家？（当……时候）
   B：_____。

3. 長城　　　　　　　　　　　　　　　　　　　　　　　　47

3. A：秦始皇為甚麼要修長城？（為了）
　　　秦始皇为什么要修长城？（为了）
　B：_____。

4. A：湯姆為甚麼要學中文？（為了）
　　　汤姆为什么要学中文？（为了）
　B：_____。

5. A：甚麼人知道中國的長城？（只要……就）
　　　什么人知道中国的长城？（只要……就）
　B：_____。

6. A：明天不下雨，我們可以出去玩嗎？（只要……就）
　　　明天不下雨，我们可以出去玩吗？（只要……就）
　B：_____。

7. A：哪個國家的人知道中國的長城？（不管……都）
　　　哪个国家的人知道中国的长城？（不管……都）
　B：_____。

8. A：你喜歡中國飯，還是喜歡日本飯？（不管……都）
　　　你喜欢中国饭，还是喜欢日本饭？（不管……都）
　B：_____。

二、用所給的詞語改寫句子

1. 別人說上中文課可以認識中國女孩子，所以我選了中文。（為了）
　別人说上中文课可以认识中国女孩子，所以我选了中文。（为了）
　_____。

2. 湯姆要去北京看小燕的父母，所以他現在學習中文。（為了）
　汤姆要去北京看小燕的父母，所以他现在学习中文。（为了）
　_____。

3. 有水字旁的字都跟水有關係。（只要……就）

有水字旁的字都跟水有关系。(只要……就)

_____。

4. 會說中文的人很容易找到工作。(只要……就)
   会说中文的人很容易找到工作。(只要……就)

_____。

5. 我喜歡吃美國飯，也喜歡吃日本飯，還喜歡吃中國飯。(不管……都)
   我喜欢吃美国饭，也喜欢吃日本饭，还喜欢吃中国饭。(不管……都)

_____。

6. 小張住在地下室，白天也要開燈。(不管……都)
   小张住在地下室，白天也要开灯。(不管……都)

_____。

三、用所給的詞語填空 (一個詞語可以用多次)

當……時候、不管……都、為了、只要……就
当……时候、不管……都、为了、只要……就

1. 這些小國家_____防止別的國家侵略，就在自己的邊界上修建起了城牆。
   这些小国家_____防止别的国家侵略，就在自己的边界上修建起了城墙。

2. 湯姆_____去看趙小燕的父母，他開始學中文了。
   汤姆_____去看赵小燕的父母，他开始学中文了。

3. 人們_____說到長城，_____會說到秦始皇，說秦始皇修長城害死了很多人。
   人们_____说到长城，_____会说到秦始皇，说秦始皇修长城害死了很多人。

4. _____去過中國的人_____知道中國的長城。
   _____去过中国的人_____知道中国的长城。

3. 長城　　　　　　　　　　　　　　　　　　　　　49

5. _____哪個朝代修建長城，累死的_____是老百姓。
   _____哪个朝代修建长城，累死的_____是老百姓。

6. _____學甚麼語言，_____要學聽、説、讀、寫。
   _____学什么语言，_____要学听、说、读、写。

7. _____我沒有錢的_____，我就想媽媽了。
   _____我没有钱的_____，我就想妈妈了。

8. _____老師開始講課的_____，他還在睡覺呢。
   _____老师开始讲课的_____，他还在睡觉呢。

四、用所給的詞語造句

1. 為了
   为了
   _____。

2. 只要……就
   只要……就
   (handwritten notes: If A happens then B [controller]; 只要 A 就 B; 只有 A 才 B; B will only happen if A happens first)
   _____。

3. 不管……都
   不管……都
   _____。

4. 當……時候
   当……时候
   _____。

5. 連起來
   连起来
   _____。

五、翻譯

1. When Mengjiangnü went to take her husband some winter clothes, she found he had already died of exhaustion and was buried under the Great Wall.

   _____

   _____ 。

2. In order to stop invasions by northern minorities, Emperor Qin linked together the original walls and built some new walls, thus forming the first Great Wall of China.

   _____

   _____ 。

3. Although many people were killed during its construction, the Chinese people nowadays are very proud of the Great Wall. Anyone who knows about China will know about the Great Wall.

   _____

   _____ 。

六、根據課文回答問題

1. 當時那些國家為甚麼要修建城牆？
   当时那些国家为什么要修建城墙？

   _____

   _____ 。

2. 萬里長城是甚麼人修建的？
   万里长城是什么人修建的？

   _____

   _____ 。

3. "孟姜女哭長城"說的是一個甚麼故事？

3. 長城

"孟姜女哭长城"说的是一个什么故事？

_____

_____ 。

4. 為甚麼長城很有名？
   为什么长城很有名？

_____

_____ 。

閱讀

大運河

不管哪一個國家的人，只要去過中國就知道中國的長城，長城很有名、很偉大。其實，和長城同樣有名、同樣偉大的還有"大運河"。

長城是人們用磚一塊一塊壘起來的，從東到西壘了一萬三千四百多里；運河是人們用鍬一鍬一鍬挖出來的，從南到北挖了三千五百多里。

書上說，最早的一條運河是春秋時期修建的，後來一些朝代也都修建過運河。到了隋朝，隋朝的皇帝為了把各地的糧食和物品運到國都西安，就讓老百姓又挖了許多新的河道，然後把它們連起來，這就是中國有名的大運河。

為甚麼要挖運河呢？那是因為古時候沒有火車和飛機，交通運輸的工具只有馬車和船。馬車上山下山的時候很不方便，所以大家都願意坐船。可是中國的河流都是從西向東流的，沒有從南到北的河流。人們為了南北交通方便，就從南到北挖了這條大運河。

後來，因為有了火車和海上運輸，大運河的作用就不大了，慢慢地一些河道斷流了、乾涸了。今天，在中國南方雖然有些河道還在使用，但她只是靜靜地在那裏流淌着。現在很少有人知道過去那條很有名、很偉大的"大運河"了。

阅读

大运河

不管哪一个国家的人,只要去过中国就知道中国的长城,长城很有名、很伟大。其实,和长城同样有名、同样伟大的还有"大运河"。

长城是人们用砖一块一块垒起来的,从东到西垒了一万三千四百多里;运河是人们用锹一锹一锹挖出来的,从南到北挖了三千五百多里。

书上说,最早的一条运河是春秋时期修建的,后来一些朝代也都修建过运河。到了隋朝,隋朝的皇帝为了把各地的粮食和物品运到国都西安,就让老百姓又挖了许多新的河道,然后把它们连起来,这就是中国有名的大运河。

为什么要挖运河呢?那是因为古时候没有火车和飞机,交通运输的工具只有马车和船。马车上山下山的时候很不方便,所以大家都愿意坐船。可是中国的河流都是从西向东流的,没有从南到北的河流。人们为了南北交通方便,就从南到北挖了这条大运河。

后来,因为有了火车和海上运输,大运河的作用就不大了,慢慢地一些河道断流了、干涸了。今天,在中国南方虽然有些河道还在使用,但她只是静静地在那里流淌着。现在很少有人知道过去那条很有名、很伟大的"大运河"了。

生 詞

大運河	大运河	Dàyùnhé		the Grand Canal
磚	砖	zhuān	n.	brick
壘	垒	lěi	v.	build by piling up bricks
鍁	锨	xiān	n.	shovel
挖	挖	wā	v.	dig
條	条	tiáo	m.	measure word for rivers
春秋時期	春秋时期	Chūnqiū shíqī		Spring and Autumn period (770–476 B.C.)
隋朝	隋朝	Suícháo		the Sui dynasty (581–618)
皇帝	皇帝	huángdì	n.	emperor
國都	国都	guódū	n.	capital city
糧食	粮食	liángshi	n.	grain
物品	物品	wùpǐn	n.	products; goods
運	运	yùn	v.	transport
西安	西安	Xī'ān		name of a city in China
交通	交通	jiāotōng	v.	transportation; traffic; communications
運輸	运输	yùnshū	v.	transportation
工具	工具	gōngjù	n.	means
馬車	马车	mǎchē	n.	carriage; cart
船	船	chuán	n.	boat; ship
方便	方便	fāngbiàn	adj.	convenient
海	海	hǎi	n.	sea
作用	作用	zuòyòng	n.	function

河道	河道	hédào	n.	river course
斷流	断流	duànliú		stop flowing
乾涸	干涸	gānhé	v.	dry up; run dry
南方	南方	nánfāng	n.	the south
使用	使用	shǐyòng	v.	use
靜靜地	静静地	jìng jìng de	adv.	quietly
流淌	流淌	liútǎng	v.	flow

問題

1. 為甚麼說大運河和長城同樣有名？
   为什么说大运河和长城同样有名？
   _____
   _____。

2. 中國人為甚麼要挖大運河？
   中国人为什么要挖大运河？
   _____
   _____。

3. 為甚麼現在大運河的作用不大了呢？
   为什么现在大运河的作用不大了呢？
   _____
   _____。

4

中國的名稱
How Names for China and the Chinese Have Changed

學習大綱

通過學習本課，學生應該能夠：

1. 掌握這些句型和詞語的意思和用法："於是"、"認為"和"以為"、"住"和"居住"、"才"、"連……也/都/還"、"改 V"。
2. 認識和運用課文以及閱讀文章內的生詞。
3. 明白中國的名稱是怎麼來的，以及這些名稱跟哪些因素有關係。
4. 了解"中國"的英文名稱"China"一詞的來源。

Study Outline

After studying this chapter, students should:

1. Have a good command of the meaning and usage of these sentence patterns and terms: "yúshì" (and then; hence), "rènwéi" and "yǐwéi" (think; consider), "zhù" and "jūzhù" (live; reside), "cái" ([not] until), "lián ... yě/dōu/hái" (even), "gǎi V" (change; instead of).
2. Be familiar with the meaning and usage of the vocabulary introduced in the text and the reading.
3. Be aware how names for China and the Chinese have changed and what caused these changes.
4. Know how the word "China" came to be used as the English name for *Zhongguo*.

課文

五千年前,在黃河中下游一帶有兩個原始部落:炎帝部落和黃帝部落。中國人認為炎帝和黃帝是自己的祖先,自己是"炎黃子孫"。

在春秋時期,炎黃的子孫們把自己叫做"華夏族"。"華"是繁榮的意思;"夏"這個字形就像一個中國人的樣子。那時候,華夏族的四周有其他少數民族,那些人的穿着打扮和華夏族不一樣,於是華夏族就用"夏"字來表示自己。

當時,華夏族以為他們居住在大地的中心,所以就把他們居住的地方叫做"中華"、"中國"。華夏族是中國最早的民族,到現在中國人還都說自己是"華人"、"華夏後裔"。

漢朝是歷史上一個非常強大的朝代。從漢朝起,華夏族又把自己叫做"漢族",把自己的語言和文字叫做"漢語"和"漢字"。唐朝也是一個很強大的朝代,有許多外國人把中國人就叫做"唐人",後來居住在國外的華僑,也把自己住的那幾條街叫做"唐人街"。

1912年中華民國成立以後,"中國"才正式成為國家的名稱。從那個時候開始,漢族和其他的少數民族都叫做中國人。今天,不但很多人把漢語改叫做"中文",就連唐人街也都改叫做"中國城"了。

课文

五千年前，在黄河中下游一带有两个原始部落：炎帝部落和黄帝部落。中国人认为炎帝和黄帝是自己的祖先，自己是"炎黄子孙"。

在春秋时期，炎黄的子孙们把自己叫做"华夏族"。"华"是繁荣的意思；"夏"这个字形就像一个中国人的样子。那时候，华夏族的四周有其他少数民族，那些人的穿着打扮和华夏族不一样，于是华夏族就用"夏"字来表示自己。

当时，华夏族以为他们居住在大地的中心，所以就把他们居住的地方叫做"中华"、"中国"。华夏族是中国最早的民族，到现在中国人还都说自己是"华人"、"华夏后裔"。

汉朝是历史上一个非常强大的朝代。从汉朝起，华夏族又把自己叫做"汉族"，把自己的语言和文字叫做"汉语"和"汉字"。唐朝也是一个很强大的朝代，有许多外国人把中国人就叫做"唐人"，后来居住在国外的华侨，也把自己住的那几条街叫做"唐人街"。

1912年中华民国成立以后，"中国"才正式成为国家的名称。从那个时候开始，汉族和其他的少数民族都叫做中国人。今天，不但很多人把汉语改叫做"中文"，就连唐人街也都改叫做"中国城"了。

生詞

名稱	名称	míngchēng	n.	name
中下游	中下游	zhōng-xiàyóu	n.	middle and lower reaches (of a river)
一帶	一带	yīdài	n.	area
原始部落	原始部落	yuánshǐ bùluò	n.	primitive tribe
炎帝黃帝	炎帝黄帝	Yándì Huángdì		Emperor Yan and Yellow Emperor, legendary rulers of ancient China (2737–2697 B.C.)
認為	认为	rènwéi	v.	think; consider
祖先	祖先	zǔxiān	n.	ancestors
子孫	子孙	zǐsūn	n.	descendants
華夏	华夏	Huáxià		an ancient name for China
繁榮	繁荣	fánróng	adj.	prosperous
四周	四周	sìzhōu	n.	all around
穿著打扮	穿着打扮	chuānzhuó dǎbàn		way of dressing; style
於是	于是	yúshì	conj.	and then; hence
民族	民族	mínzú	n.	nation; nationality
以為	以为	yǐwéi	v.	think; consider
居住	居住	jūzhù	v.	live; reside
大地	大地	dàdì	n.	world; earth
中心	中心	zhōngxīn	n.	center
後裔	后裔	hòuyì	n.	descendants
漢朝	汉朝	Hàncháo		the Han dynasty (206 B.C.–A.D. 220)
強大	强大	qiángdà	adj.	strong and powerful

唐朝	唐朝	Tángcháo		the Tang dynasty (618–907)
華僑	华侨	huáqiáo	n.	overseas Chinese
唐人街	唐人街	Tángrén jiē		Chinatown
中華民國	中华民国	Zhōnghuá Mínguó		the Republic of China
才	才	cái	adv.	not until; only then
正式	正式	zhèngshì	adj.	formal; official
成為	成为	chéngwéi	v.	turn into; become
改	改	gǎi	v.	change / correct
連……也	连……也	lián ... yě	conj.	even

語法和詞語註釋

一、於是   and then; hence

This is used at the beginning of the second clause of a sentence to indicate that a situation or action is caused by a matter mentioned in the first clause.

1. 少數民族和華夏族的穿著打扮不一樣,於是華夏族就用"夏"來表示自己。
   少数民族和华夏族的穿着打扮不一样,于是华夏族就用"夏"来表示自己。
   The minorities dressed differently from Huaxia tribe. Hence Huaxia tribe used "Xia" to represent themselves.

2. 作業做完了,於是我就去看電視了。
   作业做完了,于是我就去看电视了。
   I finished my homework and then went to watch TV.

3. 沒有現金了,於是我就用爸爸的信用卡。
   没有现金了,于是我就用爸爸的信用卡。
   I had no money left, so I used my Dad's credit card.

二、"認為"and"以為"   think; consider

"認為"and"以為"are used as verbs equivalent to "think" in English.

Sometimes, however, they are not changeable in Chinese.

"認為" in the following sentences indicates the speaker's judgment or belief.

1. 中國人認為自己是炎黃的子孫。
   中国人认为自己是炎黄的子孙。
   Chinese people consider themselves to be descendants of the Emperor Yan and the Yellow Emperor.

2. 現在很多人都認為學中文很有用。
   现在很多人都认为学中文很有用。
   These days many people think that learning Chinese is very useful.

3. 老師認為聽、說、讀、寫都很重要。
   老师认为听、说、读、写都很重要。
   The professor thinks listening, speaking, reading and writing are all very important.

"以為" on the other hand carries assumptions which might be erroneous.

4. 以前中國人以為自己住在大地的中心，所以把自己住的地方叫中國。
   以前中国人以为自己住在大地的中心，所以把自己住的地方叫中国。
   A long time ago Chinese people thought they lived in the center of the world, and thus called the place where they were living "The Middle Kingdom".

5. 我以為你回家了呢，你怎麼還在這兒？
   我以为你回家了呢，你怎么还在这儿？
   I thought you'd gone home. How come you are still here?

6. 湯姆以為只要學會聽中文就可以了。
   汤姆以为只要学会听中文就可以了。
   Tom thought that as long as he could understand Chinese by listening, he would be OK.

三、"住" and "居住"　　　live; reside

Both "居住" and "住" refer to an extended period of residence, but "住" can also be used to refer to a short stay.

1. 以前中國人以為自己居住在大地的中心，所以把自己住的地方叫中國。
   以前中国人以为自己居住在大地的中心，所以把自己住的地方叫中国。
   A long time ago Chinese people thought they lived in the center of the world, and thus called the place where they were living "The Middle Kingdom".

2. 很多居住在美國的華人還是喜歡吃中國飯。
   很多居住在美国的华人还是喜欢吃中国饭。
   Many Chinese people living in the U.S. still like to eat Chinese food.

3. 湯姆去北京的時候，在趙小燕家裏住了一兩天。
   汤姆去北京的时候，在赵小燕家里住了一两天。
   When Tom was in Beijing, he stayed at Zhao Xiaoyan's home for a few days.

4. 我朋友來看我的時候，就住在我家的客廳裏。
   我朋友来看我的时候，就住在我家的客厅里。
   When my friends came to visit me, they stayed in my living room.

四、才　　　(not) until

This is used after time expressions and indicates that something happens later than expected.

1. 1912年中華民國成立以後，"中國"才正式成為國家的名稱。
   1912年中华民国成立以后，"中国"才正式成为国家的名称。
   Only since 1912 when the Republic of China was founded, has China become the official name of the country.

2. 昨天晚上做中文作業，做到十二點才睡覺。
   昨天晚上做中文作业，做到十二点才睡觉。
   I did my Chinese homework last night and didn't go to bed until 12:00 p.m.

3. 他的衣服太髒了，洗了兩個小時才洗乾淨。
他的衣服太脏了，洗了两个小时才洗干净。
His clothes were extremely dirty and had to be washed for two hours to get them clean.

五、連……也/都/還　even

The "連……也" structure is used to emphasize whatever occurs between them. "也" can be replaced by "都" or "還".

1. 今天，不但很多人把漢語改叫做中文，就連唐人街也都改叫做中國城了。
今天，不但很多人把汉语改叫做中文，就连唐人街也都改叫做中国城了。
Today, many people call Chinese "Zhongwen" instead of "Hanyu", and even Chinatown is called "Zhongguocheng" instead of "Tangrenjie".

2. 他起來晚了，連早飯也沒有吃就去上課了。
他起来晚了，连早饭也没有吃就去上课了。
He got up late, and went to school without even having breakfast.

3. 這道數學題很容易，連小學生都會做。
这道数学题很容易，连小学生都会做。
This math problem is very easy, even elementary school students can solve it.

六、改 V　change; instead of

1. 後來人們把唐人街改叫做中國城了。
后来人们把唐人街改叫做中国城了。
Later, people call it "Zhongguocheng" instead of "Tangrenjie".

2. 我以前用左手寫字，現在改用右手了。
我以前用左手写字，现在改用右手了。
I used to write with my left hand but now I use my right hand.

3. 以前中國人用刀叉吃飯，後來改用筷子了。
以前中国人用刀叉吃饭，后来改用筷子了。

Chinese people used to eat with knives and forks, but later they changed to using chopsticks.

練 習

一、用所給的詞語完成對話

1. A：＂中國＂甚麼時候正式作為國家的名稱的？（才）
   ＂中国＂什么时候正式作为国家的名称的？（才）

   B：＿＿＿＿＿＿＿＿＿＿＿＿＿＿＿＿＿＿＿＿＿＿＿＿＿＿＿＿＿＿。

2. A：你昨天晚上是幾點鐘睡覺的？（才）
   你昨天晚上是几点钟睡觉的？（才）

   B：＿＿＿＿＿＿＿＿＿＿＿＿＿＿＿＿＿＿＿＿＿＿＿＿＿＿＿＿＿＿。

3. A：華夏族為甚麼把自己住的地方叫中國？（以為）
   华夏族为什么把自己住的地方叫中国？（以为）

   B：＿＿＿＿＿＿＿＿＿＿＿＿＿＿＿＿＿＿＿＿＿＿＿＿＿＿＿＿＿＿。

4. A：你昨天為甚麼不來上課？（以為）
   你昨天为什么不来上课？（以为）

   B：＿＿＿＿＿＿＿＿＿＿＿＿＿＿＿＿＿＿＿＿＿＿＿＿＿＿＿＿＿＿。

5. A：現在人們把唐人街叫做甚麼？（改V）
   现在人们把唐人街叫做什么？（改V）

   B：＿＿＿＿＿＿＿＿＿＿＿＿＿＿＿＿＿＿＿＿＿＿＿＿＿＿＿＿＿＿。

6. A：你以前用左手寫字，現在呢？（改V）
   你以前用左手写字，现在呢？（改V）

   B：＿＿＿＿＿＿＿＿＿＿＿＿＿＿＿＿＿＿＿＿＿＿＿＿＿＿＿＿＿＿。

二、用所給的詞語造句

1. 連……也

連……也

_____。

2. 才
　才

_____。

3. 於是
　于是

_____。

4. 改V
　改V

_____。

5. 以為
　以为

_____。

三、用所給的詞語填空（一個詞語可以用一次）

連……也、改、於是、才、以為、認為
连……也、改、于是、才、以为、认为

1. 以前人們_____城牆可以防止別的國家侵略，_____就在自己的邊界上修建起了城牆。現在人們_____城牆不能防止別的國家侵略。
　以前人们_____城墙可以防止别的国家侵略，_____就在自己的边界上修建起了城墙。现在人们_____城墙不能防止别的国家侵略。

2. 在中國_____小孩子_____知道自己是炎黃子孫。1912年以後，"中國"_____正式成為國家的名稱，漢族和其他少數民族都_____叫做中國人了。
　在中国_____小孩子_____知道自己是炎黄子孙。1912年以后，"中国"_____正式成为国家的名称，汉族和其他少数民族都_____叫做中国人了。

四、用下面的詞語說說你們國家的名稱是怎麼來的

認為、祖先、子孫、把……叫做、當時、那時候、居住、穿着打扮、於是、是表示……的意思、從……開始

认为、祖先、子孙、把……叫做、当时、那时候、居住、穿着打扮、于是、是表示……的意思、从……开始

_____
_____
_____。

五、翻譯

1. In the past, the Chinese thought they lived in the center of the world, and thus called the place where they were living "The Middle Kingdom".

    _____
    _____。

2. Since the Han dynasty, the Huaxia tribe has called themselves "the Han people", and even their language has been called "the Han language".

    _____
    _____。

3. In China, you can see many ethnic minority groups. They dress totally differently from the Han people.

    _____
    _____。

六、根據課文回答問題

1. 中國人為甚麼說自己是炎黃子孫、華夏後裔？
   中国人为什么说自己是炎黄子孙、华夏后裔？

    _____

_____ 。

2. 華夏族為甚麼把他們居住的地方叫做"中國"?
   华夏族为什么把他们居住的地方叫做"中国"?
   _____
   _____ 。

3. 從甚麼時候開始華夏族把自己的語言叫做"漢語"的?
   从什么时候开始华夏族把自己的语言叫做"汉语"的?
   _____
   _____ 。

4. 為甚麼華人住的地方叫做"唐人街"?
   为什么华人住的地方叫做"唐人街"?
   _____
   _____ 。

5. 甚麼時候把漢語改叫做"中文"的?
   什么时候把汉语改叫做"中文"的?
   _____
   _____ 。

閱 讀

中國和瓷器

英文裏"china"有兩個意思：一個是瓷器；一個是中國。有的人說"china"最早的意思是瓷器，後來才是中國。

瓷器是古代中國發明的。古時候人們的日常生活離不開瓷器：從舀湯的湯勺，到盛飯的碗盤；從喝茶的茶壺，到放花的花瓶；從最小的酒杯，到最大的水缸；就連睡覺的枕頭和坐的墩子都是用瓷做的。

到了唐朝和宋朝的時候，瓷器已經做得非常漂亮了。那時來中國的外國商人都很喜歡中國的瓷器，他們買了許多帶回去。從那以後，不但中國的瓷器大量地運到了國外，就連製作的方法也傳到了各個國家。

當時世界上許多人都知道東亞有一個大國，這個國家會做很漂亮的瓷器。那個時候外國人把瓷器叫做"china"，後來他們把製作瓷器的國家也叫做"china"，就這樣，瓷器就成了中國的名字。

如果你不相信，你可以去查字典。字典上"china"的第一個意思是瓷器，第二個意思是中國。

有人認為這種說法不對。他們說中國以前就叫"china"。當瓷器第一次運到外國的時候，外國人不知道瓷器叫甚麼，但是他們知道這些漂亮的瓷器是從中國來的，於是就把瓷器也叫做了"china"。

阅 读

中国和瓷器

英文里"china"有两个意思：一个是瓷器；一个是中国。有的人说"china"最早的意思是瓷器，后来才是中国。

瓷器是古代中国发明的。古时候人们的日常生活离不开瓷器：从舀汤的汤勺，到盛饭的碗盘；从喝茶的茶壶，到放花的花瓶；从最小的酒杯，到最大的水缸；就连睡觉的枕头和坐的墩子都是用瓷做的。

到了唐朝和宋朝的时候，瓷器已经做得非常漂亮了。那时来中国的外国商人都很喜欢中国的瓷器，他们买了许多带回去。从那以后，不但中国的瓷器大量地运到了国外，就连制作的方法也传到了各个国家。

当时世界上许多人都知道东亚有一个大国，这个国家会做很漂亮的瓷器。那个时候外国人把瓷器叫做"china"，后来他们把制作瓷器的国家也叫做"china"，就这样，瓷器就成了中国的名字。

如果你不相信，你可以去查字典。字典上"china"的第一个意思是瓷器，第二个意思是中国。

有人认为这种说法不对。他们说中国以前就叫"china"。当瓷器第一次运到外国的时候，外国人不知道瓷器叫什么，但是他们知道这些漂亮的瓷器是从中国来的，于是就把瓷器也叫做了"china"。

4. 中國的名稱

生詞

瓷器	瓷器	cíqì	n.	china
發明	发明	fāmíng	v.	invent
日常	日常	rìcháng	n.	daily; day-to-day
舀	舀	yǎo	v.	dip; ladle; scoop
湯	汤	tāng	n.	soup
杓	勺	sháo	n.	spoon; ladle
盛	盛	chéng	v.	fill (a bowl)
碗	碗	wǎn	n.	bowl
盤	盘	pán	n.	plate
茶壺	茶壶	cháhú	n.	tea pot
花瓶	花瓶	huāpíng	n.	vase
杯	杯	bēi	n.	cup
缸	缸	gāng	n.	big ceramic storage jar
枕頭	枕头	zhěntou	n.	pillow
墩子	墩子	dūnzi	n.	block
宋朝	宋朝	Sòngcháo		the Song dynasty (960–1280)
商人	商人	shāngrén	n.	merchant; businessman
大量	大量	dàliàng	adj.	in great quantities
製作	制作	zhìzuò	v.	manufacture
傳	传	chuán	v.	pass on; transmit; convey
世界	世界	shìjiè	n.	world
東亞	东亚	Dōngyà		East Asia
相信	相信	xiāngxìn	v.	believe
說法	说法	shuōfa	n.	statement; version; argument

問 題

1. 中國瓷器甚麼時候傳到外國的？
   中国瓷器什么时候传到外国的？
   _____
   _____ 。

2. 你能說出幾件中國人常用的瓷器嗎？
   你能说出几件中国人常用的瓷器吗？
   _____
   _____ 。

3. 為甚麼外國人把瓷器叫 "china"？
   为什么外国人把瓷器叫 "china"？
   _____
   _____ 。

4. 你認為 "china" 最早的意思是甚麼？
   你认为 "china" 最早的意思是什么？
   _____
   _____ 。

附錄

中國歷史朝代簡表
中国历史朝代简表

夏	夏	Xià	Xia	2205–1766 B.C.
商	商	Shāng	Shang	1766–1122 B.C.
周	周	Zhōu	Zhou	1122–221 B.C.
春秋	春秋	Chūnqiū	Spring and Autumn period	770–476 B.C.
戰國	战国	Zhànguó	Warring States	476–221 B.C.
秦	秦	Qín	Qin	221–206 B.C.
漢	汉	Hàn	Han	206 B.C.–A.D. 220
三國	三国	Sānguó	Three Kingdoms	220–280
晉	晋	Jìn	Jin	265–420
南北朝	南北朝	Nánběicháo	Northern and Southern Dynasties	420–581
隋	隋	Suí	Sui	581–618
唐	唐	Táng	Tang	618–907
五代十國	五代十国	Wǔdài shíguó	Five Dynasties and Ten Kingdoms	907–960
宋	宋	Sòng	Song	960–1280
元	元	Yuán	Yuan	1280–1368
明	明	Míng	Ming	1368–1644
清	清	Qīng	Qing	1644–1911

5

婚姻介紹
Matchmaking

學習大綱

通過學習本課，學生應該能夠：

1. 掌握這些句型和詞語的意思和用法："只有……才"和"只要……就"、"至於"、"(時間)來"、"越來越"、"讓"、"X方"、"幫忙"和"幫助"。
2. 認識和運用課文以及閱讀文章內的生詞。
3. 了解以前中國的媒婆介紹婚姻的方法。
4. 了解成語"走馬觀花"的意思和故事。

Study Outline

After studying this chapter, students should:

1. Have a good command of the meaning and usage of these sentence patterns and terms: "zhǐyǒu ... cái" (only when; not until) and "zhǐyào ... jiù" (as long as), "zhìyú" (as to; as for), "(time period) lái", "yuèláiyuè ..." (the more ..., the more ...), "ràng" (let; make), "X fāng" (X side), "bāngmáng" and "bāngzhù" (help).
2. Be familiar with the meaning and usage of the vocabulary introduced in the text and the reading.
3. Know how the matchmaking worked in ancient China.
4. Know the meaning and the origin of the expression "zǒumǎ-guānhuā" (know only from cursory observation).

課文

　　很久以前，中國有一種人叫"媒婆"，她專門給人做媒，也就是介紹婚姻。人們要結婚的時候都去找她幫忙。媒婆先到男方家說有一個女孩非常漂亮，再去女方家說有個男孩特別聰明。媒婆花言巧語說得雙方的父母都滿意了，這門婚事就說成了。

　　那時候，兒女的婚姻只要父母滿意就行了，兒女自己願意不願意、喜歡不喜歡都沒關係。許多人在結婚前甚至連面都沒有見過。新郎只有到結婚那天晚上，才知道自己娶的媳婦漂亮不漂亮；新娘也只有這個時候，才看到自己嫁的是一個甚麼樣的男人。

　　當然不管是漂亮還是醜、聰明還是笨都已經太晚了，至於他倆有沒有愛情，他們的婚姻幸福不幸福，從來就沒有人去想這些事情。

　　這種介紹婚姻的方法在中國已經千百年了。千百年來，造成了很多不幸的家庭，媒婆的名聲於是也就越來越不好了。

　　最近幾十年來，媒婆換了一個好聽的名字叫"紅娘"。介紹的方法也有了改變。紅娘讓男女雙方先見面，等到他們兩人都滿意了以後再結婚。

　　紅娘幫助許多人組成了幸福的家庭，這些人都很感激紅娘。紅娘的名聲越來越好了，找紅娘幫忙的人也越來越多了。紅娘們就成立了一個專門介紹婚姻的大公司，叫做"婚姻介紹所"。

课文

很久以前，中国有一种人叫"媒婆"，她专门给人做媒，也就是介绍婚姻。人们要结婚的时候都去找她帮忙。媒婆先到男方家说有一个女孩非常漂亮，再去女方家说有个男孩特别聪明。媒婆花言巧语说得双方的父母都满意了，这门婚事就说成了。

那时候，儿女的婚姻只要父母满意就行了，儿女自己愿意不愿意、喜欢不喜欢都没关系。许多人在结婚前甚至连面都没有见过。新郎只有到结婚那天晚上，才知道自己娶的媳妇漂亮不漂亮；新娘也只有这个时候，才看到自己嫁的是一个什么样的男人。

当然不管是漂亮还是丑、聪明还是笨都已经太晚了，至于他俩有没有爱情，他们的婚姻幸福不幸福，从来就没有人去想这些事情。

这种介绍婚姻的方法在中国已经千百年了。千百年来，造成了很多不幸的家庭，媒婆的名声于是也就越来越不好了。

最近几十年来，媒婆换了一个好听的名字叫"红娘"。介绍的方法也有了改变。红娘让男女双方先见面，等到他们两人都满意了以后再结婚。

红娘帮助许多人组成了幸福的家庭，这些人都很感激红娘。红娘的名声越来越好了，找红娘帮忙的人也越来越多了。红娘们就成立了一个专门介绍婚姻的大公司，叫做"婚姻介绍所"。

生 詞

婚姻	婚姻	hūnyīn	n.	marriage
久	久	jiǔ	adj.	for a long time
媒婆	媒婆	méipó	n.	female matchmaker
專門	专门	zhuānmén	adv.	specialize in; specially
做媒	做媒	zuò méi		be a matchmaker
__方	__方	__fāng		__side
花言巧語	花言巧语	huāyán qiǎoyǔ		honeyed and deceiving words
雙方	双方	shuāngfāng	n.	both sides
滿意	满意	mǎnyì	adj.	satisfied
成	成	chéng	v.	accomplish; succeed
甚至	甚至	shènzhì	adv.	even; (go) so far as to ...
新郎	新郎	xīnláng	n.	bridegroom
娶	娶	qǔ	v.	(of a man) marry
媳婦	媳妇	xífu	n.	wife
新娘	新娘	xīnniáng	n.	bride
只有……才	只有……才	zhǐyǒu ... cái	conj.	only when; not until
嫁	嫁	jià	v.	(of a woman) marry
醜	丑	chǒu	adj.	ugly
笨	笨	bèn	adj.	stupid; foolish
至於	至于	zhìyú	prep.	as to; as for
愛情	爱情	àiqíng	n.	love
幸福	幸福	xìngfú	adj.	happy
從來	从来	cónglái	adv.	at all times; always
造成	造成	zàochéng	v.	create

5. 婚姻介紹

不幸	不幸	bùxìng		unfortunate; unhappy
名聲	名声	míngshēng	n.	reputation
越來越	越来越	yuèláiyuè	adv.	the more ..., the more ...
紅娘	红娘	hóngniáng	n.	female matchmaker
改變	改变	gǎibiàn	v.	change
讓	让	ràng	v.	let; make
感激	感激	gǎnjī	v.	appreciate
公司	公司	gōngsī	n.	company
所	所	suǒ	n.	place; "agency"

語法和詞語註釋

①A 和 B 结婚
②新郎（娶）了新娘
③新娘嫁新郎

一、只有……才　　only when; not until

"只有" indicates the only condition required for certain circumstances to appear. It is followed by "才".

1. 新娘只有這時候，才看到自己嫁的是一個甚麼樣的男人。
   新娘只有这时候，才看到自己嫁的是一个什么样的男人。
   Only at this moment can the bride know what kind of man she has been married to.

2. 只有沒錢的時候，我才想家。
   只有没钱的时候，我才想家。
   I am homesick only when I have no money.

3. 湯姆只有學好中文，才可以去北京見小燕的父母。
   汤姆只有学好中文，才可以去北京见小燕的父母。
   Tom can go to Beijing to see Xiaoyan's parents only when he has learned Chinese well.

"只要……就" and "只有……才"

The difference between "只要……就" and "只有……才" is that "只有"

indicates the only condition, while "只要" provides a necessary condition or minimum requirement.

4. 只要體育好就可以上好大學。(學習好也可以、音樂好也可以。)
   只要体育好就可以上好大学。(学习好也可以、音乐好也可以。)
   You can get into college as long as you're good at sports. (Being good at sports is one of the conditions that is necessary for entering college.)

5. 只有體育好才可以上好大學。(學習好不可以、音樂好不可以。)
   只有体育好才可以上好大学。(学习好不可以、音乐好不可以。)
   You can get into college only if you're good at sports. (Being good at sports is the only condition for entering college.)

二、至於　as to; as for

"至於" is used at the beginning of a sentence to introduce a new topic.

1. 至於他們的婚姻幸福不幸福，沒有人去想這件事。
   至于他们的婚姻幸福不幸福，没有人去想这件事。
   As to whether their marriage was happy or not, no one cared.

2. 我跟她說過了，至於她聽不聽，我就不管了。
   我跟她说过了，至于她听不听，我就不管了。
   I've talked to her. As to whether she will listen to me, it has nothing to do with me.

3. 只要能上大學就可以，至於學得好不好，沒關係。
   只要能上大学就可以，至于学得好不好，没关系。
   It's good enough if I can enter college. It's not important as to how well I'll do in study.

三、(時間) 來

This is used after a word or phrase to indicate the period of time up to a particular moment.

5. 婚姻介紹

1. 千百年來，媒婆造成了很多不幸的家庭。
   千百年来，媒婆造成了很多不幸的家庭。
   For thousands of years, female matchmakers created many unfortunate families.

2. 這兩年來，我看了不少中國電影。
   这两年来，我看了不少中国电影。
   I've seen many Chinese movies in the past two years.

3. 十多天來，我一直覺得不舒服。
   十多天来，我一直觉得不舒服。
   I've been feeling unwell for more than ten days.

四、越來越　　the more ..., the more ...

"越來越" is used before an adjective to indicate the degree of the adjective is increased over time.

1. 媒婆的名聲越來越不好了。
   媒婆的名声越来越不好了。
   The reputation of female matchmakers became worse.

2. 他越來越老了。
   他越来越老了。
   He is getting old.

3. 我們學的生詞越來越多了。
   我们学的生词越来越多了。
   We've learned more and more new words.

五、讓　　let; make

1. 紅娘讓男女雙方先接觸一段時間。
   红娘让男女双方先接触一段时间。
   Female matchmakers let the male side and the female side have some contact for a period of time at the beginning.

2. 讓所有的人都有飯吃。
   让所有的人都有饭吃。
   Let everyone have food to eat.

3. 我的老師常常讓我頭疼。
   我的老师常常让我头疼。
   My teacher often makes my head ache.

六、__方　　__ side

男方	女方	雙方	兩方
男方	女方	双方	两方
male side	female side	both sides	both sides

我方	對方	甲方	乙方
我方	对方	甲方	乙方
our side	the other side	first party	second party

七、"幫忙"and"幫助"　　help

> The differences between "幫忙" and "幫助" are that "幫助" can be followed by an object but "幫忙" cannot, and that other words can be inserted between "幫" and "忙", but that is not the case with "幫助".

1. 請你幫我一個忙，幫我做作業。
   请你帮我一个忙，帮我做作业。
   Please do me a favor and help me do my homework.

2. 我幫助你學中文。
   我帮助你学中文。
   I help you study Chinese.

   我幫忙你學中文。(×)
   我帮忙你学中文。(×)

5. 婚姻介紹　　　　　　　　　　　　　　　　　　　　　　　　　　　　83

練 習

一、用所給的詞語回答問題

1. A：新娘甚麼時候能看到自己嫁的男人。（只有……才）
   新娘什么时候能看到自己嫁的男人。（只有……才）

   B：_____。

2. A：甚麼人明天可以不來考試。（只有……才）
   什么人明天可以不来考试。（只有……才）

   B：_____。

3. A：甚麼時候媒婆改叫做紅娘的？（……來）
   什么时候媒婆改叫做红娘的？（……来）

   B：_____。

4. A：人們甚麼時候開始用電腦做中文作業的？（……來）
   人们什么时候开始用电脑做中文作业的？（……来）

   B：_____。

5. A：媒婆做媒的時候，要去甚麼地方？（……方）
   媒婆做媒的时候，要去什么地方？（……方）

   B：_____。

6. A：後來媒婆的名聲怎麼樣了呢？（越來越）
   后来媒婆的名声怎么样了呢？（越来越）

   B：_____。

7. A：這幾天的天氣怎麼樣？（越來越）
   这几天的天气怎么样？（越来越）

   B：_____。

8. A：你告訴他開車不要喝酒，他記住了嗎？（至於）
   你告诉他开车不要喝酒，他记住了吗？（至于）

B：＿＿＿＿＿＿＿＿＿＿＿＿＿＿＿＿＿＿＿＿＿＿＿＿＿＿＿＿＿＿＿＿＿＿＿＿＿。

9. A：紅娘介紹婚姻的方法和媒婆有甚麼不一樣？（讓）
   红娘介绍婚姻的方法和媒婆有什么不一样？（让）
   B：＿＿＿＿＿＿＿＿＿＿＿＿＿＿＿＿＿＿＿＿＿＿＿＿＿＿＿＿＿＿＿＿＿。

10. A：我不知道今天的作業是甚麼，老師昨天是怎麼說的？（讓）
    我不知道今天的作业是什么，老师昨天是怎么说的？（让）
    B：＿＿＿＿＿＿＿＿＿＿＿＿＿＿＿＿＿＿＿＿＿＿＿＿＿＿＿＿＿＿＿＿＿。

二、用所給的詞語填空（一個詞語只可以用一次）

幫助、幫忙、至於、越來越、只有……才、讓
帮助、帮忙、至于、越来越、只有……才、让

1. 老師＿＿＿＿＿大家考試前一定要認真複習，＿＿＿＿＿認真複習的人＿＿＿＿＿可以考好。
   老师＿＿＿＿＿大家考试前一定要认真复习，＿＿＿＿＿认真复习的人＿＿＿＿＿可以考好。

2. 老師說有問題的人可以去找老師＿＿＿＿＿，但是老師不＿＿＿＿＿從來不複習的人。
   老师说有问题的人可以去找老师＿＿＿＿＿，但是老师不＿＿＿＿＿从来不复习的人。

3. 老師說寫漢字一定不可以寫錯，＿＿＿＿＿寫得好看不好看，沒關係。後來，同學們寫的字都＿＿＿＿＿難看了。
   老师说写汉字一定不可以写错，＿＿＿＿＿写得好看不好看，没关系。后来，同学们写的字都＿＿＿＿＿难看了。

三、用所給的詞語造句

1. 越來越
   越来越
   ＿＿＿＿＿＿＿＿＿＿＿＿＿＿＿＿＿＿＿＿＿＿＿＿＿＿＿＿＿＿＿＿＿＿＿＿＿＿＿。

2. 至於
   至于
   _____。

3. 只有……才
   只有……才
   _____。

四、翻譯

1. Now people think that only when both the bridegroom and the bride are satisfied with the marriage, can it be a happy one.
   _____
   _____。

2. When a man is looking for a wife, he usually considers whether the girl is beautiful or not. Whether or not she's smart is not important.
   _____
   _____。

3. The method of having matchmakers arrange a marriage was not a good one. It created a lot of unhappy families, and therefore the reputation of matchmakers became worse and worse.
   _____
   _____。

五、根據課文回答問題

1. 媒婆是做甚麼的？
   媒婆是做什么的？
   _____
   _____。

2. 媒婆是怎麼給人做媒的？
   媒婆是怎么给人做媒的？
   _____
   _____。

3. 那時要結婚的男女甚麼時候才可以見面？
   那时要结婚的男女什么时候才可以见面？
   _____
   _____。

4. 媒婆介紹的婚姻為甚麼不幸福？
   媒婆介绍的婚姻为什么不幸福？
   _____
   _____。

5. 媒婆和紅娘介紹婚姻的方法有甚麼不同？
   媒婆和红娘介绍婚姻的方法有什么不同？
   _____
   _____。

六、課堂討論

介紹婚姻的好處和壞處？
介绍婚姻的好处和坏处？
_____
_____。

閱讀

走馬觀花

"走馬觀花"現在的意思是說人們看東西的時候不仔細、不認真,其實,"走馬觀花"是古代傳說中的一個媒婆騙人的故事。

以前有個英俊的小伙子,三十歲了還沒有娶上媳婦;有一個漂亮的大姑娘,二十多了也沒有找到婆家。為甚麼呢?原來小伙子的腿有一點兒跛,可他想找一個漂亮的媳婦;大姑娘的鼻子有點兒歪,她也要找一個英俊的丈夫。到後來,他們的年齡越來越大,對象也越來越難找。

這兩個人的父母聽說有個媒婆很能幹,就都去求那個媒婆幫忙。他們的父母對媒婆說:只要能讓孩子結婚就行,至於跟甚麼樣的人結婚那都沒甚麼關係。媒婆想:這兩個人都有缺陷,就讓他倆結婚好了。但是最好讓他倆結婚前先見一面,他們自己滿意了,以後就不能怪我了。

於是,媒婆就讓姑娘站在家門口,手裏拿着一束鮮花,把花放在鼻子前面;讓小伙子騎着一匹大馬,在姑娘面前慢慢地跑過。小伙子看到的是一個拿着鮮花的漂亮姑娘,姑娘看到的是一個騎着大馬的英俊小伙兒,兩人不但非常滿意,而且是一見鍾情。

到結婚的那天晚上,新娘新郎入了洞房以後,他倆才發現都上了媒婆的當了。這時他們很後悔、很難過,可是生米已經煮成了熟飯,後悔也沒有用了。他們雖然怨恨媒婆騙人,但是也怪自己太粗心大意了。

阅 读

走马观花

"走马观花"现在的意思是说人们看东西的时候不仔细、不认真,其实,"走马观花"是古代传说中的一个媒婆骗人的故事。

以前有个英俊的小伙子,三十岁了还没有娶上媳妇;有一个漂亮的大姑娘,二十多了也没有找到婆家。为什么呢?原来小伙子的腿有一点儿跛,可他想找一个漂亮的媳妇;大姑娘的鼻子有点儿歪,她也要找一个英俊的丈夫。到后来,他们的年龄越来越大,对象也越来越难找。

这两个人的父母听说有个媒婆很能干,就都去求那个媒婆帮忙。他们的父母对媒婆说:只要能让孩子结婚就行,至于跟什么样的人结婚那都没什么关系。媒婆想:这两个人都有缺陷,就让他俩结婚好了。但是最好让他俩结婚前先见一面,他们自己满意了,以后就不能怪我了。

于是,媒婆就让姑娘站在家门口,手里拿着一束鲜花,把花放在鼻子前面;让小伙子骑着一匹大马,在姑娘面前慢慢地跑过。小伙子看到的是一个拿着鲜花的漂亮姑娘,姑娘看到的是一个骑着大马的英俊小伙儿,两人不但非常满意,而且是一见钟情。

到结婚的那天晚上,新娘新郎入了洞房以后,他俩才发现都上了媒婆的当了。这时他们很后悔、很难过,可是生米已经煮成了熟饭,后悔也没有用了。他们虽然怨恨媒婆骗人,但是也怪自己太粗心大意了。

5. 婚姻介紹

生詞

走馬觀花	走马观花	zǒumǎ-guānhuā		look at flowers while riding on horseback — gain a superficial understanding through cursory observation
仔細	仔细	zǐxì	adj.	careful
認真	认真	rènzhēn	adj.	conscientious; serious
傳說	传说	chuánshuō	n.	legend
騙	骗	piàn	v.	deceive
英俊	英俊	yīngjùn	adj.	handsome
小伙子	小伙子	xiǎohuǒzi	n.	young man
大姑娘	大姑娘	dàgūniang	n.	young woman
婆家	婆家	pójiā	n.	husband's family
腿	腿	tuǐ	n.	leg
跛	跛	bǒ	adj.	lame; cripple
鼻子	鼻子	bízi	n.	nose
年齡	年龄	niánlíng	n.	age
對象	对象	duìxiàng	n.	marriage partner
求	求	qiú	v.	seek [help]; beg
缺陷	缺陷	quēxiàn	n.	defect
怪	怪	guài	v.	blame
束	束	shù	m.	a bunch of
鮮花	鲜花	xiānhuā	n.	fresh flowers
騎	骑	qí	v.	ride
匹	匹	pǐ	m.	measure word for horse
一見鍾情	一见钟情	yī jiàn zhōngqíng		fall in love at first sight

洞房	洞房	dòngfáng	n.	bridal chamber
發現	发现	fāxiàn	v.	find, discover
上當	上当	shàng dàng		be tricked; be fooled
後悔	后悔	hòuhuǐ	v.	regret
難過	难过	nánguò	v.	feel bad
生米煮成熟飯	生米煮成熟饭	shēngmǐ zhǔ chéng shúfàn		The rice is already cooked — what's done can't be undone
怨恨	怨恨	yuànhèn	v.	resent; hate
粗心大意	粗心大意	cūxīn dàyì		careless

問題

1. 那兩個人為甚麼那麼大了還沒有結婚？
   那两个人为什么那么大了还没有结婚？
   _____
   _____。

2. 媒婆為甚麼要讓他們兩個先見上一面？
   媒婆为什么要让他们两个先见上一面？
   _____
   _____。

3. 他們兩人是怎麼見面的？
   他们两人是怎么见面的？
   _____
   _____。

4. 他們怨恨誰？
   他们怨恨谁？
   _____
   _____。

6

麻煩的同音字
The Trouble with Homophones

學習大綱

通過學習本課，學生應該能夠：

1. 掌握這些句型和詞語的意思和用法："或者"、"老是"、"由於……因此/所以"、"既……又"、"無論……還是……都"、"不過"、"一點兒都/也（不/沒有）"。
2. 認識和運用課文以及閱讀文章內的生詞。
3. 簡單了解中國人在日常生活中受同音字影響的情況。
4. 初步了解中國人的姓名以及其中的含義。

Study Outline

After studying this chapter, students should:

1. Have a good command of the meaning and usage of these sentence patterns and terms: "huòzhě" (or), "lǎoshì" (always), "yóuyú ... yīncǐ/suǒyǐ" (by reason of; therefore; as a result), "jì ... yòu" (both ... and; as well as), "wúlùn ... háishì ... dōu" (no matter how/whether, etc.), "bùguò" (but; however), "yīdiǎnr dōu/yě (bù/méiyǒu)" (not ... at all; not at all ...).
2. Be familiar with the meaning and usage of the vocabulary introduced in the text and the reading.
3. Have some understanding of how homophones affect Chinese people in their daily lives.
4. Know about Chinese names and their meanings.

課文

中文有很多同音字，同音字有時候讓人喜歡，有時候讓人討厭。

做生意的人，喜歡用"八"和"六"這樣的數字，做自己的電話號碼或者汽車牌照號碼，因為"八"和發財的"發"聲音相近，"八八"聽起來就像是"發發"；"六六六"會讓你覺得賺錢時順順溜溜。

在船上生活的人，他們最不喜歡聽的就是"沉"啊、"翻"啊那些字。中國人吃飯用的筷子，在幾百年以前叫"箸"(zhù)；後來由於人們不願意船老是停住不動，希望船能快快地走，因此就把"箸"改叫做"筷"(快)了。

在中國的家庭裏，一家人從來不願意分吃一個梨，因為"分梨"聽起來就像是要分離。過年、過生日送禮物的時候，不可以給夫妻倆送傘(散)，也不能給老人們送鐘(終)。

蜘蛛和蝙蝠一點兒都不好看，可是中國畫兒裏常常有蜘蛛和蝙蝠。這是因為蜘蛛也叫"喜蛛"，蝙蝠的"蝠"和福氣的"福"聲音一樣。人們喜歡聽"喜"和"福"這些字音，於是就把它們畫在了畫兒裏面。

喜鵲和烏鴉長得都是黑黑的，叫的聲音也都很難聽。不過由於喜鵲的名字好聽，因此大家都喜歡喜鵲，不喜歡烏鴉。

同音字真的很麻煩，人們既喜歡它又討厭它。其實，無論喜歡還是討厭，這都是一種迷信。

6. 麻烦的同音字

课文

中文有很多同音字，同音字有时候让人喜欢，有时候让人讨厌。

做生意的人，喜欢用"八"和"六"这样的数字，做自己的电话号码或者汽车牌照号码，因为"八"和发财的"发"声音相近，"八八"听起来就像是"发发"；"六六六"会让你觉得赚钱时顺顺溜溜。

在船上生活的人，他们最不喜欢听的就是"沉"啊、"翻"啊那些字。中国人吃饭用的筷子，在几百年以前叫"箸"(zhù)，后来由于人们不愿意船老是停住不动，希望船能快快地走，因此就把"箸"改叫做"筷"(快)了。

在中国的家庭里，一家人从来不愿意分吃一个梨，因为"分梨"听起来就像是要分离。过年、过生日送礼物的时候，不可以给夫妻俩送伞(散)，也不能给老人们送钟(终)。

蜘蛛和蝙蝠一点儿都不好看，可是中国画儿里常常有蜘蛛和蝙蝠。这是因为蜘蛛也叫"喜蛛"，蝙蝠的"蝠"和福气的"福"声音一样。人们喜欢听"喜"和"福"这些字音，于是就把它们画在了画儿里面。

喜鹊和乌鸦长得都是黑黑的，叫的声音也都很难听。不过由于喜鹊的名字好听，因此大家都喜欢喜鹊，不喜欢乌鸦。

同音字真的很麻烦，人们既喜欢它又讨厌它。其实，无论喜欢还是讨厌，这都是一种迷信。

生詞

繁體	简体	拼音	詞性	英文
麻煩	麻烦	máfan	adj.	troublesome; problematic
同音字	同音字	tóngyīnzì	n.	homonym; homophone
討厭	讨厌	tǎoyàn	v.	loathe; be sick of
做生意	做生意	zuò shēngyi		do business
號碼	号码	hàomǎ	n.	number
或者	或者	huòzhě	conj.	or
牌照	牌照	páizhào	n.	license plate; license tag
發財	发财	fā cái		get rich
相近	相近	xiāng jìn	adj.	close; near
賺錢	赚钱	zhuàn qián		make money
順順溜溜	顺顺溜溜	shùnshun liūliu	adj.	smoothly
沉	沉	chén	v.	sink
翻	翻	fān	v.	turn over; capsize
由於……因此	由于……因此	yóuyú ... yīncǐ		because, due to ..., therefore
老是	老是	lǎoshì	adv.	always; at all times
停住	停住	tíngzhù	v.	stop; anchor
分	分	fēn	v.	divide
梨	梨	lí	n.	pear
分離	分离	fēnlí	v.	separate; sever
夫妻	夫妻	fūqī	n.	husband and wife
散	散	sàn	v.	break up; disperse
送終	送终	sòng zhōng		attend upon a dying parent or other senior member of one's family

6. 麻煩的同音字

蜘蛛	蜘蛛	zhīzhū	n.	spider
蝙蝠	蝙蝠	biānfú	n.	bat
一點兒都(不/沒有)	一点儿都(不/没有)	yīdiǎnr dōu (bū/méiyǒu)	adv.	not ... at all
福氣	福气	fúqì	n.	good luck
喜鵲	喜鹊	xǐquè	n.	magpie
烏鴉	乌鸦	wūyā	n.	crow
不過	不过	bùguò	conj.	but; however
既……又	既……又	jì ... yòu	conj.	both ... and; as well as
無論	无论	wúlùn	conj.	no matter what
還是	还是	háishì	conj.	or
迷信	迷信	míxìn	n.	superstition

語法和詞語註釋

一、或者　　or

"或者" is used to connect coordinate elements of a sentence.

1. 用八和六做電話號碼或者汽車牌照號碼。
   用八和六做电话号码或者汽车牌照号码。
   Use eight and six in telephone numbers or car license plate numbers.

2. 在圖書館看書或者做作業。
   在图书馆看书或者做作业。
   Reading or doing homework in the library.

3. 這個問題你查詞典或者去問老師。
   这个问题你查词典或者去问老师。
   To solve this problem, you should look it up in the dictionary or ask the professor.

二、老是　　always

1. 那條船老是停住不動。
   那条船老是停住不动。
   That boat always lies at anchor there and doesn't move.

2. 我的女朋友老是給我打電話。
   我的女朋友老是给我打电话。
   My girlfriend rings me up all the time.

3. 他上課老是遲到。
   他上课老是迟到。
   He is always late for class.

三、由於……因此/所以　　by reason of; therefore; as a result

"由於" is only used at the beginning of the first clause to indicate a cause or reason, while "因此" or "所以" comes in the second clause to indicate the result.

1. 由於喜鵲的名字好聽，因此人們喜歡喜鵲。
   由于喜鹊的名字好听，因此人们喜欢喜鹊。
   Because the name "magpie" sounds nice, everyone likes magpies.

2. 由於拼音可以幫助我們發音，因此要學會拼音。
   由于拼音可以帮助我们发音，因此要学会拼音。
   Because Pinyin can help with our pronunciation, we have to learn it.

3. 由於下雨了，所以今天的比賽取消了。
   由于下雨了，所以今天的比赛取消了。
   Because it is raining, today's game has been canceled.

四、既……又　　both ... and; as well as

"既……又" connects two adjectives or phrases indicating that two states of affairs exist simultaneously.

1. 人們既喜歡同音字又討厭同音字。

6. 麻煩的同音字

人们既喜欢同音字又讨厌同音字。

People like homonyms, but they hate them as well.

2. 我的女朋友既聰明又漂亮。

我的女朋友既聪明又漂亮。

My girlfriend is smart, and pretty as well.

3. 學中文既要學拼音又要學漢字。

学中文既要学拼音又要学汉字。

Learning Chinese requires you to learn Pinyin as well as Chinese characters.

五、無論……還是……都　　no matter how/whether, etc.

This indicates that no matter what the circumstances are the result remains unchanged.

1. 無論是喜歡還是討厭，這都是一種迷信。

无论是喜欢还是讨厌，这都是一种迷信。

No matter whether it is loved or hated, it's all superstition.

2. 無論中國人還是外國人，都知道中國的長城。

无论中国人还是外国人，都知道中国的长城。

No matter who they are, Chinese or foreigners, everyone knows of China's Great Wall.

3. 無論是漢族還是其他少數民族，都叫做中國人。

无论是汉族还是其他少数民族，都叫做中国人。

No matter whether they belong to the Han or other minority groups, they are all called Chinese.

When "還是" is used with conjunctions such as "無論" or "不管", it is equivalent to "或者".

4. 無論颱風還是下雨，他都來上課。

无论刮风还是下雨，他都来上课。

No matter whether it's windy or raining, he always comes to class.

5. 不管颱風或者下雨，他都來上課。

不管刮风或者下雨，他都来上课。

No matter whether it's windy or raining, he always comes to class.

> In making choices, "或者" can only be used in narrative sentences; "還是" is used in interrogative sentences.

6. 做生意的人喜歡用八和六做電話號碼或者汽車牌照號碼。

做生意的人喜欢用八和六做电话号码或者汽车牌照号码。

Businessmen like to use *ba* (eight) and *liu* (six) in telephone numbers or car license plate numbers.

做生意的人喜歡用八和六做電話號碼還是汽車牌照號碼。（×）

做生意的人喜欢用八和六做电话号码还是汽车牌照号码。（×）

7. 你暑假想去北京學中文還是去臺北學中文？

你暑假想去北京学中文还是去台北学中文？

This summer, do you want to go to Beijing or Taibei to learn Chinese?

你暑假想去北京學中文或者去臺北學中文？（×）

你暑假想去北京学中文或者去台北学中文？（×）

六、不過　　but; however

> "不過" introduces a concessive statement which is usually contrasting with what precedes it.

1. 喜鵲和烏鴉長的都是黑黑的，不過由於喜鵲的名字好聽，因此人們都喜歡喜鵲。

喜鹊和乌鸦长的都是黑黑的，不过由于喜鹊的名字好听，因此人们都喜欢喜鹊。

Magpies and crows are both black. However, because the name "magpie" sounds nice, everyone likes magpies.

2. 你説的很對，不過我還是有些不相信。

你说的很对，不过我还是有些不相信。

What you said is absolutely right. However, I'm still rather dubious.

3. 中國飯很好吃，不過裏面的油太多。

   中国饭很好吃，不过里面的油太多。

   Chinese food is delicious, but there is too much oil in it.

七、一點兒都/也(不/沒有)　　not ... at all; not at all ...

1. 蜘蛛和蝙蝠一點兒都不好看。

   蜘蛛和蝙蝠一点儿都不好看。

   Spiders and bats are not good-looking at all.

2. 這一課的漢字一點兒都不難。

   这一课的汉字一点儿都不难。

   The Chinese characters in this lesson are not at all hard.

3. 我的小弟弟一點兒都不聽話。

   我的小弟弟一点儿都不听话。

   My little brother is not obedient at all.

練習

一、用所給的詞語回答問題

1. A：你每天去甚麼地方看書？(或者)

   你每天去什么地方看书？(或者)

   B：_____。

2. A：你做了多少作業了？(一點兒都"沒有")

   你做了多少作业了？(一点儿都"没有")

   B：_____。

3. A：你為甚麼不喜歡小燕？(老是)

   你为什么不喜欢小燕？(老是)

   B：_____。

4. A：你為甚麼要學中文？(由於……因此)
　　你为什么要学中文？(由于……因此)
　B：_____。

5. A：學中文只學拼音，不學漢字可以嗎？(既……又)
　　学中文只学拼音，不学汉字可以吗？(既……又)
　B：_____。

6. A：老師講的你都聽見了嗎？(不過)
　　老师讲的你都听见了吗？(不过)
　B：_____。

7. A：你是不是只會寫拼音，不會寫漢字？(無論……還是……都)
　　你是不是只会写拼音，不会写汉字？(无论……还是……都)
　B：_____。

二、用所給的詞語填空(一個詞語可以用多次)

　既……又、由於……因此、或者、還是、不過
　既……又、由于……因此、或者、还是、不过

1. _____有些字的音相同，_____過年、過生日送禮物的時候，一定要當心。
　 _____有些字的音相同，_____过年、过生日送礼物的时候，一定要当心。

2. 中國人都喜歡用"八"和"六"做電話號碼_____汽車牌照的號碼。因為無論是"八"_____"六"，都會讓人覺得可以發財。
　 中国人都喜欢用"八"和"六"做电话号码_____汽车牌照的号码。因为无论是"八"_____"六"，都会让人觉得可以发财。

3. 我最喜歡學中文了。我每天在圖書館_____在教室做中文練習。我_____學拼音_____學漢字。我覺得無論是聽說_____讀寫我都能學好。_____我的朋友告訴我說，_____中文是東方的語言，_____比別的語言要難學一些。
　 我最喜欢学中文了。我每天在图书馆_____在教室做中文练习。我

_____学拼音_____学汉字。我觉得无论是听说_____读写我都能学好。_____我的朋友告诉我说，_____中文是东方的语言，_____比别的语言要难学一些。

三、用所給的詞語造句

1. 由於⋯⋯因此
   由于⋯⋯因此
   _____。

2. 既⋯⋯又
   既⋯⋯又
   _____。

3. 老是
   老是
   _____。

4. 無論⋯⋯還是⋯⋯都
   无论⋯⋯还是⋯⋯都
   _____。

5. 一點兒都(不/沒有)
   一点儿都(不/没有)
   _____。

6. 不過
   不过
   _____。

四、翻譯

1. Because money is an inseparable part of people's lives, having too little or too much can cause a lot of problems. Therefore people love money, but they hate money as well.

_____
_____ 。

2. Businessmen are very superstitious. They like to use "eight" or "six" in their telephone numbers or car license plate numbers, because they think these numbers can bring them a big fortune.
_____
_____ 。

3. In Chinese, the pronunciation of the word "pear" (*li*) sounds like *li* in *fenli* "separate". Therefore husband and wife do not like to share a pear by cutting it apart.
_____
_____ 。

五、根據課文回答問題

1. 做生意的人為甚麼喜歡用"八"和"六"這兩個數字？
   做生意的人为什么喜欢用"八"和"六"这两个数字？
   _____
   _____ 。

2. 筷子這個詞是怎麼來的？以前叫甚麼？
   筷子这个词是怎么来的？以前叫什么？
   _____
   _____ 。

3. 為甚麼不能給新婚夫婦送傘，給老人送鐘？
   为什么不能给新婚夫妇送伞，给老人送钟？
   _____
   _____ 。

4. 人們為甚麼喜歡蝙蝠、蜘蛛、喜鵲？
   人们为什么喜欢蝙蝠、蜘蛛、喜鹊？
   _____
   _____。

5. 為甚麼說喜歡和討厭同音字是迷信？
   为什么说喜欢和讨厌同音字是迷信？
   _____
   _____。

六、課堂討論

1. 人們為甚麼既喜歡又討厭同音字？
   人们为什么既喜欢又讨厌同音字？
   _____
   _____
   _____。

2. 你為甚麼覺得同音字是或者不是迷信？
   你为什么觉得同音字是或者不是迷信？
   _____
   _____
   _____。

3. 在你的生活中有哪些迷信的東西？
   在你的生活中有哪些迷信的东西？
   _____
   _____
   _____。

閱讀

中國人的姓名

中國人的姓名分兩部分，前面是姓，後面是名字。大多數人的姓都是一個字的單姓；名字既有一個字的單名，又有兩個字的雙名。

由於父母都希望自己的孩子將來有一個好的生活，因此他們在給孩子起名字時就特別用心，他們把自己的希望寄托在孩子的名字上。

父母如果希望孩子將來有出息，把孩子的名字就叫做大偉、大海；要是想讓孩子長大後做生意發財，孩子的名字就叫金發、進財；還有的父母只希望孩子一輩子平平安安，所以就叫小平、小安。

女孩子喜歡漂亮，她們的名字裏面常常有美啊、麗啊或者是花啊、玉啊這些字。只要是漂亮的東西，無論是天上的彩霞還是地上的冰雪，甚至就連空中細細的小雨，都可以成為女孩子的名字。

樂器能發出好聽的聲音，有的女孩子就叫小琴、小鈴和小笛；小鳥的叫聲也好聽，有人就叫小鶯、小燕和小鷗。

龍和鳳是傳說中的動物，很多男孩子叫小龍、大龍；很多女孩子叫小鳳、大鳳。老虎和牛都很有力氣，有的男孩子就叫小虎、大牛。

中國有十二億多人，可是常用的姓只有幾百個，所以同姓的人有成千上萬個；每一個父母都想給孩子起一個好名字，很多父母都想出了一樣的名字，於是就有許多同名同姓的人。在中國人中間，你可能會碰到一千個張燕，一萬個李小龍。

阅读

中国人的姓名

中国人的姓名分两部分，前面是姓，后面是名字。大多数人的姓都是一个字的单姓；名字既有一个字的单名，又有两个字的双名。

由于父母都希望自己的孩子将来有一个好的生活，因此他们在给孩子起名字时就特别用心，他们把自己的希望寄托在孩子的名字上。

父母如果希望孩子将来有出息，把孩子的名字就叫做大伟、大海；要是想让孩子长大后做生意发财，孩子的名字就叫金发、进财；还有的父母只希望孩子一辈子平平安安，所以就叫小平、小安。

女孩子喜欢漂亮，她们的名字里面常常有美啊、丽啊或者是花啊、玉啊这些字。只要是漂亮的东西，无论是天上的彩霞还是地上的冰雪，甚至就连空中细细的小雨，都可以成为女孩子的名字。

乐器能发出好听的声音，有的女孩子就叫小琴、小铃和小笛；小鸟的叫声也好听，有人就叫小莺、小燕和小鸥。

龙和凤是传说中的动物，很多男孩子叫小龙、大龙；很多女孩子叫小凤、大凤。老虎和牛都很有力气，有的男孩子就叫小虎、大牛。

中国有十二亿多人，可是常用的姓只有几百个，所以同姓的人有成千上万个；每一个父母都想给孩子起一个好名字，很多父母都想出了一样的名字，于是就有许多同名同姓的人。在中国人中间，你可能会碰到一千个张燕，一万个李小龙。

生 詞

大多數	大多数	dàduōshù	n.	majority
單	单	dān	n.	single
雙	双	shuāng	n.	two; double
希望	希望	xīwàng	v.	wish; hope
將來	将来	jiānglái	n.	future
起(名字)	起(名字)	qǐ (míngzì)	v.	give (name)
用心	用心	yòngxīn		do something diligently and attentively
寄託	寄托	jìtuō	v.	place (one's hope) in
有出息	有出息	yǒu chūxi		successful
偉	伟	wěi	adj.	great
一輩子	一辈子	yībèizi	n.	all one's life
平平安安	平平安安	píngpíng-ān'ān		safe and sound
玉	玉	yù	n.	jade
彩霞	彩霞	cǎixiá	n.	rosy clouds
冰雪	冰雪	bīngxuě	n.	ice and snow
空中	空中	kōngzhōng	n.	in the air
細	细	xì	adj.	thin
樂器	乐器	yuèqì	n.	musical instrument
發	发	fā	v.	generate
琴	琴	qín	n.	a general name for certain musical instruments
鈴	铃	líng	n.	bell
笛	笛	dí	n.	flute; pipe
鳥	鸟	niǎo	n.	bird

鶯	莺	yīng	n.	warbler; oriole
鷗	鸥	ōu	n.	sea-gull
龍	龙	lóng	n.	dragon
鳳	凤	fèng	n.	phoenix
動物	动物	dòngwù	n.	animal
老虎	老虎	lǎohǔ	n.	tiger
牛	牛	niú	n.	ox
億	亿	yì	num.	a hundred million
成千上萬	成千上万	chéngqiān-shàngwàn		thousands upon thousands
碰到	碰到	pèngdào	v.	meet

問題

1. 中國人是怎麼給孩子起名字的?
   中国人是怎么给孩子起名字的?
   _____
   _____。

2. 你知道哪些名字有特別的意思?
   你知道哪些名字有特别的意思?
   _____
   _____。

3. 為甚麼說從孩子的名字上能看到父母的希望?
   为什么说从孩子的名字上能看到父母的希望?
   _____
   _____。

4. 女孩子的名字跟男孩子的有甚麼不一樣?
   女孩子的名字跟男孩子的有什么不一样?

_____

_____。

5. 女孩子的名字一般都有哪些字？
   女孩子的名字一般都有哪些字？

   _____

   _____。

6. 為甚麼會有許多同名同姓的人？
   为什么会有许多同名同姓的人？

   _____

   _____。

7. 你的名字有甚麼意思？
   你的名字有什么意思？

   _____

   _____。

7

在中國上大學
Going to College in China

學習大綱

通過學習本課，學生應該能夠：

1. 掌握這些句型和詞語的意思和用法："恰巧"、"只好"、"不是……就是"、"除了……（以外）"、"卻"、"即使……也/還"、"大都"和"大多數"。
2. 認識和運用課文以及閱讀文章內的生詞。
3. 知道在中國考大學的經過，和中國的大學在錄取學生的制度上有哪些問題。
4. 了解中國人對讀書人的看法。

Study Outline

After studying this chapter, students should:

1. Have a good command of the meaning and usage of these sentence patterns and terms: "qiàqiǎo" (by chance; happen to), "zhǐhǎo" (have to), "bùshì ... jiùshì" (either ... or; if not A ... then B), "chúle ... (yǐwài)" (besides; apart from), "què" (but), "jíshǐ ... yě/hái" (even if), "dàdū" and "dàduōshù" (most of; mostly).
2. Be familiar with the meaning and usage of the vocabulary introduced in the text and the reading.
3. Know how students in China get into college, and the problems with the college admission policy in China.
4. Understand something of Chinese attitudes towards scholars.

課文

每年七月的七、八、九號三天,是中國高中畢業生考大學的日子。學生們學了那麼多年,最後能不能上大學全看這三天的考試了。雖然中學要求學生德、智、體全面發展,可是大學錄取學生的時候,卻只看考試的成績,別的甚麼體育啊、音樂啊、社會活動全都沒關係。

考大學一年只有一次,有的學生平時學得很好,如果恰巧那幾天生病了,沒有考好,那就只好等到下一年了。

中國考大學競爭得非常厲害,每年報考的人很多,可是錄取的名額卻很少。在高中的最後一年,學生們每天從早到晚,不是做習題就是背單詞。他們除了吃飯睡覺以外,其他的時間全都用來準備考試。有些父母還花錢讓孩子去上補習班,也有的父母請大學生來家裏輔導孩子。

上大學這麼難,但是有些學生進大學以後卻不那麼用功了。學校規定報考大學的時候必須選定專業,入學以後即使你不喜歡這個專業,也不能再改了,因此有些學生對自己的專業一點兒興趣都沒有。

不過,不管你有沒有興趣,也不管你用功不用功,大學裏每門功課只要能及格就可以畢業。所以有人說中國大學進門雖難,出門卻容易。

中國現在的大學大都是自費的。大多數的學生得依靠父母給他們付學費。許多學生為了減輕家裏的負擔,就去打工賺錢。暑假的時候,在學校門口和書店旁邊有很多拿着牌子的大學生,牌子上寫着"我可以教您孩子數學和英文"、"我可以輔導您孩子考大學"。

课文

　　每年七月的七、八、九号三天，是中国高中毕业生考大学的日子。学生们学了那么多年，最后能不能上大学全看这三天的考试了。虽然中学要求学生德、智、体全面发展，可是大学录取学生的时候，却只看考试的成绩，别的什么体育啊、音乐啊、社会活动全都没关系。

　　考大学一年只有一次，有的学生平时学得很好，如果恰巧那几天生病了，没有考好，那就只好等到下一年了。

　　中国考大学竞争得非常厉害，每年报考的人很多，可是录取的名额却很少。在高中的最后一年，学生们每天从早到晚，不是做习题就是背单词。他们除了吃饭睡觉以外，其他的时间全都用来准备考试。有些父母还花钱让孩子去上补习班，也有的父母请大学生来家里辅导孩子。

　　上大学这么难，但是有些学生进大学以后却不那么用功了。学校规定报考大学的时候必须选定专业，入学以后即使你不喜欢这个专业，也不能再改了，因此有些学生对自己的专业一点儿兴趣都没有。

　　不过，不管你有没有兴趣，也不管你用功不用功，大学里每门功课只要能及格就可以毕业。所以有人说中国大学进门虽难，出门却容易。

　　中国现在的大学大都是自费的。大多数的学生得依靠父母给他们付学费。许多学生为了减轻家里的负担，就去打工赚钱。暑假的时候，在学校门口和书店旁边有很多拿着牌子的大学生，牌子上写着"我可以教您孩子数学和英文"、"我可以辅导您孩子考大学"。

生　詞

畢業生	毕业生	bìyèshēng	n.	graduate
全	全	quán	adv.	completely; entirely
要求	要求	yāoqiú	v.	require; request
德智體	德智体	dé-zhì-tǐ	n.	virtue, intellectual and physical capabilities
全面	全面	quánmiàn	adj.	whole; overall
發展	发展	fāzhǎn	v.	develop
錄取	录取	lùqǔ	v.	admit; enroll
卻	却	què	adv.	but
體育	体育	tǐyù	n.	physical education
社會活動	社会活动	shèhuì huódòng	n.	social activities
恰巧	恰巧	qiàqiǎo	adv.	by chance; happen to
只好	只好	zhǐhǎo	adv.	have to
競爭	竞争	jìngzhēng	v.	compete
厲害	厉害	lìhai	adj.	intense
報考	报考	bàokǎo	v.	enter oneself for an examination
名額	名额	míng'é	n.	quota of people
不是……就是	不是……就是	bùshì ... jiùshì	conj.	either ... or; if not A ... then B ...
除了……以外	除了……以外	chúle ... yǐwài	conj.	apart from
補習班	补习班	bǔxíbān	n.	preparation class
輔導	辅导	fǔdǎo	v.	assist; tutor
用功	用功	yònggōng		diligent
規定	规定	guīdìng	v.	define; stipulate

選定	选定	xuǎndìng	v.	decide
專業	专业	zhuānyè	n.	major; concentration
即使	即使	jíshǐ	conj.	even if
興趣	兴趣	xìngqù	n.	interest
大都	大都	dàdōu	adv.	mostly
自費	自费	zìfèi	n.	at one's own expense
依靠	依靠	yīkào	v.	rely on; depend on
付	付	fù	v.	pay
學費	学费	xuéfèi	n.	tuition
減輕	减轻	jiǎnqīng	v.	lighten; alleviate
負擔	负担	fùdān	n.	burden
打工	打工	dǎ gōng		work
牌子	牌子	páizi	n.	sign

語法和詞語註釋

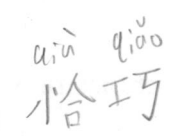

一、恰巧   by chance; happen to

1. 他平時學得很好，恰巧考試的時候生病了，結果沒有考好。
   他平时学得很好，恰巧考试的时候生病了，结果没有考好。
   He usually does very well in his studies, but he happened to be sick at the time of the examination, so he didn't do well in it.

2. 他來找我的時候，恰巧我出去吃飯去了。
   他来找我的时候，恰巧我出去吃饭去了。
   I just happened to have gone out for lunch when he came to see me.

3. 做作業時有個題我不會做，恰巧黃老師來了。
   做作业时有个题我不会做，恰巧黄老师来了。

Just when I had a problem in doing the homework, Professor Huang came over.

二、只好　　have to

> "只好" is used to indicate there is no other choice.

1. 今年考大學沒考好，只好等到明年了。
   今年考大学没考好，只好等到明年了。
   (He) didn't do well in the college entrance exam this year. He has to wait till next year.

2. 我的錢都花完了，今天只好在學校食堂吃飯了。
   我的钱都花完了，今天只好在学校食堂吃饭了。
   I've spent all my money. I have to eat at the school cafeteria today.

3. 學生為了減輕家裏的負擔，只好暑假去打工賺錢。
   学生为了减轻家里的负担，只好暑假去打工赚钱。
   In order to lighten the burden on their families, students have to work in the summer vacations to earn money.

三、不是……就是　　either ... or; if not A ... then B

> "不是……就是" denotes a choice between two possibilities.

1. 每天不是做習題就是背單詞。
   每天不是做习题就是背单词。
   Everyday I either do homework or memorize words.

2. 我周末不是洗衣服就是整理房間。
   我周末不是洗衣服就是整理房间。
   Every weekend I either do my laundry or clean my room.

3. 我的女朋友不是讓我請她吃飯，就是讓我陪她看電影。
   我的女朋友不是让我请她吃饭，就是让我陪她看电影。
   If my girlfriend isn't asking me to treat her to dinner, she's asking me to go to the movies with her.

四、除了……(以外)　　besides; apart from

"除了……(以外)" indicates an exception when it is followed by "都" in the second clause, but when it is followed by "還" or "也", it is equivalent to "in addition to" or "besides" in English.

1. 學生們除了吃飯睡覺以外，其他時間全都用來準備考試。
   学生们除了吃饭睡觉以外，其他时间全都用来准备考试。
   Apart from eating and sleeping, students spend all their time preparing for the exams.

2. 他除了認識王老師以外，不認識別的老師。
   他除了认识王老师以外，不认识别的老师。
   He doesn't know any other teachers apart from Professor Wang.

3. 趙小燕除了湯姆以外，還有別的男朋友。
   赵小燕除了汤姆以外，还有别的男朋友。
   Zhao Xiaoyan has other boyfriends besides Tom.

五、卻　　but

"卻" is often used after the subject of the second clause of a sentence. Like "可是" or "但是" it indicates a contrastive situation, but is used more often in writing.

1. 考大學的人很多，錄取的名額卻很少。
   考大学的人很多，录取的名额却很少。
   There are many people taking the college entrance exam, but the admission quota is very low.

2. 有人進大學以後卻不那麼用功了。
   有人进大学以后却不那么用功了。
   Some people don't work so hard any more once they get into college.

3. 今天考試這麼容易，我卻沒有考好。
   今天考试这么容易，我却没有考好。

Today's exam was so easy, but I didn't do well.

六、即使……也/還是　　even if

"即使" is used with "也/還是" to express a hypothetical situation or concession.

1. 入學以後即使你不喜歡你的專業也不能改了。
   入学以后即使你不喜欢你的专业也不能改了。
   After matriculation, even if you don't like your major, you can't transfer to another.

2. 即使下雨我也要去跑步。
   即使下雨我也要去跑步。
   Even if it rains, I'll go jogging.

3. 即使給我一百萬,我也不和你結婚。
   即使给我一百万,我也不和你结婚。
   Even if you gave me a million dollars, I still wouldn't marry you.

七、"大都"and"大多數"　　most of; mostly

"大都" is an adverb. It can only be followed by a verb, adjective, or "是". It cannot be followed by nouns. "大多數" can be followed by a verb, adjective, or "是". It can also be followed by nouns.

1. 現在的大學大都是自費的。
   现在的大学大都是自费的。
   Now most universities require self-financing.

2. 老師講的我大都能聽懂。
   老师讲的我大都能听懂。
   I can mostly understand what the teacher says.

3. 樹上大多數蘋果都紅了。
   树上大多数苹果都红了。
   Most of the apples on the tree have turned red.

4. 大多數的同學都有中文名字。

大多数的同学都有中文名字。

Most of my classmates have a Chinese name.

大都同學有中文名字。(×)

大都同学有中文名字。(×)

練 習

一、用所給的詞語回答問題

1. A：你今天晚上只做中文作業嗎？(除了……以外)

   你今天晚上只做中文作业吗？(除了……以外)

   B：＿＿＿＿＿＿＿＿＿＿＿＿＿＿＿＿＿＿＿＿＿＿＿。

2. A：你每天在宿舍做甚麼？(不是……就是)

   你每天在宿舍做什么？(不是……就是)

   B：＿＿＿＿＿＿＿＿＿＿＿＿＿＿＿＿＿＿＿＿＿＿＿。

3. A：我給你很多錢，你跟我結婚吧？(即使……也)

   我给你很多钱，你跟我结婚吧？(即使……也)

   B：＿＿＿＿＿＿＿＿＿＿＿＿＿＿＿＿＿＿＿＿＿＿＿。

4. A：你一點兒都沒有複習，你還要去考試嗎？(即使……也)

   你一点儿都没有复习，你还要去考试吗？(即使……也)

   B：＿＿＿＿＿＿＿＿＿＿＿＿＿＿＿＿＿＿＿＿＿＿＿。

5. A：這次考試你準備了很長時間，一定考得很好吧？(卻)

   这次考试你准备了很长时间，一定考得很好吧？(却)

   B：＿＿＿＿＿＿＿＿＿＿＿＿＿＿＿＿＿＿＿＿＿＿＿。

6. A：今天學的生詞你都記住了嗎？(大多數)

   今天学的生词你都记住了吗？(大多数)

   B：＿＿＿＿＿＿＿＿＿＿＿＿＿＿＿＿＿＿＿＿＿＿＿。

7. A：你每天在哪兒吃飯？（大都）
　　你每天在哪儿吃饭？（大都）
　B：_____。

二、用所給的詞語填空（一個詞語可以用多次）

除了……以外、即使……也、大都、大多數、恰巧、只好、卻
除了……以外、即使……也、大都、大多數、恰巧、只好、却

1. 我_____上課_____，_____的時間都在圖書館。_____周末_____要去圖書館。
   我_____上课_____，_____的时间都在图书馆。_____周末_____要去图书馆。

2. 上課的時候，老師講的我_____能聽懂，考試的時候我_____常常看不懂問題。
   上课的时候，老师讲的我_____能听懂，考试的时候我_____常常看不懂问题。

3. 我在學校門口等了她很長時間，可是她來的時候，我_____上廁所去了。她找不着我，_____一個人又回去了。
   我在学校门口等了她很长时间，可是她来的时候，我_____上厕所去了。她找不着我，_____一个人又回去了。

4. 這幾課很容易，_____幾個特別難的生詞_____，_____的字我都會寫。_____是沒有學過的課，我_____可以看懂。可是昨天老師考聽寫的時候，_____考的是那幾個特別難的生詞，我一個字都寫不出來，_____交給老師一張白紙。
   这几课很容易，_____几个特别难的生词_____，_____的字我都会写。_____是没有学过的课，我_____可以看懂。可是昨天老师考听写的时候，_____考的是那几个特别难的生词，我一个字都写不出来，_____交给老师一张白纸。

三、用所給的詞語造句

1. 不是……就是

   不是……就是

   _____。

2. 除了……以外

   除了……以外

   _____。

3. 恰巧

   恰巧

   _____。

4. 即使……也

   即使……也

   _____。

5. 只好

   只好

   _____。

四、翻譯

1. Middle schools require students to develop morally, intellectually and physically, but universities only consider exam grades when accepting students.

   _____

   _____。

2. The college entrance exam is coming up. To lessen their children's burden, parents do not let their children do anything except prepare for the exam.

   _____

   _____。

3. Nowadays most Chinese college students rely on their parents to pay their tuition. Therefore they have to work in the summer vacations to make money in order to lighten the burden on their families.
   _____
   _____ 。

五、根據課文回答問題

1. 大學錄取學生的時候只看甚麼？
   大学录取学生的时候只看什么？
   _____
   _____ 。

2. 為甚麼考大學競爭得很厲害？
   为什么考大学竞争得很厉害？
   _____
   _____ 。

3. 父母怎麼樣幫助孩子考大學？
   父母怎么样帮助孩子考大学？
   _____
   _____ 。

4. 為甚麼說：中國的大學進門雖難，出門卻容易？
   为什么说：中国的大学进门虽难，出门却容易？
   _____
   _____ 。

5. 大學生為甚麼要去打工賺錢？
   大学生为什么要去打工赚钱？
   _____
   _____ 。

六、課堂討論

1. 你認為最好的考大學的方法。
   你认为最好的考大学的方法。

   _____
   _____
   _____。

2. 你們國家考大學的方法和中國有甚麼不一樣？
   你们国家考大学的方法和中国有什么不一样？

   _____
   _____
   _____。

七、小作文

你考大學的經過。
你考大学的经过。

_____
_____
_____
_____
_____。

閱讀

讀書人

　　從隋朝開始，只有讀書的人才可以考試做官。那個時候人們讀書也只是為了做官。這些人整天不是唸書就是寫文章，他們除了埋頭學習以外不做別的事情。當時有一首詩說："書中自有黃金屋，書中自有顏如玉。"意思是說：書讀好了就可以做官，做官就可以有權勢和金錢，有權勢和金錢就可以有漂亮的女人。

　　那時還有一句話叫做："萬般皆下品，唯有讀書高"，是說社會上有各種各樣的人，做各種各樣的工作，但是只有讀書人的地位最高。只有讀不了書的人才去做工、種地、當兵、做買賣甚麼的。

　　考試做官的制度雖然在清朝末年就被取消了，但是一直到現在，大多數的中國人還是覺得讀書人最有出息。

　　前些年，中國開放改革，做生意的人大都發了財。於是有一些原先想做學問、想做研究的人，就不願意再讀書了。他們認為現在讀書需要花錢，將來即使讀好了也不一定能掙到很多錢。

　　以前，中國人大都看不起商人，說他們身上有一種錢的臭味。可是在這個時候，許多人又覺得商人最了不起了。因為大家都想去賺大錢，所以有些人就離開學校和研究所去做生意了。當時有一句很時髦的話叫做"下海"。意思是離開自己原來的工作，下到做買賣的商海裏去。

　　不過，聽說最近又有許多人想回學校讀書了，報考研究所的人也多起來了。為甚麼呢？他們說現在不管你做甚麼，都得要讀書學習。

阅 读

读书人

从隋朝开始，只有读书的人才可以考试做官。那个时候人们读书也只是为了做官。这些人整天不是念书就是写文章，他们除了埋头学习以外不做别的事情。当时有一首诗说："书中自有黄金屋，书中自有颜如玉。"意思是说：书读好了就可以做官，做官就可以有权势和金钱，有权势和金钱就可以有漂亮的女人。

那时还有一句话叫做："万般皆下品，唯有读书高"，是说社会上有各种各样的人，做各种各样的工作，但是只有读书人的地位最高。只有读不了书的人才去做工、种地、当兵、做买卖什么的。

考试做官的制度虽然在清朝末年就被取消了，但是一直到现在，大多数的中国人还是觉得读书人最有出息。

前些年，中国开放改革，做生意的人大都发了财。于是有一些原先想做学问、想做研究的人，就不愿意再读书了。他们认为现在读书需要花钱，将来即使读好了也不一定能挣到很多钱。

以前，中国人大都看不起商人，说他们身上有一种钱的臭味。可是在这个时候，许多人又觉得商人最了不起了。因为大家都想去赚大钱，所以有些人就离开学校和研究所去做生意了。当时有一句很时髦的话叫做"下海"。意思是离开自己原来的工作，下到做买卖的商海里去。

不过，听说最近又有许多人想回学校读书了，报考研究所的人也多起来了。为什么呢？他们说现在不管你做什么，都得要读书学习。

生　詞

做官	做官	zuò guān		to be an official
整天	整天	zhěngtiān	n.	all day
埋頭	埋头	mái tóu		immerse oneself in
自有	自有	zìyǒu	adv.	naturally have
黃金	黄金	huáng jīn	n.	gold
顏如玉	颜如玉	yán rú yù		a face as beautiful as jade — a beautiful woman
權勢	权势	quánshì	n.	power and influence
金錢	金钱	jīnqián	n.	money
萬般	万般	wànbān		all the different kinds
皆	皆	jiē	adv.	all; each; every
下品	下品	xiàpǐn		low-grade
唯有	唯有	wéiyǒu	adv.	only
讀書高	读书高	dú shū gāo		being literate is superior
萬般皆下品，唯有讀書高	万般皆下品，唯有读书高	wànbān jiē xiàpǐn, wéiyǒu dú shū gāo		to be a scholar is to be at the top of society
各種各樣	各种各样	gèzhǒng gèyàng		various kinds; all sorts of
做工	做工	zuò gōng		do manual work
種地	种地	zhòng dì		cultivate land
當兵	当兵	dāng bīng		be a soldier
做買賣	做买卖	zuò mǎimài		do business
制度	制度	zhìdù	n.	system
清朝	清朝	Qīngcháo		the Qing dynasty (1644–1911)
末年	末年	mònián	n.	the last years
取消	取消	qǔxiāo	v.	abolish

做學問	做学问	zuò xuéwen		do research
掙(錢)	挣(钱)	zhèng(qián)	v.	earn (money)
看不起	看不起	kànbuqǐ		look down upon
臭味	臭味	chòuwèi	n.	offensive odor
了不起	了不起	liǎobuqǐ		amazing; impressive
研究所	研究所	yánjiūsuǒ	n.	graduate school
時髦	时髦	shímáo	adj.	fashionable
下海	下海	xià hǎi		plunge into the (business) sea
商	商	shāng	n.	commerce; trade

問題

1. 從隋朝開始，人們為甚麼要讀書？
   从隋朝开始，人们为什么要读书？

   _____。

2. "書中自有黃金屋，書中自有顏如玉"的意思是甚麼？
   "书中自有黄金屋，书中自有颜如玉"的意思是什么？

   _____。

3. "萬般皆下品，唯有讀書高"是甚麼意思？
   "万般皆下品，唯有读书高"是什么意思？

   _____。

4. 一般人認為讀不了書的人去做甚麼？
   一般人认为读不了书的人去做什么？

   _____

_____

5. 為甚麼那個時候大家最看不起商人？
   为什么那个时候大家最看不起商人？
   _____
   _____

6. 為甚麼大家現在反而都覺得商人最了不起？
   为什么大家现在反而都觉得商人最了不起？
   _____
   _____

7. 甚麼是"下海"？
   什么是"下海"？
   _____
   _____

8

計劃生育和人權
Birth Control and Human Rights

學習大綱

通過學習本課,學生應該能夠:

1. 掌握這些句型和詞語的意思和用法:"原來"和"本來"、"這樣一來/那樣一來"、"尤其"和"特別"、"非……不可/不成/不行"、"對於/對"、"又……呢?"、"哪裏還……呢?"。
2. 認識和運用課文以及閱讀文章內的生詞。
3. 明白中國政府推行計劃生育政策的原因有哪些,在推行時採用了哪些方法。
4. 了解計劃生育與侵犯人權之間有甚麼關係。
5. 了解中國人教育孩子的情況。

Study Outline

After studying this chapter, students should:

1. Have a good command of the meaning and usage of these sentence patterns and terms: "yuánlái" and "běnlái" (originally; essentially), "zhèyàng yīlái/nàyàng yīlái" (in this case; thus), "yóuqí" and "tèbié" (especially; particularly), "fēi ... bùkě/bùchéng/bùxíng" (insist on; must; have to), "duìyú/duì" (for; to; with regard to), "yòu ... ne?" (could it be ...?), "nǎli hái ... ne?" (how could it be ...?).
2. Be familiar with the meaning and usage of the vocabulary introduced in the text and the reading.
3. Understand the reasons for the need for birth control in China and what the Chinese government has done to carry out its birth control policy.
4. Understand the relationship between birth control and the issue of human rights violation.
5. Know how children are brought up in China.

課 文

　　在中國的大街上常常可以看到一些宣傳畫，上面畫着一個媽媽抱着一個女娃娃，下面寫着"媽媽只生我一個"、"只生一個好"。許多外國人都覺得很奇怪，為甚麼中國人要把生孩子的事情寫在大街上呢？

　　原來這些畫是在宣傳計劃生育。中國正在推行一項控制人口的計劃生育政策，為了讓人們都知道這個政策，於是就在公共場合掛起了計劃生育的宣傳畫。計劃生育本來是個人的事情，可是現在中國的人口太多了，有十二億多，這樣一來，生孩子就成了國家的大事了。

　　政府採用各種方法來控制人口的增長：一是宣傳教育，讓人們明白人口太多了對國家和個人都不好；二是推廣避孕和節育的方法；三是規定除了少數民族和有特殊情況的人以外，一個家庭只能生一個孩子。

　　雖然政府規定一家只生一個孩子，可是有些人就是想多生幾個。中國人的傳統觀念是多子多福、養兒防老。很多人不願意只生一個孩子，尤其不願意只生一個女孩子，他們非要生第二胎、第三胎不可。

　　對於這些人，只靠宣傳和教育就不行了，於是政府就用一些別的辦法來制裁他們。比方說：當官的撤銷官職，有工作的開除公職，還有罰款甚麼的。

　　有的外國人指責中國政府的這種做法是侵犯人權，可是不這麼做又能怎麼辦呢？要是大家想生多少就生多少的話，人口就會大爆炸。那樣一來，人們就會沒有飯吃、沒有水喝、沒地方住、沒有衣服穿。如果一個人連活都活不下去了，哪裏還有甚麼人權可談呢！

课文

在中国的大街上常常可以看到一些宣传画，上面画着一个妈妈抱着一个女娃娃，下面写着"妈妈只生我一个"、"只生一个好"。许多外国人都觉得很奇怪，为什么中国人要把生孩子的事情写在大街上呢？

原来这些画是在宣传计划生育。中国正在推行一项控制人口的计划生育政策，为了让人们都知道这个政策，于是就在公共场合挂起了计划生育的宣传画。计划生育本来是个人的事情，可是现在中国的人口太多了，有十二亿多，这样一来，生孩子就成了国家的大事了。

政府采用各种方法来控制人口的增长：一是宣传教育，让人们明白人口太多了对国家和个人都不好；二是推广避孕和节育的方法；三是规定除了少数民族和有特殊情况的人以外，一个家庭只能生一个孩子。

虽然政府规定一家只生一个孩子，可是有些人就是想多生几个。中国人的传统观念是多子多福、养儿防老。很多人不愿意只生一个孩子，尤其不愿意只生一个女孩子，他们非要生第二胎、第三胎不可。

对于这些人，只靠宣传和教育就不行了，于是政府就用一些别的办法来制裁他们。比方说：当官的撤销官职，有工作的开除公职，还有罚款什么的。

有的外国人指责中国政府的这种做法是侵犯人权，可是不这么做又能怎么办呢？要是大家想生多少就生多少的话，人口就会大爆炸。那样一来，人们就会没有饭吃、没有水喝、没有地方住、没有衣服穿。如果一个人连活都活不下去了，哪里还有什么人权可谈呢！

生詞

計劃生育	计划生育	jìhuà shēngyù		birth control
人權	人权	rénquán	n.	human rights
宣傳	宣传	xuānchuán	n.	publicity; public information; propaganda
抱	抱	bào	v.	hold; carry
娃娃	娃娃	wáwa	n.	baby; child (colloquial)
奇怪	奇怪	qíguài	adj.	strange
推行	推行	tuīxíng	v.	carry out; pursue
項	项	xiàng	m.	measure word for policies
控制	控制	kòngzhì	v.	control
人口	人口	rénkǒu	n.	population
政策	政策	zhèngcè	n.	policy
公共場合	公共场合	gōnggòng chǎnghé	n.	public place
本來	本来	běnlái	adv.	originally
個人	个人	gèrén	n.	individual (person); personal
這樣一來	这样一来	zhèyàng yī lái		in this case
採用	采用	cǎiyòng	v.	adopt
推廣	推广	tuīguǎng	v.	extend; spread
避孕	避孕	bì yùn		contraception
節育	节育	jié yù		birth control
方法	方法	fāngfǎ	n.	way, method
特殊	特殊	tèshū	adj.	special; unusual
情況	情况	qíngkuàng	n.	situation
傳統	传统	chuántǒng	n.	tradition
觀念	观念	guānniàn	n.	idea; concept

8. 計劃生育和人權

多子多福	多子多福	duō zǐ duō fú		the more children one has, the more happiness
養兒防老	养儿防老	yǎng ér fáng lǎo		raise sons to provide against (for) old age
尤其	尤其	yóuqí	adv.	especially
非……不可	非……不可	fēi ... bùkě	adv.	insist on; must; have to
胎	胎	tāi	n.	fetus (but here it is a measure word for births)
對於	对于	duìyú	prep.	for; to; with regard to
靠	靠	kào	v.	depend on
辦法	办法	bànfǎ	n.	way; method
制裁	制裁	zhìcái	v.	place sanctions on; punish
撤銷	撤销	chèxiāo	v.	dismiss
官職	官职	guānzhí	n.	official position
開除	开除	kāichú	v.	fire; discharge from
公職	公职	gōngzhí	n.	public employment
罰款	罚款	fá kuǎn		fine; punish by levying fine
指責	指责	zhǐzé	v.	criticize; censure
做法	做法	zuòfǎ	n.	way of doing or making a thing; method of work
侵犯	侵犯	qīnfàn	v.	violate
爆炸	爆炸	bàozhà	v.	explode

語法和詞語註釋

一、"原來" and "本來"　　originally; essentially

Both "原來" and "本來" mean "originally", but "原來" sometimes indicates a situation that one did not know before and has suddenly become aware of.

1. 計劃生育本來 (原來) 是每個家庭的事,可是人口太多了,政府只好控制人口。

   计划生育本来 (原来) 是每个家庭的事,可是人口太多了,政府只好控制人口。

   Birth control is essentially a family issue, but the population is now so large that the government has had control it.

2. 我原來 (本來) 想學日文,可是我父母要我學中文。

   我原来 (本来) 想学日文,可是我父母要我学中文。

   Originally, I wanted to learn Japanese, but my parents wanted me to learn Chinese.

3. 大街上有很多宣傳畫,原來是政府在推行計劃生育政策。

   大街上有很多宣传画,原来是政府在推行计划生育政策。

   There are many publicity posters on the streets. It turns out that the government is promoting its birth control policy.

4. 我以為張老師回家了呢,原來他還在教室。

   我以为张老师回家了呢,原来他还在教室。

   I thought Professor Zhang had gone home. Now I see he's still in the classroom!

   我以為張老師回家了呢,本來他還在教室。(×)

   我以为张老师回家了呢,本来他还在教室。(×)

二、這樣一來/那樣一來　　in this case; thus

"這樣一來" and "那樣一來" are used between two sentences to connect the context in the discourse.

1. 雖然生孩子是每個家庭的事,可是中國人口太多造成很多問題。這樣一來,生孩子就成了國家大事了。

   虽然生孩子是每个家庭的事,可是中国人口太多造成很多问题。这样一来,生孩子就成了国家大事了。

   Although having children is a family issue, China's big population has created a lot of problems. Thus, having children has become a national issue.

2. 如果不控制人口，人口就會大爆炸。那樣一來，人們就會沒吃沒喝。
   如果不控制人口，人口就会大爆炸。那样一来，人们就会没吃没喝。
   If we don't control the population, the population will explode. In that case, people will starve.

3. 考大學的人多，錄取的人少。這樣一來，在中國上大學競爭得就非常厲害。
   考大学的人多，录取的人少。这样一来，在中国上大学竞争得就非常厉害。
   Many people take the college entrance exam, but very few are admitted, and thus entering college in China has become very competitive.

三、尤其   especially; particularly

1. 許多人不願意只生一個孩子，尤其不願意只生一個女孩子。
   许多人不愿意只生一个孩子，尤其不愿意只生一个女孩子。
   Many people are not willing to have only one child, especially when that child is a girl.

2. 很多人想多生孩子，尤其是那些有傳統觀念的人。
   很多人想多生孩子，尤其是那些有传统观念的人。
   Many people want more children, especially those people with traditional ideas.

3. 東方語言都很難學，尤其是中文。
   东方语言都很难学，尤其是中文。
   Asian languages are hard to learn, especially Chinese.

> **"尤其"and"特別"**
>
> "尤其" and "特別" both mean "especially". However, "尤其" is used to show something is outstanding in a group, so it is used in the second clause.

四、非……不可/不成/不行   insist on; must; have to

> "非……不可" indicates that something is imperative. "不可" can be omitted in spoken Chinese.

1. 他們非生第二胎、第三胎不可。
   他们非生第二胎、第三胎不可。
   They insist on having a second and a third baby.

2. 你不讓我去，我非要去。
   你不让我去，我非要去。
   You won't let me go, but I simply must.

3. 我有很多作業，今天晚上非做完不行。
   我有很多作业，今天晚上非做完不行。
   I have so much homework. I have to finish it tonight.

五、對於/對　　for; to; with regard to

Both "對於" and "對" take noun phrases, and can be used before or after the subject of a sentence.

1. 對於多生孩子的人政府採取一些辦法來制裁他們。
   对于多生孩子的人政府采取一些办法来制裁他们。
   The government has adopted some measures to punish those people who have more than one child.

2. 我對計劃生育這個政策不太清楚。
   我对计划生育这个政策不太清楚。
   I'm not very clear about the birth control policy.

3. 對於少數民族政府也有規定，他們也不能想生多少就生多少。
   对于少数民族政府也有规定，他们也不能想生多少就生多少。
   The government also has rules for minorities. They can't have as many children as they want either.

六、又……呢？　　could it be ...?

"又……呢？" is used with the interrogative pronouns "甚麼/誰/怎麼" to form rhetorical questions.

1. 雖然侵犯了人權，可是不這麼做又能怎麼辦呢？

虽然侵犯了人权，可是不这么做又能怎么办呢？
Although this violates human rights, if (China) doesn't do it, what else can it do?

2. 你自己不來上課，考試沒有考好，又能怨誰呢？
你自己不来上课，考试没有考好，又能怨谁呢？
You didn't come to class, and you didn't do well in the exams. Who can you blame it on?

3. 只要我們倆有愛情，結婚不結婚又有甚麼關係呢？
只要我们俩有爱情，结婚不结婚又有什么关系呢？
As long as we have love, does it matter whether we marry or not?

七、哪裏還……呢？　　how could it be ...?

哪里还……呢？

"哪裏還……呢？" introduces a rhetorical question.

1. 如果連活都活不下去了，哪裏還有甚麼人權可談呢？
如果连活都活不下去了，哪里还有什么人权可谈呢？
If their very survival is at issue, how can they talk about "human rights"?

2. 我的功課都作不完，哪裏還有時間看電影呢？
我的功课都作不完，哪里还有时间看电影呢？
I can't even finish my homework, how could I have time to go to movies?

3. 你不上課不做作業，哪裏還像個學生呢。
你不上课不做作业，哪里还像个学生呢。
You neither go to class nor do your homework. Just what sort of student are you?

練 習

一、用所給的詞語回答問題

1. A：我以為那個女孩子是你妹妹。(原來)
　　　我以为那个女孩子是你妹妹。(原来)

　　B：_____。

2. A：你喜歡看愛情電影嗎？(對於)
   你喜欢看爱情电影吗？(对于)
   B：_____。

3. A：我們班上是不是很多人都會寫漢字？(尤其)
   我们班上是不是很多人都会写汉字？(尤其)
   B：_____。

4. A：今天的考試你一定要去嗎？(非……不可)
   今天的考试你一定要去吗？(非……不可)
   B：_____。

5. A：你是中國人，你會說中文嗎？(本來)
   你是中国人，你会说中文吗？(本来)
   B：_____。

6. A：明天是期末考試，你今天要不要和我去看電影？(哪裏還……呢？)
   明天是期末考试，你今天要不要和我去看电影？(哪里还……呢？)
   B：_____。

二、選擇合適的詞語填空

1. _____我常常不去上課，_____考試的時候很多題都不會做。
   _____我常常不去上课，_____考试的时候很多题都不会做。
   a. 雖然……但是　　b. 因為……所以　　c. 不但……而且
   　虽然……但是　　　因为……所以　　　不但……而且

2. _____是男孩子_____女孩子，一個家庭只能生一個孩子。
   _____是男孩子_____女孩子，一个家庭只能生一个孩子。
   a. 如果……那麼　　b. 無論……還是　　c. 由於……因此
   　如果……那么　　　无论……还是　　　由于……因此

3. 老師說_____學好中文，_____可以到中國去工作。

老师说_____学好中文，_____可以到中国去工作。
a. 只要……就　　b. 即使……也　　c. 不管……也
　只要……就　　　即使……也　　　不管……也

4. 我們的中文作業，_____造句和填空_____，還要做很多翻譯。
　我们的中文作业，_____造句和填空_____，还要做很多翻译。
a. 除了……以外　　b. 不是……就是　　c. 非……不可
　除了……以外　　　不是……就是　　　非……不可

5. 雖然他每次考試都得一個C，可是他_____不生氣。
　虽然他每次考试都得一个C，可是他_____不生气。
a. 越來越　　b. 一點兒都　　c. 這樣一來
　越来越　　　一点儿都　　　这样一来

6. 現在_____小學生_____會用電腦寫作業了。
　现在_____小学生_____会用电脑写作业了。
a. 只有……才　　b. 連……也　　c. 既……又
　只有……才　　　连……也　　　既……又

三、用所給的詞語造句

1. 非……不可
　非……不可
　_____。

2. 哪裏還……呢
　哪里还……呢
　_____。

3. 這樣一來
　这样一来
　_____。

4. 對於
   对于
   _____。

5. 本來
   本来
   _____。

四、翻譯

1. How many children they want to have is essentially a matter for the individual family, but China has such a big population that having children has become a major issue for the state.

   _____
   _____
   _____。

2. The government has adopted some measures to punish those people who insist on having more than one child, especially if they are government officials.

   _____
   _____
   _____。

3. The Chinese government should educate its people and make it widely known that having too many children will do harm to both the state and the individual.

   _____
   _____
   _____。

五、根據課文回答問題

1. 為甚麼要把生孩子的事情寫在大街上？
   为什么要把生孩子的事情写在大街上？
   _____
   _____。

2. 為甚麼生孩子成了國家的大事了？
   为什么生孩子成了国家的大事了？
   _____
   _____。

3. 中國政府為了控制人口用了哪些辦法？
   中国政府为了控制人口用了哪些办法？
   _____
   _____。

4. 為甚麼有人想多生幾個？
   为什么有人想多生几个？
   _____
   _____。

5. 要是大家想生幾個就生幾個的話就會怎麼樣？
   要是大家想生几个就生几个的话就会怎么样？
   _____
   _____。

六、課堂討論

1. 計劃生育和人權的關係。
   计划生育和人权的关系。
   _____
   _____

2. 生孩子是家庭的事情還是國家的事情？
   生孩子是家庭的事情还是国家的事情？

   _____
   _____
   _____。

七、小作文

1. 你認為應該怎樣控制人口。
   你认为应该怎样控制人口。

   _____
   _____
   _____
   _____
   _____
   _____。

2. 你認為政府應該不應該管人們生孩子的事情。
   你认为政府应该不应该管人们生孩子的事情。

   _____
   _____
   _____
   _____
   _____
   _____。

閱讀

望子成龍

"望子成龍"就是父母希望孩子長大以後能有出息。大多數的中國人在孩子剛出生的時候，甚至還沒有出生的時候，就開始計劃今後怎樣教育孩子，怎樣把孩子培養成一個有出息的人。

中國以前有一個習俗叫抓周。"抓周"是在孩子周歲的那天，在一個盤子裏放上弓箭、紙筆、玩具、糖果、針線等等各種不同的東西，讓小孩子去抓，看他先抓甚麼。父母都希望孩子去抓紙和筆，抓紙和筆說明孩子喜歡讀書。中國的傳統思想認為，只有讀書的人才有出息。

為了讓孩子將來有出息，中國的父母對孩子管教得都很嚴。尤其現在每家都是獨生子女，父母的希望全都寄托在這一個孩子的身上。他們讓孩子學這、學那，如果孩子不好好學，父母就會批評甚至打罵孩子。

2000年1月17號，中國一個高中二年級的男孩子，期中考試沒有考好，成績從第十名後退到了第十八名。他的媽媽很生氣，不但打了他一頓，而且還非要他期末考試考回到前十名不可。這樣一來，那個孩子就感到非常傷心，他一時糊塗拿起榔頭就把自己的媽媽打死了。

孩子殺害自己的父母是犯罪，但是有人說中國父母管教孩子的方法也有問題。父母不應該打罵孩子，不應該對孩子的要求太高。就是因為中國人望子成龍的想法太強了，所以才發生了這樣的悲劇。

也有人說幾千年來中國人都是這樣管教孩子的，不能因為這件事情就說中國人望子成龍的想法不對，也不能說中國人管教孩子的方法全都錯了。如果孩子不聽話，除了打罵以外，又有甚麼別的好辦法呢？

阅读

望子成龙

"望子成龙"就是父母希望孩子长大以后能有出息。大多数的中国人在孩子刚出生的时候，甚至还没有出生的时候，就开始计划今后怎样教育孩子，怎样把孩子培养成一个有出息的人。

中国以前有一个习俗叫抓周。"抓周"是在孩子周岁的那天，在一个盘子里放上弓箭、纸笔、玩具、糖果、针线等等各种不同的东西，让小孩子去抓，看他先抓什么。父母都希望孩子去抓纸和笔，抓纸和笔说明孩子喜欢读书。中国的传统思想认为，只有读书的人才有出息。

为了让孩子将来有出息，中国的父母对孩子管教得都很严。尤其现在每家都是独生子女，父母的希望全都寄托在这一个孩子的身上。他们让孩子学这、学那，如果孩子不好好学，父母就会批评甚至打骂孩子。

2000年1月17号，中国一个高中二年级的男孩子，期中考试没有考好，成绩从第十名后退到了第十八名。他的妈妈很生气，不但打了他一顿，而且还非要他期末考试考回到前十名不可。这样一来，那个孩子就感到非常伤心，他一时糊涂拿起榔头就把自己的妈妈打死了。

孩子杀害自己的父母是犯罪，但是有人说中国父母管教孩子的方法也有问题。父母不应该打骂孩子，不应该对孩子的要求太高。就是因为中国人望子成龙的想法太强了，所以才发生了这样的悲剧。

也有人说几千年来中国人都是这样管教孩子的，不能因为这件事情就说中国人望子成龙的想法不对，也不能说中国人管教孩子的方法全都错了。如果孩子不听话，除了打骂以外，又有什么别的好办法呢？

生 詞

望子成龍	望子成龙	wàng zǐ chéng lóng		hope one's child will have a bright future; have great ambitions for one's child.
出生	出生	chūshēng	v.	be born
計劃	计划	jìhuà	v.	plan
今後	今后	jīnhòu	n.	later; in future
培養	培养	péiyǎng	v.	foster, train; develop
習俗	习俗	xísú	n.	custom
周歲	周岁	zhōusuì	n.	one full year (of age)
弓箭	弓箭	gōng jiàn	n.	bow and arrow
玩具	玩具	wán jù	n.	toy
糖果	糖果	tángguǒ	n.	candy
針線	针线	zhēnxiàn	n.	needle and thread
等等	等等	děngděng	par.	et cetera
說明	说明	shuōmíng	v.	illustrate; show
管教	管教	guǎn jiào	v.	subject sb. to discipline
嚴	严	yán	adj.	strict
批評	批评	pīpíng	v.	scold; blame; criticize
打罵	打骂	dǎmà	v.	beat and scold
期中	期中	qīzhōng	n.	mid-term
後退	后退	hòutuì	v.	lag behind; retrogress
期末	期末	qīmò	n.	end of term
頓	顿	dùn	m.	measure word for beatings
感到	感到	gǎndào	v.	feel
一時	一时	yīshí	n.	temporarily; momentarily

榔頭	榔头	lángtou	n.	hammer
殺害	杀害	shāhài	v.	kill
犯罪	犯罪	fàn zuì		commit a crime
問題	问题	wèntí	n.	problem
應該	应该	yīnggāi	aux.	should; ought to
強	强	qiáng	adj.	strong
發生	发生	fāshēng	v.	happen; take place
悲劇	悲剧	bēi jù	n.	tragedy
聽話	听话	tīng huà		obedient

問題

1. 中國父母甚麼時候開始計劃培養孩子？
   中国父母什么时候开始计划培养孩子？
   _____
   _____。

2. 甚麼是抓周？
   什么是抓周？
   _____
   _____。

3. 為甚麼父母都希望孩子去抓紙和筆？
   为什么父母都希望孩子去抓纸和笔？
   _____
   _____。

4. 中國父母怎樣管教孩子的？
   中国父母怎样管教孩子的？
   _____
   _____。

5. 那個男孩子的媽媽為甚麼生氣？
   那个男孩子的妈妈为什么生气？
   _____
   _____。

6. 中國人的望子成龍的想法對不對？
   中国人的望子成龙的想法对不对？
   _____
   _____。

9

繁體字和簡體字
Complex Characters and Simplified Characters

學習大綱

通過學習本課，學生應該能夠：

1. 掌握這些句型和詞語的意思和用法："受(到)"、"某"、"以及"、"自從"、"從前"和"以前"、"比"、"到底"和"究竟"。
2. 認識和運用課文以及閱讀文章內的生詞。
3. 明白為甚麼中文會有繁體字和簡體字的問題。
4. 了解漢字標音的歷史。

Study Outline

After studying this chapter, students should:

1. Have a good command of the meaning and usage of these sentence patterns and terms: "shòu (dào)" (get; receive), "mǒu" (some [unspecified]; [a] certain), "yǐ jí" (along with; as well as), "zìcóng" (since), "cóngqián" and "yǐqián" (before; previously), "bǐ" (compared with; than), "dàodǐ" and "jiū jìng" (exactly; after all).
2. Be familiar with the meaning and usage of the vocabulary introduced in the text and the reading.
3. Understand why there are both complex characters and simplified characters in Chinese.
4. Know about the history of the phonetic representation of Chinese characters.

課文

　　從前，中國沒有人講甚麼繁體字和簡體字，大家只說正體字和俗體字。那時官方文件和書籍用正體字；老百姓日常生活中用俗體字。俗體字省了很多筆劃，寫起來比較容易，所以受到大家的歡迎。

　　上世紀初，有許多學者不斷地在報紙和雜誌上寫文章說，應該把俗體字作為正式字來使用。1935年中華民國教育部公佈了三百二十四個俗體字的《簡體字表》。可是還不到一年就因為某些人的反對而被迫取消了。1952年開始，大陸的政府陸續整理出來了兩千多個俗體字，作為正式的字體，叫做"簡化字"，同時廢除了繁體字和異體字。

　　可是一直到今天，在臺灣和香港以及海外，許多人還在使用繁體字和異體字。幾十年來，臺灣方面不承認大陸推行的簡化字，大陸方面也不願意倒退回去重新用繁體字。

　　幾十年以前，海外的中文教學都是用繁體字，自從中國大陸開放以後，從大陸到海外教中文的人越來越多，去大陸學中文的學生也越來越多，於是海外的中文教學就出現了兩種字體同時存在的現象。

　　這樣一來，給學中文的學生造成了許多麻煩。從臺灣、香港來的學生不認識簡體字，從大陸來的學生不認識繁體字。本來薄薄的一本書，因為要同時用繁、簡兩種字體，於是就變成了厚厚的一本，既浪費了紙張，又提高了價錢。

　　其實，漢字從古到今一直都是在不斷地簡化，現在的繁體字比更早以前的字體已經簡化了很多。學中文的人都要問：繁體簡體的問題到底應該怎麼解決？繁體簡體同時存在的現象究竟還會有多久？

课文

从前，中国没有人讲什么繁体字和简体字，大家只说正体字和俗体字。那时官方文件和书籍用正体字；老百姓日常生活中用俗体字。俗体字省了很多笔划，写起来比较容易，所以受到大家的欢迎。

上世纪初，有许多学者不断地在报纸和杂志上写文章说，应该把俗体字作为正式字来使用。1935年中华民国教育部公布了三百二十四个俗体字的《简体字表》。可是还不到一年就因为某些人的反对而被迫取消了。1952年开始，大陆的政府陆续整理出来了两千多个俗体字，作为正式的字体，叫做"简化字"，同时废除了繁体字和异体字。

可是一直到今天，在台湾和香港以及海外，许多人还在使用繁体字和异体字。几十年来，台湾方面不承认大陆推行的简化字，大陆方面也不愿意倒退回去重新用繁体字。

几十年以前，海外的中文教学都是用繁体字，自从中国大陆开放以后，从大陆到海外教中文的人越来越多，去大陆学中文的学生也越来越多，于是海外的中文教学就出现了两种字体同时存在的现象。

这样一来，给学中文的学生造成了许多麻烦。从台湾、香港来的学生不认识简体字，从大陆来的学生不认识繁体字。本来薄薄的一本书，因为要同时用繁、简两种字体，于是就变成了厚厚的一本，既浪费了纸张，又提高了价钱。

其实，汉字从古到今一直都是在不断地简化，现在的繁体字比更早以前的字体已经简化了很多。学中文的人都要问：繁体简体的问题到底应该怎么解决？繁体简体同时存在的现象究竟还会有多久？

生 詞

正體字	正体字	zhèngtǐzì	n.	standardized form of Chinese characters
俗體字	俗体字	sútǐzì	n.	popular or simplified form of Chinese characters
官方	官方	guānfāng	n.	official
文件	文件	wénjiàn	n.	document
書籍	书籍	shūjí	n.	books
省	省	shěng	v.	leave out; omit
受到	受到	shòudào		get; receive
上世紀	上世纪	shàng shì jì	n.	last century
初	初	chū	n.	the beginning of
學者	学者	xuézhě	n.	scholar
雜誌	杂志	zázhì	n.	magazine
教育部	教育部	jiàoyùbù	n.	Ministry of Education
公佈	公布	gōngbù	v.	promulgate; publish
表	表	biǎo	n.	table; form
某	某	mǒu	n.	some (unspecified); (a) certain
反對	反对	fǎnduì	v.	object; oppose
被迫	被迫	bèipò	v.	be compelled to
陸續	陆续	lùxù	adv.	in succession
整理	整理	zhěnglǐ	v.	put in order; sort out
廢除	废除	fèichú	v.	abolish
異體字	异体字	yìtǐzì	n.	a variant form of a Chinese character
自從	自从	zìcóng	prep.	since

以及	以及	yǐ jí	conj.	as well as; along with
海外	海外	hǎiwài	n.	overseas
承認	承认	chéngrèn	v.	admit; recognize
倒退	倒退	dàotuì	v.	reverse; retrogress
重新	重新	chóngxīn	adv.	again
存在	存在	cúnzài	v.	exist
現象	现象	xiànxiàng	n.	phenomenon
薄	薄	báo	adj.	thin
厚	厚	hòu	adj.	thick
浪費	浪费	làngfèi	v.	waste
紙張	纸张	zhǐzhāng	n.	paper
提高	提高	tígāo	v.	raise; heighten
價錢	价钱	jiàqián	n.	price
比	比	bǐ	prep.	compared with; than
解決	解决	jiějué	v.	solve
到底	到底	dàodǐ	adv.	exactly; after all
究竟	究竟	jiūjìng	adv.	exactly; after all

語法和詞語註釋

一、受(到)　　get; receive

This indicates the passive voice.

1. 簡化字受到大家的歡迎。
   简化字受到大家的欢迎。
   Simplified characters have been well received by everyone.

2. 計劃生育的政策受到某些外國人的反對。
   计划生育的政策受到某些外国人的反对。

Birth control policy is opposed by some foreigners.

3. 我在家老是受妹妹的氣。

   我在家老是受妹妹的气。

   I'm always bullied at home by my younger sister.

二、某　　some (unspecified); (a) certain

"某" is used before a noun or a measure word to indicate a certain person, date, place, and so on.

1. 我想再看一下這本書的某些地方。

   我想再看一下这本书的某些地方。

   I want to read some parts of this book again.

2. 我知道某人拿了我的東西。

   我知道某人拿了我的东西。

   I know someone took my stuff away.

3. 某些事到現在我還忘不了。

   某些事到现在我还忘不了。

   There are some things which, even now, I still can't forget.

三、以及　　along with; as well as

"以及" connects nouns, verbs and phrases. It is used before the last of the items to be connected. It is more often used in written language.

1. 香港、臺灣以及海外的華人現在還用繁體字。

   香港、台湾以及海外的华人现在还用繁体字。

   The Chinese in Hong Kong and Taiwan, and those living overseas, still use complex Chinese characters.

2. 開學的時候，我買了電腦、電視以及小電冰箱。

   开学的时候，我买了电脑、电视以及小电冰箱。

   At the beginning of this term, I bought a computer, a TV and a small refrigerator.

3. 昨天我和王小龍、張大偉以及李玉鳳去看了一場電影。

昨天我和王小龙、张大伟以及李玉凤去看了一场电影。

Yesterday, I went to see a movie with Wang Xiaolong, Zhang Dawei and Li Yufeng.

四、自從　　since

"自從" shows the starting point of a period in the past. It is also often used with "以後", which indicates a period of time from a point in the past up to now.

1. 自從上了大學，我12點以前沒有睡過覺。

自从上了大学，我12点以前没有睡过觉。

Since entering college, I've never gone to bed before 12:00 a.m.

2. 自從他有了女朋友以後，他的錢花得很快。

自从他有了女朋友以后，他的钱花得很快。

Since he's had a girlfriend, his money has gone very quickly.

3. 自從考試得了A以後，他學中文更用功了。

自从考试得了A以后，他学中文更用功了。

Since he got an A in the exam, he has been studying Chinese even harder.

五、"從前"and"以前"　　before; previously

The adverbs "從前" and "以前" both indicate time in the past, but "從前" cannot be preceded by any time words.

1. 從前(以前)我住在紐約。

从前(以前)我住在纽约。

I used to live in New York.

2. 她是我從前(以前)的女朋友。

她是我从前(以前)的女朋友。

She's my ex-girlfriend.

3. 天黑以前我得回家。

天黑以前我得回家。

I have to go home before it gets dark.

4. 她是我兩年以前的女朋友。

   她是我两年以前的女朋友。

   She's my ex-girlfriend of two years ago.

   她是我兩年從前的女朋友。(×)

   她是我两年从前的女朋友。(×)

六、比   compared with; than

"比" is used to make comparison of two things or persons with regard to a particular quality.

1. 繁體字比以前的字已經簡化了不少。

   繁体字比以前的字已经简化了不少。

   When compared to the characters of ancient times, even complex characters are simpler.

2. 妹妹長得比我漂亮。

   妹妹长得比我漂亮。

   My younger sister is prettier than I am.

3. 大學的課比中學的難。

   大学的课比中学的难。

   College courses are harder than high school courses.

七、"到底"and"究竟"   exactly; after all

"到底"and"究竟"are used in interrogative sentences to indicate further exploration of a topic or an attempt to get a definitive answer.

1. 簡化字繁體字的問題到底(究竟)怎麼辦？

   简化字繁体字的问题到底(究竟)怎么办？

   How on earth can the problem of simplified characters and complex characters be dealt with?

2. 昨天晚上給你打電話的那個男人到底(究竟)是誰？

   昨天晚上给你打电话的那个男人到底(究竟)是谁？

   Who on earth was the guy who called you last night?

3. 你為甚麼不去上課，你到底(究竟)還想不想學中文？

   你为什么不去上课，你到底(究竟)还想不想学中文？

   Why didn't you come to class? Do you still want to learn Chinese or not?

> "到底" also indicates that a final result has been realized after much time and effort.

4. 這篇文章寫了兩個星期到底寫完了。

   这篇文章写了两个星期到底写完了。

   After two weeks' work, the article was finally finished.

5. 等了很長時間，她到底收到男朋友的信了。

   等了很长时间，她到底收到男朋友的信了。

   After waiting for a very long time, she finally received her boyfriend's letter.

練 習

一、用所給的詞語回答問題

1. A：你是甚麼時候開始學繁體字的？(自從)

      你是什么时候开始学繁体字的？(自从)

   B：_____。

2. A：你妹妹漂亮還是你漂亮？(比)

      你妹妹漂亮还是你漂亮？(比)

   B：_____。

3. A：為甚麼很多人都要學中文？(受到)

      为什么很多人都要学中文？(受到)

   B：_____。

4. A：你一直都住在這兒嗎？(從前)
   你一直都住在这儿吗？(从前)

   B：_____。

二、選擇合適的詞語填空

1. 我_____住在中國，我是十年_____從中國來的。
   我_____住在中国，我是十年_____从中国来的。
   a. 從前　从前　　b. 以前　以前

2. 請大家_____她一下，她需要大家_____。
   请大家_____她一下，她需要大家_____。
   a. 幫忙　帮忙　　b. 幫助　帮助

3. 我現在吃飯_____看電視？吃飯_____看電視都可以。
   我现在吃饭_____看电视？吃饭_____看电视都可以。
   a. 或者　或者　　b. 還是　还是

4. 人們_____會寫簡體字，_____的人都認識繁體字。
   人们_____会写简体字，_____的人都认识繁体字。
   a. 大都　大都　　b. 大多數　大多数

5. 他不知道_____應該學繁體字還是簡體字，所以他_____寫拼音。
   他不知道_____应该学繁体字还是简体字，所以他_____写拼音。
   a. 老是　老是　　b. 到底　到底

6. 以前大家_____中文容易學，現在他們_____學中文一點兒都不容易。
   以前大家_____中文容易学，现在他们_____学中文一点儿都不容易。
   a. 認為　认为　　b. 以為　以为

7. 東方的語言_____難學，_____是中文。
   东方的语言_____难学，_____是中文。
   a. 尤其　尤其　　b. 特別　特别

9. 繁體字和簡體字　　　　　　　　　　　　　　　　　　　157

8. 我學中文是_____和我奶奶說話，_____我奶奶不會說英文。
   我学中文是_____和我奶奶说话，_____我奶奶不会说英文。
   a. 因為　因为　　b. 為了　为了

9. 老師說只要會寫漢字就行，_____寫甚麼沒關係，_____大家都寫簡體字。
   老师说只要会写汉字就行，_____写什么没关系，_____大家都写简体字。
   a. 於是　于是　　b. 至於　至于

10. 湯姆_____學中文才能去北京，他_____開始學中文了。
    汤姆_____学中文才能去北京，他_____开始学中文了。
    a. 只有　只有　　b. 只好　只好

三、用所給的詞語造句

1. 以及
   以及
   _____。

2. 自從
   自从
   _____。

3. 受到
   受到
   _____。

4. 到底
   到底
   _____。

5. 比
   比
   _____。

四、翻譯

1. Since the Mainland promulgated simplified characters, books, newspapers and magazines there all have to use simplified characters. Elementary schools, middle schools and colleges must teach simplified characters as well.

   _____
   _____
   _____ 。

2. After simplified characters were promulgated, they were well received by everyone. However, many old people still like writing complex characters. They say simplified characters are easier to write than complex ones, but are hard to memorize and don't look nice.

   _____
   _____
   _____ 。

3. Ten years ago I learned simplified characters in the Mainland. Now I'm learning complex characters in the U.S. It is troublesome when complex characters and simplified characters are used together. Sometimes I really don't know what to write.

   _____
   _____
   _____ 。

五、根據課文回答問題

1. 甚麼是俗體字？
   什么是俗体字？

   _____
   _____ 。

2. 人們為甚麼要寫俗體字？

人们为什么要写俗体字？
_____
_____。

3. 簡化字是怎麼來的？
   简化字是怎么来的？
   _____
   _____。

4. 海外為甚麼會出現兩種字體同時存在的現象？
   海外为什么会出现两种字体同时存在的现象？
   _____
   _____。

5. 兩種字體同時存在為甚麼不好？
   两种字体同时存在为什么不好？
   _____
   _____。

六、課堂討論

1. 你覺得應該怎樣解決這兩種字體同時存在的現象？
   你觉得应该怎样解决这两种字体同时存在的现象？
   _____
   _____
   _____。

2. 應該學一種字體，還是兩種字體？
   应该学一种字体，还是两种字体？
   _____
   _____
   _____。

七、小作文

你喜歡繁體字(簡體字)的原因。

你喜欢繁体字(简体字)的原因。

_____
_____
_____
_____
_____
_____。

閱讀

拼音的歷史

大約漢代的時候，人們要說明一個字的讀音，就在這個字的後邊注明"讀若～、讀如～"。意思是說前面這個字的音，應該像後面那個字的音一樣，讀作～。例如："妍，讀若研"。就是說"妍"字要和後面研究的"研"一樣，讀作"yán"。那時還有一種"直音法"，是用一個字來表示另一個字的讀音。比方說："童，音同"，意思是說兒童的"童"的讀音和"同"一樣。這種方法到現在還有人用。

後來，人們又發明了"反切"。反切是用兩個字給一個字標音。它用前一個字的聲母和後一個字的韻母以及聲調，來拼讀另外一個字。例如："含，胡男切(胡男反)"。"切"和"反"是"拼讀"的意思。如果用現代漢語普通話來解釋，就是說用"胡"的聲母"h"跟"男"的韻母"an"以及它的聲調"ˊ"(第二聲)，可以拼成"含"字的讀音"hán"。

前面這三種標音的方法都有一個共同的缺點，就是用來標音的字必須是大家都熟悉的常用字，如果不是常用字的話，很多人就會不認識。如果連標音的字都不認識，那就沒有辦法去讀前面那個被標音的字了。

1918年，當時的中國政府公佈了一套用漢字筆劃式符號來標音的新方法，叫"注音符號"。這種用符號標音的方法比以前那些用漢字標音的方法好用多了，到現在臺灣還在使用這種"注音符號"。

1958年大陸公佈了"漢語拼音方案"。漢語拼音是用國際通用的拉丁字母給漢字標音的。漢語拼音在教學以及電腦輸入方面，比注音字母好用，所以很受歡迎。現在除了大陸以外，海外很多地方也在使用漢語拼音。最近，臺灣某些學者也提出要用拉丁字母拼音來替代注音字母。

阅 读

拼音的历史

大约汉代的时候，人们要说明一个字的读音，就在这个字的后边注明"读若～、读如～"。意思是说前面这个字的音，应该像后面那个字的音一样，读作～。例如："妍，读若研"。就是说"妍"字要和后面研究的"研"一样，读作"yán"。那时还有一种"直音法"，是用一个字来表示另一个字的读音。比方说："童，音同"，意思是说儿童的"童"的读音和"同"一样。这种方法到现在还有人用。

后来，人们又发明了"反切"。反切是用两个字给一个字标音。它用前一个字的声母和后一个字的韵母以及声调，来拼读另外一个字。例如："含，胡男切（胡男反）"。"切"和"反"是"拼读"的意思。如果用现代汉语普通话来解释，就是说用"胡"的声母"h"跟"男"的韵母"an"以及它的声调"ˊ"（第二声），可以拼成"含"字的读音"hán"。

前面这三种标音的方法都有一个共同的缺点，就是用来标音的字必须是大家都熟悉的常用字，如果不是常用字的话，很多人就会不认识。如果连标音的字都不认识，那就没有办法去读前面那个被标音的字了。

1918年，当时的中国政府公布了一套用汉字笔划式符号来标音的新方法，叫"注音符号"。这种用符号标音的方法比以前那些用汉字标音的方法好用多了，到现在台湾还在使用这种"注音符号"。

1958年大陆公布了"汉语拼音方案"。汉语拼音是用国际通用的拉丁字母给汉字标音的。汉语拼音在教学以及电脑输入方面，比注音字母好用，所以很受欢迎。现在除了大陆以外，海外很多地方也在使用汉语拼音。最近，台湾某些学者也提出要用拉丁字母拼音来替代注音字母。

9. 繁體字和簡體字

生 詞

繁體	簡體	拼音	詞性	英文
大約	大约	dàyuē	adv.	approximately; about
注明	注明	zhùmíng	v.	make a footnote; annotate
讀若	读若	dú ruò		be pronounced as
讀如	读如	dú rú		be pronounced as
妍	妍	yán	adj.	beautiful
直音法	直音法	zhíyīnfǎ	n.	a method of representing the pronunciation of Chinese characters
另	另	lìng		another
兒童	儿童	értóng	n.	child(ren)
反切	反切	fǎnqiè	n.	a method of representing the pronunciation of Chinese characters
標音	标音	biāo yīn		indicate the sound by using phonetic symbols
拼讀	拼读	pīndú	v.	spell
含	含	hán	v.	keep in the mouth
解釋	解释	jiěshì	v.	explain
共同	共同	gòngtóng	n.	common
缺點	缺点	quēdiǎn	n.	defect
必須	必须	bìxū	adv.	must
熟悉	熟悉	shúxī	adj.	be familiar with
套	套	tào	m.	a suit of; a series of
筆劃式	笔划式	bǐhuàshì	n.	strokes of a Chinese character
符號	符号	fúhào	n.	symbol
注音符號	注音符号	Zhùyīn fúhào		the National Phonetic Script (for Mandarin)

漢語拼音方案	汉语拼音方案	Hànyǔ Pīnyīn Fāng'àn		the Scheme for the Chinese Phonetic Alphabet
國際	国际	guójì	n.	international
通用	通用	tōngyòng	adj.	commonly used
拉丁字母	拉丁字母	Lādīng zìmǔ		Latin alphabet; the Roman alphabet
教學	教学	jiàoxué	v.	teaching
提出	提出	tíchū	v.	put forward; advance
替代	替代	tìdài	v.	substitute for; replace

問 題

1. 你知道以前人們是用甚麼方法來給漢字標音的嗎？
   你知道以前人们是用什么方法来给汉字标音的吗？
   _____
   _____ 。

2. 以前的標音的方法有甚麼缺點？
   以前的标音的方法有什么缺点？
   _____
   _____ 。

3. 注音符號是甚麼時候開始使用的？
   注音符号是什么时候开始使用的？
   _____
   _____ 。

4. 漢語拼音是用甚麼字母組成的？
   汉语拼音是用什么字母组成的？
   _____
   _____ 。

5. 從古代到現在一共有幾種標音的方法？
   从古代到现在一共有几种标音的方法？
   _____
   _____ 。

6. 你覺得哪一種標音方法好？
   你觉得哪一种标音方法好？
   _____
   _____ 。

10

一字多義的問題
Characters with More Than One Meaning

學習大綱

通過學習本課，學生應該能夠：

1. 掌握這些句型和詞語的意思和用法："以上"和"以下"、"根本"、"不過……罷了"、"一……就"、"結果"、"便"、"以至"、"弄"和"搞"。
2. 認識和運用課文以及閱讀文章內的生詞。
3. 明白甚麼是"一字多義"和一字多義引起的麻煩。
4. 認識中文裏一些互相通用卻又很麻煩的字。

Study Outline

After studying this chapter, students should:

1. Have a good command of the meaning and usage of these sentence patterns and terms: "yǐshàng" (more than; above), "yǐxià" (less than; below), "gēnběn" (at all; simply), "bùguò ... bàle" (only; just), "yī ... jiù" (once; as soon as), "jiéguǒ" (as a result; in the end; finally), "biàn" (then), "yǐzhì" (so ... that ...; as a result), "nòng" and "gǎo" (do; make).
2. Be familiar with the meaning and usage of the vocabulary introduced in the text and the reading.
3. Comprehend what kinds of misunderstanding have been caused by characters with more than one meaning.
4. Be familiar with some characters that can be used interchangeably and be aware of the problems caused by such interchangeable use.

課 文

　　一字多義是說一個字有兩個或以上的意思。例如："快"在"愉快"、"快樂"的裏面是高興的意思；在"快吃"、"快跑"的裏面是速度高的意思。"慢"在"傲慢"、"怠慢"的裏面表示態度冷淡；在"慢走"、"慢跑"的裏面表示速度低。

　　有人說它們不是一字多義，說它們根本就是兩個不同的字，只不過是讀音和字形一樣罷了。不管它們是甚麼，這些字形一樣、意思不一樣的字給讀書的人帶來了許多麻煩。因為人們在看書的時候，一不注意就會弄錯，就會誤解它的意思。現在的人常常弄錯，古代的人也會弄錯。古書上就講過這樣一個故事。

　　虞舜時代，舜認為音樂可以教育人民，可以改變社會風氣。於是他要大家幫他找一個懂音樂的人來整理音樂，製作樂曲。有人給舜推薦了一個名叫"夔(kuí)"的人。夔這個人特別能幹，他不但很快地整理好了音樂，而且還製作出了許多美妙的樂曲。這些樂曲一傳到民間，社會風氣很快就變好了。

　　後來有人再給舜推薦別的人的時候，舜說："夔一足也。"舜的意思是說："像夔這麼能幹的人，有一個就足夠了。"當時寫書的人就把這件事情記了下來。

　　很多年以後，有一個人在讀這本書的時候，沒有仔細地看上下文，結果把"夔一足"理解成了"夔只有一隻腳"。他覺得自己很聰明，發現了別人沒有發現的事情。於是便很得意地告訴了別人。大家一傳十，十傳百，以至於後來所有的人都以為夔只有一隻腳。

　　為甚麼他會搞錯了呢？就是因為"足"這個字有兩個意思：一個是"足夠"，一個是"腳"。

课文

一字多义是说一个字有两个或以上的意思。例如："快"在"愉快"、"快乐"的里面是高兴的意思；在"快吃"、"快跑"的里面是速度高的意思。"慢"在"傲慢"、"怠慢"的里面表示态度冷淡；在"慢走"、"慢跑"的里面表示速度低。

有人说它们不是一字多义，说它们根本就是两个不同的字，只不过是读音和字形一样罢了。不管它们是什么，这些字形一样、意思不一样的字给读书的人带来了许多麻烦。因为人们在看书的时候，一不注意就会弄错，就会误解它的意思。现在的人常常弄错，古代的人也会弄错。古书上就讲过这样一个故事。

虞舜时代，舜认为音乐可以教育人民，可以改变社会风气。于是他要大家帮他找一个懂音乐的人来整理音乐，制作乐曲。有人给舜推荐了一个名叫"夔(kuí)"的人。夔这个人特别能干，他不但很快地整理好了音乐，而且还制作出了许多美妙的乐曲。这些乐曲一传到民间，社会风气很快就变好了。

后来有人再给舜推荐别的人的时候，舜说："夔一足也。"舜的意思是说："像夔这么能干的人，有一个就足够了。"当时写书的人就把这件事情记了下来。

很多年以后，有一个人在读这本书的时候，没有仔细地看上下文，结果把"夔一足"理解成了"夔只有一只脚"。他觉得自己很聪明，发现了别人没有发现的事情。于是便很得意地告诉了别人。大家一传十，十传百，以至于后来所有的人都以为夔只有一只脚。

为什么他会搞错了呢？就是因为"足"这个字有两个意思：一个是"足够"，一个是"脚"。

生　詞

一字多義	一字多义	yī zì duō yì		one character with two or more different meanings
快樂	快乐	kuàilè	adj.	happy
愉快	愉快	yúkuài	adj.	happy
速度高	速度高	sùdù gāo		high speed
速度低	速度低	sùdù dī		low speed
傲慢	傲慢	àomàn	adj.	arrogant; haughty
怠慢	怠慢	dàimàn	v.	neglect; slight
態度	态度	tàidu	n.	attitude
冷淡	冷淡	lěngdàn	adj.	indifferent; cold
根本	根本	gēnběn	adv.	entirely; at all
不過……罷了	不过……罢了	bùguò ... bàle	adv.	only
一……就	一……就	yī ... jiù		as soon as ...; once
弄	弄	nòng	v.	make; do
誤解	误解	wù jiě	v.	misunderstand
虞	虞	Yú		dynasty founded by Shun
舜	舜	Shùn		the name of a legendary monarch in ancient China around 2200 B.C.
時代	时代	shídài	n.	times; age; era
風氣	风气	fēngqì	n.	common practice
樂曲	乐曲	yuèqǔ	n.	music
推薦	推荐	tuī jiàn	v.	recommend
夔	夔	Kuí		name of a person

也	也	yě	par.	(here) classical Chinese word
足夠	足够	zúgòu	adj.	enough
上下文	上下文	shàng-xiàwén	n.	context
結果	结果	jiéguǒ	n.	(as a) result
理解	理解	lǐjiě	v.	understand
便	便	biàn	adv.	then
得意	得意	déyì	adj.	proud of oneself
以至	以至	yǐzhì	conj.	as a result; so ... that ...
搞	搞	gǎo	v.	do; be engaged in

語法和詞語註釋

一、以上　　more than; above
　　以下　　less than; below

"以上" means more than a certain number or above a certain point. "以下" means less than a certain number or below a certain point.

1. 一字多義是一個字有兩個或兩個以上的意思。
   一字多义是一个字有两个或两个以上的意思。
   Yi zi duo yi means one character with two or more different meanings.

2. 現在大學的學費都在三萬塊錢以上。
   现在大学的学费都在三万块钱以上。
   Now all college tuition is more than $30,000.

3. 二十一歲以下的人不能喝酒。
   二十一岁以下的人不能喝酒。
   No one under twenty-one years of age can drink alcohol.

二、根本　　at all; simply

"根本" is used in a negative sentence to make the negative more strongly emphatic.

1. 其實一字多義根本就是兩個不同的字。
   其实一字多义根本就是两个不同的字。
   A character with two meanings is actually two different words.

2. 誰說她是我的女朋友，我根本就不認識她。
   谁说她是我的女朋友，我根本就不认识她。
   Who said she is my girlfriend. I don't know her at all.

3. 今天的課我根本就沒有聽懂。
   今天的课我根本就没有听懂。
   I didn't understand today's class at all.

三、不過……罷了　　only; just

"不過……罷了" refers to a scope or range, and indicates that something is as unimportant as possible.

1. 它們根本就是兩個不同的字，只不過字體和聲音一樣罷了。
   它们根本就是两个不同的字，只不过字体和声音一样罢了。
   They are actually two different words. They just have the same character and sound.

2. 我跟陳龍不熟悉，只不過在晚會上見過一兩次罷了。
   我跟陈龙不熟悉，只不过在晚会上见过一两次罢了。
   I'm not familiar with Chen Long. I've only met him once or twice at parties.

3. 我只不過想問一下罷了，沒有別的意思。
   我只不过想问一下罢了，没有别的意思。
   I just wanted to ask you. I didn't mean anything else.

四、一……就　　once; as soon as

"一……就" indicates that some extent is reached or result obtained once the action in question has taken place.

1. 寫字的時候一不注意就會弄錯。

10. 一字多義的問題　　　　　　　　　　　　　　　　　　173

写字的时候一不注意就会弄错。

As soon as you stop paying attention when writing, it's easy to make mistakes.

2. 湯姆不能喝酒，他一喝酒就醉。

汤姆不能喝酒，他一喝酒就醉。

Tom can't drink. Once he drinks, he gets drunk easily.

3. 王麗很聰明，不管甚麼東西她一學就會。

王丽很聪明，不管什么东西她一学就会。

Wang Li is very smart. No matter what it is, once she gets into it, she can learn it very fast.

五、結果　　as a result; in the end; finally

This is used in the second clause and means "consequently" or "as a result".

1. 讀書的時候沒有注意，結果把"夔一足"理解成了"夔有一隻腳"。

读书的时候没有注意，结果把"夔一足"理解成了"夔有一只脚"。

Someone didn't pay attention when reading and consequently misunderstood "Only one Kui is enough" as "Kui has only one foot".

2. 老師讓他做第五課的作業，結果他做的是第六課的作業。

老师让他做第五课的作业，结果他做的是第六课的作业。

The teacher asked him to do the homework for Lesson 5, but in the end he did the homework for Lesson 6.

3. 他說他要請我吃飯，我等了很長時間，結果他沒來。

他说他要请我吃饭，我等了很长时间，结果他没来。

He said he would invite me to dinner. I waited for him for a long time, but in the end he never came.

六、便　　then

This is used like "就", but more often appears in written language.

1. 他便很得意地把這件事告訴了別人。

   他便很得意地把这件事告诉了别人。

   Then he told other people about it very proudly.

2. 他一上床便睡着了。

   他一上床便睡着了。

   He fell asleep as soon as he went to bed.

3. 只要我請客,他便願意跟我去吃飯。

   只要我请客,他便愿意跟我去吃饭。

   As long as I treat him, he likes to have dinner with me.

七、以至   so ... that ...; as a result

"以至" is used (with "於" or without "於") in the second clause of a sentence and indicates a result caused by the previous situation.

1. 大家一傳十,十傳百,以至於所有的人都以為夔只有一隻腳。

   大家一传十,十传百,以至于所有的人都以为夔只有一只脚。

   It spread so quickly that (almost) everyone thought Kui had only one foot.

2. 上課的時候老師講的真沒有意思,以至於很多同學都睡着了。

   上课的时候老师讲的真没有意思,以至于很多同学都睡着了。

   What the teacher said in class was so boring that many students fell asleep.

3. 小燕長得太漂亮了,以至每個人都要回頭看她一眼。

   小燕长得太漂亮了,以至每个人都要回头看她一眼。

   Xiaoyan is so beautiful that everyone turns round to have a look at her.

八、弄、搞   do; make

"弄" and "搞" are special verbs, which can substitute for various other verbs. Their meanings often change according to the different objects they take.

1. 你一不注意就會弄錯。

你一不注意就会弄错。

As soon as you stop paying attention, you'll make mistakes.

2. 找一個搞音樂的人來整理音樂。

找一个搞音乐的人来整理音乐。

Find a person who specializes in music to sort out the music.

3. 我餓了，幫我弄點兒吃的來。

我饿了，帮我弄点儿吃的来。

I feel hungry. Please find me something to eat.

練習

一、用所給的詞語改寫句子

1. A：我見過王麗一兩次面，跟她不熟悉。(不過……罷了)

   我见过王丽一两次面，跟她不熟悉。(不过……罢了)

   B：_____。

2. A：昨天上課來的學生太多了，很多人只好站在教室外面聽課。(以至)

   昨天上课来的学生太多了，很多人只好站在教室外面听课。(以至)

   B：_____。

3. A：我的同屋請我去飯館吃飯，可是他突然頭疼，沒有去成。(結果)

   我的同屋请我去饭馆吃饭，可是他突然头疼，没有去成。(结果)

   B：_____。

4. A：每次看見老師的時候，我的頭會疼。(一……就)

   每次看见老师的时候，我的头会疼。(一……就)

   B：_____。

5. A：這次考試有很多題從來沒有學過。(根本)

   这次考试有很多题从来没有学过。(根本)

   B：_____。

6. A：國家規定還沒有過二十一歲生日的人不可以喝酒。(以上、以下)
　　　國家规定还没有过二十一岁生日的人不可以喝酒。(以上、以下)
　　B：_____。

二、用所給的詞語填空 (一個詞語可以用多次)

以上、一……就、越來越、根本、不過……罷了、自從、以前、其實、一點兒、結果、以至

以上、一……就、越来越、根本、不过……罢了、自从、以前、其实、一点儿、结果、以至

1. 大家說我_____很聰明，老師講的課，我_____聽_____會。不知道為甚麼，現在我不聰明了。_____，我以前_____不聰明，_____比別人用功一些_____。
   大家说我_____很聪明，老师讲的课，我_____听_____会。不知道为什么，现在我不聪明了。_____，我以前_____不聪明，_____比别人用功一些_____。

2. _____上大學以後，我每天看書要看八個小時_____，看書看得太多了，_____把眼睛都看壞了。上課時我_____就看不見黑板上的字。_____，學習_____不好了。
   _____上大学以后，我每天看书要看八个小时_____，看书看的太多了，_____把眼睛都看坏了。上课时我_____就看不见黑板上的字。_____，学习_____不好了。

三、用所給的詞語造句

1. 不過……罷了
   不过……罢了
   _____。

2. 結果
   结果
   _____。

3. 以至
   以至
   _____。

4. 根本
   根本
   _____。

5. 以上
   以上
   _____。

四、翻譯

1. If one word has two or more meanings, it is a *duo yi zi*. Actually *duo yi zi* are not hard at all. We only have to give them more attention in reading.

   _____
   _____
   _____。

2. A character is a wrong one if it's written by one person by mistake. If the wrong character is written by many people and has been wrong for a long time, and even the dictionaries have this wrong character listed, this character is no longer a wrong one.

   _____
   _____
   _____。

3. He didn't refer to the context carefully, and consequently misunderstood what it meant. However, he didn't know he was wrong, and thought he had discovered something unknown to other people.

   _____

五、根據課文回答問題

1. "快"和"慢"有哪幾個意思？
   "快"和"慢"有哪几个意思？
   _____
   _____。

2. 舜為甚麼要別人幫他找一個懂音樂的人來整理音樂？
   舜为什么要别人帮他找一个懂音乐的人来整理音乐？
   _____
   _____。

3. 舜說"夔一足也。"是甚麼意思？
   舜说"夔一足也。"是什么意思？
   _____
   _____。

4. 那個讀書人把"夔一足"理解成了甚麼意思？
   那个读书人把"夔一足"理解成了什么意思？
   _____
   _____。

5. "足"字有兩個甚麼意思？
   "足"字有两个什么意思？
   _____
   _____。

六、課堂討論

1. 為甚麼讀這些多義字的時候，一不注意就會弄錯？

为什么读这些多义字的时候，一不注意就会弄错？
_____
_____
_____ 。

2. 遇到多義字的時候，怎樣才不會弄錯？
   遇到多义字的时候，怎样才不会弄错？
_____
_____
_____ 。

七、小作文

學中文的麻煩。（同音字、多義字以及寫錯字的問題。）
学中文的麻烦。（同音字、多义字以及写错字的问题。）
_____
_____
_____
_____
_____
_____ 。

閱讀

互相通用的字

"做"和"作"聲音一樣,字體不一樣,有時候可以互相通用,有時候不能互相通用。去朋友家玩,可以寫成"做客",也可以寫成"作客";做餃子的方法,可以寫成"做法",也可以寫成"作法"。可是做文章、做詩的時候一定要寫成"做";而作曲、作畫只能用"作"。

從"做"和"作"組合的詞來看,做一個具體的東西多用"做",比如:做飯、做夢、做禮拜、做買賣;而做抽象的事情時多用"作",比如:作假、作弊、作證。大概因為"作"的不是具體的東西,所以和"作"組合的詞大都是名詞,例如:作業、作文、作品、作者、工作。

除了"做"和"作"以外,"像"和"象"有時也能通用。例如:"妹妹象爸爸,弟弟像媽媽","我好像弄懂了,又好象沒弄懂"。可是在表示"照着人物做成的形象"的意思時,如畫像、塑像,卻只能用"像"而不能用"象"。不過因為"像"有表示人物形象的意思,所以它和表示相貌的"相"又可以通用,有人就把"照相"寫成"照像";把"相片"寫成"像片"。

這些字有的是語言發展過程中詞義擴展造成的,有的是人們錯讀和錯寫造成的。例如:形容一件事情難辦,本來只有"棘手"一詞。棘手的意思是說:這件難辦的事情就像荊棘一樣扎手。棘手的"棘"和辣椒的"辣"很像,荊棘扎手和辣椒辣手的感覺也差不多一樣,結果有人就弄錯了,把棘手讀成了辣手。不知道為甚麼,大家都喜歡說辣手,以至於後來字典上也就將錯就錯地列出了"辣手"一詞。

如果一個人寫錯了一個字,這個字便是錯字;很多人都把這個字寫錯了,而且錯了很長時間,那麼這個字便不是錯字了。

阅 读

互相通用的字

"做"和"作"声音一样,字体不一样,有时候可以互相通用,有时候不能互相通用。去朋友家玩,可以写成"做客",也可以写成"作客";做饺子的方法,可以写成"做法",也可以写成"作法"。可是做文章、做诗的时候一定要写成"做";而作曲、作画只能用"作"。

从"做"和"作"组合的词来看,做一个具体的东西多用"做",比如:做饭、做梦、做礼拜、做买卖;而做抽象的事情时多用"作",比如:作假、作弊、作证。大概因为"作"的不是具体的东西,所以和"作"组合的词大都是名词,例如:作业、作文、作品、作者、工作。

除了"做"和"作"以外,"像"和"象"有时也能通用。例如:"妹妹象爸爸,弟弟像妈妈","我好像弄懂了,又好象没弄懂"。可是在表示"照着人物做成的形象"的意思时,如画像、塑像,却只能用"像"而不能用"象"。不过因为"像"有表示人物形象的意思,所以它和表示相貌的"相"又可以通用,有人就把"照相"写成"照像";把"相片"写成"像片"。

这些字有的是语言发展过程中词义扩展造成的,有的是人们错读和错写造成的。例如:形容一件事情难办,本来只有"棘手"一词。棘手的意思是说:这件难办的事情就像荆棘一样扎手。棘手的"棘"和辣椒的"辣"很像,荆棘扎手和辣椒辣手的感觉也差不多一样,结果有人就弄错了,把棘手读成了辣手。不知道为什么,大家都喜欢说辣手,以至于后来字典上也就将错就错地列出了"辣手"一词。

如果一个人写错了一个字,这个字便是错字;很多人都把这个字写错了,而且错了很长时间,那么这个字便不是错字了。

生 詞

互相	互相	hùxiāng	adv.	mutual; each other
通用	通用	tōngyòng	v.	use interchangeably
做客	做客	zuò kè		be a guest
做詩	做诗	zuò shī		write a poem
作曲	作曲	zuò qǔ		compose music
作畫	作画	zuò huà		paint
組合	组合	zǔhé	v.	constitute; make up
具體	具体	jùtǐ	adj.	specific; concrete
做夢	做梦	zuò mèng		have a dream
做禮拜	做礼拜	zuò lǐbài		go to church
抽象	抽象	chōuxiàng	adj.	abstract
作假	作假	zuò jiǎ		falsify; counterfeit
作弊	作弊	zuò bì		practice fraud
作證	作证	zuò zhèng		bear witness
作品	作品	zuòpǐn	n.	works (of literature and art)
作者	作者	zuòzhě	n.	author; writer
人物	人物	rénwù	n.	figure; character
形象	形象	xíngxiàng	n.	image
畫像	画像	huàxiàng	n.	portrait
塑像	塑像	sùxiàng	n.	statue
相貌	相貌	xiàngmào	n.	appearance
照相	照相	zhào xiàng		take a picture
相片	相片	xiàngpiān	n.	picture; photograph
形容	形容	xíngróng	v.	describe

難辦	难办	nán bàn		hard to do
棘手	棘手	jíshǒu		thorny; troublesome
荊棘	荆棘	jīng jí	n.	brambles; thorns
扎手	扎手	zhā shǒu		prick the hand
辣椒	辣椒	là jiāo	n.	hot pepper
辣	辣	là	adj.	spicy; hot
感覺	感觉	gǎn jué	n.	feeling
將錯就錯	将错就错	jiāngcuò jiùcuò		leave a mistake uncorrected and make the best of it
列出	列出	lièchū	v.	list

問題

1. 你知道和"做"組成的詞有哪些？
   你知道和"做"组成的词有哪些？

   _____
   _____。

2. 你知道和"作"組成的詞有哪些？
   你知道和"作"组成的词有哪些？

   _____
   _____。

3. 你知道和"作"組合的詞大都是動詞還是名詞？
   你知道和"作"组合的词大都是动词还是名词？

   _____
   _____。

4. "像"在表示甚麼意思的時候不可以和"象"互相通用？
   "像"在表示什么意思的时候不可以和"象"互相通用？

_____

_____ 。

5. 為甚麼把棘手寫成了"辣手"？
   为什么把棘手写成了"辣手"？

   _____

   _____ 。

6. 在甚麼情況下錯字不再是錯字了？
   在什么情况下错字不再是错字了？

   _____

   _____ 。

11

中國年和壓歲錢
Chinese New Year and New Year Money

學習大綱

通過學習本課，學生應該能夠：

1. 掌握這些句型和詞語的意思和用法："指"、"根據"、"每當"、"不僅……而且/也/還"、"頭"、"而"、形容詞重疊、"據說"和"聽說"。
2. 認識和運用課文以及閱讀文章內的生詞。
3. 了解中國人過年主要有哪些活動，這些活動有甚麼特別的意義。
4. 了解中國人為甚麼過年的時候喜歡舞龍、舞獅子。

Study Outline

After studying this chapter, students should:

1. Have a good command of the meaning and usage of these sentence patterns and terms: "zhǐ" (refer to; mean), "gēnjù" (according to), "měidāng" (when; whenever; every time), "bùjǐn... érqiě/yě/hái" (not only..., but also), "tóu" (first), "ér" (but), adjective reduplication, "jùshuō" and "tīngshuō" (it is said).
2. Be familiar with the meaning and usage of the vocabulary introduced in the text and the reading.
3. Know how the Chinese celebrate the Chinese New Year and be aware of the special meaning behind these activities.
4. Understand why the Chinese like lion and dragon dancing at the Chinese New Year.

課文

　　中國有兩個新年：一個是陽曆一月一號的元旦；一個是農曆一月一號的春節。中國人說過年一般都是指農曆的新年。

　　過年的習俗據說早就有了。根據歷史學家的研究，三千年前的甲骨文裏就有"年"字，"年"字上面是"禾"，下面是"人"，意思是人們揹着糧食回家。過年就是大家高高興興地舉行慶祝糧食豐收的活動。

　　不知甚麼時候開始，"年"又被說成是一個魔怪，說它每當過年的時候就出來害人。人們聽說魔怪怕響聲，也怕紅顏色，於是過年的那天晚上，大家不但在門外放鞭炮，還在門兩邊貼上大紅的春聯。

　　新年的前一天叫"大年三十"，三十的晚上叫"除夕"。除夕的晚上全家人要在一起吃"年飯"。年飯是一年中最好吃的一頓飯，不僅有酒、有肉，還一定要有一條魚。這一條魚不可以全部吃完，要留一點兒到明天，也就是明年，這叫做"年年有魚(餘)"，意思是說每年的收入都有節餘。

　　新年的頭一天是"大年初一"，初一的早上有的人家吃餃子，有的人家吃湯圓，餃子和湯圓都表示團團圓圓的意思。差不多所有的人家這一天都要吃年糕，年糕(高)表示人們的生活水平一年比一年高。

　　過年最高興的是小孩子，他們在給爺爺奶奶拜年的時候，可以得到很多"壓歲錢"。壓歲的意思是壓住一年中不好的東西。給小孩子壓歲錢是為了讓他們在新的一年裏平平安安。

　　很早以前，過年給孩子的不是真的錢，而是一種叫做"壓勝錢"的假錢。壓勝錢的形狀跟錢一樣，上面畫着龍和鳳，寫着"長命富貴"。人們說把它掛在身上可以避邪消災。後來為了讓小孩子高興，爺爺奶奶就把不能買東西的假錢換成了真錢，這錢的名字也就變成了壓歲錢。

课文

中国有两个新年：一个是阳历一月一号的元旦；一个是农历一月一号的春节。中国人说过年一般都是指农历的新年。

过年的习俗据说早就有了。根据历史学家的研究，三千年前的甲骨文里就有"年"字，"年"字上面是"禾"，下面是"人"，意思是人们背着粮食回家。过年就是大家高高兴兴地举行庆祝粮食丰收的活动。

不知什么时候开始，"年"又被说成是一个魔怪，说它每当过年的时候就出来害人。人们听说魔怪怕响声，也怕红颜色，于是过年的那天晚上，大家不但在门外放鞭炮，还在门两边贴上大红的春联。

新年的前一天叫"大年三十"，三十的晚上叫"除夕"。除夕的晚上全家人要在一起吃"年饭"。年饭是一年中最好吃的一顿饭，不仅有酒、有肉，还一定要有一条鱼。这一条鱼不可以全部吃完，要留一点儿到明天，也就是明年，这叫做"年年有鱼（余）"，意思是说每年的收入都有节余。

新年的头一天是"大年初一"，初一的早上有的人家吃饺子，有的人家吃汤圆，饺子和汤圆都表示团团圆圆的意思。差不多所有的人家这一天都要吃年糕，年糕（高）表示人们的生活水平一年比一年高。

过年最高兴的是小孩子，他们在给爷爷奶奶拜年的时候，可以得到很多"压岁钱"。压岁的意思是压住一年中不好的东西。给小孩子压岁钱是为了让他们在新的一年里平平安安。

很早以前，过年给孩子的不是真的钱，而是一种叫做"压胜钱"的假钱。压胜钱的形状跟钱一样，上面画着龙和凤，写着"长命富贵"。人们说把它挂在身上可以避邪消灾。后来为了让小孩子高兴，爷爷奶奶就把不能买东西的假钱换成了真钱，这钱的名字也就变成了压岁钱。

生詞

壓歲錢	压岁钱	yāsuìqián	n.	money given to children as New Year's gift
陽曆	阳历	yánglì	n.	the Gregorian calendar
元旦	元旦	yuándàn	n.	New Year's day
農曆	农历	nónglì	n.	lunar calendar
春節	春节	chūnjié	n.	Spring Festival
指	指	zhǐ	v.	refer to; mean
據說	据说	jùshuō		it is said
根據	根据	gēnjù	prep.	according to
歷史學家	历史学家	lìshǐxuéjiā	n.	historian
甲骨文	甲骨文	jiǎgǔwén	n.	inscriptions on bones or tortoise shells from the Shang dynasty; oracle-bone script
禾	禾	hé	n.	standing grain
揹	背	bēi	v.	carry on the back
舉行	举行	jǔxíng	v.	hold (ceremony, celebration)
慶祝	庆祝	qìngzhù	v.	celebrate
豐收	丰收	fēngshōu	n.	good harvest
活動	活动	huódòng	n.	activity
魔怪	魔怪	móguài	n.	monster
害人	害人	hài rén		harm people
響聲	响声	xiǎngshēng	n.	sound; noise
放鞭炮	放鞭炮	fàng biānpào		let off firecrackers
貼	贴	tiē	v.	paste
大紅	大红	dàhóng	adj.	bright red

春聯	春联	chūnlián	n.	Spring Festival couplets
除夕	除夕	chúxī	n.	the Chinese New Year's eve
不僅……還	不仅……还	bù jǐn ... hái	conj.	not only ... but also
收入	收入	shōurù	n.	income; revenue
節餘	节余	jiéyú	n.	surplus
大年初一	大年初一	dà niánchūyī	n.	the first day of the lunar year
餃子	饺子	jiǎozi	n.	dumplings
湯圓	汤圆	tāngyuán	n.	sweet dumplings made of glutinous rice flour
團團圓圓	团团圆圆	tuántuán-yuányuán		a reunion of the whole family
年糕	年糕	niángāo	n.	sweet rice cake
水平	水平	shuǐpíng	n.	level; standard
拜年	拜年	bài nián		give new year's greetings
而	而	ér	conj.	but
壓勝錢	压胜钱	yāshèngqián	n.	money to bring luck and ward off evil
假	假	jiǎ	adj.	fake
真	真	zhēn	adj.	real; genuine
長命富貴	长命富贵	chángmìng fùguì		live long and be successful
掛	挂	guà	v.	hang; put up
避邪	避邪	bì xié		ward off evil
消災	消灾	xiāo zāi		prevent calamities

相關詞彙

| 經濟學家 | 经济学家 | jīngjìxué jiā | economist |
| 人類學家 | 人类学家 | rénlèixué jiā | anthropologist |

社會學家	社会学家	shèhuìxué jiā	sociologist
生物學家	生物学家	shēngwùxué jiā	biologist
物理學家	物理学家	wùlǐxué jiā	physicist
數學家	数学家	shùxué jiā	mathematician
化學家	化学家	huàxué jiā	chemist
政治家	政治家	zhèngzhì jiā	politician
哲學家	哲学家	zhéxué jiā	philosopher
教育家	教育家	jiàoyù jiā	educationist
科學家	科学家	kēxué jiā	scientist
藝術家	艺术家	yìshù jiā	artist
音樂家	音乐家	yīnyuè jiā	musician
畫家	画家	huà jiā	painter
作家	作家	zuò jiā	writer
專家	专家	zhuān jiā	specialist
美食家	美食家	měishí jiā	epicure

語法和詞語註釋

一、指　refer to; mean

1. 中國人說過年一般指的是農曆的新年。
   中国人说过年一般指的是农历的新年。
   When the Chinese talk about celebrating New Year, this usually refers to the lunar new year.

2. 外國人認為中文難學，主要指的是中文的發音很難。

外国人认为中文难学，主要指的是中文的发音很难。

When foreigners say they think Chinese is hard to learn, they are mostly referring to Chinese pronunciation.

3. 大家說一個人好不好，主要是指他的心好不好。

大家说一个人好不好，主要是指他的心好不好。

When people say that someone is a nice person or a nasty person, they are mostly talking about whether that person is kind or not.

二、根據　　according to　　根據 gēn jù

1. 根據專家的研究，三千年前就有"年"字了。

根据专家的研究，三千年前就有"年"字了。

According to the experts' research, the character *nian* existed 3,000 years ago.

2. 根據大家的要求，明天的考試可以帶字典。

根据大家的要求，明天的考试可以带字典。

In line with everyone's request, dictionaries will be allowed in tomorrow's exam.

3. 根據氣象臺的預報，下個星期會下大雪。

根据气象台的预报，下个星期会下大雪。

According to the forecast from the weather station, there'll be heary snow next week.

三、每當　　when; whenever; every time　　每当

1. 每當過年的時候"年"就出來害人。

每当过年的时候"年"就出来害人。

When New Year comes, the *nian* will come out and harm people.

2. 每當快要考試的時候，他就去借別人的筆記。

每当快要考试的时候，他就去借别人的笔记。

Every time an exam is imminent, he goes to borrow other people's notes.

3. 每當沒有錢的時候，就打電話給媽媽。

每当没有钱的时候，就打电话给妈妈。

Whenever I have no money, I call my mom.

四、不僅……而且/也/還　　not only ..., but also

"不僅……而且/也/還" indicates a further meaning beyond the preceding meaning. "而且/也/還" is used in the second clause and introduces a further statement. It is more often used in written language. "不僅" can also be lengthened to "不僅僅".

1. 年飯不僅有酒有肉，還一定要有魚。

年饭不仅有酒有肉，还一定要有鱼。

At the New Year's Eve dinner there must not only be wine and meat, there must also be fish.

2. 中文字不僅難認而且難唸。

中文字不仅难认而且难念。

Chinese characters are not only hard to recognize but also hard to read aloud.

3. 學中文不僅僅是學聽說，還要學寫文章。

学中文不仅仅是学听说，还要学写文章。

Learning Chinese is not only a matter of learning to listen and speak, but also of learning to write.

五、頭　　first

This is used before a numeral.

1. 新年的頭一天是大年初一。

新年的头一天是大年初一。

The first day of the Lunar New Year is *da nianchuyi*.

2. 每天的頭一節課，我常常遲到。

每天的头一节课，我常常迟到。

I'm often late for the first class of the day.

3. 來美國的頭幾年，我一句英文都不會說。

   来美国的头几年，我一句英文都不会说。

   During the first few years after I came to the U.S., I couldn't speak any English at all.

六、而   but

"而" is used at the beginning of the second clause of a sentence to connect two clauses which are contrary or opposite to each other in meaning. It is chiefly used in written language.

1. 過年給孩子的不是壓歲錢，而是一種叫做"壓勝錢"的假錢。

   过年给孩子的不是压岁钱，而是一种叫做"压胜钱"的假钱。

   At New Year, what children received was not *yasuiqian*, but a kind of fake money called *yashengqian*.

2. 你不小心碰到別人的時候，不應該說"沒關係"，而應該說"對不起"。

   你不小心碰到别人的时候，不应该说"没关系"，而应该说"对不起"。

   When you bump into someone accidentally, you should say "I'm sorry" and not "That's OK".

3. 簡體字有簡體字的好處，而繁體字有繁體字的好處。

   简体字有简体字的好处，而繁体字有繁体字的好处。

   Simplified characters have their own advantages, but complex characters have theirs as well.

七、形容詞重疊   adjective reduplication

In Chinese two-syllable adjectives can be reduplicated into four-syllable words, for example "高興", "團圓", "平安" can become "高高興興", "團團圓圓", "平平安安", producing a casual and lively effect.

1. 過年就是大家高高興興舉行慶祝糧食豐收的活動。

   过年就是大家高高兴兴举行庆祝粮食丰收的活动。

   New Year festivities were activities put on by people to celebrate happily a bumper grain harvest.

2. 餃子和湯圓都表示團團圓圓的意思。

   饺子和汤圆都表示团团圆圆的意思。

   Dumplings and sweet dumplings both represent family reunions.

3. 壓歲錢是為了讓小孩子在新的一年裏平平安安。

   压岁钱是为了让小孩子在新的一年里平平安安。

   The purpose of *yasuiqian* is to wish children safe and sound in the New Year.

八、"據說"and"聽說"　　it is said

"據說" is used like "聽說" to introduce hearsay, but "據說" cannot be used after the subject in a sentence.

1. 據說過年的習俗早就有了。

   据说过年的习俗早就有了。

   It is said that the custom of celebrating New Year already existed a long time ago.

2. 人們聽說魔怪怕響聲也怕紅顏色。

   人们听说魔怪怕响声也怕红颜色。

   People heard that the monster was afraid of noise and of the color red.

3. 我聽說小張的女朋友很漂亮。

   我听说小张的女朋友很漂亮。

   I've heard Xiao Zhang's girlfriend is very beautiful.

   我據說小張的女朋友很漂亮。(×)

   我据说小张的女朋友很漂亮。(×)

練習

一、用所給的詞語填空（一個詞語可以用多次）

每當、大多數、一……就、根據、不僅……還、非……不可

每当、大多数、一……就、根据、不仅……还、非……不可

1. _____天氣預報説，明天_____要下大雨_____會颳大風。我們這個地方_____天氣不好的時候，_____的人都不去工作，如果有人_____去工作_____，他就得特別小心地開車，因為_____不小心_____會出車禍。
_____天气预报说，明天_____要下大雨_____会刮大风。我们这个地方_____天气不好的时候，_____的人都不去工作，如果有人_____去工作_____，他就得特别小心地开车，因为_____不小心_____会出车祸。

2. 今天晚上，我_____要練習語法_____要記生詞。因為_____別的班的同學説，這次考試_____的題以前都沒有做過。所以_____得認真準備_____，我這個人最怕考試，_____要考試的時候，我就睡不着覺，而且_____進教室_____頭疼。
今天晚上，我_____要练习语法_____要记生词。因为_____别的班的同学说，这次考试_____的题以前都没有做过。所以_____得认真准备_____，我这个人最怕考试，_____要考试的时候，我就睡不着觉，而且_____进教室_____头疼。

二、用所給的詞語造句

1. 不僅……還
   不仅……还
   _____。

2. 根據
   根据
   _____。

3. 每當
   每当
   _____。

4. 而
   而
   _____。

5. 據說
   据说
   _____。

三、根據課文來完成句子

1. 過年小孩子高興的原因是
   过年小孩子高兴的原因是
   _____。

2. 爺爺奶奶把假錢換成真錢的原因是
   爷爷奶奶把假钱换成真钱的原因是
   _____。

3. 過年放鞭炮和貼春聯的原因是
   过年放鞭炮和贴春联的原因是
   _____。

4. 除夕年飯不可以把魚吃完的原因是
   除夕年饭不可以把鱼吃完的原因是
   _____。

5. 大年初一吃餃子和湯圓的原因是
   大年初一吃饺子和汤圆的原因是
   _____。

6. 過年吃年糕的原因是
   过年吃年糕的原因是
   _____。

四、翻譯

1. It is said that the *nian* is not only afraid of noise, but also of the color red. Therefore, when New Year comes, people not only paste Spring Festival couplets on either side of their doors, they also let off firecrackers in their yards.

11. 中國年和壓歲錢　　　　　　　　　　　　　　　　　　　　　　　197

_____
_____
_____ 。

2. During the first day or two of the New Year, people happily eat dumplings and sweet dumplings. Eating dumplings and sweet dumplings represents the reunion of each family.

_____
_____
_____ 。

3. According to research done by historians, there was no real *yasuiqian* a long time ago. At New Year, grandparents would give children a kind of fake money that could not be used to buy things, but could ward off evil and keep the children safe.

_____
_____
_____ 。

五、根據課文回答問題

1. "年"的意思是甚麼？
   "年"的意思是什么？

   _____
   _____ 。

2. 為甚麼過年的時候大家要貼春聯，放鞭炮？
   为什么过年的时候大家要贴春联，放鞭炮？

   _____
   _____ 。

3. 為甚麼不可以把魚全部吃完？
   为什么不可以把鱼全部吃完？
   _____
   _____。

4. 甚麼是"壓歲錢"？
   什么是"压岁钱"？
   _____
   _____。

5. 為甚麼要把"壓勝錢"掛在孩子的身上？
   为什么要把"压胜钱"挂在孩子的身上？
   _____
   _____。

六、課堂討論

人們為甚麼要過年？
人们为什么要过年？
_____
_____
_____。

七、小作文

寫一下你過新年的活動。
写一下你过新年的活动。
_____
_____
_____
_____
_____。

閱讀

龍和獅子

中國人過年的時候不僅喜歡舞龍，而且也喜歡舞獅子。

龍不是真的動物，它是一種傳說中的動物。在中國歷史上，龍是權威的象徵。畫着龍的衣服只有皇帝才可以穿，皇帝睡覺的床叫做龍床。那時候人們都認為皇帝就是天上的龍。今天，龍成為中華民族的象徵，每一個中國人都說自己是龍的傳人。

過去，人們以為龍掌管着下雨和颱風，所以每當天旱，莊稼快要乾死的時候，人們就去求龍快一點兒下雨；而當大雨成災，莊稼快要淹死的時候，又去求龍不要再下雨了。等到糧食豐收了，大家都說這是龍王的功勞。

龍是人們的救星卻又給人們帶來災難，大家既喜歡牠又怕牠。為了感謝龍讓人們平平安安地過了一年，同時又求牠下一年也不要給人們帶來災難，所以到過年的時候大家都要來祭拜龍。

可是，人們都不知道龍到底長得是甚麼樣子，幾千年來沒有人見過真的龍，於是大家就根據閃電的形狀，用黃綢布做成一條由蛇的身子、馬的頭、雞的爪子、魚的鱗組成的龍。過年時把這條又大、又長、又兇惡的龍抬出來讓大家祭拜。這種抬着龍到處讓人們來祭拜的活動，慢慢地就變成了過年時的一種娛樂了。

獅子據說是漢代才從國外運進來的。動物中最厲害的是獅子，許多有錢的人都希望獅子能夠保護自己，可是獅子不能像貓、狗那樣的養在家裏，因此他們就做了一些銅獅子、石獅子擺在自家的大門口。

後來一些練功夫的人為了炫耀自己的本領跟獅子一樣厲害，就用大紅綢布製作成一頭兇惡的大獅子。他們把獅子抬出來像舞龍那樣地舞來舞去。漸漸地舞獅子也成了人們過年時的娛樂了。

阅 读

龙和狮子

中国人过年的时候不仅喜欢舞龙,而且也喜欢舞狮子。

龙不是真的动物,它是一种传说中的动物。在中国历史上,龙是权威的象征。画着龙的衣服只有皇帝才可以穿,皇帝睡觉的床叫做龙床。那时候人们都认为皇帝就是天上的龙。今天,龙成为中华民族的象征,每一个中国人都说自己是龙的传人。

过去,人们以为龙掌管着下雨和刮风,所以每当天旱,庄稼快要干死的时候,人们就去求龙快一点儿下雨;而当大雨成灾,庄稼快要淹死的时候,又去求龙不要再下雨了。等到粮食丰收了,大家都说这是龙王的功劳。

龙是人们的救星却又给人们带来灾难,大家既喜欢它又怕它。为了感谢龙让人们平平安安地过了一年,同时又求它下一年也不要给人们带来灾难,所以到过年的时候大家都要来祭拜龙。

可是,人们都不知道龙到底长得是什么样子,几千年来没有人见过真的龙,于是大家就根据闪电的形状,用黄绸布做成一条由蛇的身子、马的头、鸡的爪子、鱼的鳞组成的龙。过年时把这条又大、又长、又凶恶的龙抬出来让大家祭拜。这种抬着龙到处让人们来祭拜的活动,慢慢地就变成了过年时的一种娱乐了。

狮子据说是汉代才从国外运进来的。动物中最厉害的是狮子,许多有钱的人都希望狮子能够保护自己,可是狮子不能像猫、狗那样的养在家里,因此他们就做了一些铜狮子、石狮子摆在自家的大门口。

后来一些练功夫的人为了炫耀自己的本领跟狮子一样厉害,就用大红绸布制作成一头凶恶的大狮子。他们把狮子抬出来像舞龙那样地舞来舞去。渐渐地舞狮子也成了人们过年时的娱乐了。

生詞

獅子	狮子	shīzi	n.	lion
權威	权威	quánwēi	n.	authority
象徵	象征	xiàngzhēng	n.	symbol
龍的傳人	龙的传人	lóng de chuánrén		dragon's descendants
莊稼	庄稼	zhuāngjia	n.	crops
掌管	掌管	zhǎngguǎn	v.	control; take charge of
天旱	天旱	tiān hàn		drought
乾死	干死	gānsǐ		dying of drought
淹死	淹死	yānsǐ		drown
功勞	功劳	gōngláo	n.	contribution; credit
救星	救星	jiùxīng	n.	liberator; emancipator
災難	灾难	zāinàn	n.	calamity
牠	它	tā	pn.	it (used when the antecedent is an animal)
祭拜	祭拜	jìbài	v.	sacrifice to; worship
閃電	闪电	shǎndiàn	n.	lightning
綢布	绸布	chóubù	n.	silk
蛇	蛇	shé	n.	snake
馬	马	mǎ	n.	horse
雞	鸡	jī	n.	chicken
爪	爪	zhuǎ	n.	claw
魚鱗	鱼鳞	yúlín	n.	scale
兇惡	凶恶	xiōng'è	adj.	ferocious
抬	抬	tái	v.	lift up; (of two or more persons) carry
娛樂	娱乐	yúlè	n.	amusement; entertainment

舞龍	舞龙	wǔ lóng		dragon dance (a team of men dancing with a cloth dragon at Chinese festivals)
保護	保护	bǎohù	v.	safeguard; protect
銅	铜	tóng	n.	bronze
擺	摆	bǎi	v.	put
練	练	liàn	v.	practice
武功	武功	wǔgōng	n.	martial arts
炫耀	炫耀	xuànyào	v.	show off
本領	本领	běnlǐng	n.	skill; ability
舞獅子	舞狮子	wǔ shīzi		lion dance (a two-man team dancing inside a cloth lion at Chinese festivals)
漸漸地	渐渐地	jiàn jiàn de	adv.	gradually

問題

1. 以前龍象徵着甚麼？
   以前龙象征着什么？

   _____
   _____。

2. 人們為甚麼去求龍？
   人们为什么去求龙？

   _____
   _____。

3. 為甚麼大家既喜歡龍又怕龍？
   为什么大家既喜欢龙又怕龙？

   _____
   _____。

4. 人們做出來的龍是甚麼樣的？
   人们做出来的龙是什么样的？

   _____

   _____ 。

5. 舞龍是怎麼形成的？
   舞龙是怎么形成的？

   _____

   _____ 。

6. 為甚麼許多人家的門口要擺一些銅獅子、石獅子？
   为什么许多人家的门口要摆一些铜狮子、石狮子？

   _____

   _____ 。

7. 為甚麼要舞獅子？
   为什么要舞狮子？

   _____

   _____ 。

12

中國的情人節
Chinese Valentine's Day

學習大綱

通過學習本課，學生應該能夠：

1. 掌握這些句型和詞語的意思和用法："V於"、"V不起，V得起"、"趁"、"眼看"、"往"、"這麼"、"相V"、"差不多"和"幾乎"。
2. 認識和運用課文以及閱讀文章內的生詞。
3. 知道中國情人節的來歷。
4. 初步了解中國人對婚姻的看法。

Study Outline

After studying this chapter, students should:

1. Have a good command of the meaning and usage of these sentence patterns and terms: "V yú" (from; in), "V bùqǐ, V déqǐ" (cannot V; can V), "chèn" (while), "yǎnkàn" (soon; in a moment), "wàng" (toward), "zhème" (such; so), "xiāng V" (V each other), "chàbuduō" and "jīhū" (almost).
2. Be familiar with the meaning and usage of the vocabulary introduced in the text and the reading.
3. Know about the origin of the Chinese Valentine's Day.
4. Have some idea of what the Chinese view of marriage is.

課文

中國的情人節是農曆的七月七號，它來源於一個美麗動人的傳說。

以前，有一個男孩子叫牛郎。牛郎很窮，連媳婦都娶不起。他每天放牛回來以後還得自己做飯、洗衣服。天上的七仙女看到牛郎很可憐，要去幫助牛郎。一天，她趁媽媽不注意偷偷地來到了牛郎家。七仙女織布織得很好，大家都叫她織女。牛郎和織女一個織布、一個放牛，他們兩個人生活得很幸福。不久，他們還生了一兒一女。

沒過幾年，織女的事情被她媽媽王母娘娘發現了。王母娘娘非常生氣，她不願意讓自己的女兒嫁給一個窮人，就把織女抓回去了。

牛郎看到織女被抓走了，趕緊領着兩個孩子拼命地追上天去。眼看就要追上了，王母娘娘拔下頭上的簪子往身後一劃，在織女和牛郎的中間劃出了一條很寬很寬的銀河。寬寬的銀河把牛郎和織女分開了。

多少年過去了，織女一直守在河那邊盼着牛郎，牛郎帶着孩子也在河這邊苦苦地等着織女。王母娘娘看到織女這麼癡心地愛着牛郎，只好讓他們在七月七號晚上見一次面。

七月七號這天晚上好心的喜鵲都飛到銀河上，牠們用自己的身體搭成一座橋，牛郎帶着孩子和織女就在鵲橋上相會。

那天夜裏差不多每個女孩子都不睡覺，她們躲在葡萄架下偷聽織女牛郎的悄悄話。要是這天恰巧下雨了，她們說這是織女傷心的眼淚。

雖然這是一個傳說，可是幾乎所有的人都願意相信它是真的。在銀河的兩岸真的有兩顆閃亮的大星星。西邊的那顆是織女，東邊的這顆是牛郎，緊挨在牛郎邊上的兩顆小星星，就是他們那一對可愛的小兒女！

七月七號是牛郎織女相聚的日子，世上相愛的人也喜歡在這一天相聚，漸漸地這一天就成了中國的情人節。

课文

中国的情人节是农历的七月七号,它来源于一个美丽动人的传说。

以前,有一个男孩子叫牛郎。牛郎很穷,连媳妇都娶不起。他每天放牛回来以后还得自己做饭、洗衣服。天上的七仙女看到牛郎很可怜,要去帮助牛郎。一天,她趁妈妈不注意偷偷地来到了牛郎家。七仙女织布织得很好,大家都叫她织女。牛郎和织女一个织布、一个放牛,他们两个人生活得很幸福。不久,他们还生了一儿一女。

没过几年,织女的事情被她妈妈王母娘娘发现了。王母娘娘非常生气,她不愿意让自己的女儿嫁给一个穷人,就把织女抓回去了。

牛郎看到织女被抓走了,赶紧领着两个孩子拼命地追上天去。眼看就要追上了,王母娘娘拔下头上的簪子往身后一划,在织女和牛郎的中间划出了一条很宽很宽的银河。宽宽的银河把牛郎和织女分开了。

多少年过去了,织女一直守在河那边盼着牛郎,牛郎带着孩子也在河这边苦苦地等着织女。王母娘娘看到织女这么痴心地爱着牛郎,只好让他们在七月七号晚上见一次面。

七月七号这天晚上好心的喜鹊都飞到银河上,它们用自己的身体搭成一座桥,牛郎带着孩子和织女就在鹊桥上相会。

那天夜里差不多每个女孩子都不睡觉,她们躲在葡萄架下偷听织女牛郎的悄悄话。要是这天恰巧下雨了,她们说这是织女伤心的眼泪。

虽然这是一个传说,可是几乎所有的人都愿意相信它是真的。在银河的两岸真的有两颗闪亮的大星星。西边的那颗是织女,东边的这颗是牛郎,紧挨在牛郎边上的两颗小星星,就是他们那一对可爱的小儿女!

七月七号是牛郎织女相聚的日子,世上相爱的人也喜欢在这一天相聚,渐渐地这一天就成了中国的情人节。

生詞

繁體	簡體	拼音	詞性	英文
情人節	情人节	qíngrén jié	n.	Valentine's Day
於	于	yú	prep.	from; in
美麗動人	美丽动人	měilì-dòngrén		lovely and affecting
牛郎	牛郎	Niúláng	n.	Herd-boy
窮	穷	qióng	adj.	poor
娶不起	娶不起	qǔbùqǐ		cannot afford to marry
七仙女	七仙女	Qīxiānnǚ		the 7th Fairy
可憐	可怜	kělián	adj.	pitiful
趁	趁	chèn	prep.	while
偷偷地	偷偷地	tōutōu de	adv.	by stealth; secretly
織布	织布	zhī bù		weave
生活	生活	shēnghuó	v.	live
王母娘娘	王母娘娘	Wángmǔ niángniang		Queen of Heaven
趕緊	赶紧	gǎn jǐn	adv.	hastily; in a hurry
拼命地	拼命地	pīnmìng de	adv.	exerting the utmost strength
領着	领着	lǐngzhe	v.	bring(ing)
追	追	zhuī	v.	chase
眼看	眼看	yǎnkàn	adv.	soon; in a moment
拔	拔	bá	v.	pull out/up
簪子	簪子	zānzi	n.	hair clasp
往	往	wǎng	prep.	toward
劃	划	huá	v.	draw; scratch
寬	宽	kuān	adj.	wide
銀河	银河	Yínhé		the Milky Way

守	守	shǒu	v.	keep watch
盼着	盼着	pànzhe	v.	look forward to
苦苦地	苦苦地	kǔkǔ de	adj.	bitterly
這麼	这么	zhème	pn.	such; so
癡心地	痴心地	chīxīn de	adv.	infatuatedly
搭成	搭成	dāchéng		put up (temporary structure)
橋	桥	qiáo	n.	bridge
相會	相会	xiānghuì	v.	meet each other (for lovers)
躲	躲	duǒ	v.	hide, dodge
葡萄架	葡萄架	pútáo jià	n.	grape arbor
偷聽	偷听	tōutīng		eavesdrop (偷看 = secretly look at)
悄悄話	悄悄话	qiāoqiāohuà	n.	whispered sweet talk
幾乎	几乎	jīhū	adv.	almost
閃亮	闪亮	shǎnliàng	adj.	sparkling; shining
緊挨	紧挨	jǐn'āi		be next to
一對	一对	yī duì		pair
相聚	相聚	xiāng jù	v.	get together
相愛	相爱	xiāng'ài	v.	love each other

語法和詞語註釋

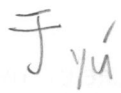

一、V 於 (yú)   from; in

"於" is used after a verb to indicate the place where the action happens or stems from. It occurs more frequently in written language.

1. 中國的情人節來源於一個美麗動人的傳說。
   中国的情人节来源于一个美丽动人的传说。
   Chinese Valentine's Day originates from a beautiful and moving legend.

2. 我畢業於北京大學。
   我毕业于北京大学。
   I graduated from Beijing University.

3. 他一九八二年生於北京。
   他一九八二年生于北京。
   He was born in Beijing in 1982.

二、V 不起，V 得起　　cannot V, can V

"不起" is used after a verb to mean "cannot afford to do something", while "V 得起" means "can afford to do something".

1. 牛郎很窮，連媳婦都娶不起。
   牛郎很穷，连媳妇都娶不起。
   The Herd-boy was so poor that he couldn't afford to get married.

2. 這個遊戲機太貴了，我買不起。
   这个游戏机太贵了，我买不起。
   This games console is so expensive that I can't afford it.

3. 大學的學費這麼高，我爸爸說他付不起。
   大学的学费这么高，我爸爸说他付不起。
   The college tuition is so expensive that my father said he couldn't afford to pay it.

三、趁　　while

趁 chen

"趁" is used in the first clause to mean "using the condition or taking the opportunity".

1. 織女趁着她媽媽不注意，偷偷地來到了牛郎家。
   织女趁着她妈妈不注意，偷偷地来到了牛郎家。
   The Fairy Maiden secretly came to the Herd-boy's home while her mom was inattentive.

2. 趁着放假的時候，我去了北京和上海。

趁着放假的时候，我去了北京和上海。

I went to Beijing and Shanghai while I was on vacation.

3. 趁老師還沒有來，我趕快又複習了一下。

趁老师还没有来，我赶快又复习了一下。

While the teacher was not here, I quickly did another review.

四、眼看　　soon; in a moment

眼看 yǎnkàn

1. 眼看牛郎就要追上了。

眼看牛郎就要追上了。

It seemed the Herd-boy would soon catch up with them.

2. 眼看就要畢業了。

眼看就要毕业了。

We are going to graduate very soon.

3. 眼看就要大考了，我還一點兒都沒有準備。

眼看就要大考了，我还一点儿都没有准备。

I've got my final (exam) very soon, but I've done hardly any preparation.

五、往　　toward

"往" indicates the direction in which an action is carried out.

1. 王母娘娘拔下頭上的簪子往身後一劃，在織女和牛郎的中間劃出一條大河。

王母娘娘拔下头上的簪子往身后一划，在织女和牛郎的中间划出一条大河。

The Queen of Heaven pulled out her hair clasp and drew a line behind her. A big river appeared between the Fairy Maiden and the Herd-boy.

2. 他把車往後一倒，碰到了我的車。

他把车往后一倒，碰到了我的车。

When he was backing his car, his car bumped into mine.

3. 往前看，前面就是你的宿舍。

往前看，前面就是你的宿舍。

If you look ahead, your dormitory is in front of you.

六、這麼　　such; so

> "這麼" modifies a verb or adjective to express a particular state, degree, or quality.

1. 王母娘娘看到織女這麼癡心地愛着牛郎，就只好讓他們見一面。
   王母娘娘看到织女这么痴心地爱着牛郎，就只好让他们见一面。
   When the Queen of Heaven saw the Fairy Maiden was deeply in love with the Herd-boy, she had to let them see each other once.

2. 我沒有想到中文這麼容易。
   我没有想到中文这么容易。
   I did not expect Chinese to be this easy.

3. 湯姆的女朋友這麼漂亮！
   汤姆的女朋友这么漂亮！
   Tom's girlfriend is so beautiful!

> "那麼" is used the same way as "這麼" in situations such as the following.

4. 我沒有想到中文那麼容易。
   我没有想到中文那么容易。
   I did not expect Chinese to be that easy.

> If "這麼" and "那麼" appear at the same time, "這麼" refers to something close to the speaker, while "那麼" refers to something further away.

5. 我們家沒有你們家這麼大，但是你們家沒有我們家那麼乾淨。
   我们家没有你们家这么大，但是你们家没有我们家那么干净。
   Our house is not as big as yours, but your house is not as clean as ours.

6. 湯姆的女朋友沒有你長得這麼漂亮，但是你沒有湯姆女朋友那麼聰明！
   汤姆的女朋友没有你长得这么漂亮，但是你没有汤姆女朋友那么聪明！
   Tom's girlfriend is not as beautiful as you are, but you are not as smart as she is!

七、相 V　　V each other

1. 牛郎帶着孩子和織女就在鵲橋上相會。

   牛郎带着孩子和织女就在鹊桥上相会。

   The Herd-boy brought the children and met the Fairy Maiden on the bridge put up by the magpies.

2. 相愛的人都喜歡在七月七號這一天相聚。

   相爱的人都喜欢在七月七号这一天相聚。

   All lovers like to get together on the seventh day of the seventh lunar month.

3. 我們相愛很久了。

   我们相爱很久了。

   We have been in love with each other for a long time.

八、"差不多"and"幾乎"　　almost

> "差不多"and "幾乎" can be used in similar ways, both of them meaning "almost" or "nearly", but "差不多" can also be used as an adjective to answer a question independently and can occur at the end of a sentence.

1. 那天夜裏差不多(幾乎)每一個女孩子都不睡覺。

   那天夜里差不多(几乎)每一个女孩子都不睡觉。

   On that night almost no girls will go to sleep.

2. 老師講的我差不多(幾乎)都懂了。

   老师讲的我差不多(几乎)都懂了。

   I have understood almost everything that the teacher taught us.

3. 我們倆的中文水平差不多。

   我们俩的中文水平差不多。

   Our standard of Chinese is roughly the same.

   我們倆的中文水平幾乎。(×)

   我们俩的中文水平几乎。(×)

練 習

一、根據課文來完成句子

1. 織女來到牛郎家，是因為
   织女来到牛郎家，是因为
   _____。

2. 王母娘娘把織女抓回去，是因為
   王母娘娘把织女抓回去，是因为
   _____。

3. 織女一直守在河邊盼着牛郎，是因為
   织女一直守在河边盼着牛郎，是因为
   _____。

4. 那天夜裏女孩子不睡覺，是因為
   那天夜里女孩子不睡觉，是因为
   _____。

5. 人們都願意相信這個傳說是真的，是因為
   人们都愿意相信这个传说是真的，是因为
   _____。

6. 七月七號是情人節，是因為
   七月七号是情人节，是因为
   _____。

二、找出和例句意思相同的句子

1. 牛郎眼看就要追上織女了。
   牛郎眼看就要追上织女了。

   a. 牛郎看見織女要追上來了。
      牛郎看见织女要追上来了。
   b. 牛郎馬上就要追上織女了。

牛郎马上就要追上织女了。
c. 牛郎馬上看見織女追來了。
牛郎马上看见织女追来了。

2. 織女非要跟牛郎結婚不可。
织女非要跟牛郎结婚不可。

   a. 織女非常不願意和牛郎結婚。
   织女非常不愿意和牛郎结婚。
   b. 織女不一定願意和牛郎結婚。
   织女不一定愿意和牛郎结婚。
   c. 織女除了牛郎不和別人結婚。
   织女除了牛郎不和别人结婚。

3. 牛郎太窮了連媳婦都娶不起。
牛郎太穷了连媳妇都娶不起。

   a. 牛郎太窮了連媳婦都不願意娶。
   牛郎太穷了连媳妇都不愿意娶。
   b. 牛郎太窮了沒有辦法去娶媳婦。
   牛郎太穷了没有办法去娶媳妇。
   c. 牛郎太窮了要找個有錢的媳婦。
   牛郎太穷了要找个有钱的媳妇。

4. 在中國幾乎沒有人不知道牛郎織女的故事。
在中国几乎没有人不知道牛郎织女的故事。

   a. 在中國差不多每個人都知道牛郎織女的故事。
   在中国差不多每个人都知道牛郎织女的故事。
   b. 在中國差不多沒有人知道牛郎和織女的故事。
   在中国差不多没有人知道牛郎和织女的故事。
   c. 在中國幾乎每個人都不知道牛郎織女的故事。
   在中国几乎每个人都不知道牛郎织女的故事。

5. 王母娘娘看到織女這麼癡心地愛着牛郎。
王母娘娘看到织女这么痴心地爱着牛郎。

a. 王母娘娘看到織女癡心地愛着這個牛郎。
　　王母娘娘看到织女痴心地爱着这个牛郎。
b. 王母娘娘看到織女非常癡心地愛着牛郎。
　　王母娘娘看到织女非常痴心地爱着牛郎。
c. 王母娘娘看到這個織女癡心地愛着牛郎。
　　王母娘娘看到这个织女痴心地爱着牛郎。

三、翻譯

1. The Fairy Maiden's mom caught the Fairy Maiden and brought her back by stealth while the Herd-boy was not at home. At the moment when the Herd-boy seemed about to catch up with the Fairy Maiden, her mom pulled out her hair clasp and drew a line behind her. A very wide river appeared.

2. I don't know what kind of a story the western Valentine's Day originates from, but I do know Chinese Valentine's Day originates from a beautiful and moving legend.

3. The Herd-boy used to be very poor. He couldn't afford to buy clothes, he couldn't afford to buy meat and he couldn't even afford to get married. After the Fairy Maiden came to his home, they ate meat and wore new clothes almost everyday.

四、根據課文回答問題

1. 織女為甚麼要去幫助牛郎?
   织女为什么要去帮助牛郎?
   _____
   _____。

2. 王母娘娘為甚麼要把織女帶回去?
   王母娘娘为什么要把织女带回去?
   _____
   _____。

3. 許多年輕的女孩子七月七號那天晚上做甚麼?
   许多年轻的女孩子七月七号那天晚上做什么?
   _____
   _____。

4. 在銀河的兩岸可以看到甚麼?
   在银河的两岸可以看到什么?
   _____
   _____。

5. 為甚麼人們都願意相信這個傳說是真的?
   为什么人们都愿意相信这个传说是真的?
   _____
   _____。

五、課堂討論

1. 愛情和金錢哪一個重要?
   爱情和金钱哪一个重要?
   _____
   _____
   _____。

2. 你父母不喜歡你的女朋友/男朋友，你怎麼辦？
   你父母不喜欢你的女朋友/男朋友，你怎么办？
   _____
   _____
   _____。

六、小作文

1. 最幸福的婚姻。
   最幸福的婚姻。
   _____
   _____
   _____
   _____
   _____
   _____。

2. 金錢和婚姻。
   金钱和婚姻。
   _____
   _____
   _____
   _____
   _____
   _____。

閱讀

結髮夫妻白頭到老

根據國家的統計，現在中國離婚的人越來越多了。為甚麼這麼多人離婚呢？這些人當初結婚的時候，想沒想過將來要離婚的事？

一般來說，要結婚的人一定不會去想要離婚的事情；要結婚的人想的只是你愛我、我愛你，兩人永遠相愛，海枯石爛都不變心。

以前人們結婚的時候，男女雙方要各自剪下一綹頭髮，把它們結紮在一起保存起來。意思是兩個人要永遠生活在一起，永遠不分離。那時人們把頭髮結紮在一起的夫妻叫做"結髮夫妻"。

也有人說結髮夫妻是指第一次結婚的夫妻。古時候小孩子的頭髮都是隨便披在頭上的。當男孩子長到二十歲、女孩子長到十五歲的時候，他們就得把頭髮用帶子紮起來，這叫做"結髮"。

結髮表示一個人已經成年了，那時候規定只有結了髮的人才可以結婚。人們把剛一結髮就結婚的人叫做結髮夫妻。因為結髮夫妻都是第一次結婚，所以大家說結髮夫妻就是指第一次結婚的夫妻。

過去每當有人要結婚的時候，親戚朋友們總是要送給新郎新娘一對繡着鴛鴦的枕頭，或者是畫着兩隻鴛鴦的畫兒。

中國人認為鴛鴦是代表愛情的鳥，鴛鴦幾乎都是雌雄成雙成對地在一起，永遠不分離。大家給新婚夫婦送鴛鴦畫兒的意思，就是祝願他們能像鴛鴦那樣相親相愛、白頭到老。

"白頭到老"就是說兩個人結婚了以後永遠在一起，即使是彼此的頭髮都白了也不分離。人們都說這是世界上最好的婚姻。

多少年過去了，人們的傳統觀念早都改變了。雖然現在還有人給新婚夫婦送畫有鴛鴦的畫兒，也還有人說結髮夫妻要白頭到老，但是離婚的人卻是越來越多了。

阅读

结发夫妻白头到老

根据国家的统计，现在中国离婚的人越来越多了。为什么这么多人离婚呢？这些人当初结婚的时候，想没想过将来要离婚的事？

一般来说，要结婚的人一定不会去想要离婚的事情；要结婚的人想的只是你爱我、我爱你，两人永远相爱，海枯石烂都不变心。

以前人们结婚的时候，男女双方要各自剪下一绺头发，把它们结扎在一起保存起来。意思是两个人要永远生活在一起，永远不分离。那时人们把头发结扎在一起的夫妻叫做"结发夫妻"。

也有人说结发夫妻是指第一次结婚的夫妻。古时候小孩子的头发都是随便披在头上的。当男孩子长到二十岁、女孩子长到十五岁的时候，他们就得把头发用带子扎起来，这叫做"结发"。

结发表示一个人已经成年了，那时候规定只有结了发的人才可以结婚。人们把刚一结发就结婚的人叫做结发夫妻。因为结发夫妻都是第一次结婚，所以大家说结发夫妻就是指第一次结婚的夫妻。

过去每当有人要结婚的时候，亲戚朋友们总是要送给新郎新娘一对绣着鸳鸯的枕头，或者是画着两只鸳鸯的画儿。

中国人认为鸳鸯是代表爱情的鸟，鸳鸯几乎都是雌雄成双成对地在一起，永远不分离。大家给新婚夫妇送鸳鸯画儿的意思，就是祝愿他们能像鸳鸯那样相亲相爱、白头到老。

"白头到老"就是说两个人结婚了以后永远在一起，即使是彼此的头发都白了也不分离。人们都说这是世界上最好的婚姻。

多少年过去了，人们的传统观念早都改变了。虽然现在还有人给新婚夫妇送画有鸳鸯的画儿，也还有人说结发夫妻要白头到老，但是离婚的人却是越来越多了。

生 詞

結髮	结发	jié fà		weave hair
白頭到老	白头到老	báitóudàolǎo		live to old age in conjugal bliss
統計	统计	tǒngjì	n.	statistics
離婚	离婚	lí hūn		divorce
當初	当初	dāngchū	n.	originally; at the beginning
永遠	永远	yǒngyuǎn	adj.	forever
海枯石爛不變心	海枯石烂不变心	hǎikū shílàn bù biàn xīn		The sea may run dry and the rocks may crumble, but our hearts will always remain loyal
各自	各自	gèzì	pn.	each; by oneself; respective
剪	剪	jiǎn	v.	cut (hair etc.) with scissors
綹	绺	liǔ	m.	lock; tuft; skein
結紮	结扎	jiézā	v.	tie together
保存	保存	bǎocún	v.	preserve; conserve
披散	披散	pīsan		(of hair) hang down loosely
帶子	带子	dàizi	n.	band; belt
紮	扎	zā	v.	bind
成年	成年	chéngnián	v.	grow up; be of age
剛	刚	gāng	adv.	just
親戚	亲戚	qīnqī	n.	relative
總是	总是	zǒngshì	adv.	always
繡	绣	xiù	v.	embroider
鴛鴦	鸳鸯	yuānyāng	n.	mandarin duck
代表	代表	dàibiǎo	v.	represent
雄	雄	xióng	n.	male

雌	雌	cí	n.	female
成雙成對	成双成对	chéngshuāng-chéngduì		in pairs
祝願	祝愿	zhùyuàn	v.	wish (someone something)
相親相愛	相亲相爱	xiāngqīn-xiāng'ài		love each other
彼此	彼此	bǐcǐ	pn.	each other

問題

1. 一般來說,要結婚的人他們想甚麼?
   一般来说,要结婚的人他们想什么?

   _____
   _____ 。

2. 為甚麼有人說結髮夫妻是指第一次結婚的夫妻?
   为什么有人说结发夫妻是指第一次结婚的夫妻?

   _____
   _____ 。

3. 從前有人要結婚時,親戚朋友為甚麼要送畫有鴛鴦的畫兒?
   从前有人要结婚时,亲戚朋友为什么要送画有鸳鸯的画儿?

   _____
   _____ 。

4. 甚麼是白頭到老?
   什么是白头到老?

   _____
   _____ 。

5. 為甚麼中國人認為白頭到老的婚姻是世界上最好的婚姻?
   为什么中国人认为白头到老的婚姻是世界上最好的婚姻?

   _____

_____。

6. 現在人們的傳統觀念是不是都改變了？
   现在人们的传统观念是不是都改变了？

   _____
   _____。

13

婦女能頂半邊天
"Women Can Hold Up Half the Sky"

學習大綱

通過學習本課，學生應該能夠：

1. 掌握這些句型和詞語的意思和用法："凡是"、"看"、"再……也"、"反正"、"由於……緣故"、"從來"和"一直"、"反而"。
2. 認識和運用課文以及閱讀文章內的生詞。
3. 簡單地了解中國的"男女平等"問題。
4. 了解過去中國女人纏小腳、男人留辮子的歷史。

Study Outline

After studying this chapter, students should:

1. Have a good command of the meaning and usage of these sentence patterns and terms: "fánshì" (every; all; any), "kàn" (look after; take care of), "zài ... yě" (even if; even though), "fǎnzhèng" (anyway; anyhow), "yóuyú ... yuángù" (due to; as a result of), "cónglái" and "yīzhí" (always), "fǎn'ér" (on the contrary; instead).
2. Be familiar with the meaning and usage of the vocabulary introduced in the text and the reading.
3. Have some understanding of the issue of the "equality of the sexes" in China.
4. Know about the history of women's foot-binding and men's wearing of pigtails in China.

課文

近幾十年來，中國有一句很流行的話，叫做"婦女能頂半邊天"。這句話的意思是說：女人和男人是平等的。女人跟男人一樣能幹，凡是男人能做的事情，女人都可以做。

在很早以前，中國的男女是不平等的。當時不管是城市還是鄉下，上學讀書、出外做工、當兵打仗的全都是男人，女人只能在家裏做飯、做衣服、看孩子。那個時候女人做飯做得再香，做衣服做得再漂亮也不能去外面做。所以，街上飯店裏的廚師和服裝店裏的裁縫全都是男人。

晉朝的時候，有一個女孩子叫祝英台。她非常想讀書學習，可是那時的學校不收女孩子，於是她就穿上男孩子的衣服，裝扮成一個男孩子的樣子，去學校讀了三年書。

南北朝時，有一個叫花木蘭的女孩子，她的爸爸已經老了，而弟弟年紀還小，她也是女扮男裝才出去替父親當兵打仗的。

雖然中國從來都是重男輕女的，但是在一千多年前的唐代，也出現過像武則天那樣的女皇帝，清代的慈禧實際上也是皇帝。不管後來的人們說她們好還是壞，反正女人當了皇帝。在那個時候，大家又都覺得應該是重女輕男了。

由於重男輕女的緣故，中國的家庭一直都是男主外，女主內。也就是說男人管外面的大事，女人只管家裏做飯、洗衣服、照顧孩子這些小事。現在男女平等了，很多女人跟男人一樣到外面去工作。然而千百年來，中國人都已經習慣女主內了，所以女人下班回家以後，再累也還得去做飯、洗衣服、照顧孩子。

本來是為了改變重男輕女的舊觀念、提高婦女的地位，大家才說"婦女能頂半邊天"的，結果現在男女平等了反而加重了婦女的負擔，現在的婦女實際上頂的是"大半個天"。

课文

　　近几十年来,中国有一句很流行的话,叫做"妇女能顶半边天"。这句话的意思是说:女人和男人是平等的。女人跟男人一样能干,凡是男人能做的事情,女人都可以做。

　　在很早以前,中国的男女是不平等的。当时不管是城市还是乡下,上学读书、出外做工、当兵打仗的全都是男人,女人只能在家里做饭、做衣服、看孩子。那个时候女人做饭做得再香,做衣服做得再漂亮也不能去外面做。所以,街上饭店里的厨师和服装店里的裁缝全都是男人。

　　晋朝的时候,有一个女孩子叫祝英台。她非常想读书学习,可是那时的学校不收女孩子,于是她就穿上男孩子的衣服,装扮成一个男孩子的样子,去学校读了三年书。

　　南北朝时,有一个叫花木兰的女孩子,她的爸爸已经老了,而弟弟年纪还小,她也是女扮男装才出去替父亲当兵打仗的。

　　虽然中国从来都是重男轻女的,但是在一千多年前的唐代,也出现过像武则天那样的女皇帝,清代的慈禧实际上也是皇帝。不管后来的人们说她们好还是坏,反正女人当了皇帝。在那个时候,大家又都觉得应该是重女轻男了。

　　由于重男轻女的缘故,中国的家庭一直都是男主外,女主内。也就是说男人管外面的大事,女人只管家里做饭、洗衣服、照顾孩子这些小事。现在男女平等了,很多女人跟男人一样到外面去工作。然而千百年来,中国人都已经习惯女主内了,所以女人下班回家以后,再累也还得去做饭、洗衣服、照顾孩子。

　　本来是为了改变重男轻女的旧观念、提高妇女的地位,大家才说"妇女能顶半边天"的,结果现在男女平等了反而加重了妇女的负担,现在的妇女实际上顶的是"大半个天"。

生 詞

	婦女	妇女	fùnǚ	n.	woman
	頂	顶	dǐng	v.	support from below; hold up
	半邊天	半边天	bànbiāntiān	n.	half of the sky
	流行	流行	liúxíng	adj.	prevalent; popular
	平等	平等	píngděng	adj.	equal
	凡是	凡是	fánshì	adv.	every; all; any
	城市	城市	chéngshì	n.	city
	鄉下	乡下	xiāngxià	n.	countryside
	看	看	kān	v.	look after; take care of
	再……也	再……也	zài ... yě		even if; even though
	廚師	厨师	chúshī	n.	cook; chef
	裁縫	裁缝	cáifeng	n.	tailor; dressmaker
	晉朝	晋朝	Jìn cháo		the Jin dynasty (265–420)
	祝英台	祝英台	Zhù Yīngtái		name of a person
	裝扮	装扮	zhuāngbàn	v.	disguise; masquerade
	南北朝	南北朝	Nánběicháo		the Northern and Southern Dynasties (420–581)
	花木蘭	花木兰	Huā Mùlán		name of a person
	女扮男裝	女扮男装	nǚbànnánzhuāng		a woman disguised as a man
	替	替	tì	v.	take the place of
	重男輕女	重男轻女	zhòngnán-qīngnǚ		favor the male and regard the female as less important
	出現	出现	chūxiàn	v.	appear; emerge
	武則天	武则天	Wǔ Zétiān		name of an empress
	慈禧	慈禧	Cíxǐ		empress dowager of the Qing dynasty

13. 婦女能頂半邊天   229

反正	反正	fǎnzhèng	adv.	anyway; anyhow
緣故	缘故	yuángù	n.	cause; reason
主	主	zhǔ	v.	preside over
下班	下班	xià bān	v.	come or go off work
地位	地位	dìwèi	n.	position; status
反而	反而	fǎn'ér	adv.	on the contrary; instead
加重	加重	jiāzhòng		aggravate
實際	实际	shí jì	adj.	real(ly); actual(ly)

語法和詞語註釋

一、凡是   every; all; any

"凡是" occurs before a noun phrase and is often used in conjunction with "都" to indicate inclusiveness: "whatever", "whoever", etc.

1. 凡是男人能做的事情，女人都可以做。
   凡是男人能做的事情，女人都可以做。
   Whatever can be done by men can also be done by women.

2. 凡是作業寫得不整齊的人都必須重寫。
   凡是作业写得不整齐的人都必须重写。
   Anyone who didn't write the homework neatly must redo it.

3. 凡是多生孩子的人都會受到政府的制裁。
   凡是多生孩子的人都会受到政府的制裁。
   Anyone who has more than one child will be punished by the government.

二、看   look after; take care of

1. 女人在家看孩子。
   女人在家看孩子。
   The women would look after the children at home.

2. 暑假的時候我幫朋友看房子。

暑假的时候我帮朋友看房子。

During the summer vacation, I looked after my friend's house for him.

3. 看住牠，別讓牠跑出去。

看住它，别让它跑出去。

Keep an eye on the cat/dog and don't let it escape.

三、再……也　　even if; even though

"再……也"emphasizes that no matter what the situation is, the result will never be changed.

1. 女人做飯做得再香，衣服做得再漂亮也不能去外面做。

女人做饭做得再香，衣服做得再漂亮也不能去外面做。

Even if women could cook delicious food and make beautiful clothes, they couldn't do this outside.

2. 她們下班回家再累也得做飯、洗衣服、照顧孩子。

她们下班回家再累也得做饭、洗衣服、照顾孩子。

Even if they are very tired after work, they have to cook, do the laundry and look after the children.

3. 她再吃也吃不胖。

她再吃也吃不胖。

Even if she eats a lot, she doesn't gain weight.

四、反正　　anyway; anyhow

"反正"is often used in the second clause of a sentence to emphasize that a situation will not change under any circumstances. The first clause usually starts with"不管"or"無論".

1. 不管後來的人們說武則天和慈禧是好還是壞，反正這兩個女人當了皇帝。

不管后来的人们说武则天和慈禧是好还是坏，反正这两个女人当了皇帝。

No matter whether people afterwards say Wu Zetian and Cixi are good or bad, these two women had become the empresses.

2. 無論你怎麼說，反正我不聽你的。
   无论你怎么说，反正我不听你的。
   No matter what you say, I won't listen to you anyway.

3. 不管他是好人還是壞人，反正我要跟他結婚。
   不管他是好人还是坏人，反正我要跟他结婚。
   No matter whether he is a good man or a bad man, I want to marry him anyway.

五、由於……緣故　　due to; as a result of

> "由於……緣故" is used in the same way as "因為……原因" to introduce a cause or reason for something, but it more often appears in written language.

1. 由於重男輕女的緣故，中國人的家庭都是男主外，女主內。
   由于重男轻女的缘故，中国人的家庭都是男主外，女主内。
   Due to the fact that males are favored and females are seen as less important, in Chinese families it is the men who are responsible for matters outside the home and the women who see to things inside.

2. 由於他常常不來上課的緣故，所以有些問題他一點兒都不懂。
   由于他常常不来上课的缘故，所以有些问题他一点儿都不懂。
   Because he missed a lot of classes, there were some problems he could hardly understand at all.

3. 由於天氣的緣故，比賽取消了。
   由于天气的缘故，比赛取消了。
   Due to the bad weather, the match was canceled.

六、"從來" and "一直"　　always

> "從來" and "一直" are interchangeable when they indicate continuous action from the past up to the present. However, for short periods of time, only "一直" is used, and "從來" is more often used in negative sentences.

1. 我從來 (一直) 不吸煙。
   我从来 (一直) 不吸烟。
   I never smoke.

2. 他從來 (一直) 就是這樣對人沒有禮貌。
   他从来 (一直) 就是这样对人没有礼貌。
   He is always impolite to people like this.

3. 這兩天小王一直發燒。
   这两天小王一直发烧。
   Xiao Wang has had a fever for the past few days.

   這兩天小王從來發燒。(×)
   这两天小王从来发烧。(×)

七、反而　　on the contrary; instead

"反而" indicates that the result of a situation is contrary to expectations or to the normal situation.

1. 男女平等了反而加重了婦女的負擔。
   男女平等了反而加重了妇女的负担。
   Contrary to what one might expect, with equality of the sexes the burden on women has increased.

2. 我幫她做作業，她不但不感謝我，反而生我的氣。
   我帮她做作业，她不但不感谢我，反而生我的气。
   I did the homework for her. Instead of being grateful, she got angry with me.

3. 今天的考試，難的題我都會做，容易的反而做錯了。
   今天的考试，难的题我都会做，容易的反而做错了。
   I could do all the hard questions in today's exam, but I got the easy ones wrong.

練 習

一、用所給的詞語回答問題

1. A：聽說下學期的中文很難，你還要學嗎？（再……也）
   听说下学期的中文很难，你还要学吗？（再……也）

   B：_____。

2. A：明天有考試，你為甚麼不複習準備？（反正）
   明天有考试，你为什么不复习准备？（反正）

   B：_____。

3. A：今天的考試怎麼樣？（反而）
   今天的考试怎么样？（反而）

   B：_____。

4. A：你為甚麼要轉到別的學校？（由於……緣故）
   你为什么要转到别的学校？（由于……缘故）

   B：_____。

5. A：甚麼人知道中國的長城？（凡是）
   什么人知道中国的长城？（凡是）

   B：_____。

6. A：你聽說過中國的大運河嗎？（從來）
   你听说过中国的大运河吗？（从来）

   B：_____。

二、從課文中找出正確的答案

男人能做的事情和男人不願意做的事情	女人能做的事情和女人不能做的事情	哪幾位女人做了人們認為女人不能做的事情
男人能做的事情和男人不愿意做的事情	女人能做的事情和女人不能做的事情	哪几位女人做了人们认为女人不能做的事情

三、選擇合適的詞語填空

1. 小王_____沒有忘記你，這幾天_____說要給你寫信呢。
   小王_____没有忘记你，这几天_____说要给你写信呢。
   a. 一直　一直　　b. 從來　从来

2. 姐姐和妹妹長得_____一樣，高低胖瘦看起來都好像_____。
   姐姐和妹妹长得_____一样，高低胖瘦看起来都好像_____。
   a. 差不多　差不多　　b. 幾乎　几乎

3. _____碰到不認識的字，他_____來問我。
   _____碰到不认识的字，他_____来问我。
   a. 凡是　凡是　　b. 總是　总是

4. 我_____王小龍病了，_____是喝酒喝病的。
   我_____王小龙病了，_____是喝酒喝病的。
   a. 據說　据说　　b. 聽説　听说

四、用所給的詞語造句

1. 反正
   反正
   _____。

2. 反而
   反而
   _____。

3. 凡是
   凡是
   _____。

4. 從來
   从来
   _____。

5. 再……也
   再……也
   _____。

五、翻譯

1. Even if chefs in restaurants can cook very well, they are unwilling to cook at home. No matter how beautiful the clothes are that women make at home, they cannot go and make them in clothes shops in town.

   _____
   _____
   _____。

2. When women became empresses, no one dared to speak in front of them that women couldn't be empresses.

   _____
   _____
   _____ 。

3. The meaning of "Women can hold up half the sky" is that men and women are equal. Contrary to what one might expect, with equality of the sexes the burden on women has increased.

   _____
   _____
   _____ 。

六、根據課文回答問題

1. 為甚麼以前的廚師和裁縫都是男人？
   为什么以前的厨师和裁缝都是男人？

   _____
   _____ 。

2. 甚麼是男主外，女主內？
   什么是男主外，女主内？

   _____
   _____ 。

3. 為甚麼現在很多女人都跟男人一樣出外工作？
   为什么现在很多女人都跟男人一样出外工作？

   _____
   _____ 。

4. 為甚麼要提出"婦女能頂半邊天"？
   为什么要提出"妇女能顶半边天"？

5. 為甚麼說現在的婦女頂的是"大半個天"?
   为什么说现在的妇女顶的是"大半个天"?

七、課堂討論

有沒有真正的男女平等？
有没有真正的男女平等？

八、小作文

你對男女平等的看法。
你对男女平等的看法。

閱讀

小腳和辮子

在一些描寫中國歷史的電影裏，人們常常看到裹着小腳的女人和留着大辮子的男人。很多外國人都覺得很奇怪，中國女人為甚麼要纏小腳呢？中國男人又為甚麼要留辮子呢？纏小腳和留辮子的習俗是甚麼時候開始的，又是甚麼時候結束的呢？

中國女人纏小腳的習俗，據古書上說從唐代的時候就開始了。

纏小腳是一件非常痛苦的事情。當小女孩四、五歲的時候，她的媽媽就用一條布帶把她的小腳纏裹起來，纏了一圈又一圈，纏得緊緊的。在纏的過程中，一雙白嫩的小腳不但被纏得皮破肉爛，連腳骨也都被折斷了。纏到最後，整個腳只有三寸那麼大，路都走不穩，這時候大家反而都說這腳好看，說這一雙小腳是"三寸金蓮"。還說這女孩子很有福氣，將來一定能找到一個好婆家。

纏腳這麼痛苦，為甚麼還一定要纏呢？原來在古時候，男人喜歡女人的腳小，他們覺得女人的小腳好看，小腳的女人漂亮。女人要是腳大的話，別人就會笑話她，大腳的姑娘找不到婆家。

中國女人的小腳一直纏了一千多年。清朝初年的時候，清朝政府曾經禁止過女人纏小腳，可是大家還是偷偷地纏。大概是到了清朝末年，人們才開始覺悟，才知道女人不應該纏小腳。

中國男人從來都是留長頭髮的。他們說身體和頭髮都是父母給的，不可以傷害。不過，那時人們是把頭髮束在頭頂上用帶子紮起來的。

男人們梳大辮子是從清朝才開始的。當時清朝政府要求所有的人都得把前額的頭髮剃乾淨，在後腦勺梳上一條粗粗的大辮子。凡是不留辮子的人就要被殺頭。清朝滅亡以後，大家才把辮子都剪掉了。

男人留那麼長的辮子，一定很麻煩、很不方便，但是他們卻沒有像中國女人纏小腳那樣吃那麼多的苦、受那麼大的罪。

阅 读

小脚和辫子

在一些描写中国历史的电影里，人们常常看到裹着小脚的女人和留着大辫子的男人。很多外国人都觉得很奇怪，中国女人为什么要缠小脚呢？中国男人又为什么要留辫子呢？缠小脚和留辫子的习俗是什么时候开始的，又是什么时候结束的呢？

中国女人缠小脚的习俗，据古书上说从唐代的时候就开始了。

缠小脚是一件非常痛苦的事情。当小女孩四、五岁的时候，她的妈妈就用一条布带把她的小脚缠裹起来，缠了一圈又一圈，缠得紧紧的。在缠的过程中，一双白嫩的小脚不但被缠得皮破肉烂，连脚骨也都被折断了。缠到最后，整个脚只有三寸那么大，路都走不稳，这时候大家反而都说这脚好看，说这一双小脚是"三寸金莲"。还说这女孩子很有福气，将来一定能找到一个好婆家。

缠脚这么痛苦，为什么还一定要缠呢？原来在古时候，男人喜欢女人的脚小，他们觉得女人的小脚好看，小脚的女人漂亮。女人要是脚大的话，别人就会笑话她，大脚的姑娘找不到婆家。

中国女人的小脚一直缠了一千多年。清朝初年的时候，清朝政府曾经禁止过女人缠小脚，可是大家还是偷偷地缠。大概是到了清朝末年，人们才开始觉悟，才知道女人不应该缠小脚。

中国男人从来都是留长头发的。他们说身体和头发都是父母给的，不可以伤害。不过，那时人们是把头发束在头顶上用带子扎起来的。

男人们梳大辫子是从清朝才开始的。当时清朝政府要求所有的人都得把前额的头发剃干净，在后脑勺梳上一条粗粗的大辫子。凡是不留辫子的人就要被杀头。清朝灭亡以后，大家才把辫子都剪掉了。

男人留那么长的辫子，一定很麻烦、很不方便，但是他们却没有像中国女人缠小脚那样吃那么多的苦、受那么大的罪。

生詞

辮子	辫子	biànzi	n.	braid
描寫	描写	miáoxiě	v.	describe
裹	裹	guǒ	v.	wrap
留	留	liú	v.	keep
纏	缠	chán	v.	twine; bind
布帶	布带	bùdài	n.	a strip of cloth
圈	圈	quān	n.	circle; round
緊緊的	紧紧的	jǐn jǐn de	adj.	tightly
過程	过程	guòchéng	n.	process
嫩	嫩	nèn	adj.	delicate; tender
皮破肉爛	皮破肉烂	pípò-ròulàn		skin broken and flesh rotting
腳骨	脚骨	jiǎogǔ	n.	foot bone
折斷	折断	zhéduàn	v.	break
寸	寸	cùn	n.	inch
穩	稳	wěn	adj.	steady
三寸金蓮	三寸金莲	sāncùn jīnlián		three-inch "golden lotuses": describes a woman's beautiful bound feet
痛苦	痛苦	tòngkǔ	adj.	suffering; agony
笑話	笑话	xiàohuà	v.	ridicule; laugh at
吃苦	吃苦	chī kǔ		suffer
受罪	受罪	shòu zuì		suffering; hardship
禁止	禁止	jìnzhǐ	v.	prohibit
覺悟	觉悟	juéwù	v.	become aware of
傷害	伤害	shānghài	v.	harm

梳	梳	shū	v.	comb
束	束	shù	v.	bundle
頭頂	头顶	tóudǐng	n.	the top of head
前額	前额	qián'é	n.	forehead
剃	剃	tì	v.	shave
後腦勺	后脑勺	hòunǎosháo	n.	the back of the head
粗	粗	cū	adj.	thick
殺頭	杀头	shā tóu		behead; decapitate
滅亡	灭亡	mièwáng	v.	perish; die out
剪掉	剪掉	jiǎndiào	v.	cut off

問題

1. 小腳是怎麼纏的?
   小脚是怎么缠的?

   _____
   _____。

2. 女孩子為甚麼一定得纏小腳呢?
   女孩子为什么一定得缠小脚呢?

   _____
   _____。

3. 大家都說腳小的女孩子怎麼樣?
   大家都说脚小的女孩子怎么样?

   _____
   _____。

4. 甚麼時候才開始不纏小腳的？
   什么时候才开始不缠小脚的？

   _____

   _____。

14

家家有老人
Every Family Has Its Elderly Members

學習大綱

通過學習本課，學生應該能夠：

1. 掌握這些句型和詞語的意思和用法："把……V在……上"、"V來V去"、"誰、哪兒、甚麼、幾"、"Adj起來"、"不再……了"、量詞重疊、動詞重疊。
2. 認識和運用課文以及閱讀文章內的生詞。
3. 簡單地了解中國老年人的生活。
4. 簡單地了解中國老年人有甚麼樣的娛樂和鍛煉活動。

Study Outline

After studying this chapter, students should:

1. Have a good command of the meaning and usage of these sentence patterns and terms: "bǎ ... V zài ... shàng" (V ... on ...), "V lái V qù" (an action occurred repeatedly), "shéi, nǎr, shěnme, jǐ" (who, where, what, when), "Adj qǐlái", "bùzài ... le" (not anymore, no longer), measure word reduplication, verb reduplication.
2. Be familiar with the meaning and usage of the vocabulary introduced in the text and the reading.
3. Know something of the lives of the elderly members in China.
4. Have some idea of the favorite recreational activities and exercises of elderly people in China.

課文

家家有老人,人人都會老。老人問題是每個家庭都會遇到的問題。

世界上一些發達的國家裏有很多養老院,當老人年齡太大、行動不方便的時候,兒女們通常就把他們送到養老院去。中國也有養老院,但是中國的老人一般不願意去養老院,住養老院的只是一些無兒無女的老人。

中國人認為如果有兒有女的老人住在養老院裏,那一定是他的兒女不孝順。中國人特別講究要孝順老人。如果兒女對老人不好,他們就會受到社會上的譴責,要是虐待老人的話,他們還可能去坐牢。

一般來說中國的家庭很少發生虐待兒童的事情,但是虐待老人的情況卻很多。古書上就講過這樣一個故事。

從前有一個兒子經常打罵他的老父親,而他的父親卻特別疼愛自己的孫子。鄰居問他:"你兒子整天打你、罵你,你為甚麼對他的兒子還這麼好呢?"老人說:"我盼望我的孫子快快長大。等他長大以後,他也會像他爸爸對待我那樣去對待他的爸爸。"

以前大概是因為經濟上的原因,許多做兒女的把錢都花在自己孩子的身上,而對老人的生活卻關心不夠。尤其當老人長期生病,特別需要兒女照顧的時候,他們反倒對老人惡聲惡氣。有的老人雖然還有其他的子女,但那些子女也都是互相推來推去,誰都不願意照顧有病的父母。

近幾十年來,中國的經濟好起來了,老人在生活上不再有甚麼問題了,可是他們在精神上卻常常感到孤獨和苦悶。

為了讓老人能夠愉快地生活,讓他們有一個幸福的晚年,人們就開辦了很多"老年大學"。讓老人去學學書法,學學畫畫兒,學學跳舞甚麼的。同時在許多城市也設立了"老年娛樂活動中心"。在那裏,老人們可以下下棋、打打牌,聊聊天、散散心。還有的地方成立了"老年婚姻介紹所",專門為鰥寡老人介紹對象。

课文

家家有老人，人人都会老。老人问题是每个家庭都会遇到的问题。

世界上一些发达的国家里有很多养老院，当老人年龄太大、行动不便的时候，儿女们通常就把他们送到养老院去。中国也有养老院，但是中国的老人一般不愿意去养老院，住养老院的只是一些无儿无女的老人。

中国人认为如果有儿有女的老人住在养老院里，那一定是他的儿女不孝顺。中国人特别讲究要孝顺老人。如果儿女对老人不好，他们就会受到社会上的谴责，要是虐待老人的话，他们还可能去坐牢。

一般来说中国的家庭很少发生虐待儿童的事情，但是虐待老人的情况却很多。古书上就讲过这样一个故事。

从前有一个儿子经常打骂他的老父亲，而他的父亲却特别疼爱自己的孙子。邻居问他："你儿子整天打你、骂你，你为什么对他的儿子还这么好呢？"老人说："我盼望我的孙子快快长大。等他长大以后，他也会像他爸爸对待我那样去对待他的爸爸。"

以前大概是因为经济上的原因，许多做儿女的把钱都花在自己孩子的身上，而对老人的生活却关心不够。尤其当老人长期生病，特别需要儿女照顾的时候，他们反倒对老人恶声恶气。有的老人虽然还有其他的子女，但那些子女也都是互相推来推去，谁都不愿意照顾有病的父母。

近几十年来，中国的经济好起来了，老人在生活上不再有什么问题了，可是他们在精神上却常常感到孤独和苦闷。

为了让老人能够愉快地生活，让他们有一个幸福的晚年，人们就开办了很多"老年大学"。让老人去学学书法，学学画画儿，学学跳舞什么的。同时在许多城市也设立了"老年娱乐活动中心"。在那里，老人们可以下下棋、打打牌，聊聊天、散散心。还有的地方成立了"老年婚姻介绍所"，专门为鳏寡老人介绍对象。

生詞

發達	发达	fādá	adj.	developed; flourishing
養老院	养老院	yǎnglǎoyuàn	n.	home for the elderly
行動	行动	xíngdòng	n.	movement; action
通常	通常	tōngcháng	adj.	generally; often
無	无	wú	v.	do not have; without
孝順	孝顺	xiàoshùn	v.	show filial obedience
講究	讲究	jiǎngjiū	v.	stress; value
譴責	谴责	qiǎnzé	v.	denounce; condemn
虐待	虐待	nüèdài	v.	ill-treat
坐牢	坐牢	zuò láo		go to jail
罵	骂	mà	v.	abuse; curse
疼愛	疼爱	téng'ài	v.	be very fond of; love dearly
孫子	孙子	sūnzi	n.	grandson
盼望	盼望	pànwàng	v.	expect; look forward to
對待	对待	duìdài	v.	treat; approach
經濟	经济	jīngjì	n.	economy
關心	关心	guānxīn	v.	care (about)
需要	需要	xūyào	v.	be in need of
反倒	反倒	fǎndào	adv.	on the contrary, same as "反而"
惡聲惡氣	恶声恶气	èshēng'èqì		speak in a nasty way
推來推去	推来推去	tuīlái tuīqù		push responsibility onto others
精神	精神	jīngshén	n.	spirit
孤獨	孤独	gūdú	adj.	lonely
苦悶	苦闷	kǔmèn	adj.	dejected; feeling low
晚年	晚年	wǎnnián	n.	old age

開辦	开办	kāibàn	v.	set up; start
書法	书法	shūfǎ	n.	calligraphy
跳舞	跳舞	tiào wǔ		dancing
設立	设立	shèlì	v.	set up
下棋	下棋	xià qí		play chess
打牌	打牌	dǎ pái		play cards
聊天	聊天	liáo tiān		chat
散心	散心	sàn xīn		relieve boredom; relax
鰥寡	鳏寡	guānguǎ	n.	widowers and widows

語法和詞語註釋

一、把……V在……上　　V ... on ...

"把……V在……上" indicates the aspect or place (which may not be a physical place) on which an action focuses.

1. 他們把錢花在孩子身上。
   他们把钱花在孩子身上。
   They spend money on their children.

2. 孩子把時間用在學習上。
   孩子把时间用在学习上。
   Children spend time on their studies.

3. 我爸爸把精力放在工作上。
   我爸爸把精力放在工作上。
   My father concentrates his energy on his work.

二、V來V去　　an action occurring repeatedly

1. 子女之間也是推來推去，誰也不願意照顧老人。
   子女之间也是推来推去，谁也不愿意照顾老人。

Sons and daughters push the responsibility onto each other, and none of them is willing to take care of their elderly parents.

2. 這本書他看來看去，也不明白書裏講的是甚麼。

这本书他看来看去，也不明白书里讲的是什么。

He read this book again and again, but still couldn't understand what it was about.

3. 媽媽問來問去，還是不知道兒子的女朋友是誰。

妈妈问来问去，还是不知道儿子的女朋友是谁。

The mother asked her son again and again, but still couldn't find out who his girlfriend was.

三、誰、哪兒、甚麼、幾　　who, where, what, when

"誰", "哪兒", "甚麼", "幾" when used in conjunction with "也" or "都" mean that there is no exception.

1. 那些子女互相推來推去，誰也不願意照顧生病的老人。

那些子女互相推来推去，谁也不愿意照顾生病的老人。

The sons and daughters push responsibility onto each other, and no one is willing to take care of their sick elderly parents.

2. 二十一歲以前，誰都不可以喝酒。

二十一岁以前，谁都不可以喝酒。

No one is allowed to drink before he/she is twenty-one years old.

3. 除了生病的同學以外，明天誰都得來開會。

除了生病的同学以外，明天谁都得来开会。

Everyone must come to the meeting tomorrow, except those students who are sick.

4. 我只想睡覺了，哪兒也不想去。

我只想睡觉了，哪儿也不想去。

I just want to sleep. I don't want to go anywhere.

5. 我有點兒惡心，甚麼都不想吃。

我有点儿恶心，什么都不想吃。

I'm feeling a bit sick. I don't want to eat anything.

6. 明天我在家，你幾點來都行。

明天我在家，你几点来都行。

I'll be at home tomorrow. You can come anytime you want.

四、Adj 起來

"Adj 起來" indicates that the degree of the state described by the adjective is increasing.

1. 近十年中國的經濟好起來了。

近十年中国的经济好起来了。

China's economy has begun to improve over the last ten years.

2. 秋天來了，天氣冷起來了。

秋天来了，天气冷起来了。

The fall is coming. It's getting cold.

3. 這一學期的課文難起來了。

这一学期的课文难起来了。

This semester's lessons are getting harder.

五、不再……了　　not any more; no longer

"不再 …… 了" indicates that a situation will not be repeated again.

1. 經濟好了，老人的生活不再有甚麼問題了。

经济好了，老人的生活不再有什么问题了。

The economy has improved and there are no longer any problems in the liver of the elderly.

2. 自從上次他罵了我以後，我不再理他了。

自从上次他骂了我以后，我不再理他了。

I'm not speaking to him any more, since he swore at me that time.

3. 這一學期學完以後，我不再學中文了。

這一学期学完以后，我不再学中文了。

After this semester, I won't study Chinese any longer.

六、量詞重疊　　Measure word reduplication

Measure word reduplication indicates a uniform situation with no exceptions. Here "家家"、"人人"、"年年" are measure words.

1. 家家有老人，人人都會老。

家家有老人，人人都会老。

There are elderly people in every family, and every one of us will grow old.

2. 除夕晚上吃年飯的時候，不要把魚吃完，意思是說年年有餘。

除夕晚上吃年饭的时候，不要把鱼吃完，意思是说年年有余。

At the New Year's Eve dinner, the fish is not supposed to be eaten up, implying that there is surplus every year.

3. 我們班上的同學個個都很聰明。

我们班上的同学个个都很聪明。

Every single student in our class is very smart.

七、動詞重疊　　Verb reduplication

Verb reduplication indicates the action is carried out in a casual and easy manner.

1. 讓老人學學書法，學學畫畫兒，學學跳舞甚麼的。

让老人学学书法，学学画画儿，学学跳舞什么的。

Let the elderly learn calligraphy, painting and dancing, etc.

2. 老人們可以在那裏下下棋、聊聊天、散散心。

老人们可以在那里下下棋、聊聊天、散散心。

The elders can play chess, chat and relax there.

3. 過年在家，我每天只是看看電視、打打電話。

过年在家，我每天只是看看电视、打打电话。

Over Chinese New Year, all I did was watch TV and make phone calls at home every day.

練習

一、根據課文來完成句子

1. 中國老人不願意去養老院是因為
   中国老人不愿意去养老院是因为
   _____。

2. 兒女受到社會指責是因為
   儿女受到社会指责是因为
   _____。

3. 那個老人特別疼愛自己的孫子是因為
   那个老人特别疼爱自己的孙子是因为
   _____。

4. 兒女對老人生活關心不夠是因為
   儿女对老人生活关心不够是因为
   _____。

5. 開辦"老年大學"和"老年活動中心"是因為
   开办"老年大学"和"老年活动中心"是因为
   _____。

6. 成立"老年婚姻介紹所"是因為
   成立"老年婚姻介绍所"是因为
   _____。

二、用所給的語法形式造句

1. V來V去　　舉例：媽媽說來說去，就是不喜歡我的女朋友。
   V来V去　　举例：妈妈说来说去，就是不喜欢我的女朋友。

2. 量詞重疊　　舉例：我們班上的同學個個都很聰明。
　　量词重叠　　举例：我们班上的同学个个都很聪明。

　　_____。

3. 動詞重疊　　舉例：我喜歡晚飯後到外面散散步。
　　动词重叠　　举例：我喜欢晚饭后到外面散散步。

　　_____。

三、把下面句子按照順序連成一段文章

黃昏戀

Huánghūnliàn

Romance of Two Elderly People

(　) 張大爺從來沒有結過婚，
(　) 他們為了每天都能見面，
(　) 王大媽也非常喜歡張大爺，
(　) 這幾十年來他一直都是一個人生活。
(　) 王媽媽十幾年前就跟她的丈夫離婚了，
(　) 張大爺特別喜歡王大媽，
(　) 最近王媽媽和張大爺建立了新的家庭，
(　) 但是平常家裏只有王大媽一個人。
(　) 雖然她的兒女過年過節的時候都回來看她，
(　) 一天不見就想她。
(　) 於是倆人都去上老年大學。
(　) 天天都想去看他。
(13) 他們有了一個幸福而愉快的晚年。

　　黄昏恋

(　) 张大爷从来没有结过婚，
(　) 他们为了每天都能见面，
(　) 王大妈也非常喜欢张大爷，

(　)这几十年来他一直都是一个人生活。
(　)王妈妈十几年前就跟她的丈夫离婚了，
(　)张大爷特别喜欢王大妈，
(　)最近王妈妈和张大爷建立了新的家庭，
(　)但是平常家里只有王大妈一个人。
(　)虽然她的儿女过年过节的时候都回来看她，
(　)一天不见就想她。
(　)于是俩人都去上老年大学。
(　)天天都想去看他。
(13)他们有了一个幸福而愉快的晚年。

四、翻譯

1. There are elderly people in every family, and every one of us will become old. If we speak to the elderly in a nasty way and do not take good care of them now, our children will not take care of us when we are old.

2. When elderly people have money, everyone likes to take care of them. When they don't have money, their sons and daughters try to push the responsibility onto each other and none of them is willing to take care of them.

3. Now China's economy is improving, and there are no longer any problems in the lives of the elderly. They spend more time exercising, and everyday they take a walk, dance, play cards, or play chess.

_____
_____。

五、根據課文回答問題

1. 為甚麼中國有兒女的老人不願意住在養老院裏？
   为什么中国有儿女的老人不愿意住在养老院里？
   _____
   _____。

2. 如果兒女們不孝順老人、虐待老人的話會怎麼樣？
   如果儿女们不孝顺老人、虐待老人的话会怎么样？
   _____
   _____。

3. 那個老父親為甚麼特別疼愛自己孫子？
   那个老父亲为什么特别疼爱自己孙子？
   _____
   _____。

4. 許多兒女是怎樣對待孩子和老人的？
   许多儿女是怎样对待孩子和老人的？
   _____
   _____。

5. 當老人長期生病特別需關心照顧的時候，兒女是怎樣做的？
   当老人长期生病特别需关心照顾的时候，儿女是怎样做的？
   _____
   _____。

6. 為甚麼要成立"老年娛樂活動中心"？
   为什么要成立"老年娱乐活动中心"？
   _____

六、課堂討論

1. 老人應該住在家裏還是住在養老院？為甚麼？
   老人应该住在家里还是住在养老院？为什么？
   _____
   _____
   _____。

2. 比較一下中國的老人生活和你們國家的老人生活有甚麼不同。
   比较一下中国的老人生活和你们国家的老人生活有什么不同。
   _____
   _____
   _____。

3. 為甚麼會有虐待老人的問題？
   为什么会有虐待老人的问题？
   _____
   _____
   _____。

七、小作文

等你老了以後，你想怎樣生活？
等你老了以后，你想怎样生活？
_____
_____
_____
_____
_____。

〈黃昏戀〉的答案

（1）張大爺從來沒有結過婚，
（2）這幾十年來他一直都是一個人生活。
（3）王媽媽十幾年前就跟她的丈夫離婚了，
（4）雖然兒女過年過節的時候都回來看她，
（5）但是平常家裏只有王大媽一個人。
（6）張大爺特別喜歡王大媽，
（7）一天不見就想她。
（8）王大媽也非常喜歡張大爺，
（9）天天都想去看他。
（10）他們為了每天都能見面，
（11）於是都去上老年大學。
（12）最近王媽媽和張大爺建立了新的家庭，
（13）他們有了一個幸福而愉快的晚年。

（1）张大爷从来没有结过婚，
（2）这几十年来他一直都是一个人生活。
（3）王妈妈十几年前就跟她的丈夫离婚了，
（4）虽然儿女过年过节的时候都回来看她，
（5）但是平常家里只有王大妈一个人。
（6）张大爷特别喜欢王大妈，
（7）一天不见就想她。
（8）王大妈也非常喜欢张大爷，
（9）天天都想去看他。
（10）他们为了每天都能见面，
（11）于是都去上老年大学。
（12）最近王妈妈和张大爷建立了新的家庭，
（13）他们有了一个幸福而愉快的晚年。

閱讀

老人的娛樂和鍛煉

　　每天早上在公園裏、廣場上，甚至馬路邊上都聚集着許多老人。他們有的在做操，有的在打拳，還有的在跳舞，這是老人們在鍛煉身體。老人知道"生命在於運動"這個道理，知道自己老了更需要運動，所以他們退休以後把注意力都放在鍛煉身體上。

　　以前老人們鍛煉只是散散步、打打拳，做做操，最近幾年不知為甚麼，老人們都喜歡跳舞了。不過，老人們跳舞不是天黑了以後在舞廳裏跳，而是一大早起來在外面跳。老奶奶跳，老爺爺也跳。有的人跳的是傳統的"秧歌"舞，有的人跳的是老年"迪斯科"，還有的人只是隨便地扭來扭去，誰也不知道他們跳的是甚麼。

　　老人們不管自己跳得好不好看，也不在乎別人覺得好看不好看。他們認為只要自己跳得高興，只要能跳得渾身出汗就行。以前許多身體不好的老人跳舞以後，發現自己的身體漸漸地好起來了。老人們都說跳舞是很好的活動，它既是一種鍛煉也是一種娛樂。

　　以前老人們的娛樂大都是打打撲克，或者下下象棋。現在大多數的老人不再喜歡打牌下棋了，他們發現麻將比撲克和象棋有意思。

　　麻將現在是中國最普遍的娛樂活動。這幾年，打麻將跟跳舞一樣特別受老年人的歡迎。老人們每天吃完了晚飯以後，他們就聚集在一起，一邊打麻將一邊聊天。麻將讓老人消磨時間，也給老人們帶來了很多樂趣。

　　因為麻將的排列組合變化無窮，所以打麻將的時候得動腦子認真思考。據說有人專門做過研究，說打麻將對老人的大腦思維有幫助，能防止老人得老年性癡呆症。

　　中國老人真的是很有福氣，他們喜歡跳舞，跳舞既能鍛煉身體又能娛樂；他們喜歡打麻將，打麻將既能娛樂又能防病。

阅 读

老人的娱乐和锻炼

　　每天早上在公园里、广场上，甚至马路边上都聚集着许多老人。他们有的在做操，有的在打拳，还有的在跳舞，这是老人们在锻炼身体。老人知道"生命在于运动"这个道理，知道自己老了更需要运动，所以他们退休以后把注意力都放在锻炼身体上。

　　以前老人们锻炼只是散散步、打打拳，做做操，最近几年不知为什么，老人们都喜欢跳舞了。不过，老人们跳舞不是天黑了以后在舞厅里跳，而是一大早起来在外面跳。老奶奶跳，老爷爷也跳。有的人跳的是传统的"秧歌"舞，有的人跳的是老年"迪斯科"，还有的人只是随便地扭来扭去，谁也不知道他们跳的是什么。

　　老人们不管自己跳得好不好看，也不在乎别人觉得好看不好看。他们认为只要自己跳得高兴，只要能跳得浑身出汗就行。以前许多身体不好的老人跳舞以后，发现自己的身体渐渐地好起来了。老人们都说跳舞是很好的活动，它既是一种锻炼也是一种娱乐。

　　以前老人们的娱乐大都是打打扑克，或者下下象棋。现在大多数的老人不再喜欢打牌下棋了，他们发现麻将比扑克和象棋有意思。

　　麻将现在是中国最普遍的娱乐活动。这几年，打麻将跟跳舞一样特别受老年人的欢迎。老人们每天吃完了晚饭以后，他们就聚集在一起，一边打麻将一边聊天。麻将让老人消磨时间，也给老人们带来了很多乐趣。

　　因为麻将的排列组合变化无穷，所以打麻将的时候得动脑子认真思考。据说有人专门做过研究，说打麻将对老人的大脑思维有帮助，能防止老人得老年性痴呆症。

　　中国老人真的是很有福气，他们喜欢跳舞，跳舞既能锻炼身体又能娱乐；他们喜欢打麻将，打麻将既能娱乐又能防病。

14. 家家有老人

生 詞

鍛煉	锻炼	duànliàn	v.	exercising for health
公園	公园	gōngyuán	n.	park
廣場	广场	guǎngchǎng	n.	public square
馬路邊	马路边	mǎlù biān	n.	roadside
聚集	聚集	jùjí	v.	gather; assemble
做操	做操	zuò cāo		doing calisthenics
打拳	打拳	dǎ quán		practice (Chinese) boxing
生命	生命	shēngmìng	n.	life
運動	运动	yùndòng	v.	exercise; sports
道理	道理	dàolǐ	n.	argument; principle
退休	退休	tuìxiū	v.	retire
注意力	注意力	zhùyìlì	n.	attention
舞廳	舞厅	wǔtīng	n.	ballroom
一大早	一大早	yīdàzǎo		early morning
空地	空地	kòngdì	n.	open space/area
秧歌	秧歌	yāngge	n.	name of a type of popular rural folk dance
迪斯科	迪斯科	dísīkē	n.	disco
扭來扭去	扭来扭去	niǔlái niǔqù		swing; roll
不在乎	不在乎	bùzàihu		not mind; not care about
渾身	浑身	húnshēn		all over one's body
出汗	出汗	chū hàn		sweat
撲克	扑克	pūkè	n.	poker
象棋	象棋	xiàngqí	n.	(Chinese) chess
麻將	麻将	má jiàng	n.	mahjong

普遍	普遍	pǔbiàn	adj.	common
消磨	消磨	xiāomó	v.	while away
歡迎	欢迎	huānyíng	n.	welcome
排列組合	排列组合	páiliè zǔhé		arrange and assemble
無窮	无穷	wúqióng		infinite
動腦子	动脑子	dòng nǎozi		use one's brains
思考	思考	sīkǎo	v.	ponder
大腦	大脑	dànǎo	n.	cerebrum
思維	思维	sīwéi	n.	thinking
老年性癡呆症	老年性痴呆症	lǎoniánxìng chīdāizhèng		senile dementia
防病	防病	fáng bìng		prevent disease

問題

1. 老人為甚麼要鍛煉身體？
   老人为什么要锻炼身体？
   _____
   _____。

2. 老人們跳舞的時候是怎麼想的？
   老人们跳舞的时候是怎么想的？
   _____
   _____。

3. 為甚麼老人喜歡跳舞？
   为什么老人喜欢跳舞？
   _____
   _____。

4. 以前老人們是怎麼娛樂的？
   以前老人们是怎么娱乐的？

   _____
   _____ 。

5. 為甚麼老人喜歡麻將？
   为什么老人喜欢麻将？

   _____
   _____ 。

6. 為甚麼說中國老人很有福氣？
   为什么说中国老人很有福气？

   _____
   _____ 。

15

節日的食品
Special Foods for Festivals and Holidays

學習大綱

通過學習本課，學生應該能夠：

1. 掌握這些句型和詞語的意思和用法："儘管……還是"、單音節形容詞＋雙音後綴、"V好"、"則"、"原先……後來"、"V下來/下去"。
2. 認識和運用課文以及閱讀文章內的生詞。
3. 簡單了解元宵節、中秋節和端午節時，中國人吃甚麼樣的食品，這些食品在節日裏又有甚麼特別的意義。
4. 簡單了解中國菜的種類和特色。

Study Outline

After studying this chapter, students should:

1. Have a good command of the meaning and usage of these sentence patterns and terms: "jínguǎn ... háishì" (although; despite), single syllable adjectives + two-syllable suffixes, "V hǎo" (verb complement used after a verb), "zé" (then), "yuánxiān ... hòulái" (formerly ... later; originally ... after), "V xiàlái/xiàqù" (directional complement).
2. Be familiar with the meaning and usage of the vocabulary introduced in the text and the reading.
3. Have some knowledge of what special foods the Chinese eat during the Lantern Festival, the Mid-Autumn Festival and the Dragon Boat Festival, and their implications.
4. Have a simple understanding of the different types of Chinese cuisines and their characteristics.

課文

　　中國有很多節日，也有很多節日食品。人們在不同的節日裏吃不同的東西，例如元宵節吃元宵，端午節吃糉子，中秋節吃月餅。

　　元宵節是新年後的第一個圓月夜。當圓圓的月亮升起來的時候，大街小巷掛滿了各種各樣的燈籠。燈籠上寫着許多謎語。儘管這時外面冰天雪地、寒風刺骨，大家都還是要出去看燈籠、猜謎語。

　　這天晚上，街上到處都在賣元宵。元宵是用米粉做的，裏面包着核桃、芝麻和花生。在冰天雪地中遊玩的大人和小孩，只要吃上一碗剛煮好的熱騰騰、香噴噴的元宵，就一點兒也不覺得冷了。

　　元宵節漢代就有了，不過吃元宵的習俗卻是從宋代才開始的。人們說元宵既表示團圓又表示圓滿。如果自己家人在一起吃元宵，那是希望家人能夠團圓；如果送給朋友，則是祝願朋友事事圓滿。

　　八月十五是中秋節。每月的十五月亮都會圓，但是八月十五的月亮最圓。這天晚上人們要吃月餅。圓圓的月餅就像是天上圓圓的月亮，吃月餅是表示家家戶戶都團團圓圓。月餅是用麪做的，裏面的餡是蓮蓉、豆沙和火腿等等。據說唐朝就已經有中秋節吃月餅的習俗了。

　　端午節吃糉子，人們傳說是為了紀念屈原的。

　　屈原是戰國時期的楚國人。他原先幫助楚國國王治理國家，後來有人嫉妒他，在楚王面前說他的壞話，楚王漸漸地就疏遠了他，最後把他流放到了很遠的地方。屈原看到楚國一天天地衰落下去，感到很難過，於是就在五月初五這天跳到江裏自殺了。

　　屈原死了以後，人們都很懷念他。到了五月初五這天，大家把米飯包在竹葉或者蘆葦葉裏，投到江裏去祭奠屈原，後來這一天慢慢地就變成了一個節日，包糉子的習俗也流傳了下來。

　　糉子大都是甜的，裏面是白糖、紅棗和豆沙，也有人喜歡吃有肉的鹹糉子。不過現在人們包糉子不再投到江裏去了，而是留着自己吃了。

课文

中国有很多节日，也有很多节日食品。人们在不同的节日里吃不同的东西，例如元宵节吃元宵，端午节吃粽子，中秋节吃月饼。

元宵节是新年后的第一个圆月夜。当圆圆的月亮升起来的时候，大街小巷挂满了各种各样的灯笼。灯笼上写着许多谜语。尽管这时外面冰天雪地、寒风刺骨，大家都还是要出去看灯笼、猜谜语。

这天晚上，街上到处都在卖元宵。元宵是用米粉做的，里面包着核桃、芝麻和花生。在冰天雪地中游玩的大人和小孩，只要吃上一碗刚煮好的热腾腾、香喷喷的元宵，就一点儿也不觉得冷了。

元宵节汉代就有了，不过吃元宵的习俗却是从宋代才开始的。人们说元宵既表示团圆又表示圆满。如果自己家人在一起吃元宵，那是希望家人能够团圆；如果送给朋友，则是祝愿朋友事事圆满。

八月十五是中秋节。每月的十五月亮都会圆，但是八月十五的月亮最圆。这天晚上人们要吃月饼。圆圆的月饼就像是天上圆圆的月亮，吃月饼是表示家家户户都团团圆圆。月饼是用面做的，里面的馅是莲蓉、豆沙和火腿等等。据说唐朝就已经有中秋节吃月饼的习俗了。

端午节吃粽子，人们传说是为了纪念屈原的。

屈原是战国时期的楚国人。他原先帮助楚国国王治理国家，后来有人嫉妒他，在楚王面前说他的坏话，楚王渐渐地就疏远了他，最后把他流放到了很远的地方。屈原看到楚国一天天地衰落下去，感到很难过，于是就在五月初五这天跳到江里自杀了。

屈原死了以后，人们都很怀念他。到了五月初五这天，大家把米饭包在竹叶或者芦苇叶里，投到江里去祭奠屈原，后来这一天慢慢地就变成了一个节日，包粽子的习俗也流传了下来。

粽子大都是甜的，里面是白糖、红枣和豆沙，也有人喜欢吃有肉的咸粽子。不过现在人们包粽子不再投到江里去了，而是留着自己吃了。

生　詞

食品	食品	shípǐn	n.	foodstuff
元宵	元宵	yuánxiāo	n.	sweet dumplings made of glutinous rice flour
月餅	月饼	yuèbǐng	n.	moon cake
糉子	粽子	zòngzi	n.	a pyramid-shaped dumpling made of glutinous rice wrapped in bamboo or reed leaves
大街小巷	大街小巷	dà jiē-xiǎoxiàng	n.	all streets
燈籠	灯笼	dēnglong	n.	lantern
謎語	谜语	míyǔ	n.	riddle
儘管……還是	尽管……还是	jǐnguǎn ... háishì	conj.	although; despite
冰天雪地	冰天雪地	bīngtiān-xuědì		a world of ice and snow
寒風刺骨	寒风刺骨	hánfēng-cìgǔ		the cold wind chills one to the bone
猜	猜	cāi	v.	guess
米粉	米粉	mǐfěn	n.	rice flour
包	包	bāo	v.	wrap
核桃	核桃	hétao	n.	walnuts
芝麻	芝麻	zhīma	n.	sesame
花生	花生	huāshēng	n.	peanut
遊玩	游玩	yóuwán	v.	go sight-seeing
熱騰騰	热腾腾	rètēngtēng	adj.	steaming hot
香噴噴	香喷喷	xiāngpēnpēn	adj.	deliciously scented; appetizing
圓滿	圆满	yuánmǎn	adj.	satisfactory; complete

則	则	**zé**	*conj.*	then
餡	馅	**xiàn**	*n.*	stuffing; filling
蓮蓉	莲蓉	**liánróng**	*n.*	lotus bean paste
豆沙	豆沙	**dòushā**	*n.*	sweetened bean paste
火腿	火腿	**huǒtuǐ**	*n.*	ham
紀念	纪念	**jìniàn**	*v.*	memorialize; commemorate
屈原	屈原	**Qū Yuán**		name of a person
楚國	楚国	**Chǔ guó**		the state of Chu
原先	原先	**yuánxiān**	*adj.*	originally
國王	国王	**guówáng**	*n.*	king
治理	治理	**zhìlǐ**	*v.*	administer; manage
嫉妒	嫉妒	**jídù**	*v.*	be jealous of
壞話	坏话	**huàihuà**	*n.*	vicious talk
疏遠	疏远	**shūyuǎn**	*v.*	become estranged; stand off
流放	流放	**liúfàng**	*v.*	exile
衰落	衰落	**shuāiluò**	*v.*	be on the wane; decline
自殺	自杀	**zìshā**	*v.*	commit suicide
懷念	怀念	**huáiniàn**	*v.*	cherish the memory of
竹葉	竹叶	**zhúyè**	*n.*	bamboo leaves
蘆葦葉	芦苇叶	**lúwěiyè**	*n.*	reed leaves
投	投	**tóu**	*v.*	throw
祭奠	祭奠	**jìdiàn**	*v.*	hold a memorial ceremony for
流傳	流传	**liúchuán**	*v.*	hand down
白糖	白糖	**báitáng**	*n.*	white sugar
紅棗	红枣	**hóngzǎo**	*n.*	red jujube
鹹	咸	**xián**	*adj.*	salted

相關詞彙

元旦	元旦	yuándàn	New Year's Day
春節	春节	chūn jié	Spring Festival
元宵節	元宵节	yuánxiāo jié	the Lantern Festival (the fifteenth day of the first lunar month)
清明節	清明节	qīngmíng jié	the Festival of Pure Brightness (the fifth day of the fourth lunar month)
端午節	端午节	duānwǔ jié	the Dragon Boat Festival (the fifth day of the fifth lunar month)
中秋節	中秋节	zhōngqiū jié	the Mid-Autumn Festival (the fifteenth day of the eighth lunar month)
重陽節	重阳节	chóngyáng jié	the Double Ninth Festival (the ninth day of the ninth lunar month)

語法和詞語註釋

一、儘管……還是   although; despite

"儘管" often implies a concession of some kind and it is often used in conjunction with "還是" in the second clause. "儘管" can be used either before or after the subject, but "還是" appears after the subject only.

1. 儘管外面冰天雪地寒風刺骨，大家都還是出去看花燈、猜謎語。

   尽管外面冰天雪地寒风刺骨，大家都还是出去看花灯、猜谜语。

   Despite the fact that outside everything is covered with ice and snow and the wind is chilly, people still go out to see the lanterns and try to guess the riddles.

2. 他儘管不喜歡我，我還是要跟他去看電影。

他尽管不喜欢我，我还是要跟他去看电影。

Even though he doesn't like me, I still want to go to the movie with him.

3. 儘管我懂了，我還是認真地聽老師講。

尽管我懂了，我还是认真地听老师讲。

Although I'd understood, I still listened carefully to the professor.

二、單音節形容詞＋雙音後綴

> Single syllable adjectives can be followed by two syllable suffixes to make the tone of speaking lively, for example "熱騰騰", "香噴噴".

1. 只要吃上一碗剛煮好的熱騰騰、香噴噴的元宵就一點兒也都不覺得冷了。

只要吃上一碗刚煮好的热腾腾、香喷喷的元宵就一点儿也都不觉得冷了。

You won't feel cold at all if only you eat a bowl of appetizing, newly-boiled, steaming hot, sweet dumplings.

2. 放假了，同學們都回家了，宿舍裏冷清清的只有我一個人。

放假了，同学们都回家了，宿舍里冷清清的只有我一个人。

It's the vacation. All my classmates have gone home, and I have been left all alone in the dormitory.

3. 小張笑嘻嘻地告訴我，他的女朋友來了。

小张笑嘻嘻地告诉我，他的女朋友来了。

Xiao Zhang smiled broadly and told me that his girlfriend had arrived.

三、V 好　　verb complement

> "好" is a verb complement, which is used after a verb to indicate the completion of an action.

1. 來吃飯吧，飯做好了。

来吃饭吧，饭做好了。

Come and eat. The meal is ready.

2. 你的作業做好了嗎？
   你的作业做好了吗？
   Have you finished your homework?

3. 暑假去哪裏學中文想好了嗎？
   暑假去哪里学中文想好了吗？
   Have you decided where to study Chinese this summer?

四、則   then

> "則" is used more often in the written language. It indicates a relation of causality or reasoning between two clauses, but is often left untranslated in the English version of the sentences.

1. 如果送給朋友，則是祝願朋友事事圓滿如意。
   如果送给朋友，则是祝愿朋友事事圆满如意。
   If you buy them for your friends, (then) it means you are wishing everything goes well for your friends.

2. SAT考到一千五百分的人則可以上好大學。
   SAT考到一千五百分的人则可以上好大学。
   If you get a SAT score higher than 1,500, you can get into a good university.

3. 水一百度以上會變成水蒸汽，零度以下則變成冰。
   水一百度以上会变成水蒸汽，零度以下则变成冰。
   Water becomes steam above 100 ℃, and becomes ice below 0 ℃.

五、原先……後來   formerly ... later; originally ... after

> "原先……後來" connects two sentences in a time sequence.

1. 屈原原先在楚國做官，後來有人嫉妒他，在楚王面前說他的壞話。
   屈原原先在楚国做官，后来有人嫉妒他，在楚王面前说他的坏话。
   Qu Yuan was originally an official in the state of Chu, but later on someone who was jealous of him slandered him in front of the king of Chu.

2. 我原先想大學畢業以後上研究所，後來我想先掙錢，所以就工作了。

我原先想大学毕业以后上研究所，后来我想先挣钱，所以就工作了。
I was originally planning to go into a research institute after graduation, but later I thought I'd earn some money first, so I got a job.

3. 我原先學的是日文，後來看到很多人學中文，於是我也決定學中文了。
我原先学的是日文，后来看到很多人学中文，于是我也决定学中文了。
Originally I studied Japanese, but later on I saw a lot of people were studying Chinese, so I decided to study Chinese too.

六、V下來/下去　　directional complement

> When "下來" is used after a verb, it indicates the continuation of an activity from the past until the present, but "下去" indicates the continuation of an activity without any reference to time.

1. 到後來，這一天慢慢地變成了一個節日，包糭子的習俗也流傳了下來。
到后来，这一天慢慢地变成了一个节日，包粽子的习俗也流传了下来。
Gradually this day became a festival, and the custom of wrapping *zongzi* was handed down.

2. 他知道中文很難學，可是他還是堅持下來了。
他知道中文很难学，可是他还是坚持下来了。
He knows Chinese is very hard to learn, but he has persevered with it up till now.

3. 屈原看到楚國一天天地衰落下去。
屈原看到楚国一天天地衰落下去。
Qu Yuan saw that the state of Chu was declining day by day.

4. 我願意和你一直生活下去。
我愿意和你一直生活下去。
I'd like to live with you forever.

> "V下來/下去" also express direction of movement. For example, "下去" is used to indicate movement downward and away from the speaker. "下來" indicates movement downward and towards the speaker.

5. 弟弟在樓上對我說："我把籃球給你扔下去。"我說："好，你扔下來吧。"
   弟弟在楼上对我说："我把篮球给你扔下去。"我说："好，你扔下来吧。"
   My brother upstairs said to me: "I'm throwing the basketball to you." I said: "OK. Throw it to me."

練習

一、根據課文來完成句子

1. 中秋節吃月餅是表示
   中秋节吃月饼是表示
   _____。

2. 端午節包糉子原先是為了
   端午节包粽子原先是为了
   _____。

3. 元宵節晚上人們出去是為了
   元宵节晚上人们出去是为了
   _____。

4. 楚王疏遠屈原是因為
   楚王疏远屈原是因为
   _____。

5. 把元宵送給朋友是為了
   把元宵送给朋友是为了
   _____。

二、用所給的詞語填空 (一個詞語只能用一次)

只要……就、儘管……還是、原先……後來、只不過……罷了、為了、不再……了
只要……就、尽管……还是、原先……后来、只不过……罢了、为了、不再……了

我_____喜歡吸煙,_____不吸煙了。因為我有了一個新女朋友,她不讓我吸煙。所以_____和她在一起,我_____不能吸煙。有的時候_____我特別想吸煙,但是我_____不能吸。我不吸煙是_____不讓我女朋友生氣。我的同學笑話我,説我很怕我的女朋友。其實我不是怕她,_____是很愛她_____。當然她也説了,要是她發現我再吸煙,她就_____喜歡我_____。

我_____喜欢吸烟,_____不吸烟了。因为我有了一个新女朋友,她不让我吸烟。所以_____和她在一起,我_____不能吸烟。有的时候_____我特别想吸烟,但是我_____不能吸。我不吸烟是_____不让我女朋友生气。我的同学笑话我,说我很怕我的女朋友。其实我不是怕她,_____是很爱她_____。当然她也说了,要是她发现我再吸烟,她就_____喜欢我_____。

三、寫出三種節日食品開始的年代和代表的意義

元宵　元宵	月餅　月饼	糉子　粽子

四、根據課文寫出這三種食品是用甚麼做的、有甚麼味道

1. 元宵
   元宵
   _____。

2. 月餅
   月饼
   _____。

3. 糉子
   粽子
   _____。

五、翻譯

1. On the evening of New Year's Eve, although outside is a world of ice and snow and the wind is chilly, children still run out in great excitement to set off firecrackers.

   _____
   _____
   _____。

2. The custom of eating moon cakes, sweet dumplings and *zongzi* at festivals has been handed down from ancient times. Because all the food at these festivals is so delicious, the custom will be handed down forever.

   _____
   _____
   _____。

3. Although I don't like eating sweet things, I still bought a pack of sweet dumplings on the day of the Lantern Festival. As I ate the deliciously scented and steaming hot sweet dumplings, I thought of my parents.

   _____
   _____
   _____。

六、根據課文回答問題

1. 元宵節那天晚上人們做甚麼？
   元宵节那天晚上人们做什么？
   _____

2. 為甚麼元宵節要吃元宵？
   为什么元宵节要吃元宵？
   _____
   _____

3. 屈原為甚麼要自殺？
   屈原为什么要自杀？
   _____
   _____

4. 端午節是怎麼來的？
   端午节是怎么来的？
   _____
   _____

5. 糉子是怎麼來的？
   粽子是怎么来的？
   _____
   _____

6. 為甚麼月餅和元宵都是圓圓的？
   为什么月饼和元宵都是圆圆的？
   _____
   _____

七、課堂討論

談一下你們國家的節日食品有甚麼特點、有甚麼意義。
谈一下你们国家的节日食品有什么特点、有什么意义。
_____
_____

_____。

八、小作文

介紹你們國家某一個節日裏的食品。

介绍你们国家某一个节日里的食品。

_____
_____
_____
_____
_____
_____。

閱讀

中國的飯菜

最早的時候，人們吃飯只是為了生存。那時候只要能把肚子吃飽，至於吃甚麼、怎麼吃都沒有甚麼關係。

後來社會進步了，經濟發達了，人們的生活水平提高了，吃飯對於人們來說，已經不只是為了生存，而變成一種生活享受了。這時候人們對吃甚麼、怎麼吃有了很多講究。人們要求飯菜不僅要有營養，而且還要求色味香俱全。

在中國，飯菜的烹調早已經成為一門學問、一門學科，甚至是一門藝術。中國有許多烹飪學校，還有各種講解烹調的書。

中國地方很大，東、西、南、北、中，各個地方都有自己不同的烹調方法。人們根據不同的味道，把中國菜分為山東菜、四川菜、湖南菜等八個不同的菜系。

做飯的時候，儘管人們烹調的方法都是蒸、煮、煎、炸、炒；用的都是油、鹽、醬、醋、糖；做好的菜也都是酸、甜、麻、辣、鹹，可是不知道為甚麼，大家都說不同菜系的飯菜味道就是不一樣。

每一個地方除了一般的飯菜以外，還有許多獨特的風味食品。比方說北京的烤鴨、西安的羊肉泡饃、臺灣的蚵仔麵線、四川的麻辣火鍋、天津的狗不理包子、上海的春卷、桂林的炒米粉等等。

這些獨特風味的地方食品，大都是從古代傳下來的。因為它們既好吃又便宜，所以很受歡迎。無論是誰，只要說到熱騰騰的狗不理包子、香噴噴的北京烤鴨以及那又麻又辣的四川火鍋，都會饞得流口水。

雖然每一個地方都有許多不同的飯菜，但是各個地方也有很多相同的食品。

在中國不管你走到哪一個城市，都可以吃到油條豆漿、燒餅稀飯和餃子餛飩。而且過年、過節的時候，不管甚麼地方的人，也都要吃年糕、元宵、月餅和糉子這些節日的食品。

阅 读

中国的饭菜

最早的时候，人们吃饭只是为了生存。那时候只要能把肚子吃饱，至于吃什么、怎么吃都没有什么关系。

后来社会进步了，经济发达了，人们的生活水平提高了，吃饭对于人们来说，已经不只是为了生存，而变成一种生活享受了。这时候人们对吃什么、怎么吃有了很多讲究。人们要求饭菜不仅要有营养，而且还要求色味香俱全。

在中国，饭菜的烹调早已经成为一门学问、一门学科，甚至是一门艺术。中国有许多烹饪学校，还有各种讲解烹调的书。

中国地方很大，东、西、南、北、中，各个地方都有自己不同的烹调方法。人们根据不同的味道，把中国菜分为山东菜、四川菜、湖南菜等八个不同的菜系。

做饭的时候，尽管人们烹调的方法都是蒸、煮、煎、炸、炒；用的都是油、盐、酱、醋、糖；做好的菜也都是酸、甜、麻、辣、咸，可是不知道为什么，大家都说不同菜系的饭菜味道就是不一样。

每一个地方除了一般的饭菜以外，还有许多独特的风味食品。比方说北京的烤鸭、西安的羊肉泡馍、台湾的蚵仔面线、四川的麻辣火锅、天津的狗不理包子、上海的春卷、桂林的炒米粉等等。

这些独特风味的地方食品，大都是从古代传下来的。因为它们既好吃又便宜，所以很受欢迎。无论是谁，只要说到热腾腾的狗不理包子、香喷喷的北京烤鸭以及那又麻又辣的四川火锅，都会馋得流口水。

虽然每一个地方都有许多不同的饭菜，但是各个地方也有很多相同的食品。

在中国不管你走到哪一个城市，都可以吃到油条豆浆、烧饼稀饭和饺子馄饨。而且过年、过节的时候，不管什么地方的人，也都要吃年糕、元宵、月饼和粽子这些节日的食品。

15. 節日的食品

生 詞

生存	生存	shēngcún	v.	survive; live
肚子	肚子	dùzi	n.	stomach
社會	社会	shèhuì	n.	society
進步	进步	jìnbù	v.	advance; progress
享受	享受	xiǎngshòu	n.	enjoyment; pleasure
營養	营养	yíngyǎng	n.	nourishment
色味香	色味香	sè-wèi-xiāng	n.	color, taste and smell
烹調	烹调	pēngtiáo	v.	cook
學科	学科	xuékē	n.	branch of learning
藝術	艺术	yìshù	n.	art
烹飪	烹饪	pēngrèn	n.	cuisine; cooking
味道	味道	wèidao	n.	taste; flavor
山東	山东	Shāndōng		name of a province in China
四川	四川	Sìchuān		name of a province in China
湖南	湖南	Hú'nán		name of a province in China
菜系	菜系	càixì	n.	culinary systems
蒸	蒸	zhēng	v.	steam
煮	煮	zhǔ	v.	boil
煎	煎	jiān	v.	fry
炸	炸	zhá	v.	deep fry
炒	炒	chǎo	v.	stir fry
油	油	yóu	n.	oil
鹽	盐	yán	n.	salt
醬	酱	jiàng	n.	soy sauce
醋	醋	cù	n.	vinegar

酸	酸	suān	adj.	sour
麻	麻	má	adj.	numbing to the mouth
獨特	独特	dútè	adj.	unique
風味	风味	fēngwèi	n.	special flavor; characteristic of a particular place
烤鴨	烤鸭	kǎoyā	n.	roast duck
羊肉泡饃	羊肉泡馍	yángròu pàomó	n.	pancakes cooked in lamb soup
蚵仔麵線	蚵仔面线	kèzǐ miànxiàn	n.	noodles with oyster
天津	天津	Tiānjīn		name of a city in China
狗不理包子	狗不理包子	Gǒubùlǐ bāozi	n.	Goubuli stuffed steam bun
火鍋	火锅	huǒguō	n.	chafing dish
春卷	春卷	chūnjuǎn	n.	spring roll
桂林	桂林	Guìlín		name of a city in China
便宜	便宜	piányi	adj.	cheap
饞	馋	chán	adj.	greedy
流口水	流口水	liú kǒushuǐ		dribble; drool; salivate
油條	油条	yóutiáo	n.	deep-fried dough sticks
豆漿	豆浆	dòujiāng	n.	soy-bean milk
燒餅	烧饼	shāobǐng	n.	sesame seed bun
稀飯	稀饭	xīfàn	n.	rice porridge; gruel
餛飩	馄饨	húntún	n.	wonton

問題

1. 為甚麼很早以前人們不講究吃？
   为什么很早以前人们不讲究吃？

_____

_____ 。

2. 後來人們是怎麼講究吃的？
   后来人们是怎么讲究吃的？
   _____
   _____。

3. 為甚麼說在中國飯菜的烹調成為一門學問？
   为什么说在中国饭菜的烹调成为一门学问？
   _____
   _____。

4. 你知道中國飯菜是怎麼烹調的嗎？
   你知道中国饭菜是怎么烹调的吗？
   _____
   _____。

5. 你知道或者吃過哪些地方小吃？
   你知道或者吃过哪些地方小吃？
   _____
   _____。

6. 不同的地方有哪些相同的食品？
   不同的地方有哪些相同的食品？
   _____
   _____。

附錄

cài dān
菜 單 Menu

tānglèi
湯類 Soups

suānlàtāng
酸辣湯 hot sour soup 1.50

dànhuātāng
蛋花湯 egg drop soup 1.50

hǎixiāntāng
海鮮湯 seafood delight soup 1.50

càilèi
菜類 Dishes

qīngzhēng yú
清蒸魚 steamed fish 15.95

hóngshāo ròu
紅燒肉 pork braised in brown sauce . 8.95

tángcù páigǔ
糖醋排骨 sweet and sour spare ribs . 8.95

Mápó dòufu
麻婆豆腐 Mapo bean curd 6.95

jiāoyán dàxiā
椒鹽大蝦 spiced salt shrimp 12.95

Zuǒgōng jī
左公雞 General Zuo's chicken 9.95

chǎo bōcài
炒菠菜 stir-fried spinach 5.95

zhǔshí
主食 Staple food

mǐfàn
米飯 rice 1.50

jīdàn chǎo mǐfàn
雞蛋炒米飯 egg fried rice 1.50

mántou
饅頭 steamed bun 1.50

fēngwèi xiǎochī
風味小吃 Local flavor snacks

dàndàn miàn
擔擔麵 Sichuan noodles with hot sauce . 4.95

zhá jiàng miàn
炸醬麵 noodles served with fried bean
        sauce and minced meat 4.95

xiǎolóng bāozi
小籠包子 steamed stuffed bun 6.95

yángròu guōtiē
羊肉鍋貼 fried mutton dumplings ... 6.95

xiānròu húntún
鮮肉餛飩 pork wonton 4.95

jiǔshuǐ
酒水 Beverages

lùchá	Qīngdǎo pí jiǔ	Máotái jiǔ
綠茶	青島啤酒	茅臺酒
green tea	Qingdao beer	Maotai
2.00	7.00	500.00

15. 節日的食品

附 录

cài dān
菜 单 Menu

tānglèi
汤类　Soups

suānlà tāng
酸辣汤 hot sour soup......................1.50

dànhuā tāng
蛋花汤 egg drop soup.....................1.50

hǎixiān tāng
海鲜汤 seafood delight soup.........1.50

càilèi
菜类　Dishes

qīngzhēng yú
清蒸鱼 steamed fish......................15.95

hóngshāo ròu
红烧肉 pork braised in brown sauce.8.95

tángcù páigǔ
糖醋排骨 sweet and sour spare ribs.8.95

Mápó dòufu
麻婆豆腐 Mapo bean curd............6.95

jiāoyán dàxiā
椒盐大虾 spiced salt shrimp........12.95

Zuǒgōng jī
左公鸡 General Zuo's chicken.......9.95

chǎo bōcài
炒菠菜 stir-fried spinach................5.95

zhǔshí
主食　Staple food

mǐfàn
米饭 rice...1.50

jīdàn chǎo mǐfàn
鸡蛋炒米饭 egg fried rice.................1.50

mántou
馒头 steamed bun............................1.50

fēngwèi xiǎochī
风味小吃　Local flavor snacks

dàndàn miàn
担担面 Sichuan noodles with hot sauce.4.95

zhá jiàng miàn
炸酱面 noodles served with fried bean sauce and minced meat........4.95

xiǎolóng bāozi
小笼包子 steamed stuffed bun.........6.95

yángròu guōtiē
羊肉锅贴 fried mutton dumplings....6.95

xiānròu húntún
鲜肉馄饨 pork wonton......................4.95

jiǔshuǐ
酒水　Beverages

lùchá	Qīngdǎo pí jiǔ	Máotái jiǔ
绿茶	青岛啤酒	茅台酒
green tea	Qingdao beer	Maotai
2.00	7.00	500.00

16

到中國旅遊
Touring Around China

學習大綱

通過學習本課，學生應該能夠：

1. 掌握這些句型和詞語的意思和用法："之前、之後、之中"、"以北、以南"、"不要說……，就是……也"、"……得V也V不Adj"、"不妨"、"沿著"、"使得"。
2. 認識和運用課文以及閱讀文章內的生詞。
3. 了解中國的幾個旅遊名城：北京、西安、桂林、上海，以及這些城市的特色。
4. 簡單了解旅客在中國看病時要留意的事情。

Study Outline

After studying this chapter, students should:

1. Have a good command of the meaning and usage of these sentence patterns and terms: "zhīqián, zhīhòu, zhīzhōng" (before, after, within), "yǐ béi, yǐ nán" ([to the] north of, [to the] south of), "bùyàoshuō ... jiùshì ... yě" (even if ... still, not to mention), "... de V yě V bu Adj" (degree complement), "bùfáng" (may [as well]; might [as well]), "yán zhe" (along), "shǐde" (make; cause; render).
2. Be familiar with the meaning and usage of the vocabulary introduced in the text and the reading.
3. Know about the most famous cities in China: Beijing, Xi'an, Guilin and Shanghai, and the tourist points of interest there.
4. Know something of what a tourist should pay attention to when seeing a doctor in China .

課文

到中國去旅遊的人，第一個要去的地方就是北京。

北京是中國的首都，在這之前也是清朝的首都。北京保存着許多像故宮、頤和園那樣的清朝皇宮的遺址。在北京以北不遠的地方，還有聞名於世界的萬里長城。所以，不要說是外國人了，就是中國人也喜歡到北京去旅遊。

接下來人們要去的地方是西安。西安是一座非常有名的古城，因為她曾經是周、秦、漢、唐等十三個朝代的首都，所以西安的名勝古蹟多得數也數不清。

在西安你可以去參觀六千年前的半坡村遺址，你也可以去看兩千年前的秦代兵馬俑和一千多年前的唐代大雁塔。如果你還有興趣，不妨登上五百年前的明代城牆，沿着城牆仔細地看一看古城西安。在西安不僅能看到各個時代的名勝古蹟，而且還能欣賞到唐代的音樂歌舞。

遊完了北京和西安之後，很多人都要坐飛機去桂林。桂林是中國最漂亮的城市。整個桂林城就在青山綠水的懷抱之中，清澈的灕江靜靜地從桂林流過，江水中倒映出兩岸秀麗的山峰。

桂林城裏有許多像大樹一樣的石峰，石峰之間是一片片像鏡子一樣的小湖。有的石峰下還有洞穴，洞穴裏有美麗的鐘乳石，有彎彎的小河流。大自然的風光把桂林打扮得非常漂亮。幾乎所有到中國的人，都會去看一看如詩如畫的桂林。

到中國旅遊的人，最後要去的是被稱作"購物天堂"的大上海。

上海是中國最大、最繁華、最熱鬧的城市。這十幾年來的改革開放使得上海更加繁華熱鬧了。尤其是十里長的南京路，那裏高樓入雲、商店林立、遊人如潮。每當夜晚到來的時候，整個南京路就是一片霓虹燈的海洋。馬上就要回家的外國人最喜歡逛的是上海的夜市，在那裏，他們可以買到許多又好又便宜的禮物，帶回去送給他們的家人和朋友。

课文

到中国去旅游的人，第一个要去的地方就是北京。

北京是中国的首都，在这之前也是清朝的首都。北京保存着许多像故宫、颐和园那样的清朝皇宫的遗址。在北京以北不远的地方，还有闻名于世界的万里长城。所以，不要说是外国人了，就是中国人也喜欢到北京去旅游。

接下来人们要去的地方是西安。西安是一座非常有名的古城，因为她曾经是周、秦、汉、唐等十三个朝代的首都，所以西安的名胜古迹多得数也数不清。

在西安你可以去参观六千年前的半坡村遗址，你也可以去看两千年前的秦代兵马俑和一千多年前的唐代大雁塔。如果你还有兴趣，不妨登上五百年前的明代城墙，沿着城墙仔细地看一看古城西安。在西安不仅能看到各个时代的名胜古迹，而且还能欣赏到唐代的音乐歌舞。

游完了北京和西安之后，很多人都要坐飞机去桂林。桂林是中国最漂亮的城市。整个桂林城就在青山绿水的怀抱之中，清澈的漓江静静地从桂林流过，江水中倒映出两岸秀丽的山峰。

桂林城里有许多像大树一样的石峰，石峰之间是一片片像镜子一样的小湖。有的石峰下还有洞穴，洞穴里有美丽的钟乳石，有弯弯的小河流。大自然的风光把桂林打扮得非常漂亮。几乎所有到中国的人，都会去看一看如诗如画的桂林。

到中国旅游的人，最后要去的是被称作"购物天堂"的大上海。

上海是中国最大、最繁华、最热闹的城市。这十几年来的改革开放使得上海更加繁华热闹了。尤其是十里长的南京路，那里高楼入云、商店林立、游人如潮。每当夜晚到来的时候，整个南京路就是一片霓虹灯的海洋。马上就要回家的外国人最喜欢逛的是上海的夜市，在那里，他们可以买到许多又好又便宜的礼物，带回去送给他们的家人和朋友。

生詞

旅遊	旅游	lǚyóu	v.	travel
之前	之前	zhī qián		before
故宮	故宫	Gùgōng		Forbidden City; Palace Museum
頤和園	颐和园	Yíhé Yuán		the Summer Palace
皇宮	皇宫	huánggōng	n.	palace
遺址	遗址	yízhǐ	n.	ruins; relics
聞名	闻名	wénmíng	adj.	well-known
接下來	接下来	jiēxiàlái		follow; go on (with)
周	周	Zhōu		the Zhou dynasty (1122–221 B.C.)
名勝古蹟	名胜古迹	míngshèng-gǔ jī		famous historic and cultural sites
數不清	数不清	shǔbùqīng		incalculable; numerous
參觀	参观	cānguān	v.	visit; look around
半坡村	半坡村	Bànpōcūn		the Banpo village in Xi'an
兵馬俑	兵马俑	Bīngmǎyǒng		clay figures of warriors and horses buried with the dead; terra-cotta soldiers and horses
大雁塔	大雁塔	Dàyàn Tǎ		Big Wild Goose Pagoda
不妨	不妨	bùfáng	adv.	may(as well); might (as well)
登	登	dēng	v.	step on; ascend; climb
欣賞	欣赏	xīnshǎng	v.	enjoy; admire
青山綠水	青山绿水	qīngshān-lǜshuǐ		blue hills and green rivers
懷抱	怀抱	huáibào	v.	embrace
清澈	清澈	qīngchè	adj.	limpid
灕江	漓江	Lí Jiāng		the Li River

倒映	倒映	dàoyìng		inverted reflection in water
秀麗	秀丽	xiùlì	adj.	delicate; graceful
石峰	石峰	shífēng	n.	rock peaks
鏡子	镜子	jìngzi	n.	mirror
洞穴	洞穴	dòngxué	n.	cave; cavern
鐘乳石	钟乳石	zhōngrǔshí	n.	stalactite
大自然	大自然	dàzìrán	n.	nature
風光	风光	fēngguāng	n.	sight; scene
如詩如畫	如诗如画	rúshī-rúhuà		as beautiful as a poem or a painting
購物	购物	gòu wù		shopping
天堂	天堂	tiāntáng	n.	heaven
繁華	繁华	fánhuá	adj.	bustling; flourishing
熱鬧	热闹	rè'nào	adj.	lively
使得	使得	shǐde	v.	make; cause; render
南京路	南京路	Nánjīng Lù		Nanjing Road
商店	商店	shāngdiàn	n.	store
林立	林立	línlì		stand in great number (like trees in a forest)
遊人如潮	游人如潮	yóurénrúcháo		many visitors like a tide
霓虹燈	霓虹灯	níhóngdēng	n.	neon light
海洋	海洋	hǎiyáng	n.	sea
逛	逛	guàng	v.	stroll
夜市	夜市	yèshì	n.	night fair; night market

語法和詞語註釋

一、之前、之後、之中　　before, after, within

> "之", when followed by nouns such as "前", "後", "中", indicates a particular time or location relative to another.

1. 北京是中國現在的首都，在這之前也是清朝的首都。
   北京是中国现在的首都，在这之前也是清朝的首都。
   Beijing is the current capital of China. Previously, it was also the capital of the Qing dynasty.

2. 每天睡覺之前，我都要洗一個熱水澡。
   每天睡觉之前，我都要洗一个热水澡。
   Every day, before going to bed, I like to take a hot bath.

3. 遊覽完北京、西安之後，許多人都要去桂林。
   游览完北京、西安之后，许多人都要去桂林。
   After visiting Beijing and Xi'an, many people like to go to Guilin.

4. 吃了止疼藥之後，我的頭不疼了。
   吃了止疼药之后，我的头不疼了。
   After I took the pain-killer, my headache went away.

5. 桂林整個城市都是在青山綠水的懷抱之中。
   桂林整个城市都是在青山绿水的怀抱之中。
   The entire city of Guilin is embraced by blue mountains and green rivers.

二、以北、以南　　(to the) north of, (to the) south of

> "以" is followed by location nouns, such as "北", "南", to indicate a particular location in relation to another.

1. 北京以北不遠的地方有世界有名的長城。
   北京以北不远的地方有世界有名的长城。
   The world-famous Great Wall is close to the north of Beijing.

2. 中國的南方是指長江以南的地方。

中国的南方是指长江以南的地方。

"South China" means places which are south of the Yangtze River.

3. 桂林在西安以南。

桂林在西安以南。

Guilin is south of Xi'an.

三、不要說……，就是……也　　even if ... still, not to mention

"不要說……，就是……也" implies a concession of some sort.

1. 不要說是外國人了，就是中國人也喜歡到北京去旅遊。

不要说是外国人了，就是中国人也喜欢到北京去旅游。

Even Chinese people like to tour Beijing, not to mention foreigners.

2. 不要說我不知道，就是我知道也不能告訴你。

不要说我不知道，就是我知道也不能告诉你。

I don't know, but even if I did I couldn't tell you.

3. 不要說是你的話我不聽，就是我爸爸媽媽的話我也不聽。

不要说是你的话我不听，就是我爸爸妈妈的话我也不听。

It's not just you I won't listen to, I won't even listen to my parents.

四、……得 V 也 V 不 Adj　　degree complement

This pattern is used to indicate that an action does not arrive at the result you expected, no matter what you do.

1. 西安的名勝古蹟多得數也數不清。

西安的名胜古迹多得数也数不清。

Xi'an's famous historic and cultural sites are too numerous to count.

2. 中文課的作業多得做也做不完。

中文课的作业多得做也做不完。

There is so much Chinese homework that I'll never get it done.

3. 衣服太髒了，(髒得) 我怎麼洗也洗不乾淨。

衣服太脏了，(脏得) 我怎么洗也洗不干净。

The clothes are so dirty that I can't wash them clean no matter how hard I try.

五、不妨　　may (as well); might (as well); no harm in V-ing

1. 如果你有興趣，不妨沿着五百年前的明代城牆走一圈。

如果你有兴趣，不妨沿着五百年前的明代城墙走一圈。

If you are interested, you may take a walk along the five hundred year old Ming dynasty city wall.

2. 聽說中文課不是很難，你不妨去試一試。

听说中文课不是很难，你不妨去试一试。

I gather that the Chinese class is not very difficult. You may have a try.

3. 要是你不着急的話，不妨再陪我坐一會兒。

要是你不着急的话，不妨再陪我坐一会儿。

If you are not in a hurry, you may sit with me for a little longer.

六、沿着　　along

1. 你也可以沿着城牆仔細地看一看古城西安。

你也可以沿着城墙仔细地看一看古城西安。

You can walk along the city wall and take a look at the old city of Xi'an.

2. 我早上起來喜歡沿着小湖跑步。

我早上起来喜欢沿着小湖跑步。

After getting up in the morning, I like jogging along beside the small lake.

3. 我想去中國沿着長城從東到西走一次。

我想去中国沿着长城从东到西走一次。

I want to go to China and walk along the Great Wall from the east to the west.

七、使得　　make; cause; render

"使得" is equivalent to "to make" or "to cause" in English, but is chiefly used in written language.

1. 這十幾年來的改革開放，使得上海更加繁華熱鬧了。

   这十几年来的改革开放，使得上海更加繁华热闹了。

   The reforms and opening of the last ten years or so have made Shanghai an even more flourishing city.

2. 小王的女朋友使得他整天坐立不安。

   小王的女朋友使得他整天坐立不安。

   Xiao Wang's girlfriend makes him restless all day.

3. 發燒使得我一點兒力氣都沒有。

   发烧使得我一点儿力气都没有。

   The fever made me feel I had no strength left.

練 習

一、從課文中找出描寫這四個城市的詞語

北京　北京	西安　西安	桂林　桂林	上海　上海

二、用一段話來比較這四個城市之間相同和不同的地方

_____

_____

_____。

三、用所給的詞語回答問題

1. A：你甚麼時候預習課文？（之前）

      你什么时候预习课文？（之前）

   B：_____。

2. A：你甚麼時候覺得家裏的飯菜好吃？（之後）
   你什么时候觉得家里的饭菜好吃？（之后）
   B：_____。

3. A：老師，還有半個小時，我要不要做翻譯題呢？（不妨）
   老师，还有半个小时，我要不要做翻译题呢？（不妨）
   B：_____。

4. A：你每天都在哪裏跑步？（沿着）
   你每天都在哪里跑步？（沿着）
   B：_____。

5. A：聽說你有很多錢，能不能借給我一些？（不要說……就是……也）
   听说你有很多钱，能不能借给我一些？（不要说……就是……也）
   B：_____。

四、翻譯

1. The nature scenery of Guilin makes it so beautiful that even Chinese people like to go there, not to mention foreigners. The views are as lovely as a poem or a painting.

   _____
   _____
   _____。

2. Xi'an has so many famous historic and cultural sites that some foreign travelers can feel puzzled about which dynasty the historic site they're visiting belongs to.

   _____
   _____
   _____。

3. If you have time tonight, you might stroll around the Nanjing Road, where

you will see how flourishing the Shanghai night-market is.

_____
_____
_____ 。

五、根據課文回答問題

1. 到中國旅遊的人喜歡去甚麼地方？
   到中国旅游的人喜欢去什么地方？
   _____
   _____ 。

2. 在西安可以看到甚麼？
   在西安可以看到什么？
   _____
   _____ 。

3. 為甚麼説桂林是一個漂亮美麗的城市？
   为什么说桂林是一个漂亮美丽的城市？
   _____
   _____ 。

4. 南京路是一條甚麼樣的大街？
   南京路是一条什么样的大街？
   _____
   _____ 。

5. 人們為甚麼最後去上海？
   人们为什么最后去上海？
   _____
   _____ 。

六、課堂討論

人們為甚麼喜歡旅遊?
人们为什么喜欢旅游?

_____
_____
_____ 。

七、小作文

描寫一個你旅遊過的地方或者你喜歡的地方。
描写一个你旅游过的地方或者你喜欢的地方。

_____
_____
_____
_____
_____
_____ 。

閱讀

在醫院看病

在中國旅遊的時候很可能會生病，不過在中國看病要比在美國方便多了。只要你覺得哪兒不舒服，隨時都可以去醫院門診部掛號看病。

醫院把不同的病分成不同的科，掛號的時候，你得知道你的病是屬於哪一個科。

一般來說，眼睛的病是眼科。嘴裏面的病是口腔科。感冒、發燒、咳嗽、拉肚子是內科。頭摔破了、手割破了是外科。腳崴了、腿斷了要去看骨科。身上長了許多疙瘩、皮膚癢得難受，那你就得去看皮膚科。當然如果是急病，不管甚麼科，也不用掛號，直接去急診室就可以了。

有些科的名字很奇怪，如傳染科、計劃生育科甚麼的。傳染科是治療肝炎、痢疾那些傳染病的。計劃生育科是專門做避孕和墮胎手術的。

中國人覺得墮胎這個詞不好聽，於是就把墮胎叫做"人流"，也就是人工流產的意思。中國一直都在推行一家一個孩子的計劃生育政策，這樣使得許多已經有了孩子的人，就要去醫院做節育手術。而且，如果她們不小心又懷孕了的話，那也一定要到醫院去做人流。

看病的時候，醫生可能要你去檢驗科化驗大小便或者血液，也可能要你去放射科透視或拍片。看完病之後，拿上醫生給你的藥方，先要去劃價處劃價，然後去收費處交錢，最後才可以去藥房取藥。

吃藥之前要仔細地讀一下藥瓶上的說明。藥瓶上寫的都是書面語，吃的藥上面寫着"口服"，皮膚外面用的藥寫着"外用"。外用藥不可以口服，有的外用藥吃下去會有危險，所以，這些藥的藥瓶上都特別注明了"切忌口服"，意思是說絕對不能吃下去。

如果看不懂那些說明，不妨去問問醫生。有些說明不要說外國人，就是中國人也常常弄不明白。以前有一幅漫畫，畫的是一個人拿了一瓶外用藥，上面寫着"切忌口服"。這個人認識的字不多，他只認識"口服"，不認識"切忌"，結果把絕對不能口服的藥喝進肚子裏去了。

阅读

在医院看病

在中国旅游的时候很可能会生病，不过在中国看病要比在美国方便多了。只要你觉得哪儿不舒服，随时都可以去医院门诊部挂号看病。

医院把不同的病分成不同的科，挂号的时候，你得知道你的病是属于哪一个科。

一般来说，眼睛的病是眼科。嘴里面的病是口腔科。感冒、发烧、咳嗽、拉肚子是内科。头摔破了、手割破了是外科。脚崴了、腿断了要去看骨科。身上长了许多疙瘩、皮肤痒得难受，那你就得去看皮肤科。当然如果是急病，不管什么科，也不用挂号，直接去急诊室就可以了。

有些科的名字很奇怪，如传染科、计划生育科什么的。传染科是治疗肝炎、痢疾那些传染病的。计划生育科是专门做避孕和堕胎手术的。

中国人觉得堕胎这个词不好听，于是就把堕胎叫做"人流"，也就是人工流产的意思。中国一直都在推行一家一个孩子的计划生育政策，这样使得许多已经有了孩子的人，就要去医院做节育手术。而且，如果她们不小心又怀孕了的话，那也一定要到医院去做人流。

看病的时候，医生可能要你去检验科化验大小便或者血液，也可能要你去放射科透视或拍片。看完病之后，拿上医生给你的药方，先要去划价处划价，然后去收费处交钱，最后才可以去药房取药。

吃药之前要仔细地读一下药瓶上的说明。药瓶上写的都是书面语，吃的药上面写着"口服"，皮肤外面用的药写着"外用"。外用药不可以口服，有的外用药吃下去会有危险，所以，这些药的药瓶上都特别注明了"切忌口服"，意思是说绝对不能吃下去。

如果看不懂那些说明，不妨去问问医生。有些说明不要说外国人，就是中国人也常常弄不明白。以前有一幅漫画，画的是一个人拿了一瓶外用药，上面写着"切忌口服"。这个人认识的字不多，他只认识"口服"，不认识"切忌"，结果把绝对不能口服的药喝进肚子里去了。

16. 到中國旅遊

生 詞

隨時	随时	suíshí	adv.	at any time
門診部	门诊部	ménzhěnbù	n.	out-patient department
掛號	挂号	guà hào		register
屬於	属于	shǔyú	v.	be part of; belong to
科	科	kē	n.	section
口腔科	口腔科	kǒuqiāngkē	n.	(department of) stomatology
眼睛	眼睛	yǎnjīng	n.	eye
感冒	感冒	gǎnmào	n.	catch a cold
發燒	发烧	fā shāo		have a temperature
咳嗽	咳嗽	késou	v.	cough
拉肚子	拉肚子	lā dùzi		have loose bowels; diarrhea
內科	内科	nèikē	n.	(department of) internal medicine
摔	摔	shuāi	v.	fall; lose one's balance
破	破	pò	v.	break
割	割	gē	v.	cut
外科	外科	wàikē	n.	surgical department
崴	崴	wǎi	v.	sprain
斷	断	duàn	v.	break
骨科	骨科	gǔkē	n.	(department of) orthopedics
疙瘩	疙瘩	gēda	n.	pimple; spots
皮膚	皮肤	pífū	n.	skin
癢	痒	yǎng	v.	itch; tickle
直接	直接	zhíjiē	adj.	directly
急病	急病	jí bìng		acute disease
急診室	急诊室	jízhěnshì	n.	emergency treatment room

傳染	传染	chuánrǎn	v.	infect
肝炎	肝炎	gānyán	n.	hepatitis
痢疾	痢疾	lìji	n.	dysentery
墮胎	堕胎	duò tāi		induced abortion
手術	手术	shǒushù	v.	surgery
人工流產	人工流产	réngōng liúchǎn		induced abortion
懷孕	怀孕	huái yùn		pregnant
檢驗科	检验科	jiǎnyànkē	n.	laboratory
化驗	化验	huàyàn	v.	laboratory test
大小便	大小便	dà-xiǎobiàn	n.	stool and urine
血液	血液	xuèyè	n.	blood
透視	透视	tòushì	v.	X-ray
拍片	拍片	pāi piàn		take X-ray
放射科	放射科	fàngshèkē	n.	X-ray department
藥方	药方	yàofāng	n.	prescription
劃價處	划价处	huà jiàchù	n.	pricing department
收費處	收费处	shōufèichù	n.	cashier
交	交	jiāo	v.	pay
藥房	药房	yàofáng	n.	pharmacy
藥瓶	药瓶	yàopíng	n.	drug bottle
書面語	书面语	shūmiànyǔ	n.	written language
口服	口服	kǒufú		take orally
外用	外用	wàiyòng		external use
危險	危险	wēixiǎn	adj.	dangerous
絕對	绝对	juéduì	adj.	absolute
切忌	切忌	qiè jì	v.	avoid by all means
漫畫	漫画	mànhuà	n.	cartoon

問 題

1. 為甚麼說在中國看病比在美國方便多了？
   为什么说在中国看病比在美国方便多了？
   _____
   _____ 。

2. 為甚麼掛號的時候你要知道你的病是屬於哪一科？
   为什么挂号的时候你要知道你的病是属于哪一科？
   _____
   _____ 。

3. 甚麼人要做避孕和墮胎手術？
   什么人要做避孕和堕胎手术？
   _____
   _____ 。

4. 取藥的時候你要注意甚麼？
   取药的时候你要注意什么？
   _____
   _____ 。

5. "口服"和"外用"是甚麼意思？
   "口服"和"外用"是什么意思？
   _____
   _____ 。

6. 那幅漫畫說的是甚麼故事？
   那幅漫画说的是什么故事？
   _____
   _____ 。

附錄一

中國各省、自治區、特別行政區以及主要城市簡表
中国各省、自治区、特别行政区以及主要城市简表

省	省	shěng	province	市	市	shì	city
				北京	北京	Běijīng	Beijing
				上海	上海	Shànghǎi	Shanghai
				天津	天津	Tiānjīn	Tianjin
				重慶	重庆	Chóngqìng	Chongqing
河北	河北	Héběi	Hebei	石家莊	石家庄	Shíjiāzhuāng	Shijiazhuang
河南	河南	Hénán	Henan	鄭州	郑州	Zhèngzhōu	Zhengzhou
湖北	湖北	Húběi	Hubei	武漢	武汉	Wǔhàn	Wuhan
湖南	湖南	Húnán	Hunan	長沙	长沙	Chángshā	Changsha
山西	山西	Shānxī	Shanxi	太原	太原	Tàiyuán	Taiyuan
陝西	陕西	Shǎnxī	Shaanxi	西安	西安	Xī'ān	Xi'an
山東	山东	Shāndōng	Shandong	濟南	济南	Jǐnán	Jinan
廣東	广东	Guǎngdōng	Guangdong	廣州	广州	Guǎngzhōu	Guangzhou
江蘇	江苏	Jiāngsū	Jiangsu	南京	南京	Nánjīng	Nanjing
安徽	安徽	Ānhuī	Anhui	合肥	合肥	Héféi	Hefei
浙江	浙江	Zhèjiāng	Zhejiang	杭州	杭州	Hángzhōu	Hángzou
江西	江西	Jiāngxī	Jiangxi	南昌	南昌	Nánchāng	Nanchang
福建	福建	Fújiàn	Fujian	福州	福州	Fúzhōu	Fuzhou
臺灣	台湾	Táiwān	Taiwan	臺北	台北	Táiběi	Taibei
甘肅	甘肃	Gānsù	Gansu	蘭州	兰州	Lánzhōu	Lanzhou
青海	青海	Qīnghǎi	Qinghai	西寧	西宁	Xīníng	Xining
四川	四川	Sìchuān	Sichuan	成都	成都	Chéngdū	Chengdu
貴州	贵州	Guìzhōu	Guizhou	貴陽	贵阳	Guìyáng	Guiyang
雲南	云南	Yúnnán	Yunnan	昆明	昆明	Kūnmíng	Kunming
海南	海南	Hǎinán	Hainan	海口	海口	Hǎikǒu	Haikou
遼寧	辽宁	Liáoníng	Liaoning	瀋陽	沈阳	Shěnyáng	Shenyang
吉林	吉林	Jílín	Jilin	長春	长春	Chángchūn	Changchun

| 黑龍江 | 黑龙江 | Hēilóngjiāng | Heilongjiang | 哈爾濱 | 哈尔滨 | Hā'ěrbīn | Harbin |

自治區	自治区	**zìzhìqū**	**autonomous region**				
西藏	西藏	Xīzàng	Xizang; Tibet	拉薩	拉萨	Lāsà	Lhasa
廣西	广西	Guǎngxī	Guangxi	南寧	南宁	Nánníng	Nanning
寧夏	宁夏	Níngxià	Ningxia	銀川	银川	Yínchuān	Yinchuan
新疆	新疆	Xīnjiāng	Xinjiang	烏魯木齊	乌鲁木齐	Wūlǔmùqí	Ürümqi
內蒙古	内蒙古	Nèiménggǔ	Nei Mongol	呼和浩特	呼和浩特	Hūhéhàotè	Huhhot

特別行政區	特别行政区	**tèbié xíngzhèngqū**	**special administrative region**
香港	香港	Xiānggǎng	Hong Kong
澳門	澳门	Àomén	Macau

附錄二

常見病及其相關詞語
常见病及其相关词语

繁體	简体	拼音	英文
頭疼	头疼	tóu téng	headache
頭暈 (昏)	头晕 (昏)	tóu yūn (hūn)	dizzy
惡心	恶心	ě xīn	nausea
嘔吐	呕吐	ǒu tù	vomit
流鼻涕	流鼻涕	liú bítì	have a running nose
鼻塞	鼻塞	bísāi	snuffle
嗓子疼	嗓子疼	sǎngzi téng	sore throat
牙疼	牙疼	yá téng	toothache
膝蓋疼	膝盖疼	xīgài téng	knee pain
關節疼	关节疼	guān jié téng	joint pain
肚子疼	肚子疼	dùzi téng	abdomen pain
胃疼	胃疼	wèi téng	stomach pain
胸疼	胸疼	xiōng téng	chest pain
背疼	背疼	bèi téng	back pain
腰疼	腰疼	yāo téng	lower back pain
抽筋	抽筋	chōu jīn	cramp
過敏	过敏	guòmǐn	allergy
哮喘	哮喘	xiàochuǎn	asthma
便秘	便秘	biànbì	constipation
暈車 (船)	晕车 (船)	yùn chē (chuán)	carsickness (seasickness)
醉	醉	zuì	drunk
酒精中毒	酒精中毒	jiǔ jīng zhòngdú	alcoholic poisoning
食物中毒	食物中毒	shíwù zhòngdú	food poisoning
受傷	受伤	shòu shāng	be injured; be wounded

流血	流血	liú xuè	bleed; shed blood
止血	止血	zhǐ xuè	stanch bleeding
中暑	中暑	zhòngshǔ	heatstroke; calenture
昏迷	昏迷	hūnmí	stupor
人工呼吸	人工呼吸	réngōng hūxī	artificial respiration
水土不服	水土不服	shuǐtǔ bùfú	the climate does not suit one
注射	注射	zhùshè	injection
按摩	按摩	ànmó	massage
針灸	针灸	zhēn jiǔ	acupuncture
消毒	消毒	xiāo dú	disinfect
包紮	包扎	bāozā	wrap up
創口貼	创口贴	chuāngkǒutiē	band-aid

神話故事
Myths and Folklore

學習大綱

通過學習本課，學生應該能夠：

1. 掌握這些句型和詞語的意思和用法："明明"、"憑"、"寧可……也"、"才"、"越……越"、"不如"、"怎麼"和"為甚麼"。
2. 認識和運用課文以及閱讀文章內的生詞。
3. 學到"愚公移山"的故事。
4. 學到有關相思樹和相思鳥的故事。

Study Outline

After studying this chapter, students should:

1. Have a good command of the meaning and usage of these sentence patterns and terms: "míngmíng" (it is obvious that), "píng" (depend on; lean on), "níngkě ... yě" (would rather; had better), "cái" (as an intensifier), "yuè ... yuè" (the more ..., the more), "bùrú" (not as good as), "zěnme" and "weìshénme" (how come; why).
2. Be familiar with the meaning and usage of the vocabulary introduced in the text and the reading.
3. Be familiar with the Chinese fable "The Foolish Old Man Who Removed the Mountain".
4. Learn the Chinese fables about the "loving trees" and the "loving birds".

課文

　　中國有許多神話故事，這些故事都是人們根據自己的想像編造出來的，例如我們前面學過的牛郎織女的故事。

　　神話故事裏面的人物在現實生活中是絕對沒有的，故事裏面的事情在現實生活中也是根本不可能發生的。也不知道為甚麼，人們明明知道這些故事是編造出來的，可是大家都還是喜歡講、喜歡聽。

　　神話故事流傳了千百年了。千百年來，人們一代又一代地重複着這些古老的故事。人們講的最多的、大家最熟悉的，除了牛郎織女的故事以外，就是愚公移山的故事了。

　　愚公移山是說一個叫愚公的老人，他帶領着兒孫們要把擋在家門口的兩座大山搬走。愚公家的隔壁住着一位寡婦，她每天都帶着孩子來幫忙。愚公的對門住着一個叫智叟的老人，他不但不來幫忙，反而笑話愚公說："您真是老糊塗了啊！您都快九十歲了，憑你們這幾個人怎麼能夠搬得走這兩座大山呢？我寧可一輩子不出門，也不做這種傻事。"

　　愚公回答說："您才是老糊塗了啊！您呀，越老越笨，笨得連那小孩子都不如。您想想，我年紀雖然很大了，可是我還有兒子，有孫子，子子孫孫是無窮盡的。這兩座山雖然很高，但它卻不會再增高了。只要我們不停地挖下去，為甚麼會搬不走呢？"

　　這件事被上帝知道了。上帝被愚公的精神感動了，於是他就派了兩個大力士把兩座大山揹走了。

　　人們喜歡神話故事，是因為人們在故事裏面寄托着自己的希望。有的人希望自己能像故事裏的人物那樣聰明、勇敢，做出一些驚天動地的大事情；有的人希望自己能像故事裏說的那樣，和自己心愛的人在一起幸福地生活。

　　在日常生活中，人們總是會遇到這樣那樣的困難，而這些古老的神話故事，可以讓人們在和困難做鬥爭的時候，感受到一股力量，感受到一個希望，感受到一份信心。

课文

中国有许多神话故事，这些故事都是人们根据自己的想象编造出来的，例如我们前面学过的牛郎织女的故事。

神话故事里面的人物在现实生活中是绝对没有的，故事里面的事情在现实生活中也是根本不可能发生的。也不知道为什么，人们明明知道这些故事是编造出来的，可是大家都还是喜欢讲、喜欢听。

神话故事流传了千百年了。千百年来，人们一代又一代地重复着这些古老的故事。人们讲的最多的、大家最熟悉的，除了牛郎织女的故事以外，就是愚公移山的故事了。

愚公移山是说一个叫愚公的老人，他带领着儿孙们要把挡在家门口的两座大山搬走。愚公家的隔壁住着一位寡妇，她每天都带着孩子来帮忙。愚公的对门住着一个叫智叟的老人，他不但不来帮忙，反而笑话愚公说："您真是老糊涂了啊！您都快九十岁了，凭你们这几个人怎么能够搬得走这两座大山呢？我宁可一辈子不出门，也不做这种傻事。"

愚公回答说："您才是老糊涂了啊！您呀，越老越笨，笨得连那小孩子都不如。您想想，我年纪虽然很大了，可是我还有儿子，有孙子，子子孙孙是无穷尽的。这两座山虽然很高，但它却不会再增高了。只要我们不停地挖下去，为什么会搬不走呢？"

这件事被上帝知道了。上帝被愚公的精神感动了，于是他就派了两个大力士把两座大山背走了。

人们喜欢神话故事，是因为人们在故事里面寄托着自己的希望。有的人希望自己能像故事里的人物那样聪明、勇敢，做出一些惊天动地的大事情；有的人希望自己能像故事里说的那样，和自己心爱的人在一起幸福地生活。

在日常生活中，人们总是会遇到这样那样的困难，而这些古老的神话故事，可以让人们在和困难做斗争的时候，感受到一股力量，感受到一个希望，感受到一份信心。

生 詞

繁體	简体	拼音	詞性	英文
神話	神话	shénhuà	n.	myth; fairy tale
想像	想象	xiǎngxiàng	v.	imagine
編造	编造	biānzào	v.	make up
現實	现实	xiànshí	n.	real; actual
明明	明明	míngmíng	adv.	obviously; plainly
重複	重复	chóngfù	v.	repeat
愚公移山	愚公移山	Yúgōng-yíshān		the Foolish Old Man removed the mountains
兒孫	儿孙	érsūn	n.	children and grandchildren
擋	挡	dǎng	v.	block
搬走	搬走	bānzǒu		take away
隔壁	隔壁	gébì	n.	next door
寡婦	寡妇	guǎfu	n.	widow
對門	对门	duìmén	n.	the house opposite
智叟	智叟	Zhìsǒu		the Wise Old Man
傻	傻	shǎ	adj.	stupid; foolish
憑	凭	píng	prep.	depend on; lean on
寧可……也	宁可……也	nìngkě ... yě	conj.	would rather; had better
不如	不如	bùrú		not as good as
無窮盡	无穷尽	wúqióng jìn		endless; inexhaustible
增高	增高	zēnggāo		heighten; raise
件	件	jiàn	m.	measure word: piece, article, etc.
上帝	上帝	Shàngdì		God
感動	感动	gǎndòng	v.	move

派	派	pài	v.	send
大力士	大力士	dàlìshì	n.	a man of unusual strength
勇敢	勇敢	yǒnggǎn	adj.	brave
驚天動地	惊天动地	jīngtiān-dòngdì		world-shaking
古老	古老	gǔlǎo	adj.	ancient
鬥爭	斗争	dòuzhēng	v.	struggle; fight
感受	感受	gǎnshòu	v.	feel
股	股	gǔ	m.	measure word for strength
力量	力量	lìliang	n.	strength
份	份	fèn	m.	measure word for confidence
信心	信心	xìnxīn	n.	confidence

語法和詞語註釋

一、明明　　it is obvious that

> "明明" is used after the subject to indicate that an action or situation is contrary to people's beliefs or expectations.

1. 人們明明知道這些故事是編造出來的，可是大家還是喜歡講、喜歡聽。
   人们明明知道这些故事是编造出来的，可是大家还是喜欢讲、喜欢听。
   People undoubtedly know that these are made-up stories, but everyone still likes to tell them and listen to them.

2. 湯姆明明知道小燕有男朋友，可是還是要請小燕去看電影。
   汤姆明明知道小燕有男朋友，可是还是要请小燕去看电影。
   Tom obviously knows Xiaoyan has a boyfriend, but he is still going to invite her to go to the movies with him.

3. 你明明知道這個題的答案，為甚麼不告訴我？
   你明明知道这个题的答案，为什么不告诉我？
   You obviously know the answer to this question. Why didn't you tell me?

二、憑　depend on; lean on

1. 憑你們這幾個人怎麼能搬得走這兩座大山呢？
   凭你们这几个人怎么能搬得走这两座大山呢？
   With only the few of you, how can these two mountains be moved away?

2. 你憑甚麼說我拿了你的書。
   你凭什么说我拿了你的书。
   On what basis do you say that I took your books?

3. 電影院、遊樂場的門口都寫着"憑票入場"。
   电影院、游乐场的门口都写着"凭票入场"。
   Movie theaters and amusement parks all have "Admission by ticket only" on the door.

三、寧可……也　would rather; had better

"寧可……也" is used to express a preference (which may not be a good choice, either) after comparing another option.

1. 我寧可一輩子不出門，也不做這種傻事。
   我宁可一辈子不出门，也不做这种傻事。
   I would rather stay at home for my entire life than do something stupid like this.

2. 我寧可死也不和你結婚。
   我宁可死也不和你结婚。
   I would rather die than marry you.

3. 寧可今天晚上不睡覺也要把作業做完。
   宁可今天晚上不睡觉也要把作业做完。
   I would rather stay up the whole night and finish my homework.

四、才　intensifier

"才" is used in exclamatory sentences for emphasis.

1. 愚公回答說："您才是老糊塗了啊！"

愚公回答说："您才是老糊涂了啊！"

The Foolish Old Man said: "It's you who are the old fool!"

2. 這麼多年來，我發現你才是真正的好人！

这么多年来，我发现你才是真正的好人！

After all these years, I've finally realized it's you who are the good guy!

3. 我才不願意跟他做朋友呢！

我才不愿意跟他做朋友呢！

I'll never make friends with him!

五、越……越　　the more ..., the more ...

"越……越" connects two words or phrases and indicates the increasing degree of one state or process as the other increases.

1. 您呀，越老越笨。

您呀，越老越笨。

The older you get, the more foolish you become.

2. 中文課越學越容易。

中文课越学越容易。

The more you study Chinese, the easier it becomes.

3. 學校餐廳的飯越吃越難吃。

学校餐厅的饭越吃越难吃。

The more you eat in the school's dining hall, the lousier you think the food is.

六、不如　　not as good as

"不如" is used in comparison sentences with the meaning "not as good as". "不如" can also appear after the object of comparison, when using "連……都不如".

1. 你笨得連那個小孩子都不如。

你笨得连那个小孩子都不如。

You're even more foolish than that child.

2. 我的中文水平連小學生都不如。

我的中文水平连小学生都不如。

The level of my Chinese is even lower than that of elementary school students.

3. 趙小燕不如王小鳳漂亮。

赵小燕不如王小凤漂亮。

Zhao Xiaoyan is not as pretty as Wang Xiaofeng.

七、"怎麼"and"為甚麼"　　why; how come

"怎麼"and"為甚麼"can both be used to inquire about the reason for something, but "怎麼"can also be used to ask about the manner of an action.

1. 只要我們不停地挖下去，為甚麼(怎麼)會搬不走呢？

只要我们不停地挖下去，为什么(怎么)会搬不走呢？

If we keep digging, why shouldn't we be able to move it away?

2. 你怎麼(為甚麼)不去上課？

你怎么(为什么)不去上课？

How come you didn't go to class?

3. 憑你們這幾個人怎麼能夠搬得走這兩座大山呢？

凭你们这几个人怎么能够搬得走这两座大山呢？

With only the few of you, how can these two mountains be moved away?

4. 這個字老師沒有教過，我不知道怎麼寫。

这个字老师没有教过，我不知道怎么写。

The teacher has never taught us this character, so I don't know how to write it.

練習

一、用所給的詞語填空(每一個詞語都要用到)

這麼、那麼、甚麼、怎麼、為甚麼

A：天已經_____黑了，外面又下着雨，你_____還不回宿舍去呢？

B：我沒有帶雨傘，我_____回去呢？

A：我沒有想到你_____笨，旁邊的教室裏有_____多的同學，你不能去借一把傘嗎？

B：你說_____？我借別人的傘，別人_____回去？

A：那你_____時候才能回宿舍呢？

B：我不知道。_____時候雨停了，_____時候我再回宿舍。

这么、那么、什么、怎么、为什么

A：天已经_____黑了，外面又下着雨，你_____还不回宿舍去呢？

B：我没有带雨伞，我_____回去呢？

A：我没有想到你_____笨，旁边的教室里有_____多的同学，你不能去借一把伞吗？

B：你说_____？我借别人的伞，别人_____回去？

A：那你_____时候才能回宿舍呢？

B：我不知道。_____时候雨停了，_____时候我再回宿舍。

二、選擇合適的量詞填空

1. 位、座、個、門、種、條(每個量詞只能用兩次)

一_____娛樂	一_____城市	一_____布帶	兩_____故事
兩_____方法	兩_____大山	兩_____辮子	一_____朝代
一_____老人	兩_____老師	兩_____功課	一_____學問

位、座、个、门、种、条(每个量词只能用两次)

一_____娱乐	一_____城市	一_____布带	两_____故事
两_____方法	两_____大山	两_____辫子	一_____朝代
一_____老人	两_____老师	两_____功课	一_____学问

2. 顆、束、隻、件、匹、項、本、頓、幅、頭、份、股(每個量詞只能用一次)

| 一_____飯 | 兩_____腳 | 三_____書 | 四_____鮮花 |
| 五_____大馬 | 六_____星星 | 七_____政策 | 八_____獅子 |

九_____事情　十_____漫畫　一_____力量　一_____信心

顆、束、只、件、匹、項、本、頓、幅、頭、份、股(每個量詞只能用一次)

一_____饭　　兩_____脚　　三_____书　　四_____鲜花
五_____大马　六_____星星　七_____政策　八_____狮子
九_____事情　十_____漫画　一_____力量　一_____信心

三、用所給的詞語造句

1. 寧可……也
   宁可……也
   _____。

2. 越……越
   越……越
   _____。

3. 連……不如
   连……不如
   _____。

4. 憑
   凭
   _____。

5. 明明
   明明
   _____。

四、翻譯

1. The older the Foolish Old Man got, the more foolish he became. He obviously knew that with only the few people in his own family, the two big mountains could never be moved away, but he still wanted to do this stupid thing.

2. People obviously know that fairy tales are made up, but they still like to read these stories. Some people say that if one reads too many fairy tales, one will become very foolish.

3. The Wise Old Man said: I'm not foolish at all. It's you who are foolish! I would rather do nothing all my life than do such a stupid thing. There are too many things in life which people cannot possibly do.

五、根據課文回答問題

1. 甚麼是神話故事？
   什么是神话故事？

2. 為甚麼說這些故事是編出來的？
   为什么说这些故事是编出来的？

3. 愚公的故事說的是甚麼？
   愚公的故事说的是什么？

4. 聽了古老的神話故事可以讓人們感受到甚麼？
   听了古老的神话故事可以让人们感受到什么？
   _____
   _____。

六、課堂討論

1. 智叟聰明還是愚公聰明？
   智叟聪明还是愚公聪明？
   _____
   _____
   _____。

2. 為甚麼人們都喜歡神話故事？
   为什么人们都喜欢神话故事？
   _____
   _____
   _____。

七、小作文

簡單地寫一個你知道的神話故事。
简单地写一个你知道的神话故事。
_____
_____
_____
_____
_____。

閱讀

相思樹和相思鳥

　　中國有一句話叫做"有情人終成眷屬"，意思是説兩個相愛的人，最後一定會生活在一起的。中國人還説："在天願做比翼鳥，在地願做連理枝"，意思是説相愛的人，活着的時候在一起，死了以後也要變成兩隻比翼齊飛的小鳥，也要變成兩棵長在一起的大樹。人們為甚麼要這樣説呢？因為古書上就記載着這樣的一個神話故事。

　　春秋時期宋國有一個人叫韓憑，他的妻子長得像仙女一樣漂亮。宋國國王是一個既兇惡又好色的人。他一看到韓憑漂亮的妻子就把她搶走了。韓憑的妻子非常傷心，她偷偷地給丈夫寫了封信説：我只愛你一個人，我寧可死也不願意和那個連禽獸都不如的壞蛋在一起生活。我們活着的時候不能在一起，那我們死了以後在一起吧。韓憑看了妻子的信以後就上吊自殺了，第二天他的妻子也從高臺上跳了下去。

　　韓憑妻子臨死前留了封遺書給宋王，她説："我活着的時候不能和我丈夫在一起，死了以後請把我們埋在一起吧。"宋王看到這封信特別生氣，他説："你們活着不能在一起，死了也不讓你們在一起。"他派人把韓憑夫婦分開來埋葬，兩座墳墓離得遠遠的，他對着墳墓説："你們要是有本事把兩座墓合在一起的話，那我就不阻攔你們了。"

　　第二天，兩座墓上各自長出了一棵樹。樹長得很快，而且樹幹都彎曲着往一起靠攏。兩棵樹越長越大，越長距離越近。不久，它們的根連在一起，樹枝也交錯在一起了，到最後，兩棵樹竟然合成了一棵大樹。

　　樹上飛來了兩隻小鳥，這兩隻鳥從早到晚不停地叫着，叫聲非常悲哀，過路人聽了都很難過。大家知道牠們是韓憑夫婦變的，都很同情牠們，於是就把這兩隻總是一起飛來飛去的鳥叫做"相思鳥"；把這兩棵連在一起的樹叫做"相思樹"。

　　從此以後，"相思"成了愛情的專用語。思念相愛的人叫做相思；因為相思而流的眼淚叫做"相思淚"；因為相思而吃不下飯、睡不着覺的人是得了"相思病"；兩顆在一起象徵愛情的紅豆叫做"相思豆"。

阅 读

相思树和相思鸟

中国有一句话叫做"有情人终成眷属",意思是说两个相爱的人,最后一定会生活在一起的。中国人还说:"在天愿做比翼鸟,在地愿做连理枝",意思是说相爱的人,活着的时候在一起,死了以后也要变成两只比翼齐飞的小鸟,也要变成两棵长在一起的大树。人们为什么要这样说呢?因为古书上就记载着这样的一个神话故事。

春秋时期宋国有一个人叫韩凭,他的妻子长得像仙女一样漂亮。宋国国王是一个既凶恶又好色的人。他一看到韩凭漂亮的妻子就把她抢走了。韩凭的妻子非常伤心,她偷偷地给丈夫写了封信说:我只爱你一个人,我宁可死也不愿意和那个连禽兽都不如的坏蛋在一起生活。我们活着的时候不能在一起,那我们死了以后在一起吧。韩凭看了妻子的信以后就上吊自杀了,第二天他的妻子也从高台上跳了下去。

韩凭妻子临死前留了封遗书给宋王,她说:"我活着的时候不能和我丈夫在一起,死了以后请把我们埋在一起吧。"宋王看到这封信特别生气,他说:"你们活着不能在一起,死了也不让你们在一起。"他派人把韩凭夫妇分开来埋葬,两座坟墓离得远远的,他对着坟墓说:"你们要是有本事把两座墓合在一起的话,那我就不阻拦你们了。"

第二天,两座墓上各自长出了一棵树。树长得很快,而且树干都弯曲着往一起靠拢。两棵树越长越大,越长距离越近。不久,它们的根连在一起,树枝也交错在一起了,到最后,两棵树竟然合成了一棵大树。

树上飞来了两只小鸟,这两只鸟从早到晚不停地叫着,叫声非常悲哀,过路人听了都很难过。大家知道它们是韩凭夫妇变的,都很同情它们,于是就把这两只总是一起飞来飞去的鸟叫做"相思鸟";把这两棵连在一起的树叫做"相思树"。

从此以后,"相思"成了爱情的专用语。思念相爱的人叫做相思;因为相思而流的眼泪叫做"相思泪";因为相思而吃不下饭、睡不着觉的人是得了"相思病";两颗在一起象征爱情的红豆叫做"相思豆"。

生詞

相思	相思	xiāngsī	v.	yearning for each other (of lovers)
終	终	zhōng	adv.	in the end; eventually; finally
眷屬	眷属	juànshǔ	n.	family dependents
有情人終成眷屬	有情人终成眷属	yǒuqíngrén zhōngchéng juànshǔ		lovers will finally get married
願	愿	yuàn	v.	wish
比翼鳥	比翼鸟	bǐyìniǎo	n.	a pair of lovebirds — a devoted couple
連理枝	连理枝	liánlǐzhī	n.	trees whose branches interlock or join together
活著	活着	huózhe		be alive
比翼齊飛	比翼齐飞	bǐyì qífēi		to fly side by side
宋國	宋国	Sòng guó		the state of Song
韓憑	韩凭	Hán Píng		name of a person
好色	好色	hào sè		lustful
搶	抢	qiǎng	v.	take away by force
禽獸	禽兽	qínshòu	n.	birds and beasts
壞蛋	坏蛋	huàidàn	n.	wicked person
封	封	fēng	m.	measure word for letters
上吊	上吊	shàng diào		hang oneself
高臺	高台	gāotái		high platform
臨死	临死	línsǐ		on one's deathbed
留下	留下	liúxià	v.	leave
遺書	遗书	yíshū	n.	a letter or note left by someone immediately before death

分開	分开	fēnkāi		divide
墳墓	坟墓	fénmù	n.	tomb
本事	本事	běnshì	n.	ability
合	合	hé	v.	join; combine
阻攔	阻拦	zǔlán	v.	block the way; stop
樹幹	树干	shùgàn	n.	trunk (of a tree)
彎曲	弯曲	wānqū	v.	bend; curve
靠攏	靠拢	kàolǒng	v.	close up
根	根	gēn	n.	root of a tree
樹枝	树枝	shùzhī	n.	branch
交錯	交错	jiāocuò	v.	interlock
竟然	竟然	jìngrán	adv.	actually; unexpectedly
偎依	偎依	wēiyī	v.	snuggle up to; lean close to
悲哀	悲哀	bēiāi	adj.	sad
過路人	过路人	guòlùrén	n.	passerby
同情	同情	tóngqíng	v.	sympathize with
專用語	专用语	zhuānyòngyǔ		special-purpose word
思念	思念	sīniàn	v.	miss
相思病	相思病	xiāngsībìng	n.	lovesickness
紅豆	红豆	hóngdòu	n.	love pea; red bean

問題

1. 宋國的國王為甚麼要把韓憑的妻子搶走？
   宋国的国王为什么要把韩凭的妻子抢走？

   _____

   _____ 。

17. 神話故事　　　323

2. 韓憑妻子的遺書裏面要宋王做甚麼？
   韩凭妻子的遗书里面要宋王做什么？
   _____
   _____ 。

3. 宋王看了韓憑妻子的遺書以後是怎麼做的？
   宋王看了韩凭妻子的遗书以后是怎么做的？
   _____
   _____ 。

4. 韓憑和他妻子墓上的兩棵樹是怎麼長的？
   韩凭和他妻子墓上的两棵树是怎么长的？
   _____
   _____ 。

5. 兩隻鳥為甚麼從早到晚不停地叫？
   两只鸟为什么从早到晚不停地叫？
   _____
   _____ 。

6. 甚麼是相思樹？
   什么是相思树？
   _____
   _____ 。

7. 甚麼是相思、相思淚、相思病？
   什么是相思、相思泪、相思病？
   _____
   _____ 。

成語的來源
The Origins of Chinese Proverbs

學習大綱

通過學習本課，學生應該能夠：

1. 掌握這些句型和詞語的意思和用法："關於"、"大致"、"自"、"所"、"往往"、"向"、"通過"。
2. 認識和運用課文以及閱讀文章內的生詞。
3. 簡單地了解中國成語的來源，和某些成語在意思上的轉變。
4. 簡單地了解甚麼是中國的詩詞。

Study Outline

After studying this chapter, students should:

1. Have a good command of the meaning and usage of these sentence patterns and terms: "guānyú" (regarding; about), "dàzhì" (generally; roughly; approximately), "zì" (from), "suǒ" (that; which; what), "wǎngwǎng" (often; frequently), "xiàng" (toward), "tōngguò" (by way of; by means of).
2. Be familiar with the meaning and usage of the vocabulary introduced in the text and the reading.
3. Have some understanding of the origins of Chinese proverbs, and of how the meanings of some of the proverbs have deviated from their original meanings.
4. Know a little about Chinese poetry.

課文

中文裏有一種由四個字組成的固定詞組叫做"成語"，比方說我們學過的"望子成龍"、"白頭到老"、"一見鍾情"、"青山綠水"、"美麗動人"、"女扮男裝"、"海枯石爛"等等。

成語很多都是從古代流傳下來的。關於成語的來源大致來說有以下幾個方面：一是來自歷史故事，如"走馬觀花"；二是出自神話寓言，例如"愚公移山"；三是由文章和詩詞演變來的，比如"水滴石穿"、"眉來眼去"；還有一些是由人們口頭常說的四字俗語形成的，如"三心二意"、"一乾二淨"等等。

人們說有些成語不大好懂，主要是因為成語所表示的含義，往往是在字面意思之外。有的時候儘管你認識成語裏所有的字，也知道每一個字的意思，但你不一定能明白整個成語所要表達的意思。

比如"水滴石穿"這個成語，它字面上的意思是說水珠滴落在大石頭上，把大石頭滴穿了。其實，它真正的意思是說人們只要有恆心，不斷努力，堅持下去，無論多麼困難的事情都一定能成功。

還有些成語，它的含義在使用的過程中發生了變化，人們今天用它來表示的意思和它原先的含義完全不一樣。

例如"眉來眼去"這個成語，它原先的意思是描寫大自然美麗的景色的。它是說當你坐船行走在山水之間的時候，你會看到遠處像彎彎的眉毛一樣的山峰慢慢地向你走來；而身邊像眼波一樣的水流漸漸地離你遠去。然而，今天眉來眼去的意思，則是指男女之間通過眉眼來傳遞相愛的感情的。

成語大多是四個字的，很少有三個字以下和五、六個字以上的，這是因為如果字太少了的話不容易表達出深刻的含義，字太多的話又不夠簡練，而且兩個雙音節的四字成語唸起來比較順口。

由於成語是一種人們已經習慣了的、固定了的詞語結構，所以一般來講，成語的詞序和字數是不能隨意變動的。

课文

中文里有一种由四个字组成的固定词组叫做"成语",比方说我们学过的"望子成龙"、"白头到老"、"一见钟情"、"青山绿水"、"美丽动人"、"女扮男装"、"海枯石烂"等等。

成语很多都是从古代流传下来的。关于成语的来源大致来说有以下几个方面:一是来自历史故事,如"走马观花";二是出自神话寓言,例如"愚公移山";三是由文章和诗词演变来的,比如"水滴石穿"、"眉来眼去";还有一些是由人们口头常说的四字俗语形成的,如"三心二意"、"一干二淨"等等。

人们说有些成语不大好懂,主要是因为成语所表示的含义,往往是在字面意思之外。有的时候尽管你认识成语里所有的字,也知道每一个字的意思,但你不一定能明白整个成语所要表达的意思。

比如"水滴石穿"这个成语,它字面上的意思是说水珠滴落在大石头上,把大石头滴穿了。其实,它真正的意思是说人们只要有恒心,不断努力,坚持下去,无论多么困难的事情都一定能成功。

还有些成语,它的含义在使用的过程中发生了变化,人们今天用它来表示的意思和它原先的含义完全不一样。

例如"眉来眼去"这个成语,它原先的意思是描写大自然美丽的景色的。它是说当你坐船行走在山水之间的时候,你会看到远处像弯弯的眉毛一样的山峰慢慢地向你走来;而身边像眼波一样的水流渐渐地离你远去。然而,今天眉来眼去的意思,则是指男女之间通过眉眼来传递相爱的感情的。

成语大多是四个字的,很少有三个字以下和五、六个字以上的,这是因为如果字太少了的话不容易表达出深刻的含义,字太多的话又不够简练,而且两个双音节的四字成语念起来比较顺口。

由于成语是一种人们已经习惯了的、固定了的词语结构,所以一般来讲,成语的词序和字数是不能随意变动的。

生詞

成語	成语	chéngyǔ	n.	proverb; idiom; set phrase
固定	固定	gùdìng	adj.	fixed
詞組	词组	cízǔ	n.	expression; phrase
關於	关于	guānyú	prep.	regarding; about
大致	大致	dàzhì	adv.	generally; roughly
自	自	zì	prep.	from
寓言	寓言	yùyán	n.	allegory; fable
詩詞	诗词	shīcí	n.	poems
演變	演变	yǎnbiàn	v.	evolve
含義	含义	hányì	n.	implication
眉來眼去	眉来眼去	méilái-yǎnqù		exchange love glances with sb.; make eyes at each other
口頭	口头	kǒutóu	adj.	oral
俗語	俗语	súyǔ	n.	common saying; folk adage
形成	形成	xíngchéng	v.	form; take shape
水滴石穿	水滴石穿	shuǐdī-shíchuān		dripping water wears through a stone — little strokes fell great oaks
三心二意	三心二意	sānxīn-èryì		half-hearted; change one's mind constantly
一乾二淨	一干二净	yīgān-'èr jìng	adj.	thorough(ly); complete(ly)
所	所	suǒ	par.	(see grammar notes)
往往	往往	wǎngwǎng	adv.	often; frequently
表達	表达	biǎodá	v.	express
滴	滴	dī	v.	drip

石	石	shí	n.	stone
穿	穿	chuān	v.	pierce through
滴落	滴落	dīluò	v.	drip down; weep
恆心	恒心	héngxīn	n.	perseverance
堅持	坚持	jiānchí	v.	uphold
多麼	多么	duōme	adv.	how; what
成功	成功	chénggōng	v.	succeed
景色	景色	jǐngsè	n.	scenery
行走	行走	xíngzǒu	v.	run; move
眉毛	眉毛	méimao	n.	eyebrow
向	向	xiàng	prep.	toward
眼波	眼波	yǎnbō	n.	(of a woman's eyes) a fluid glance
通過	通过	tōngguò	prep.	by way of; by means of
傳遞	传递	chuándì	v.	transmit; convey
雙音節	双音节	shuāngyīn jié	n.	two-syllable
順口	顺口	shùnkǒu	adj.	easy to read
深刻	深刻	shēnkè	adj.	profound; deep
簡練	简练	jiǎnliàn	adj.	concise
結構	结构	jiégòu	n.	structure
詞序	词序	cíxù	n.	word order
隨意	随意	suí yì	adv.	as one pleases
變動	变动	biàndòng	v.	change and move

語法和詞語註釋

一、關於   regarding; about

1. 關於成語的來源大致有以下幾個方面：……。
   关于成语的来源大致有以下几个方面：……。
   Where the origin of proverbs is concerned, there are roughly speaking the following kinds: ....

2. 我最近讀了幾篇關於愛情的小說。
   我最近读了几篇关于爱情的小说。
   I've recently read a few love stories.

3. 我們學的課文，有關於中國文化的，也有關於漢語知識的。
   我们学的课文，有关于中国文化的，也有关于汉语知识的。
   As for the texts that we are studying, some are to do with Chinese culture, some are to do with knowledge of the Chinese language.

二、大致   generally; roughly; approximately

1. 關於成語的來源大致有以下幾個方面：……。
   关于成语的来源大致有以下几个方面：……。
   Where the origin of proverbs is concerned, there are roughly speaking the following kinds: ....

2. 學中文的目的大致有三個。
   学中文的目的大致有三个。
   Roughly speaking, people studying Chinese with three aims in mind.

3. 班上同學的水平大致相同。
   班上同学的水平大致相同。
   Students in my class are all at approximately the same level.

三、自   from

"自" is used in written language to indicate the place or time in the past from which something starts.

1. 成語一是來自歷史故事，二是出自神話寓言。
   成语一是来自历史故事，二是出自神话寓言。
   Proverbs, firstly, are derived from historical stories; secondly, they come from fairy tales or fables.

2. 我們班的同學來自各個地方。
   我们班的同学来自各个地方。
   My classmates come from various places.

3. 湯姆出自內心地對趙小燕說：我愛你。
   汤姆出自内心地对赵小燕说：我爱你。
   Tom said to Zhao Xiaoyan from the bottom of his heart: I love you.

4. 自古以來，中國人就認為夫妻應該白頭到老。
   自古以来，中国人就认为夫妻应该白头到老。
   Since ancient times, Chinese people think husband and wife should live together till they are old and gray.

四、所　　that; which; what

> "所" is used before a verb to introduce a relative clause. It is often used in the written language.

1. 成語所表示的意思往往是在字面之外。
   成语所表示的意思往往是在字面之外。
   The meaning that a proverb expresses is often beyond the literal meaning of the characters.

2. 小燕是我所見過的最漂亮的姑娘。
   小燕是我所见过的最漂亮的姑娘。
   Xiaoyan is the most beautiful girl that I've ever seen.

3. 我們所學的課文都是關於中國語言和文化的。
   我们所学的课文都是关于中国语言和文化的。
   The texts that we are studying are all about Chinese language and culture.

五、往往　often; frequently

"往往" is used before the verb to mean "it is often the case that ", but with more focus on the regularity of the action than in English.

1. 成語所表示的意思往往是在字面之外。
   成语所表示的意思往往是在字面之外。
   The meaning that a proverb expresses is often beyond the literal meaning of the characters.

2. 我做作業往往做到半夜一兩點。
   我做作业往往做到半夜一两点。
   I often do my homework till around one or two o'clock in the morning.

3. 每次上課的時候小張都喜歡發言，不過他往往說錯。
   每次上课的时候小张都喜欢发言，不过他往往说错。
   Xiao Zhang likes to speak in class, but he often says something wrong.

六、向　toward

"向" indicates the direction of an action.

1. 像彎彎的眉毛一樣的山峰慢慢地向你走來。
   像弯弯的眉毛一样的山峰慢慢地向你走来。
   The mountain peaks which look like curved eyebrows are moving slowly toward you.

2. 兩棵大樹長得很快，而且樹幹都彎曲著向一起靠攏。
   两棵大树长得很快，而且树干都弯曲着向一起靠拢。
   The two big trees grew very fast, and the trunks bent toward each other and drew closer.

3. 水向低處流。
   水向低处流。
   Water flows downwards.

七、通過　　by way of; by means of

"通過"introduces the means by which an action is carried out.

1. 眉來眼去的意思是指男女之間通過眉眼來傳遞愛情。

   眉来眼去的意思是指男女之间通过眉眼来传递爱情。

   Meilai-yanqu refers to men and women conveying their love by exchanging loving glances.

2. 通過學習中文，我們了解了許多中國文化。

   通过学习中文，我们了解了许多中国文化。

   We learn a lot about Chinese culture by studying Chinese.

3. 我和我的女朋友是通過上網認識的。

   我和我的女朋友是通过上网认识的。

   I got to know my girlfriend through the Internet.

練習

一、用所給的詞語回答問題

1. A："牛郎織女"這個神話故事講的是甚麼？（關於）

   "牛郎织女"这个神话故事讲的是什么？（关于）

   B：_____。

2. A：明天考試你都準備好了嗎？（大致）

   明天考试你都准备好了吗？（大致）

   B：_____。

3. A：你們班上的同學都是從甚麼地方來的？（自）

   你们班上的同学都是从什么地方来的？（自）

   B：_____。

4. A：請問去圖書館怎麼走？（向）

   请问去图书馆怎么走？（向）

B：_____。

5. A：你怎麼認識你的女朋友的？(通過)
　　　你怎么认识你的女朋友的？(通过)
　　　B：_____。

6. A：你下課以後會去甚麼地方？(往往)
　　　你下课以后会去什么地方？(往往)
　　　B：_____。

二、把意思相同的成語和句子連起來

1. 年年有餘　　　　　　　(　)過去女人纏得很漂亮的小腳。
　 年年有余　　　　　　　　　过去女人缠得很漂亮的小脚。
2. 白頭到老　　　　　　　(　)看東西的時候不認真不仔細。
　 白头到老　　　　　　　　　看东西的时候不认真不仔细。
3. 一見鍾情　　　　　　　(　)夫妻倆人結婚後永遠不分離。
　 一见钟情　　　　　　　　　夫妻俩人结婚后永远不分离。
4. 望子成龍　　　　　　　(　)事情已經做錯了就錯下去吧。
　 望子成龙　　　　　　　　　事情已经做错了就错下去吧。
5. 走馬觀花　　　　　　　(　)兩個人第一次見面就愛上了。
　 走马观花　　　　　　　　　两个人第一次见面就爱上了。
6. 將錯就錯　　　　　　　(　)每一年人們賺的錢都有節餘。
　 将错就错　　　　　　　　　每一年人们赚的钱都有节余。
7. 冰天雪地　　　　　　　(　)希望孩子長大以後很有出息。
　 冰天雪地　　　　　　　　　希望孩子长大以后很有出息。
8. 如詩如畫　　　　　　　(　)到處都是冰雪天氣非常寒冷。
　 如诗如画　　　　　　　　　到处都是冰雪天气非常寒冷。
9. 三寸金蓮　　　　　　　(　)描寫那些很漂亮的自然風景。
　 三寸金莲　　　　　　　　　描写那些很漂亮的自然风景。

三、根據課文寫出答案

1. 講解成語詞序不能變動的是哪一段？
   讲解成语词序不能变动的是哪一段？
   _____。

2. 説成語比較難懂的是哪一段？
   说成语比较难懂的是哪一段？
   _____。

3. 第七段講的是甚麼？
   第七段讲的是什么？
   _____。

4. 第二段講的是甚麼？
   第二段讲的是什么？
   _____。

5. 哪一個成語的意思發生了變化？
   哪一个成语的意思发生了变化？
   _____。

四、翻譯

1. Proverbs consist of only four characters, but the meanings that they express are usually very profound. By learning proverbs, we can learn many historical stories and a lot about ancient culture.

   _____
   _____
   _____。

2. Regarding the origin of Valentine's Day, some people say it originates from ancient fairy tales, some say it's from historical stories, and some say it's imported from abroad.

3. Generally speaking there are two kinds of proverbs today: One kind has been handed down from ancient times; the other kind has been produced recently by modern society. But in neither kind can the order of the characters, or their number, be altered at will.

五、根據課文回答問題

1. 甚麼是成語？
   什么是成语？

2. 成語的來源有哪些？
   成语的来源有哪些？

3. "水滴石穿"是甚麼意思？
   "水滴石穿"是什么意思？

4. 現在"眉來眼去"表示甚麼意思？
   现在"眉来眼去"表示什么意思？

5. 成語為甚麼大多是四個字？
   成语为什么大多是四个字？
   _____
   _____。

六、課堂討論

1. 人們喜歡成語的原因。
   人们喜欢成语的原因。
   _____
   _____
   _____。

2. 你們母語裏的成語和中文的成語有哪些不同？
   你们母语里的成语和中文的成语有哪些不同？
   _____
   _____
   _____
   _____。

七、小作文

寫一個你喜歡的成語故事。
写一个你喜欢的成语故事。
_____
_____
_____
_____
_____
_____。

閱讀

詩詞

"床前明月光，疑是地上霜。舉頭望明月，低頭思故鄉。"差不多所有的中國人都會背這首名叫《靜夜思》的唐詩。

這首詩是說有一個遠離家鄉的人，一天晚上他看到床前一片白白的月光，以為是秋天的霜。當他抬頭看到天上圓圓的月亮的時候，想起了遠方的故鄉。

《靜夜思》是唐朝詩人李白寫的。中國古代有許多很有名的詩人；有許多很有名的詩詞。這些詩詞有的是描寫大自然的風光；有的是讚美純潔的愛情；也有的是敘述人生的悲歡離合。

"紅豆生南國，春來發幾枝。勸君多採擷，此物最相思。"紅豆生長在南方，春天的時候發出幾枝新芽。你多採一些帶回家去吧，這小小的紅豆代表着愛的思念。

這首《紅豆》詩是唐朝的另一位詩人王維寫的。這一首表示愛情的《紅豆》詩，千百年來不知道打動過多少少男少女的心。

宋朝的詩人蘇軾寫過一首關於月亮的詞。詞的最後一段是這樣寫的："人有悲歡離合，月有陰晴圓缺，此事古難全。但願人長久，千里共嬋娟"。

它的意思是說：人們有的時候會悲傷，有的時候會高興；有時候要分離，有時候又團圓。這就像月亮一樣，有時會遇到陰天，有時會碰到晴天；月亮有圓的時候，也有不圓的時候。從古到今，人們不可能總是高興的，家人不可能永遠團聚在一起；天也不可能總是晴的，月亮也不可能永遠是圓的。但是，只要大家都健康地活着，當你我都在看着那美麗的月亮的時候，即使彼此相隔千里之外，也好像是相聚在一起的。

詩詞大都只有短短的幾行，但是她所表達的含義卻很多。這些優美的詩詞不僅可以讓你了解到古代的歷史和文化，而且還可以讓你在精神上得到一種美的享受。當你在朗誦這些詩詞的時候，常常會陶醉在這些美妙的詩句之中。

阅读

诗词

"床前明月光，疑是地上霜。举头望明月，低头思故乡。"差不多所有的中国人都会背这首名叫《静夜思》的唐诗。

这首诗是说有一个远离家乡的人，一天晚上他看到床前一片白白的月光，以为是秋天的霜。当他抬头看到天上圆圆的月亮的时候，想起了远方的故乡。

《静夜思》是唐朝诗人李白写的。中国古代有许多很有名的诗人；有许多很有名的诗词。这些诗词有的是描写大自然的风光；有的是赞美纯洁的爱情；也有的是叙述人生的悲欢离合。

"红豆生南国，春来发几枝。劝君多采撷，此物最相思。"红豆生长在南方，春天的时候发出几枝新芽。你多采一些带回家去吧，这小小的红豆代表着爱的思念。

这首《红豆》诗是唐朝的另一位诗人王维写的。这一首表示爱情的《红豆》诗，千百年来不知道打动过多少少男少女的心。

宋朝的诗人苏轼写过一首关于月亮的词。词的最后一段是这样写的："人有悲欢离合，月有阴晴圆缺，此事古难全。但愿人长久，千里共婵娟"。

它的意思是说：人们有的时候会悲伤，有的时候会高兴；有时候要分离，有时候又团圆。这就像月亮一样，有时会遇到阴天，有时会碰到晴天；月亮有圆的时候，也有不圆的时候。从古到今，人们不可能总是高兴的，家人不可能永远团聚在一起；天也不可能总是晴的，月亮也不可能永远是圆的。但是，只要大家都健康地活着，当你我都在看着那美丽的月亮的时候，即使彼此相隔千里之外，也好像是相聚在一起的。

诗词大都只有短短的几行，但是她所表达的含义却很多。这些优美的诗词不仅可以让你了解到古代的历史和文化，而且还可以让你在精神上得到一种美的享受。当你在朗诵这些诗词的时候，常常会陶醉在这些美妙的诗句之中。

生 詞

月光	月光	yuèguāng	n.	moonlight
疑	疑	yí	v.	doubt
霜	霜	shuāng	n.	frost
舉頭	举头	jǔ tóu		raise one's head
低頭	低头	dī tóu		lower one's head
背	背	bèi	v.	recite
故鄉	故乡	gùxiāng	n.	hometown
首	首	shǒu	m.	measure word for poems
李白	李白	Lǐ Bái		name of a poet
讚美	赞美	zànměi	v.	praise; eulogize
純潔	纯洁	chún jié	adj.	pure; clean and honest
敘述	叙述	xùshù	v.	narrate
人生	人生	rénshēng	n.	life
悲歡離合	悲欢离合	bēihuān-líhé		joy and sorrows, separations and reunions
南國	南国	nánguó	n.	the southern land
發	发	fā	v.	grow; put forth
勸	劝	quàn	v.	advise; persuade
君	君	jūn	n.	you; gentleman
採擷	采撷	cǎixié	v.	pick
物	物	wù	n.	thing; object
芽	芽	yá	n.	sprout; bud
王維	王维	Wáng Wéi		name of a poet
打動	打动	dǎdòng	v.	(of emotions) move; touch

少男少女	少男少女	shàonán shàonǚ	n.	young boy and young girl
蘇軾	苏轼	Sū Shì		name of a poet
陰	阴	yīn	adj.	cloudy
晴	晴	qíng	adj.	fine; clear
缺	缺	quē	adj.	waning
長久	长久	cháng jiǔ	adj.	for a long time
共	共	gòng	adv.	share ... together
嬋娟	婵娟	chán juān		used in ancient texts referring to a lovely woman, here it refers to the moon
悲傷	悲伤	bēishāng	adj.	sad
遇到	遇到	yùdào	v.	encounter
團聚	团聚	tuán jù	v.	reunite
健康	健康	jiànkāng	adj.	healthy
相隔	相隔	xiānggé		be at a distance of; be apart
短	短	duǎn	adj.	short
行	行	háng	m.	line
了解	了解	liǎo jiě	v.	understand
朗誦	朗诵	lǎngsòng	v.	declaim
優美	优美	yōuměi	adj.	graceful; exquisite
陶醉	陶醉	táozuì	v.	be intoxicated with
美妙	美妙	měimiào	adj.	splendid; wonderful

問題

1. 《靜夜思》這首唐詩說的是甚麼？
《静夜思》这首唐诗说的是什么？

2. 甚麼是悲歡離合？
   什么是悲欢离合？
   _____
   _____。

3. 《紅豆》這首詩為甚麼能打動少男少女的心？
   《红豆》这首诗为什么能打动少男少女的心？
   _____
   _____。

4. "但願人長久，千里共嬋娟"的意思是甚麼？
   "但愿人长久，千里共婵娟"的意思是什么？
   _____
   _____。

5. 人們為甚麼喜歡詩詞？
   人们为什么喜欢诗词？
   _____
   _____。

6. 你學過哪些詩詞？
   你学过哪些诗词？
   _____
   _____。

顏色的含義
The Implications of Colors

學習大綱

通過學習本課，學生應該能夠：

1. 掌握這些句型和詞語的意思和用法："要不然"、"向來"、"按照"、"者"、"之所以……，是因為"、"化"、"既然……就"。
2. 認識和運用課文以及閱讀文章內的生詞。
3. 了解紅、黃、綠、白、黑這五種顏色在中國人的生活中有甚麼特別的含義。
4. 了解中國人對牡丹、荷花、竹子和松樹的一些特別看法。

Study Outline

After studying this chapter, students should:

1. Have a good command of the meaning and usage of these sentence patterns and terms: "yàoburán" (otherwise), "xiànglái" (always [up to the present]), "ànzhào" (according to), "zhě" (-er; -ist), "zhīsuǒyǐ ..., shì yīnwèi" (the reason why), "huà" (-ize; -ify), "jìrán ..., jiù" (since ..., [then] ...).
2. Be familiar with the meaning and usage of the vocabulary introduced in the text and the reading.
3. Understand what implications the colors red, yellow, green, white and black have in Chinese daily life.
4. Understand the unique Chinese views on the peony, water-lily, bamboo and pine tree.

課文

紅、黃、綠、白、黑這五種顏色在中國人的生活中有特別的含義。

紅色代表喜慶。中國人認為紅色可以給人帶來吉利。在喜慶的日子裏，做喜慶的事情時一定要用紅顏色，要不然就會讓人們覺得不吉利。

過年是喜慶的日子。過年時大門兩旁貼着紅色的春聯，門上貼着大紅的福字，門頭上掛着大紅燈籠。不但小孩子放的鞭炮是紅色的，就連爺爺奶奶給他們的壓歲錢，也都是用紅紙包起來的。

結婚是喜慶的事情。結婚時洞房的門上貼着大紅的喜聯，窗戶上貼着紅雙喜字。新娘要穿紅衣服、坐紅轎子、頭上還要蓋一塊紅綢布。現在結婚不興坐轎子了，但還是要在新娘的汽車上繫上一朵大紅花。

中國人向來喜歡黃色，因為黃色表示富貴。金子是黃色的，龍是黃色的，皇帝住的皇宮也是黃色的。中國人生活在黃土地上，喝的是黃河的水，自己的皮膚也都是黃色的。黃色是中國人的本色。可是不知為甚麼，在中國，黃色又代表着色情。色情笑話叫做黃色笑話，色情雜誌叫做黃色雜誌，政府取締賣淫嫖娼的活動叫做"掃黃"。

白色和黑色表示悲哀。有人去世的時候，輓聯是白色的，棺材是黑色的。按照傳統的習俗，親戚們穿白色的衣服，朋友們戴黑色的袖套，袖套上要有一朵小白花。報紙和雜誌在刊登死者的照片時，只能用黑白照片，而且還一定要在照片的四周加上粗粗的黑邊兒。

綠色是大自然的顏色。在冬天還沒有完全過去的時候，樹枝上幾片嫩綠的葉芽、地上幾棵細細的青草，給大地帶來了春天的信息。人們之所以喜歡綠色，就是因為這綠色的花草樹木，能讓人感到生命的存在，能美化人們的生活環境。

中國人喜歡穿綠顏色的衣服，但是中國人，尤其是中國的男人從來不戴綠顏色的帽子。自古以來，人們把妻子有了外遇的男人叫做"戴綠帽子"，也就是說這個人的妻子偷偷地愛上了別的男人。

綠帽子既然有這樣特別的意思，中國的男人，尤其是那些結了婚的男人，當然就不願意戴那頂綠綠的綠帽子了。

课文

　　红、黄、绿、白、黑这五种颜色在中国人的生活中有特别的含义。

　　红色代表喜庆。中国人认为红色可以给人带来吉利。在喜庆的日子里，做喜庆的事情时一定要用红颜色，要不然就会让人们觉得不吉利。

　　过年是喜庆的日子。过年时大门两旁贴着红色的春联，门上贴着大红的福字，门头上挂着大红灯笼。不但小孩子放的鞭炮是红色的，就连爷爷奶奶给他们的压岁钱，也都是用红纸包起来的。

　　结婚是喜庆的事情。结婚时洞房的门上贴着大红的喜联，窗户上贴着红双喜字。新娘要穿红衣服、坐红轿子、头上还要盖一块红绸布。现在结婚不兴坐轿子了，但还是要在新娘的汽车上扎上一朵大红花。

　　中国人向来喜欢黄色，因为黄色表示富贵。金子是黄色的，龙是黄色的，皇帝住的皇宫也是黄色的。中国人生活在黄土地上，喝的是黄河的水，自己的皮肤也都是黄色的。黄色是中国人的本色。可是不知为什么，在中国，黄色又代表着色情。色情笑话叫做黄色笑话，色情杂志叫做黄色杂志，政府取缔卖淫嫖娼的活动叫做"扫黄"。

　　白色和黑色表示悲哀。有人去世的时候，挽联是白色的，棺材是黑色的。按照传统的习俗，亲戚们穿白色的衣服，朋友们戴黑色的袖套，袖套上要有一朵小白花。报纸和杂志在刊登死者的照片时，只能用黑白照片，而且还一定要在照片的四周加上粗粗的黑边儿。

　　绿色是大自然的颜色。在冬天还没有完全过去的时候，树枝上几片嫩绿的叶芽、地上几棵细细的青草，给大地带来了春天的信息。人们之所以喜欢绿色，就是因为这绿色的花草树木，能让人感到生命的存在，能美化人们的生活环境。

　　中国人喜欢穿绿颜色的衣服，但是中国人，尤其是中国的男人从来不戴绿颜色的帽子。自古以来，人们把妻子有了外遇的男人叫做"戴绿帽子"，也就是说这个人的妻子偷偷地爱上了别的男人。

　　绿帽子既然有这样特别的意思，中国的男人，尤其是那些结了婚的男人，当然就不愿意戴那顶绿绿的绿帽子了。

生 詞

顏色	颜色	yánsè	n.	color
喜慶	喜庆	xǐqìng	adj.	auspicious or happy occasions (such as weddings, births, promotions, etc.)
吉利	吉利	jílì	n./adj.	luck; lucky; propitious
要不然	要不然	yàoburán	conj.	otherwise
門頭	门头	méntóu	n.	over the door
喜聯	喜联	xǐlián	n.	wedding couplet
轎子	轿子	jiàozi	n.	sedan chair
興	兴	xīng	v.	become popular
塊	块	kuài	m.	a piece of
朵	朵	duǒ	m.	measure word for flowers
金子	金子	jīnzi	n.	gold
富貴	富贵	fùguì	n.	riches and honor
本色	本色	běnsè	n.	natural color
向來	向来	xiànglái	adv.	always; all along
色情	色情	sèqíng	n.	pornography
笑話	笑话	xiàohua	n.	joke
取締	取缔	qǔdì	v.	clamp down
賣淫	卖淫	mài yín		prostitute oneself
嫖娼	嫖娼	piáo chāng		go whoring
掃黃	扫黄	sǎo huáng		crack down on pornography
去世	去世	qùshì		die; pass away
輓聯	挽联	wǎnlián	n.	elegiac couplet
棺材	棺材	guāncai	n.	coffin

按照	按照	ànzhào	prep.	according to
戴	戴	dài	v.	wear; put on
袖套	袖套	xiùtào	n.	armband
刊登	刊登	kāndēng	v.	publish
者	者	zhě	par.	(see grammar notes)
邊	边	biān	n.	rim; edge
嫩綠	嫩绿	nènlǜ	adj.	light green
葉芽	叶芽	yèyá	n.	a tender leaf
草	草	cǎo	n.	grass
信息	信息	xìnxī	n.	message; news
之所以	之所以	zhīsuǒyǐ	conj.	the reason why
化	化	huà	v.	-ize; -ify
美化	美化	měihuà	v.	beautify
環境	环境	huánjìng	n.	environment
外遇	外遇	wàiyù	n.	adulterer; paramour
帽子	帽子	màozi	n.	cap; hat
既然	既然	jìrán	conj.	now that; since

語法和詞語註釋

一、要不然   otherwise

"要不然" is used at the beginning of the second clause of a sentence to indicate the result or consequence which would be caused by the opposite situation or action to that introduced in the first clause.

1. 做喜慶的事情時要用紅顏色，要不然就會讓人們覺得不吉利。
   做喜庆的事情时要用红颜色，要不然就会让人们觉得不吉利。
   The red color should be used on auspicious or happy occasions. Otherwise

people would think it unlucky.

2. 出外旅遊一定要給家裏打電話，要不然父母就會擔心。
出外旅游一定要给家里打电话，要不然父母就会担心。
You should give your family a call when you're traveling, otherwise your parents will worry about you.

3. 考試一定要在 D 以上，要不然就不及格。
考试一定要在 D 以上，要不然就不及格。
You must get a D or above in the exams, otherwise you can't pass.

二、向來   always (up to the present)

"向來" indicates that a situation has always been the case from the past up to now. It often refers to habits or routines.

1. 中國人向來喜歡黃顏色。
中国人向来喜欢黄颜色。
The Chinese have always liked the color yellow.

2. 他向來不喜歡一個人散步。
他向来不喜欢一个人散步。
He never likes to go for a stroll alone.

3. 他考試向來都是 A。
他考试向来都是 A。
He has always got an A in his exams.

三、按照   according to

1. 按照傳統的習俗，有人去世的時候親戚要穿白色的衣服。
按照传统的习俗，有人去世的时候亲戚要穿白色的衣服。
When someone passes away, it is customary for his/her relatives to dress in white.

2. 按照學校的規定，一學期要選四門課。
按照学校的规定，一学期要选四门课。

According to the regulations of the school, one must take four courses each semester.

3. 按照中國的計劃生育政策，一家只能生一個孩子。
   按照中国的计划生育政策，一家只能生一个孩子。
   According to China's birth control policy, a family can only have one child.

四、者　　-er; -ist

"者" is used (1) after a noun, a verb or an adjective to indicate a person or people; (2) to indicate things that have been mentioned before.

1. 報紙和雜誌刊登死者的照片時，只能用黑白照片。
   报纸和杂志刊登死者的照片时，只能用黑白照片。
   When newspapers and magazines publish photos of the dead person, only black and white photos are used.

2. 這本書是王老師寫的，他是這本書的作者。
   这本书是王老师写的，他是这本书的作者。
   This book is written by Professor Wang. He's the author of this book.

3. 吃飯、睡覺、穿衣服，這三者是生活中必須要做的事情。
   吃饭、睡觉、穿衣服，这三者是生活中必须要做的事情。
   Eating, sleeping and getting dressed, these three things are what we have to do in life.

五、之所以……，是因為　　the reason why

"之所以" is used right after the subject in the first clause of a sentence to introduce the reason for something. "是因為" emphasizes the reason or the cause in the second clause. It is more often used in written language.

1. 人們之所以喜歡綠顏色，就是因為綠色能讓人們感覺到生命的存在。
   人们之所以喜欢绿颜色，就是因为绿色能让人们感觉到生命的存在。
   The reason why people like the color green is that it can make people aware of the existence of life.

2. 這一課之所以不難，是因為課文裏面沒有很多生詞。

　　這一课之所以不难，是因为课文里面没有很多生词。

　　The reason why this lesson is not hard is that there are not many new words in the text.

3. 我之所以學中文，是因為我的專業是東亞研究。

　　我之所以学中文，是因为我的专业是东亚研究。

　　The reason why I'm studying Chinese is that my major is East Asian Studies.

六、化　　-ize; -ify

"化" is a verbal suffix indicating a quality or state brought about after change.

1. 綠色能美化人們的生活環境。

　　绿色能美化人们的生活环境。

　　The color green can beautify people's environment.

2. 樹木和花草可以淨化空氣。

　　树木和花草可以淨化空气。

　　Trees and flowers can purify the air.

3. 現在中國人的生活越來越西化了。

　　现在中国人的生活越来越西化了。

　　Nowadays Chinese people's lives are becoming more and more westernized.

七、既然……，就　　since ..., (then) ...

"既然" is used either before or after the subject of a sentence to introduce a situation or fact which already exists, and "就" introduces the result or conclusion in the second clause.

1. 綠帽子既然有這樣的意思，中國的男人當然就不願意戴那頂綠帽子了。

　　绿帽子既然有这样的意思，中国的男人当然就不愿意戴那顶绿帽子了。

　　Since green caps mean this, Chinese men are of course not willing to wear them.

2. 你既然不舒服,那就不要去上課了吧。

你既然不舒服,那就不要去上课了吧。

Since you don't feel well, don't go to class.

3. 你既然聽不懂,就應該去問老師。

你既然听不懂,就应该去问老师。

Since you don't understand it, you should ask the teacher.

練習

一、把課文中說到的帶有顏色的東西填入表中

紅　紅	黃　黃	綠　綠	黑白　黑白

二、簡單地描述一下這五種顏色各自的含義

1. 紅　红

   _____。

2. 黃　黄

   _____。

3. 黑白　黑白

   _____。

4. 綠　绿

   _____。

三、選擇合適的詞語填空

1. 中國人_____喜歡黃顏色，_____中國人的皮膚是黃顏色的。
   中国人_____喜欢黄颜色，_____中国人的皮肤是黄颜色的。

   a. 既然……就　　b. 寧可……也　　c. 之所以……是因為

   既然……就　　　寧可……也　　　之所以……是因為

2. 我_____一輩子不結婚，_____不願意跟他結婚。
   我_____一辈子不结婚，_____不愿意跟他结婚。

   a. 既然……就　　b. 寧可……也　　c. 之所以……是因為

   既然……就　　　寧可……也　　　之所以……是因為

3. 你的病_____還沒有好，那_____不要去上課了吧！
   你的病_____还没有好，那_____不要去上课了吧！

   a. 既然……就　　b. 寧可……也　　c. 之所以……是因為

   既然……就　　　寧可……也　　　之所以……是因為

4. _____中國名稱的來源，據說有很多不同的說法。
   _____中国名称的来源，据说有很多不同的说法。

   a. 按照　　b. 通過　　c. 關於

   按照　　　通过　　　关于

5. _____學習中文，我學到了很多中國歷史文化知識。
   _____学习中文，我学到了很多中国历史文化知识。

   a. 按照　　b. 通過　　c. 關於

   按照　　　通过　　　关于

6. _____學校的規定，我們一學期只能選四門課。
   _____学校的规定，我们一学期只能选四门课。

   a. 按照　　b. 通過　　c. 關於

   按照　　　通过　　　关于

7. 我們這個課本_____分為語言和文化兩部分。

我们这个课本___A___分为语言和文化两部分。

   a. 大致   b. 向來   c. 往往

   大致   向来   往往

8. 中國人_____都認為自己是龍的傳人。

   中國人___B___都认为自己是龙的传人。

   a. 大致   b. 向來   c. 往往

   大致   向来   往往

9. 頭一天睡覺睡晚了，第二天上課_____會遲到。

   头一天睡觉睡晚了，第二天上课_____会迟到。

   a. 大致   b. 向來   c. 往往   C

   大致   向来   往往

四、翻譯

1. According to the traditional custom, a bride must dress in red at wedding. Otherwise, people would think it unlucky. Nowadays, many Chinese have become westernized, and some brides wear white dresses at their weddings.

   _____

   _____

   _____ 。

2. The Chinese have always liked the color yellow. The reason why they like it is that it is also the color of their skins. For some reason, the color yellow is also used to refer to pornography, and so pornographic novels and movies are called "yellow novels and movies".

   _____

   _____

   _____ 。

3. Now that we know some colors have special meanings, we should be very careful when presenting gifts to our friends. We should be especially careful not to give them green caps as gifts.

　　_____
　　_____
　　_____ 。

五、根據課文回答問題

1. 為甚麼過年和結婚的時候要用紅顏色？
   为什么过年和结婚的时候要用红颜色？
   　_____
   　_____ 。

2. 為甚麼說黃顏色是中國人的本色？
   为什么说黄颜色是中国人的本色？
   　_____
   　_____ 。

3. 黃色後來又有了甚麼樣的意思？
   黄色后来又有了什么样的意思？
   　_____
   　_____ 。

4. 老人去世的時候，要用甚麼顏色？
   老人去世的时候，要用什么颜色？
   　_____
   　_____ 。

5. 人們為甚麼喜歡綠色？
   人们为什么喜欢绿色？
   　_____
   　_____ 。

6. 為甚麼中國男人從來不戴綠色的帽子？
   为什么中国男人从来不戴绿色的帽子？
   _____
   _____ 。

六、課堂討論

1. 你們國家哪些顏色有特別的含義？
   你们国家哪些颜色有特别的含义？
   _____
   _____
   _____ 。

2. 顏色對人們的生活有甚麼影響？
   颜色对人们的生活有什么影响？
   _____
   _____
   _____
   _____ 。

七、小作文 *pick one*

1. 談一談顏色和生活的關係。
   谈一谈颜色和生活的关系。
   _____
   _____
   _____
   _____
   _____ 。

2. 你為甚麼喜歡這種顏色，而不喜歡那種顏色？
   你为什么喜欢这种颜色，而不喜欢那种颜色？

閱讀

牡丹、荷花、竹子、松樹

中國人向來喜愛花草樹木，不僅是因為花草樹木可以美化環境、可以淨化空氣，還因為許多花草樹木代表着特別的含義。

中國人最喜歡牡丹花。在中國人的眼裏，美麗大方的牡丹花代表着幸福美滿、榮華富貴。中國人之所以把牡丹花選為國花，就是希望自己的國家，能像盛開的牡丹花那樣繁榮昌盛。

中國人喜歡用花草樹木來比喻人的品德和性格。大家把那些生活在不好的環境中，卻沒有受環境影響的人比做荷花。因為荷花的根生長在水底下的污泥中，可是水面上的花朵卻一塵不染。人們說那些不受環境影響的人就像荷花一樣"出污泥而不染"。

竹子中間是空的、外面是直的。人們常常用它來比喻一個謙虛而正直的人。竹子不管在甚麼樣的環境裏都能夠生存，它可以從大石頭底下生長出來、它在寒冷的冬天也不會凋零。人們喜歡竹子，就是喜歡它那種堅強的性格。

老人們都喜愛松樹，因為松樹一年四季都是綠蔥蔥的。綠蔥蔥的松樹看起來就像是一個永遠年輕的人。由於松樹活的時間要比其他的樹長得多，因此人們把松樹當作長壽的象徵，把老年人比做不老松。

當老人過七十、八十、九十，甚至一百歲生日的時候，兒孫們大都會送給老人一幅畫着松樹和仙鶴的畫兒。這幅畫兒的名字叫做"松鶴延年"。"延年"是延長壽命的意思，就是希望老人能夠像松樹和仙鶴那樣長壽。

人們都喜歡交朋友，但是誰都討厭那種只是貪圖錢財、貪圖權勢的酒肉朋友；大家都願意結交在困難的時候，彼此能互相幫助、互相支持的知心朋友。

古時候，人們把松樹、竹子、梅花這三者稱作"歲寒三友"。意思是說在寒冷的冬天，當所有的花草樹木差不多都凋零的時候，松樹、竹子和梅花依然在風雪中相依為伴，它們就像三個在困難時期互相幫助、互相支持的好朋友。

阅读

牡丹、荷花、竹子、松树

中国人向来喜爱花草树木，不仅是因为花草树木可以美化环境、可以净化空气，还因为许多花草树木代表着特别的含义。

中国人最喜欢牡丹花。在中国人的眼里，美丽大方的牡丹花代表着幸福美满、荣华富贵。中国人之所以把牡丹花选为国花，就是希望自己的国家，能像盛开的牡丹花那样繁荣昌盛。

中国人喜欢用花草树木来比喻人的品德和性格。大家把那些生活在不好的环境中，却没有受环境影响的人比做荷花。因为荷花的根生长在水底下的污泥中，可是水面上的花朵却一尘不染。人们说那些不受环境影响的人就像荷花一样"出污泥而不染"。

竹子中间是空的、外面是直的。人们常常用它来比喻一个谦虚而正直的人。竹子不管在什么样的环境里都能够生存，它可以从大石头底下生长出来、它在寒冷的冬天也不会凋零。人们喜欢竹子，就是喜欢它那种坚强的性格。

老人们都喜爱松树，因为松树一年四季都是绿葱葱的。绿葱葱的松树看起来就像是一个永远年轻的人。由于松树活的时间要比其他的树长得多，因此人们把松树当作长寿的象征，把老年人比做不老松。

当老人过七十、八十、九十，甚至一百岁生日的时候，儿孙们大都会送给老人一幅画着松树和仙鹤的画儿。这幅画儿的名字叫做"松鹤延年"。"延年"是延长寿命的意思，就是希望老人能够像松树和仙鹤那样长寿。

人们都喜欢交朋友，但是谁都讨厌那种只是贪图钱财、贪图权势的酒肉朋友；大家都愿意结交在困难的时候，彼此能互相帮助、互相支持的知心朋友。

古时候，人们把松树、竹子、梅花这三者称作"岁寒三友"。意思是说在寒冷的冬天，当所有的花草树木差不多都凋零的时候，松树、竹子和梅花依然在风雪中相依为伴，它们就像三个在困难时期互相帮助、互相支持的好朋友。

19. 颜色的含義

生詞

牡丹	牡丹	mǔdan	n.	peony
荷花	荷花	héhuā	n.	lotus
竹子	竹子	zhúzi	n.	bamboo
松樹	松树	sōngshù	n.	pine
淨化	净化	jìnghuà	v.	purify
大方	大方	dàfang	adj.	natural and poised
美滿	美满	měimǎn	adj.	happy; satisfactory
榮華富貴	荣华富贵	rónghuá-fùguì		high position and great wealth
國花	国花	guóhuā	n.	national flower
盛開	盛开	shèngkāi	v.	be in full blossom
繁榮昌盛	繁荣昌盛	fánróng-chāngshèng		thriving and prosperous
比喻	比喻	bǐyù	v.	use as a metaphor
品德	品德	pǐndé	n.	moral character
性格	性格	xìnggé	n.	temperament
影響	影响	yǐngxiǎng	v.	influence; affect
比做	比做	bǐzuò	v.	be likened to
污泥	污泥	wūní	n.	dirt
水面	水面	shuǐmiàn	n.	water surface
花朵	花朵	huāduǒ	n.	flower
塵	尘	chén	n.	dust
染	染	rǎn	v.	contaminate
一塵不染	一尘不染	yīchénbùrǎn		not soiled by even a speck of dust
出污泥而不染	出污泥而不染	chū wūní ér bùrǎn		emerge unstained from the filth

空	空	kōng	adj.	empty
直	直	zhí	adj.	straight
謙虛	谦虚	qiānxū	adj.	humble
正直	正直	zhèngzhí	adj.	honest
凋零	凋零	diāolíng	v.	wither
堅強	坚强	jiānqiáng	adj.	staunch
季	季	jì	n.	season
綠葱葱	绿葱葱	lùcōngcōng	adj.	green
長壽	长寿	chángshòu	n.	long life
不老松	不老松	bùlǎosōng		evergreen pine
仙鶴	仙鹤	xiānhè	n.	red-crowned crane
松鶴延年	松鹤延年	sōnghè-yánnián		live as long as the pine and crane
壽命	寿命	shòumìng	n.	life-span; longevity
貪圖	贪图	tāntú	v.	covet; hanker after
酒肉朋友	酒肉朋友	jiǔròu péngyǒu		fair-weather friends
結交	结交	jiéjiāo	v.	associate with
支持	支持	zhīchí	v.	support
知心朋友	知心朋友	zhīxīn péngyǒu		intimate friends
梅花	梅花	méihuā	n.	plum blossom
歲寒三友	岁寒三友	suìhán-sānyǒu		the three companions of winter
依然	依然	yīrán	adv.	still; as before
相依為伴	相依为伴	xiāngyīwéi bàn		stick together and help each other in difficulties

問題

1. 人們為甚麼喜歡花草樹木？
   人们为什么喜欢花草树木？

19. 颜色的含义　　　　　　　　　　　　　　　　　　　　　　　361

_____
_____ 。

2. 中國人為甚麼把牡丹花選為國花？
   中国人为什么把牡丹花选为国花？
   _____
   _____ 。

3. 人們把甚麼人比做荷花？
   人们把什么人比做荷花？
   _____
   _____ 。

4. 中國人為甚麼喜歡竹子？
   中国人为什么喜欢竹子？
   _____
   _____ 。

5. "松鶴延年"這幅畫要送給甚麼人？
   "松鹤延年"这幅画要送给什么人？
   _____
   _____ 。

6. "歲寒三友"是甚麼樣的朋友？
   "岁寒三友"是什么样的朋友？
   _____
   _____ 。

附錄

漢語常用顏色一覽表
汉语常用颜色一览表

繁體	简体	拼音	英文
紅色	红色	hóngsè	red
大紅色	大红色	dàhóngsè	bright red
粉紅色	粉红色	fěnhóngsè	pink
黃色	黄色	huángsè	yellow
金黃色	金黄色	jīnhuángsè	golden yellow
淡黃色	淡黄色	dànhuángsè	light yellow
橘黃色	橘黄色	júhuángsè	orange
橙色	橙色	chéngsè	orange
綠色	绿色	lǜsè	green
墨綠色	墨绿色	mòlǜsè	dark green
淺綠色	浅绿色	qiǎnlǜsè	light green
嫩綠色	嫩绿色	nènlǜsè	light (soft) green; verdant
藍色	蓝色	lánsè	blue
深藍色	深蓝色	shēnlánsè	dark blue
淺藍色	浅蓝色	qiǎnlánsè	light blue; baby blue
青色	青色	qīngsè	blue or green or black
紫色	紫色	zǐsè	purple
灰色	灰色	huīsè	gray
深灰色	深灰色	shēnhuīsè	dark gray
淺灰色	浅灰色	qiǎnhuīsè	light gray
灰白色	灰白色	huībáisè	grayish-white
黑色	黑色	hēisè	black

咖啡色	咖啡色	kāfēisè	coffee color
棕色	棕色	zōngsè	brown
米色	米色	mǐsè	beige; cream-colored
奶油色	奶油色	nǎiyóusè	cream-colored

吃虧是福、難得糊塗
"To Suffer Losses Is Good Forfune" and "Ignorance Is Bliss"

學習大綱

通過學習本課，學生應該能夠：

1. 掌握這些句型和詞語的意思和用法："與"、"千萬"、"盡量/盡可能"、"難得"、"糊裏糊塗"、"所謂"、"仍然"。
2. 認識和運用課文以及閱讀文章內的生詞。
3. 明白"吃虧是福"和"難得糊塗"的文化意義。
4. 了解中國人親屬之間的稱呼。

Study Outline

After studying this chapter, students should:

1. Have a good command of the meaning and usage of these sentence patterns and terms: "yǔ" (with), "qiānwàn" (must; be sure to), "jìnliàng/ jìn kěnéng" (to the best of one's ability), "nándé" (seldom; rarely), "húlihútu" (confused; muddled), "suǒwèi" (what is called; so-called), "réngrán" (still).
2. Be familiar with the meaning and usage of the vocabulary introduced in the text and the reading.
3. Understand the cultural significance of the two phrases "chīkuī shì fú" (to suffer losses is good fortune) and "nándé hútu" (where ignorance is bliss, 'tis folly to be wise) in China.
4. Know how relatives address each other in China.

課文

中國人的家裏除了掛有山水畫、花鳥畫以外，還掛有一些字畫。這些字畫掛在牆上不僅是為了好看，更主要的是提醒人們應該怎樣對待生活、應該怎樣與別人相處。最常見的是清朝鄭板橋寫的"吃虧是福"、"難得糊塗"這兩幅字。

"吃虧是福"是說：在與別人的交往中，千萬不要想着去佔別人的便宜，無論是錢財還是別的甚麼，盡量都讓着人家點兒。這樣雖然你吃了一點兒虧，受了一些兒委屈，可是大家都覺得你是一個好人，都願意和你交往。當你遇到麻煩需要幫助的時候，大家都會來幫你，這就是你的福氣。

"難得糊塗"的意思是說：在和大家相處的時候，要盡可能地去理解別人。一個人做錯了一點兒事，你絕對不要去跟他斤斤計較，要學會原諒人。而且當你在心裏原諒別人的時候，表面上還要裝作糊裏糊塗、好像甚麼都不知道的樣子，不要讓人家看出來覺得不好意思。裝糊塗去原諒別人，一般人很難做到，所以說"難得糊塗"。

一個人只有真正懂得並且做到"吃虧是福"和"難得糊塗"，他才會有許多朋友。古人所謂"水至清則無魚，人至察則無徒"，就是這個道理。誰都知道水如果太乾淨的話，魚就沒有辦法生存；一個人要是對大大小小的事情都非常認真、都斤斤計較的話，他也就不會有甚麼朋友了！

中國有五千年的文明史。在這五千年裏，中國人創造了許多物質文明，他們發明了印刷術、指南針、火藥和紙，修建了長城和運河。與此同時，他們也在一代又一代地傳授着像"吃虧是福"、"難得糊塗"這種"精神"上的文明。

"吃虧是福"、"難得糊塗"直到今天仍然在中國流傳着，幾乎所有的中國人都懂得這兩句話所包含的深刻的意義。有人說"走後門"、"拉關係"的習俗之所以能夠在中國一直延續下來，就是因為中國人太懂得"吃虧是福"、"難得糊塗"的緣故了！

课文

中国人的家里除了挂有山水画、花鸟画以外，还挂有一些字画。这些字画挂在墙上不仅是为了好看，更主要的是提醒人们应该怎样对待生活、应该怎样与别人相处。最常见的是清朝郑板桥写的"吃亏是福"、"难得糊涂"这两幅字。

"吃亏是福"是说：在与别人的交往中，千万不要想着去占别人的便宜，无论是钱财还是别的什么，尽量都让着人家点儿。这样虽然你吃了一点儿亏，受了一些儿委屈，可是大家都觉得你是一个好人，都愿意和你交往。当你遇到麻烦需要帮助的时候，大家都会来帮你，这就是你的福气。

"难得糊涂"的意思是说：在和大家相处的时候，要尽可能地去理解别人。一个人做错了一点儿事，你绝对不要去跟他斤斤计较，要学会原谅人。而且当你在心里原谅别人的时候，表面上还要装作糊里糊涂、好像什么都不知道的样子，不要让人家看出来觉得不好意思。装糊涂去原谅别人，一般人很难做到，所以说"难得糊涂"。

一个人只有真正懂得并且做到"吃亏是福"和"难得糊涂"，他才会有许多朋友。古人所谓"水至清则无鱼，人至察则无徒"，就是这个道理。谁都知道水如果太干净的话，鱼就没有办法生存；一个人要是对大大小小的事情都非常认真、都斤斤计较的话，他也就不会有什么朋友了！

中国有五千年的文明史。在这五千年里，中国人创造了许多物质文明，他们发明了印刷术、指南针、火药和纸，修建了长城和运河。与此同时，他们也在一代又一代地传授着像"吃亏是福"、"难得糊涂"这种"精神"上的文明。

"吃亏是福"、"难得糊涂"直到今天仍然在中国流传着，几乎所有的中国人都懂得这两句话所包含的深刻的意义。有人说"走后门"、"拉关系"的习俗之所以能够在中国一直延续下来，就是因为中国人太懂得"吃亏是福"、"难得糊涂"的缘故了！

生詞

吃虧	吃亏	chī kuī		suffer losses
吃虧是福	吃亏是福	chīkuī shì fú		to suffer losses is good fortune
難得	难得	nándé	adj.	seldom; rarely
難得糊塗	难得糊涂	nándé hútu		where ignorance is bliss, 'tis folly to be wise
山水畫	山水画	shānshuǐhuà	n.	landscape painting
花鳥畫	花鸟画	huāniǎohuà	n.	traditional Chinese paintings of flowers and birds
字畫	字画	zìhuà	n.	calligraphy; painting
字	字	zì	n.	calligraphy; writing
提醒	提醒	tíxǐng	v.	remind
與	与	yǔ	prep.	with
相處	相处	xiāngchǔ	v.	get along with (each other)
鄭板橋	郑板桥	Zhèng Bǎnqiáo		name of a person
交往	交往	jiāowǎng	v.	associate with
千萬	千万	qiānwàn	adv.	must; be sure to
佔便宜	占便宜	zhàn piányi		profit at other people's expense
錢財	钱财	qiáncái	n.	wealth; money
盡量	尽量	jǐnliàng	adv.	to the best of one's abilities
讓	让	ràng	v.	yield; give ground
人家	人家	rénjia	n.	other people
委屈	委屈	wěiqu	v.	(suffer) injustice; be wronged
盡可能	尽可能	jǐn kě'néng	adv.	try one's best
斤斤計較	斤斤计较	jīn jīn jì jiào		excessively mean and small-minded

原諒	原谅	yuánliàng	v.	excuse; forgive
表面	表面	biǎomiàn	n.	surface
裝	装	zhuāng	v.	pretend
糊裏糊塗	糊里糊涂	húlihútu		confused; muddled
所謂	所谓	suǒwèi	v.	what is called; so-called
至	至	zhì	adv.	extremely
清	清	qīng	adj.	clear
察	察	chá	adj.	sharp
徒	徒	tú	n.	companion; friend
文明	文明	wénmíng	n.	civilization
印刷術	印刷术	yìnshuāshù	n.	printing; typography
指南針	指南针	zhǐnánzhēn	n.	compass
火藥	火药	huǒyào	n.	gunpowder
物質	物质	wùzhì	n.	material goods, etc.
與此同時	与此同时	yǔ cǐ tóngshí		at the same time
傳授	传授	chuánshòu	v.	pass on (knowledge)
仍然	仍然	réngrán	adv.	still; yet
包含	包含	bāohán	v.	contain; embody
走後門	走后门	zǒu hòumén		secure advantages through pull or influence (lit., "go through the back door")
拉關係	拉关系	lā guānxi		try to establish connections with important people
延續	延续	yánxù	v.	continue; go on

語法和詞語註釋

一、與　　with

> "與" has the same meaning as "跟" but it more often appears in written language.

1. 提醒人們應該怎樣對待生活、怎樣與別人相處。
   提醒人们应该怎样对待生活、怎样与别人相处。
   To remind people how to adopt a correct attitude towards life, and how to get along with others.

2. 與她相比，我一點兒都不漂亮。
   与她相比，我一点儿都不漂亮。
   Compared with her, I am not pretty at all.

3. 這件事與我無關。
   这件事与我无关。
   This matter has nothing to do with me.

二、千萬　　must; be sure to

1. 在和別人的交往中，千萬不要想着去佔別人的便宜。
   在和别人的交往中，千万不要想着去占别人的便宜。
   In your dealings with other people, never think of profiting at other people's expense.

2. 到國外旅遊的時候，千萬要注意安全。
   到国外旅游的时候，千万要注意安全。
   When you're traveling abroad, you must be careful about your personal safety.

3. 喝酒以後，千萬不要開車。
   喝酒以后，千万不要开车。
   Never drink and drive.

三、盡量/盡可能　　to the best of one's ability

1. 無論是錢財還是別的甚麼，盡量都讓着人家點兒。
   无论是钱财还是别的什么，尽量都让着人家点儿。
   No matter whether in money matters or other things, try your best to give ground to others a little.

2. 盡可能地去理解別人。
   尽可能地去理解别人。
   Try your best to understand others.

3. 寫漢字的時候，要盡量寫好。
   写汉字的时候，要尽量写好。
   When you're writing Chinese characters, you must try your best to write them well.

四、難得　　seldom; rarely

1. 難得糊塗。
   难得糊涂。
   Where ignorance is bliss, 'tis folly to be wise.

2. 我在麻州上學，我男朋友在加州上學，我們平時難得見一面。
   我在麻州上学，我男朋友在加州上学，我们平时难得见一面。
   I'm studying in Massachusetts, but my boyfriend is studying in California. It's normally hard to get to see each other.

3. 免費去中國旅遊，這種機會真是很難得。
   免费去中国旅游，这种机会真是很难得。
   The chance to travel to China free is really rare.

五、糊裏糊塗　　in disorderly fashion; act stupidly

When "裏" is inserted into certain two-syllable adjectives and the first syllable of the adjective is repeated (e.g. 糊裏糊塗), a more lively effect is produced. Frequent examples of this are:

shǎlishǎqi	luōliluōsuō	huānglihuāngzhāng
傻裏傻氣	囉裏囉嗦	慌裏慌張
傻里傻气	罗里罗嗦	慌里慌张
soft in the head	long-winded	flurried; agitated

1. 表面上要裝作糊裏糊塗的樣子。
   表面上要装作糊里糊涂的样子。
   Outwardly, you should pretend to be muddled.

2. 我媽媽常常囉裏囉嗦的，真煩人。
   我妈妈常常罗里罗嗦的，真烦人。
   My mother is always so long-winded, it's really annoying.

3. 已經都上課了，小張才慌裏慌張地跑進教室。
   已经都上课了，小张才慌里慌张地跑进教室。
   The class had already begun when Xiao Zhang ran into the classroom in a flurry.

六、所謂　　what is called; so-called

"所謂" introduces the word or phrase which will be explained in the following phrase or clause.

1. 古人所謂"水至清則無魚，人至察則無徒"，就是這個道理。
   古人所谓"水至清则无鱼，人至察则无徒"，就是这个道理。
   This truth is what the people in ancient times meant by "The cleanest water has no fish; the extremely cautious person has no friends".

2. 所謂會中文，就是指聽、說、讀、寫都會。
   所谓会中文，就是指听、说、读、写都会。
   By "knowing Chinese" we mean knowing how to listen, speak, read and write.

3. 中國人所謂的"好學生"，就是聽老師話的學生。
   中国人所谓的"好学生"，就是听老师话的学生。
   Those whom the Chinese call "good students" are students who do as their teachers say.

七、仍然　　still

"仍然" means "還", but it more often appears in written language.

1. "吃虧是福"、"難得糊塗"到今天仍然在中國流傳着。
   "吃亏是福"、"难得糊涂"到今天仍然在中国流传着。
   "To suffer losses is good fortune" and "Where ignorance is bliss, it's folly to be wise" are sayings which are still widespread in China.

2. 他中文已經說得很好了，可他仍然在學中文。
   他中文已经说得很好了，可他仍然在学中文。
   He already speaks very good Chinese, but he's still learning it.

3. 下課了，他仍然坐在教室裏。
   下课了，他仍然坐在教室里。
   The class is over, but he is still sitting in the classroom.

練習

一、根據課文來完成句子

1. 中國人家裏掛字畫是為了
   中国人家里挂字画是为了
   _____。

2. 和別人交往中盡量讓着別人是為了
   和别人交往中尽量让着别人是为了
   _____。

3. 原諒別人時要裝作糊裏糊塗是為了
   原谅别人时要装作糊里糊涂是为了
   _____。

4. 人們要做到吃虧是福、難得糊塗是為了
   人们要做到吃亏是福、难得糊涂是为了

_____。

5. 中國人走後門、拉關係的習俗能延續下來是因為
   中国人走后门、拉关系的习俗能延续下来是因为
   _____。

二、找出和例句意思不同的句子

1. 中國人的家裏除了掛有山水畫以外，還掛有字畫。
   中国人的家里除了挂有山水画以外，还挂有字画。

   a. 中國人的家裏既掛有山水畫，也掛有字畫。
      中国人的家里既挂有山水画，也挂有字画。
   b. 中國人的家裏不僅掛有山水畫，還掛有字畫。
      中国人的家里不仅挂有山水画，还挂有字画。
   c. 中國人的家裏原先掛有山水畫，後來掛有字畫。
      中国人的家里原先挂有山水画，后来挂有字画。

2. 與別人交往的時候千萬不要去佔別人的便宜。
   与别人交往的时候千万不要去占别人的便宜。

   a. 與別人交往的時候絕對不要去佔別人的便宜。
      与别人交往的时候绝对不要去占别人的便宜。
   b. 與別人交往的時候不要太多地佔別人的便宜。
      与别人交往的时候不要太多地占别人的便宜。
   c. 與別人交往的時候一定不要去佔別人的便宜。
      与别人交往的时候一定不要去占别人的便宜。

3. 人們之所以要交朋友，是因為可以走後門。
   人们之所以要交朋友，是因为可以走后门。

   a. 人們交朋友的原因，是因為可以走後門。
      人们交朋友的原因，是因为可以走后门。
   b. 人們為了走後門，所以他們都要交朋友。
      人们为了走后门，所以他们都要交朋友。
   c. 人們為了要交朋友，所以大家都走後門。
      人们为了要交朋友，所以大家都走后门。

4. 難得糊塗才會有朋友，要不然就沒有人願意和你交往。
   难得糊涂才会有朋友，要不然就没有人愿意和你交往。

   a. 難得糊塗才會有朋友，不這樣就沒有人願意和你交往。
      难得糊涂才会有朋友，不这样就没有人愿意和你交往。
   b. 難得糊塗才會有朋友，只有這樣人們才願意和你交往。
      难得糊涂才会有朋友，只有这样人们才愿意和你交往。
   c. 難得糊塗才會有朋友，既然這樣沒有人願意和你交往。
      难得糊涂才会有朋友，既然这样没有人愿意和你交往。

三、把下面句子按照順序連成一段文章

我的同屋　　　　　我的同屋

( ) 我有一個同屋叫黃小麗，　　( ) 我有一个同屋叫黄小丽，
( ) 大家都說我們是好朋友。　　( ) 大家都说我们是好朋友。
( ) 等到我需要穿裙子的時候，　( ) 等到我需要穿裙子的时候，
( ) 可從來不讓別人吃她的東西。( ) 可从来不让别人吃她的东西。
( ) 我想告訴她佔別人便宜不好，( ) 我想告诉她占别人便宜不好，
( ) 幾乎每一件裙子都是髒的。　( ) 几乎每一件裙子都是脏的。
( ) 她還經常隨便吃我買的點心，( ) 她还经常随便吃我买的点心，
( ) 要不然沒有人願意和你交往。( ) 要不然没有人愿意和你交往。
( ) 她常常穿我的裙子去跳舞，　( ) 她常常穿我的裙子去跳舞，
( ) 她非常漂亮又特別聰明。　　( ) 她非常漂亮又特别聪明。
( ) 今天學了"難得糊塗"之後， ( ) 今天学了"难得糊涂"之后，
( ) 穿過以後從來都不洗乾淨。　( ) 穿过以后从来都不洗干净。
( ) 她個子高低和我差不多，　　( ) 她个子高低和我差不多，
( ) 我想還是甚麼都不要說了吧。( ) 我想还是什么都不要说了吧。

四、翻譯

1. Some people think that in your dealings with others, you should try never to be treated unjustly. You must try your best to profit at other people's expense, and this way you won't suffer loss yourself.

_____

_____

_____ 。

2. In fact, what people in ancient times said about "To suffer losses is good fortune", and "Where ignorance is bliss, 'tis folly to be wise " is not right. When other people do something wrong, you should never pretend to be ignorant about it.

_____

_____

_____ 。

3. Now people still believe that if a person is excessively mean and small-minded, he/she won't have any friends. However, people also know that if one pretends to be muddled in everything, he won't have good friends as well.

_____

_____

_____ 。

五、根據課文回答問題

1. 中國人家裏為甚麼要掛一些字畫？
   中国人家里为什么要挂一些字画？

   _____

   _____ 。

2. 你知道"吃虧是福"是甚麼意思嗎？
   你知道"吃亏是福"是什么意思吗？

   _____

   _____ 。

3. 為甚麼喜歡佔別人便宜的人沒有朋友？
   为什么喜欢占别人便宜的人没有朋友？
   _____
   _____ 。

4. "難得糊塗"是甚麼意思？
   "难得糊涂"是什么意思？
   _____
   _____ 。

5. 為甚麼原諒別人的時候要裝做糊裏糊塗？
   为什么原谅别人的时候要装做糊里糊涂？
   _____
   _____ 。

6. 甚麼樣的人會有許多朋友？
   什么样的人会有许多朋友？
   _____
   _____ 。

7. "水至清則無魚"是甚麼意思？
   "水至清则无鱼"是什么意思？
   _____
   _____ 。

六、課堂討論

你覺得"吃虧是福"、"難得糊塗"對不對？為甚麼？
你觉得"吃亏是福"、"难得糊涂"对不对？为什么？
_____
_____
_____ 。

七、小作文

1. 你和你的朋友（同學、室友）是怎麼相處的。
   你和你的朋友（同学、室友）是怎么相处的。

   _____
   _____
   _____
   _____
   _____。

2. 怎樣才是真正的好朋友。
   怎样才是真正的好朋友。

   _____
   _____
   _____
   _____
   _____
   _____。

〈我的同屋〉的答案

（1）我有一個同屋叫黃小麗，	（1）我有一个同屋叫黄小丽，
（2）她非常漂亮又特別聰明。	（2）她非常漂亮又特别聪明。
（3）她個子高低和我差不多，	（3）她个子高低和我差不多，
（4）大家都說我們是好朋友。	（4）大家都说我们是好朋友。
（5）她常常穿我的裙子去跳舞，	（5）她常常穿我的裙子去跳舞，
（6）穿過以後從來都不洗乾淨。	（6）穿过以后从来都不洗干净。
（7）等到我需要穿裙子的時候，	（7）等到我需要穿裙子的时候，
（8）幾乎每一件裙子都是髒的。	（8）几乎每一件裙子都是脏的。
（9）她還經常隨便吃我買的點心，	（9）她还经常随便吃我买的点心，
（10）可從來不讓別人吃她的東西。	（10）可从来不让别人吃她的东西。

⑾ 我想告訴她佔別人便宜不好，
⑿ 要不然沒有人願意和你交往。
⒀ 今天學了"難得糊塗"之後，
⒁ 我想還是甚麼都不要說了吧。

⑾ 我想告诉她占别人便宜不好，
⑿ 要不然没有人愿意和你交往。
⒀ 今天学了"难得糊涂"之后，
⒁ 我想还是什么都不要说了吧。

閱讀

稱呼和禮貌

中國人親屬之間的稱呼很複雜，不要說外國人弄不清楚，就是中國人自己常常也是糊裏糊塗的。

爸爸的父母親是爺爺、奶奶；媽媽的父母親是外公、外婆。哥哥弟弟的孩子是侄子、侄女；姐姐妹妹的孩子是外甥、外甥女。兒子的孩子是孫子、孫女；女兒的孩子是外孫、外孫女。

中國家庭是根據祖父、也就是爺爺的血緣關係來繫聯的。在一個家庭裏面，與祖父有血緣關係的人都姓祖父的姓，只有姓祖父姓的人才是這個家庭裏的人；如果跟祖父沒有血緣關係、不姓祖父姓的人那就是外人，所以中國有外公、外婆、外甥、外孫這樣的稱呼。

父親的哥哥是你的伯伯；父親的弟弟是你的叔叔。伯伯和叔叔的孩子是你的堂哥、堂姐、堂弟、堂妹。

"堂"是大房子的意思。因為你的爺爺也是堂哥、堂姐的爺爺，你們都姓爺爺的姓，所以你們就像是一棟大房子裏面的兄弟姐妹。

爸爸的姐妹是你的姑姑，媽媽的兄弟姐妹是你的舅舅和姨姨。這些姑姑、舅舅、姨姨的孩子是你的表哥、表姐、表弟、表妹。

所謂"表"就是外面的意思。因為你的爺爺不是表哥、表姐他們的爺爺，你和他們不是一個姓，所以他們就不是你那棟大房子裏的兄弟姐妹，他們只是房子外面的表兄弟、表姐妹。

如果你生活在一個大家族裏，你要盡可能地弄清楚你和每一個人的關係，叫人的時候千萬不要叫錯。不管這些稱呼多麼複雜、多麼麻煩，你也要盡量地習慣。絕對不可以像外國家庭那樣直接叫家人的名字。

中國人特別講究禮貌，他們認為小孩子叫大人的名字，是最不禮貌的做法。在中國人的家裏，孩子不能叫父母的名字，更不能叫祖父、祖母和外祖父、外祖母的名字。

人們教育孩子不但在家裏要有禮貌，到了外面仍然要有禮貌。早上起來見到鄰居家的老人，你得說"爺爺奶奶，早上好！"去學校見到了老師，你也一定得叫一聲"老師好！"

阅读

称呼和礼貌

中国人亲属之间的称呼很复杂，不要说外国人弄不清楚，就是中国人自己常常也是糊里糊涂的。

爸爸的父母亲是爷爷、奶奶；妈妈的父母亲是外公、外婆。哥哥弟弟的孩子是侄子、侄女；姐姐妹妹的孩子是外甥、外甥女。儿子的孩子是孙子、孙女；女儿的孩子是外孙、外孙女。

中国家庭是根据祖父、也就是爷爷的血缘关系来系联的。在一个家庭里面，与祖父有血缘关系的人都姓祖父的姓，只有姓祖父姓的人才是这个家庭里的人；如果跟祖父没有血缘关系、不姓祖父姓的人那就是外人，所以中国有外公、外婆、外甥、外孙这样的称呼。

父亲的哥哥是你的伯伯；父亲的弟弟是你的叔叔。伯伯和叔叔的孩子是你的堂哥、堂姐、堂弟、堂妹。

"堂"是大房子的意思。因为你的爷爷也是堂哥、堂姐的爷爷，你们都姓爷爷的姓，所以你们就像是一栋大房子里面的兄弟姐妹。

爸爸的姐妹是你的姑姑，妈妈的兄弟姐妹是你的舅舅和姨姨。这些姑姑、舅舅、姨姨的孩子是你的表哥、表姐、表弟、表妹。

所谓"表"就是外面的意思。因为你的爷爷不是表哥、表姐他们的爷爷，你和他们不是一个姓，所以他们就不是你那栋大房子里的兄弟姐妹，他们只是房子外面的表兄弟、表姐妹。

如果你生活在一个大家族里，你要尽可能地弄清楚你和每一个人的关系，叫人的时候千万不要叫错。不管这些称呼多么复杂、多么麻烦，你也要尽量地习惯。绝对不可以像外国家庭那样直接叫家人的名字。

中国人特别讲究礼貌，他们认为小孩子叫大人的名字，是最不礼貌的做法。在中国人的家里，孩子不能叫父母的名字，更不能叫祖父、祖母和外祖父、外祖母的名字。

人们教育孩子不但在家里要有礼貌，到了外面仍然要有礼貌。早上起来见到邻居家的老人，你得说"爷爷奶奶，早上好！"去学校见到了老师，你也一定得叫一声"老师好！"

生詞

稱呼	称呼	chēnghu	n.	form of address
禮貌	礼貌	lǐmào	n.	courtesy; politeness
親屬	亲属	qīnshǔ	n.	relatives
外公	外公	wàigōng	n.	mother's father; grandfather
父母親	父母亲	fù-mǔqīn	n.	parents
外婆	外婆	wàipó	n.	mother's mother; grandmother
姪子	侄子	zhízi	n.	brother's son; nephew
姪女	侄女	zhínǚ	n.	brother's daughter; niece
外甥	外甥	wàisheng	n.	sister's son; nephew
外甥女	外甥女	wàishengnǚ	n.	sister's daughter; niece
孫女	孙女	sūnnǚ	n.	son's daughter; granddaughter
女兒	女儿	nǚ'ér	n.	daughter
外孫	外孙	wàisūn	n.	daughter's son; grandson
外孫女	外孙女	wàisūnnǚ	n.	daughter's daughter; granddaughter
祖父	祖父	zǔfù	n.	father's father; grandfather
血緣	血缘	xuèyuán	n.	blood relationship
繫聯	系联	xìlián	v.	relate to
外人	外人	wàirén	n.	outsider; stranger
伯伯	伯伯	bóbo	n.	father's elder brother; address for men of an age approx. that of father, but older
叔叔	叔叔	shūshu	n.	father's younger brother; address for men of an age approx. that of father
堂	堂	táng	n.	relatives born of the same grandfather; hall

堂哥、堂弟	堂哥、堂弟	tánggē tángdì	n.	male cousins from father's brothers
堂姐、堂妹	堂姐、堂妹	táng jiě tángmèi	n.	female cousins from father's brother
棟	栋	dòng	m.	measure word for house
兄弟姐妹	兄弟姐妹	xiōngdì jiěmèi	n.	brothers and sisters
姑姑	姑姑	gūgu	n.	aunt; father's sister
舅舅	舅舅	jiùjiu	n.	mother's brother
姨姨	姨姨	yíyi	n.	mother's sister
表哥、表弟	表哥、表弟	biǎogē biǎodì	n.	male cousins from father's sister or mother's brother or sister
表姐、表妹	表姐、表妹	biǎo jiě biǎomèi	n.	female cousins from father's sister or mother's brother or sister
表	表	biǎo	n.	the relationship between the children or grandchildren of a brother and a sister or sisters
家族	家族	jiāzú	n.	family; clan
祖母	祖母	zǔmǔ	n.	father's mother; grandmother
外祖父	外祖父	wàizǔfù	n.	mother's father; grandfather
外祖母	外祖母	wàizǔmǔ	n.	mother's mother; grandmother
鄰居	邻居	lín jū	n.	neighbor

問題

1. 中國家庭是根據甚麼來繫聯的？
   中国家庭是根据什么来系联的？

   _____
   _____ 。

2. 堂哥、堂姐、堂弟、堂妹的"堂"是甚麼意思？
   堂哥、堂姐、堂弟、堂妹的"堂"是什么意思？

   _____
   _____ 。

3. 表哥、表姐、表弟、表妹的"表"是甚麼意思？
   表哥、表姐、表弟、表妹的"表"是什么意思？
   _____
   _____。

4. 為甚麼中國人的家裏不能直接叫大人的名字？
   为什么中国人的家里不能直接叫大人的名字？
   _____
   _____。

5. 中國人是怎樣教育孩子有禮貌的？
   中国人是怎样教育孩子有礼貌的？
   _____
   _____。

附　錄

中國家庭親屬稱謂簡表

			爺爺	奶奶	外公	外婆	
伯伯	叔叔	姑姑	爸爸	媽媽		舅舅	姨姨
伯母	嬸嬸	姑父				舅媽	姨父
	哥哥	弟弟	我		姐姐	妹妹
	嫂嫂	弟媳			姐夫	妹夫
	侄子	侄女	兒子	女兒	外甥	外甥女
			兒媳	女婿		
			孫子	孫女	外孫	外孫女

中国家庭亲属称谓简表

			爷爷	奶奶	外公	外婆	
伯伯	叔叔	姑姑	爸爸	妈妈		舅舅	姨姨
伯母	婶婶	姑父				舅妈	姨父
	哥哥	弟弟	我		姐姐	妹妹
	嫂嫂	弟媳			姐夫	妹夫
	侄子	侄女	儿子	女儿	外甥	外甥女
			儿媳	女婿		
			孙子	孙女	外孙	外孙女

21

中國人信仰的宗教
Religious Beliefs in China

學習大綱

通過學習本課，學生應該能夠：

1. 掌握這些句型和詞語的意思和用法："隨着"、"否則"、"並 (不)"、"除非……才"、"親 (眼、耳、口、手、身)"、"無非"、"與其……，不如"、"始終"。
2. 認識和運用課文以及閱讀文章內的生詞。
3. 了解中國有哪幾種主要宗教信仰和有關的習俗。
4. 了解中國的迷信文化的一些習俗。

Study Outline

After studying this chapter, students should:

1. Have a good command of the meaning and usage of these sentence patterns and terms: "suízhe" (along with), "fǒuzé" (otherwise), "bìng (bu)" (actually [not]; [not] at all), "chúfēi ... cái" (only if), "qīn (yǎn, ěr, kǒu, shǒu, shēn)" (with one's own [eyes, ears, mouth, hands, etc.]), "wúfēi" (nothing but; no more than), "yǔqí ... bùrú" (rather ... than), "shǐzhōng" (from beginning to end).
2. Be familiar with the meaning and usage of the vocabulary introduced in the text and the reading.
3. Know about the major religious beliefs in China and the customs associated with them.
4. Know about superstitious beliefs in China and the customs associated with them.

課文

中國人信仰的宗教主要是佛教和道教，也有人信仰基督教及其他的一些宗教。

佛教是漢朝的時候從印度傳進來的。隨着佛教的傳入，中國許多地方蓋起了寺廟，許多人出家當了和尚和尼姑。

佛教的教祖是釋迦牟尼。佛教宣傳的是因果報應，意思是說做好事會有好結果。人活着的時候多做好事，死後可以上天堂，否則，死了以後就要下地獄，有的人甚至還會變成豬、狗甚麼的。

信佛的人過年、過節都要到廟裏去給佛燒香磕頭，他們認為這樣才能得到佛的保佑。有很多人平常不去燒香磕頭，只是在遇到麻煩的時候才去求佛保佑。人們說這些人"平時不燒香，急時抱佛腳"。

道教是中國人自己的宗教，是漢朝時創立的。道教的教祖是老子，道教的寺廟叫道觀，道觀裏住的男人叫道士、女人叫道姑。道教認為人只要做好事不做壞事，就可以長生不死，就可以變成神仙。

南北朝時，有人把儒家也當成了宗教。他們把儒家叫做儒教，許多地方都蓋起了祭拜孔子的孔廟。其實，儒家只是教人們怎樣學習、怎樣做一個好人、怎樣治理國家，儒家好像和鬼神並沒有甚麼關係。

早在唐朝時，西方的基督教就傳到了中國。雖然中國信仰基督教的人沒有佛教和道教那麼多，可是在一些大城市裏，還是能看到房頂上豎着十字架的教堂。

也有許多人不相信任何宗教。他們不相信世界上真的會有鬼神和上帝，他們說除非親眼看到了上帝和鬼神，他們才會相信。

其實，信不信宗教沒甚麼關係。佛經、道經、聖經裏講的，教堂裏牧師說的，無非都是要人多做好事不做壞事。去教堂做禮拜，讀佛經、聖經，與其說是接受一種宗教宣傳，還不如說是在接受一種道德教育。

信神的人以為神住在天上，所以他們把寺廟修建在高山上。中國有名的懸空寺就修建在山西恆山的懸崖峭壁上。寺內並排擺着釋迦牟尼、老子和孔子三座塑像。到那兒去燒香磕頭的人始終不明白，為甚麼外來的釋迦牟尼在中間，而中國自己的老子和孔子在兩旁。

课文

中国人信仰的宗教主要是佛教和道教，也有人信仰基督教及其他的一些宗教。

佛教是汉朝的时候从印度传进来的。随着佛教的传入，中国许多地方盖起了寺庙，许多人出家当了和尚和尼姑。

佛教的教祖是释迦牟尼。佛教宣传的是因果报应，意思是说做好事会有好结果。人活着的时候多做好事，死后可以上天堂，否则，死了以后就要下地狱，有的人甚至还会变成猪、狗什么的。

信佛的人过年、过节都要到庙里去给佛烧香磕头，他们认为这样才能得到佛的保佑。有很多人平常不去烧香磕头，只是在遇到麻烦的时候才去求佛保佑。人们说这些人"平时不烧香，急时抱佛脚"。

道教是中国人自己的宗教，是汉朝时创立的。道教的教祖是老子，道教的寺庙叫道观，道观里住的男人叫道士、女人叫道姑。道教认为人只要做好事不做坏事，就可以长生不死，就可以变成神仙。

南北朝时，有人把儒家也当成了宗教。他们把儒家叫做儒教，许多地方都盖起了祭拜孔子的孔庙。其实，儒家只是教人们怎样学习、怎样做一个好人、怎样治理国家，儒家好像和鬼神并没有什么关系。

早在唐朝时，西方的基督教就传到了中国。虽然中国信仰基督教的人没有佛教和道教那么多，可是在一些大城市里，还是能看到房顶上竖着十字架的教堂。

也有许多人不相信任何宗教。他们不相信世界上真的会有鬼神和上帝，他们说除非亲眼看到了上帝和鬼神，他们才会相信。

其实，信不信宗教没什么关系。佛经、道经、圣经里讲的，教堂里牧师说的，无非都是要人多做好事不做坏事。去教堂做礼拜，读佛经、圣经，与其说是接受一种宗教宣传，还不如说是在接受一种道德教育。

信神的人以为神住在天上，所以他们把寺庙修建在高山上。中国有名的悬空寺就修建在山西恒山的悬崖峭壁上。寺内并排摆着释迦牟尼、老子和孔子三座塑像。到那儿去烧香磕头的人始终不明白，为什么外来的释迦牟尼在中间，而中国自己的老子和孔子在两旁。

生 詞

宗教	宗教	zōng jiào	n.	religion
佛教	佛教	Fó jiào		Buddhism
道教	道教	Dào jiào		Taoism
信仰	信仰	xìnyǎng	v.	believe in
基督教	基督教	Jīdū jiào		Christianity
印度	印度	Yìndù		India
隨著	随着	suízhe	prep.	along with
寺廟	寺庙	sìmiào	n.	temple
出家	出家	chū jiā		become a monk or nun
和尚	和尚	héshang	n.	bonze; monk
尼姑	尼姑	nígū	n.	nun; priestess
教祖	教祖	jiàozǔ	n.	the founder of a religion
釋迦牟尼	释迦牟尼	Shì jiāmóuní		Sakyamuni
因果報應	因果报应	yīnguǒ bàoyìng		as a man sows, so let him reap; retributive justice
否則	否则	fǒuzé	conj.	otherwise
地獄	地狱	dìyù	n.	hell
燒香	烧香	shāo xiāng		burn joss-sticks
磕頭	磕头	kē tóu		kowtow
保佑	保佑	bǎoyòu	v.	bless
創立	创立	chuànglì	v.	found; institute
老子	老子	Lǎozǐ		Lao Zi (philosopher in the Spring and Autumn Period)
道觀	道观	dàoguàn	n.	Taoist temple
道士	道士	dàoshì	n.	Taoist priest

道姑	道姑	dàogū	n.	Taoist nun
長生不死	长生不死	chángshēng bùsǐ	v.	live forever and never die
神仙	神仙	shénxiān	n.	immortal; supernatural being
儒家	儒家	Rú jiā	n.	the Confucian school
孔子	孔子	Kǒngzǐ		Confucius
孔廟	孔庙	Kǒngmiào	n.	Confucian temple
鬼神	鬼神	guǐshén	n.	ghosts and gods
並 (+neg.)	并 (+neg.)	bìng (+neg.)	adv.	actually (not); (not) at all
豎	竖	shù	v.	erect; set upright
十字架	十字架	shízì jià	n.	crucifix; cross
教堂	教堂	jiàotáng	n.	church
除非……才	除非……才	chúfēi ... cái	conj.	only if
親眼	亲眼	qīnyǎn		see with one's eyes
佛經	佛经	fó jīng	n.	Buddhist sutra
道經	道经	dào jīng	n.	Taoist scriptures
聖經	圣经	Shèng jīng	n.	Bible
牧師	牧师	mùshī	n.	minister (in a church)
無非	无非	wúfēi	adv.	nothing but; no more than
與其……不如	与其……不如	yǔqí ... bùrú	conj.	rather ... than ...
道德	道德	dàodé	n.	ethics
恆山	恒山	Héng Shān		Mt. Heng
懸崖峭壁	悬崖峭壁	xuányá-qiàobì	n.	sheer precipice and overhanging rocks
懸空寺	悬空寺	Xuánkōng Sì		Hanging Temple
並排	并排	bìngpái		be side by side
始終	始终	shǐzhōng	adv.	from beginning to end

語法和詞語註釋

一、隨着　　along with

"隨着" is used in the first clause of a sentence to indicate the condition that makes things change in the second clause.

1. 隨着佛教的傳入，許多地方都蓋起了寺廟。
   随着佛教的传入，许多地方都盖起了寺庙。
   With Buddhism's spread to China, temples were built in many places.

2. 隨着年齡的增長，小弟弟越來越聽話了。
   随着年龄的增长，小弟弟越来越听话了。
   As he grows older, my little brother is becoming more and more obedient.

3. 隨着科學的進步，人們慢慢地不再迷信了。
   随着科学的进步，人们慢慢地不再迷信了。
   As science has developed, so people have gradually stopped being superstitious any more.

二、否則　　otherwise

"否則" is used like "要不然" to introduce the result or consequence which would be caused by the opposite situation or action.

1. 人們做好事，死後就可以上天堂，否則，死後就要下地獄。
   人们做好事，死后就可以上天堂，否则，死后就要下地狱。
   If a person does good, he can go to heaven after he dies. Otherwise, he'll go to hell.

2. 這次考試我一定要得一個A，否則，我就畢不了業。
   这次考试我一定要得一个A，否则，我就毕不了业。
   I have to get an A in this exam, otherwise I can't graduate.

3. 你先答應不生我的氣，否則，我就不告訴你。
   你先答应不生我的气，否则，我就不告诉你。

First, promise me that you won't be angry with me. Otherwise, I won't tell you.

三、並(不/沒有)　　actually (not); (not) at all

"並" can be used before "不" or "沒有" to emphasize the negative verbal phrase.

1. 儒家好像和鬼神並沒有甚麼關係。
   儒家好像和鬼神并没有什么关系。
   Confucianism seems have no connection with ghosts and gods at all.

2. 雖然我星期天去教堂，但是我並不相信甚麼鬼神。
   虽然我星期天去教堂，但是我并不相信什么鬼神。
   I go to church every Sunday, but I don't actually believe in any ghosts and gods.

3. 這一課的生詞雖然很多，但是並不難。
   这一课的生词虽然很多，但是并不难。
   There are many new words in this lesson, but it's not difficult at all.

四、除非……才　　only if

"除非" is used in the first clause of a sentence to introduce the only condition necessary for something to happen. "才" in the second clause indicates that the result can be achieved under this condition.

1. 除非親眼看到，他們才會相信。
   除非亲眼看到，他们才会相信。
   They wouldn't believe it unless they saw it with their own eyes.

2. 除非你請客，我才會跟你去吃飯。
   除非你请客，我才会跟你去吃饭。
   I won't go to dinner with you unless you treat me.

3. 除非給我獎學金，我才上這個學校。
   除非给我奖学金，我才上这个学校。
   I won't go to this school unless I'm granted a scholarship.

五、親 (眼、耳、口、手、身)　　with one's own (eyes, ears, etc.)

"親" is used before the words "眼", "耳", "口", "手", "身" to emphasize that one does things with one's own eyes, ears, mouth, hands, etc.

1. 親眼看到上帝和鬼神，他們才相信。

   亲眼看到上帝和鬼神，他们才相信。

   They won't believe it unless they see god, ghosts and spirits with their own eyes.

2. 這件衣服是媽媽親手做的。

   这件衣服是妈妈亲手做的。

   This dress was made by my mom with her own hands.

3. 昨天老師親口告訴我說，今天的考試很容易。

   昨天老师亲口告诉我说，今天的考试很容易。

   Yesterday the teacher told me personally that today's exam will be very easy.

六、無非　　nothing but; no more than

"無非" is used like "只不過" to indicate that a situation will not go beyond the speaker's expectation, and to add emphasis.

1. 牧師講的無非是教人多做好事不做壞事的話。

   牧师讲的无非是教人多做好事不做坏事的话。

   What the minister said is nothing more than asking people to do more good things and not to do bad things.

2. 學任何語言都差不多一樣，無非就是一些發音、語法和詞彙。

   学任何语言都差不多一样，无非就是一些发音、语法和词汇。

   Learning all languages is roughly the same. It's simply some pronunciation, grammar, and vocabulary.

3. 南方菜和北方菜差不多一樣，無非就是多放了一點兒糖。

   南方菜和北方菜差不多一样，无非就是多放了一点儿糖。

   Southern dishes and northern dishes are almost the same. It's just that southern dishes have a little more sugar in them.

七、與其……，不如　　rather..., than

"與其" is used at the beginning of the first clause of a sentence to indicate a choice that has been abandoned, and "不如" is used in the second clause to indicate one's preferred choice.

1. 與其說是在接受一種宗教宣傳，還不如說是在接受一種道德教育。
   与其说是在接受一种宗教宣传，还不如说是在接受一种道德教育。
   We would rather say they're receiving moral education, than say they're receiving religious propaganda.

2. 與其在電腦上找答案，還不如去問老師。
   与其在电脑上找答案，还不如去问老师。
   It's better for you to ask the teacher than to look for answers on the computer.

3. 與其等兩個小時讓他來接我，還不如自己走回去。
   与其等两个小时让他来接我，还不如自己走回去。
   I'd rather walk back myself than wait two hours for him to pick me up.

八、始終　　from beginning to end

"始終" is used before the verb in a sentence to indicate a situation that has not changed from start to finish.

1. 到那兒去燒香磕頭的人，始終不明白，為甚麼外來的釋迦牟尼在中間。
   到那儿去烧香磕头的人，始终不明白，为什么外来的释迦牟尼在中间。
   The people who go there to burn joss-sticks can never understand why Sakyamuni, who came from overseas, is in the middle.

2. 我始終弄不清楚，為甚麼漢字要有繁體和簡體兩種。
   我始终弄不清楚，为什么汉字要有繁体和简体两种。
   I can never figure out why Chinese characters have both complex forms and simplified forms.

3. 媽媽始終沒有告訴我她和爸爸離婚的原因。
   妈妈始终没有告诉我她和爸爸离婚的原因。
   Mom has always refused to tell me why she divorced dad.

練 習

一、用所給的詞語填空（每個詞語只能用一次）

千萬、與其……不如、否則、無非、隨着、除非……才、既然、按照

小麗：大偉，我媽說_____你星期天去教堂做禮拜，我_____可以和你結婚。
大偉：我很忙，功課很多。_____去聽牧師講演，還_____去做中文作業呢！
小麗：你說甚麼？_____你不願意去教堂，那咱們就分手吧！
大偉：好吧，好吧！但是你_____不能告訴我媽，_____我媽會生氣的。
小麗：你怕甚麼？你媽生氣_____罵你兩句罷了。那有甚麼可怕的？
大偉：你不知道，_____我們家的傳統，甚麼教都不信。
小麗：好吧。我想_____年齡的增長，你媽一定也會去教堂的。

千万、与其……不如、否则、无非、随着、除非……才、既然、按照

小丽：大伟，我妈说_____你星期天去教堂做礼拜，我_____可以和你结婚。
大伟：我很忙，功课很多。_____去听牧师讲演，还_____去做中文作业呢！
小丽：你说什么？_____你不愿意去教堂，那咱们就分手吧！
大伟：好吧，好吧！但是你_____不能告诉我妈，_____我妈会生气的。
小丽：你怕什么？你妈生气_____骂你两句罢了。那有什么可怕的？
大伟：你不知道，_____我们家的传统，什么教都不信。
小丽：好吧。我想_____年龄的增长，你妈一定也会去教堂的。

二、從課文中找出和這四個宗教有關係的詞語

佛敎　佛教	道敎　道教	儒敎　儒教	基督敎　基督教

三、簡單地描述一下這四個宗教各自的特點

1. 佛教　佛教

   _____ 。

2. 道教　道教

   _____ 。

3. 儒教　儒教

   _____ 。

4. 基督教　基督教

   _____ 。

四、翻譯

1. Some people say that they can't believe god or ghosts and spirits really exist unless they can see them with their own eyes. In fact this way of thinking is not necessarily right, because there are many things in the world that are invisible to ordinary people.

   _____
   _____
   _____ 。

2. With the development of science, many people no longer believe in god or spirits. They say, when you're in misfortune, you'd better help yourself out rather than sit there and wait for the god to help you.

   _____
   _____
   _____ 。

3. Generally speaking, religious teachings are nothing more than teaching people to do good things instead of bad things. The Buddhist sutras say people can go to heaven after death if they do more good things. Otherwise, they'll go to hell.

五、根據課文回答問題

1. 佛教為甚麼要人們做好事？
   佛教为什么要人们做好事？

2. "平時不燒香，急時抱佛腳"是甚麼意思？
   "平时不烧香，急时抱佛脚"是什么意思？

3. 道教說甚麼人可以變成神仙？
   道教说什么人可以变成神仙？

4. 為甚麼說儒家跟鬼神沒有關係？
   为什么说儒家跟鬼神没有关系？

5. 為甚麼說信不信宗教沒有關係？
   为什么说信不信宗教没有关系？

6. 為甚麼要把寺廟修建在高山上？
   为什么要把寺庙修建在高山上？

7. 到懸空寺燒香磕頭的人不明白甚麼？
   到悬空寺烧香磕头的人不明白什么？

   _____

   _____

六、課堂討論

1. 為甚麼有許多人要信仰宗教？
   为什么有许多人要信仰宗教？

   _____

   _____

   _____

2. 你覺得宗教有甚麼用處？
   你觉得宗教有什么用处？

   _____

   _____

   _____

七、小作文

你對宗教的看法。
你对宗教的看法。

_____

_____

_____

_____

_____

閱讀

中國人的迷信

中國許多迷信的人,他們自己其實並沒有甚麼特定的宗教信仰。他們只要看到神像,不管是佛教的還是道教的,都要去燒香磕頭。

這些人相信世界上有鬼神。他們認為不同的神管不同的事情,比方說財神管賺錢發財;觀音菩薩管生兒育女;門神管驅鬼消災。

許多人把自己需要的神像請到家裏,在神像面前擺上水果點心,天天給神燒香磕頭。以前在農村,幾乎家家都供有財神或觀音菩薩。每年的大年初一,所有人家的大門上都要貼上新的門神。

人們這樣誠心誠意地敬神,就是想得到神的保佑。但是有的人給財神燒了一輩子香,也沒有發財;給觀音菩薩磕了無數個頭,也沒有孩子;還有的人家雖然年年都貼新的門神,可家裏的災禍卻一直不斷。

有人說這是他們的命不好,說他們命裏注定就是不幸的人。很多人都相信命運這種說法,而且都特別關心自己的命運。

過年的頭幾天,人們都要去廟裏求神許願。他們在燒香磕頭之後還一定要去抽籤,看看自己今年的運氣好不好,看看自己許的那些願能不能實現。

因為人們都想知道自己的命運,於是社會上就出現了一些算卦、看相、測字等所謂能算命的人。算卦的人說:只要告訴我你出生的時間,我就能算出你的過去和將來;看相的人說:讓我看一下你的面相和手紋,我便能看出你的婚姻和壽命;測字的人說:你隨便寫一個字,從字體上我就能知道你最近有甚麼喜事、你遇到了甚麼災禍。

這些算命的人到處吹噓他們算得很準,可是親身試過的人都說他們是在騙人。那些上過當的人說,除非傻瓜才會相信他們的話,如果真有甚麼事情發生,與其花錢聽他們胡說,還不如自己去想辦法解決。

以前,由於社會落後,人們不懂得科學,所以很多人才相信迷信。現在隨着社會的進步,迷信的人應該是越來越少了。

然而,在科學已經非常發達的今天,不知為甚麼,過年、過節去廟裏燒香磕頭、求神拜佛的人反而多起來了。那些算卦、看相和測字的人甚至開始用電腦來給人們算命了。

阅读

中国人的迷信

　　中国许多迷信的人，他们自己其实并没有什么特定的宗教信仰。他们只要看到神像，不管是佛教的还是道教的，都要去烧香磕头。

　　这些人相信世界上有鬼神。他们认为不同的神管不同的事情，比方说财神管赚钱发财；观音菩萨管生儿育女；门神管驱鬼消灾。

　　许多人把自己需要的神像请到家里，在神像面前摆上水果点心，天天给神烧香磕头。以前在农村，几乎家家都供有财神或观音菩萨。每年的大年初一，所有人家的大门上都要贴上新的门神。

　　人们这样诚心诚意地敬神，就是想得到神的保佑。但是有的人给财神烧了一辈子香，也没有发财；给观音菩萨磕了无数个头，也没有孩子；还有的人家虽然年年都贴新的门神，可家里的灾祸却一直不断。

　　有人说这是他们的命不好，说他们命里注定就是不幸的人。很多人都相信命运这种说法，而且都特别关心自己的命运。

　　过年的头几天，人们都要去庙里求神许愿。他们在烧香磕头之后还一定要去抽签，看看自己今年的运气好不好，看看自己许的那些愿能不能实现。

　　因为人们都想知道自己的命运，于是社会上就出现了一些算卦、看相、测字等所谓能算命的人。算卦的人说：只要告诉我你出生的时间，我就能算出你的过去和将来；看相的人说：让我看一下你的面相和手纹，我便能看出你的婚姻和寿命；测字的人说：你随便写一个字，从字体上我就能知道你最近有什么喜事、你遇到了什么灾祸。

　　这些算命的人到处吹嘘他们算得很准，可是亲身试过的人都说他们是在骗人。那些上过当的人说，除非傻瓜才会相信他们的话，如果真有什么事情发生，与其花钱听他们胡说，还不如自己去想办法解决。

　　以前，由于社会落后，人们不懂得科学，所以很多人才相信迷信。现在随着社会的进步，迷信的人应该是越来越少了。

　　然而，在科学已经非常发达的今天，不知为什么，过年、过节去庙里烧香磕头、求神拜佛的人反而多起来了。那些算卦、看相和测字的人甚至开始用电脑来给人们算命了。

生 詞

特定	特定	tèdìng	adj.	special
神像	神像	shénxiàng	n.	the picture or statue of a god
財神	财神	cáishén	n.	the god of wealth
觀音菩薩	观音菩萨	guānyīn púsà		Bodhisattva; Goddess of Mercy
生兒育女	生儿育女	shēng'ér-yù'nǚ		give birth to children and raise them
門神	门神	ménshén	n.	door-god
驅鬼	驱鬼	qū guǐ		drive out evil spirits
水果	水果	shuǐguǒ	n.	fruit
點心	点心	diǎnxīn	n.	pastry
供	供	gòng	v.	make offerings
人家	人家	rén jiā	n.	family
誠心誠意	诚心诚意	chéngxīn-chéngyì		sincerely; faithfully
敬	敬	jìng	v.	piously worship
災禍	灾祸	zāihuò	n.	disaster
命	命	mìng	n.	fate; fortune
命裏注定	命里注定	mìnglǐzhùdìng		decreed by fate; predestined
命運	命运	mìngyùn	n.	destiny; fate
許願	许愿	xǔ yuàn		make a vow to a god
抽籤	抽签	chōu qiān		draw lots
運氣	运气	yùnqi	n.	fate; fortune
實現	实现	shíxiàn	v.	realize; come true
算卦	算卦	suàn guà		divination
看相	看相	kàn xiàng		practice physiognomy

測字	测字	**cè zì**		fortune-telling by analyzing a Chinese character
算命	算命	**suàn mìng**		fortune-telling
面相	面相	**miànxiàng**	*n.*	face
手紋	手纹	**shǒuwén**	*n.*	lines of the hand
到處	到处	**dàochù**	*adv.*	all over; everywhere
吹噓	吹嘘	**chuīxū**	*v.*	boast; crow about
準	准	**zhǔn**	*adj.*	accurate
親身	亲身	**qīnshēn**		personally; by oneself
試	试	**shì**	*v.*	try
傻瓜	傻瓜	**shǎguā**	*n.*	fool
胡說	胡说	**húshuō**		nonsense
落後	落后	**luòhòu**	*adj.*	lagging behind; backward
科學	科学	**kēxué**	*n.*	science

問題

1. 那些人把甚麼神請到自己的家裏？
   那些人把什么神请到自己的家里？
   _____
   _____。

2. 為甚麼有人敬神卻沒有得到神的保佑？
   为什么有人敬神却没有得到神的保佑？
   _____
   _____。

3. 去廟裏求神的人為甚麼要去抽籤？
   去庙里求神的人为什么要去抽签？
   _____

4. 為甚麼會出現那些算命的人？
   为什么会出现那些算命的人？
   _____
   _____。

5. 為甚麼科學發達了，迷信的人反而多起來了呢？
   为什么科学发达了，迷信的人反而多起来了呢？
   _____
   _____。

6. 你見過算命的嗎？你相信那些算命的嗎？
   你见过算命的吗？你相信那些算命的吗？
   _____
   _____。

長江三峽
The Three Gorges of the Yangtze River

學習大綱

通過學習本課，學生應該能夠：

1. 掌握這些句型和詞語的意思和用法："如此"、"難怪"、"可惜"、"若干"、"相當"、"將"、"況且"。
2. 認識和運用課文以及閱讀文章內的生詞。
3. 了解中國的第一大河流——長江和長江三峽有甚麼景色。
4. 了解中國的第二大河流——黃河和中華民族的關係。

Study Outline

After studying this chapter, students should:

1. Have a good command of the meaning and usage of these sentence patterns and terms: "rúcǐ" (such; like that), "nánguài" (no wonder), "kěxī" (it's a pity; it's too bad), "ruògān" (some; several), "xiāngdāng" (quite), "jiāng" (will; be going to be), "kuàngqiě" (besides; in addition).
2. Be familiar with the meaning and usage of the vocabulary introduced in the text and the reading.
3. Know about the Yangtze River, the longest river in China, and the scenery along the Three Gorges.
4. Know about the Yellow River, the second longest river in China, and its relationship with the Chinese people.

課 文

　　長江是中國第一大河流。她從青藏高原上的雪山上流下來，流過四川、湖北、湖南等地，最後從上海流入大海。

　　長江在四川和湖北之間穿過一座叫巫山的大山。巫山有二百多公里長。長江在巫山中穿行，形成了瞿塘峽、巫峽、西陵峽三個大峽谷。這就是人們所說的長江三峽。

　　三峽的江面很窄，兩岸都是懸崖峭壁；峽谷中水流很急，水中有許多礁石險灘。人們乘船經過這裏時都特別害怕，因為一不小心，船不是碰到礁石，就是撞上峭壁。峽谷的最窄處，你抬頭仰望，在兩岸高高的峭壁之間，只能望見那細細的一線天。這時你伸出左手，好像就要摸着那邊峭壁上的青苔；探出右手，似乎也能採到這邊石縫中的野花。

　　三峽是世界有名的風景區，在那裏你能看到各種珍奇的飛禽走獸；能看到許多像飄帶一樣的瀑布。坐船行走在峽谷之中，船隨着水走，水繞着山行。兩岸美麗的景色就像一幅幅的畫，一個接一個地展現在你的眼前，讓你覺得就像是穿行在一個奇妙無比的天然畫廊之中。

　　三峽沿岸有十二座山峰，其中最奇妙的是巫峽中的神女峰。神女峰遠遠地看去，就像是一個美麗動人的少女，靜靜地站立在山頂之上。每當船行走到神女峰下時，本來晴朗朗的天空，忽然有幾片薄薄的雲霧輕輕地飄過來，接着便有點點雨滴飄灑在你我的臉上。還不等去擦拭，那雲、那雨，又都不見了。有人說這是神女的淚珠，也有人說這是神奇的"巫山雲雨"。

　　三峽是如此的美麗，如此的神奇，難怪所有的人都喜歡她。

　　十分可惜的是，三峽現在正在建一座特別大的大水壩。若干年後，水壩建好了，江面就會變得非常寬闊。到時候相當多的名勝古蹟將會被淹沒在水底下，像"一線天"、"巫山雲雨"那樣的景色可能就再也看不到了。

　　不過，水壩建好後的三峽也一定會有另外一種美麗的景色。況且，那時候的三峽，江面寬闊、水流平緩，沒有甚麼礁石和險灘，也不會再有甚麼危險了。

课文

　　长江是中国第一大河流。她从青藏高原上的雪山上流下来，流过四川、湖北、湖南等地，最后从上海流入大海。

　　长江在四川和湖北之间穿过一座叫巫山的大山。巫山有二百多公里长。长江在巫山中穿行，形成了瞿塘峡、巫峡、西陵峡三个大峡谷。这就是人们所说的长江三峡。

　　三峡的江面很窄，两岸都是悬崖峭壁；峡谷中水流很急，水中有许多礁石险滩。人们乘船经过这里时都特别害怕，因为一不小心，船不是碰到礁石，就是撞上峭壁。峡谷的最窄处，你抬头仰望，在两岸高高的峭壁之间，只能望见那细细的一线天。这时你伸出左手，好像就要摸着那边峭壁上的青苔；探出右手，似乎也能采到这边石缝中的野花。

　　三峡是世界有名的风景区，在那里你能看到各种珍奇的飞禽走兽；能看到许多像飘带一样的瀑布。坐船行走在峡谷之中，船随着水走，水绕着山行。两岸美丽的景色就像一幅幅的画，一个接一个地展现在你的眼前，让你觉得就像是穿行在一个奇妙无比的天然画廊之中。

　　三峡沿岸有十二座山峰，其中最奇妙的是巫峡中的神女峰。神女峰远远地看去，就像是一个美丽动人的少女，静静地站立在山顶之上。每当船行走到神女峰下时，本来晴朗朗的天空，忽然有几片薄薄的云雾轻轻地飘过来，接着便有点点雨滴飘洒在你我的脸上。还不等去擦拭，那云、那雨，又都不见了。有人说这是神女的泪珠，也有人说这是神奇的"巫山云雨"。

　　三峡是如此的美丽，如此的神奇，难怪所有的人都喜欢她。

　　十分可惜的是，三峡现在正在建一座特别大的大水坝。若干年后，水坝建好了，江面就会变得非常宽阔。到时候相当多的名胜古迹将会被淹没在水底下，像"一线天"、"巫山云雨"那样的景色可能就再也看不到了。

　　不过，水坝建好后的三峡也一定会有另外一种美丽的景色。况且，那时候的三峡，江面宽阔、水流平缓，没有什么礁石和险滩，也不会再有什么危险了。

生詞

青藏	青藏	Qīng-Zàng		Qinghai and Xizang (Tibet)
高原	高原	gāoyuán	n.	plateau
湖北	湖北	Húběi		name of a province in China
巫山	巫山	Wū Shān		Mt. Wu
穿行	穿行	chuānxíng	v.	pass through
瞿塘峽	瞿塘峡	Qútáng Xiá		the Qutang Gorge
巫峽	巫峡	Wū Xiá		the Wu Gorge
西陵峽	西陵峡	Xīlíng Xiá		the Xiling Gorge
峽谷	峡谷	xiágǔ	n.	gorge
江面	江面	jiāngmiàn	n.	river surface
窄	窄	zhǎi	adj.	narrow
急	急	jí	adj.	rapid
礁石險灘	礁石险滩	jiāoshí-xiǎntān	n.	reefs and dangerous shoals
仰望	仰望	yǎngwàng	v.	look up
伸	伸	shēn	v.	stretch out
摸	摸	mō	v.	touch
青苔	青苔	qīngtái	n.	moss
探	探	tàn	v.	stretch forward; stick out
似乎	似乎	sìhū	adv.	seem; as if
石縫	石缝	shífèng	n.	crack; crevice
野花	野花	yěhuā	n.	wild flower
風景區	风景区	fēngjǐngqū	n.	scenic spot
珍奇	珍奇	zhēnqí	adj.	rare and valuable
飛禽走獸	飞禽走兽	fēiqín-zǒushòu	n.	birds and beasts
飄帶	飘带	piāodài	n.	ribbon; streamer

瀑布	瀑布	pùbù	n.	waterfall
繞	绕	rǎo	v.	go around
展現	展现	zhǎnxiàn	v.	unfold before one's eyes
奇妙	奇妙	qímiào	adj.	marvelous
無比	无比	wúbǐ	adj.	unparalleled
天然	天然	tiānrán	adj.	natural
畫廊	画廊	huàláng	n.	art gallery
沿岸	沿岸	yán'àn	n.	along the bank
神女峰	神女峰	Shénnǚ Fēng		Mt. Goddess; Goddess Peak
晴朗朗	晴朗朗	qínglǎnglang	adj.	clear; sunny
雲霧	云雾	yúnwù	n.	cloud and mist
飄	飘	piāo	v.	float
飄灑	飘洒	piāosǎ	v.	float and drip
擦拭	擦拭	cāshì	v.	wipe
淚珠	泪珠	lèizhū	n.	teardrop
神奇	神奇	shénqí	adj.	magical; miraculous
如此	如此	rúcǐ	pn.	such; like that
難怪	难怪	nánguài	adv.	no wonder
可惜	可惜	kěxī	adj.	it's a pity; it's too bad
水壩	水坝	shuǐbà	n.	dam
若干	若干	ruògān	n.	some; several
寬闊	宽阔	kuānkuò	adj.	wide
相當	相当	xiāngdāng	adv.	quite
將	将	jiāng	adv.	will
淹沒	淹没	yānmò	v.	submerge; flood
況且	况且	kuàngqiě	conj.	besides; in addition
平緩	平缓	pínghuǎn	adj.	flat and slow

語法和詞語註釋

一、如此　　such; like that

"如此" is often used in written language to refer to the situation mentioned before.

1. 三峽如此的美麗，難怪人們都喜歡她。
   三峡如此的美丽，难怪人们都喜欢她。
   The Three Gorges are so beautiful. No wonder people like them.

2. 我沒有想到我們的中文課本會如此的有意思。
   我没有想到我们的中文课本会如此的有意思。
   I didn't expect that our Chinese textbook would be so interesting.

3. 我從來沒有見過長得如此漂亮的姑娘。
   我从来没有见过长得如此漂亮的姑娘。
   I have never seen such a beautiful girl.

二、難怪　　no wonder

"難怪" is used either before or after the subject of a sentence to indicate that the speaker is not surprised by the situation after he/she has found out the cause of it.

1. 三峽如此的美麗，難怪人們都喜歡她。
   三峡如此的美丽，难怪人们都喜欢她。
   The Three Gorges are so beautiful. No wonder people like them.

2. 他生病住醫院了，難怪他這幾天沒有來上課。
   他生病住医院了，难怪他这几天没有来上课。
   He has been sick and is in hospital. No wonder he didn't come to class the past few days.

3. 湯姆的宿舍難怪這麼乾淨，原來他女朋友來了。
   汤姆的宿舍难怪这么干净，原来他女朋友来了。

No wonder Tom's room is so clean. His girlfriend has come.

三、可惜　　it's a pity; it is too bad

"可惜" means "it is to be regretted".

1. 可惜的是，三峽正在建一座大水壩。
   可惜的是，三峡正在建一座大水坝。
   It's a pity that a big dam is being built in the Three Gorges.

2. 他學了一半就退掉了，真是太可惜了。
   他学了一半就退掉了，真是太可惜了。
   It's such a pity that he gave up studying it halfway through.

3. 聽說昨天的電影特別有意思，可惜我去晚了，沒買着票。
   听说昨天的电影特别有意思，可惜我去晚了，没买着票。
   I heard that yesterday's movie was very interesting. Unfortunately I was late and didn't manage to buy a ticket.

四、若干　　some; several

"若干" is often used in written language to indicate an indefinite number.

1. 若干年後，大壩建好了，江面就會變得很寬。
   若干年后，大坝建好了，江面就会变得很宽。
   Several years from now, when the big dam has been built, the river surface will become very wide.

2. 若干年前，這裏還是一片荒地。
   若干年前，这里还是一片荒地。
   Several years ago, this was only a piece of wasteland.

3. 老師講了若干條規定，如按時交作業、不能曠課等等。
   老师讲了若干条规定，如按时交作业、不能旷课等等。
   The teacher talked about several rules, such as handing in homework on time, not skipping class, etc.

五、相當　quite

"相當" is used before an adjective to indicate a certain degree, and is not as strong as "很".

1. 相當多的名勝古蹟將會淹沒在水底下。
   相当多的名胜古迹将会淹没在水底下。
   Quite a number of scenic spots and historical sites will be submerged.

2. 學好中文以後，就會有相當多的機會去中國。
   学好中文以后，就会有相当多的机会去中国。
   After you've learned Chinese, you will have quite a lot of chances to go to China.

3. 我們班上的同學相當多的人都吃過中國飯。
   我们班上的同学相当多的人都吃过中国饭。
   Quite a number of students in my class have had Chinese food.

六、將　will; be going to be

1. 大壩建好以後，相當多的名勝古蹟將會淹沒在水底下。
   大坝建好以后，相当多的名胜古迹将会淹没在水底下。
   After the big dam has been built, quite a number of scenic spots and historical sites will be submerged.

2. 學好中文以後，將會有很多機會去中國。
   学好中文以后，将会有很多机会去中国。
   After you've learned Chinese, you will have quite a lot of chances to go to China.

3. 你說的那些話，我將永遠記在心中。
   你说的那些话，我将永远记在心中。
   I'll always remember what you've said.

七、況且　besides; in addition

"況且" is often used in conjunction with "又", "也", "還" to connect two sentences which are complementary to each other.

1. 水壩建好後的三峽會有另一種景色。況且,那時的三峽不會再有甚麼危險了。

   水坝建好后的三峡会有另一种景色。况且,那时的三峡不会再有什么危险了。

   After the dam has been built, the Three Gorges will look quite different. What's more, they will then no longer be at all dangerous.

2. 學一門語言本來就很難,況且還是一門東方語言。

   学一门语言本来就很难,况且还是一门东方语言。

   It goes without saying that learning a language is very difficult, and all the more so when it is an oriental language.

3. 已經這麼晚了,況且又下着大雨,你就不要去了吧。

   已经这么晚了,况且又下着大雨,你就不要去了吧。

   It's already so late, besides, it's raining. Just don't go.

練 習

一、用所給的詞語填空 (每一個詞語都要用到)

如此、若干、相當、無非、始終、仍然、否則、盡量

又學了一年中文了。在這一年裏面,我們學了_____多的中國文化知識,其中還有_____篇是講中國歷史的。無論是文化還是歷史,_____都是讓我們多學一些中國語言。老師要我們回家以後_____說中文,_____就會忘記的。我的中文有_____大的進步,得感謝我們的中文老師。下一學期我_____要上中文課。我_____記着老師的話,一定要把中文學好。

如此、若干、相当、无非、始终、仍然、否则、尽量

又学了一年中文了。在这一年里面,我们学了_____多的中国文化知识,其中还有_____篇是讲中国历史的。无论是文化还是历史,_____都是让我们多学一些中国语言。老师要我们回家以后_____说中文,

_____就会忘记的。我的中文有_____大的进步，得感谢我们的中文老师。下一学期我_____要上中文课。我_____记着老师的话，一定要把中文学好。

二、選擇合適的詞語填空（每個詞語只能用一次）

漸漸地、靜靜地、慢慢地、快快地、短短的、彎彎的、粗粗的、細細的、綠綠的、圓圓的、長長的、黑黑的、厚厚的、薄薄的、寬寬的、白白的

我_____明白了。　河水_____流着。　他_____睡着了。
船_____向前走。　兩條_____辮子。　兩道_____眉毛。
一片_____小草。　寫了封_____信。　一條_____布帶。
一塊_____月餅。　一條_____小狗。　兩件_____衣服。
兩本_____字典。　一條_____大街。　一條_____小河。
一片_____月光。

渐渐地、静静地、慢慢地、快快地、短短的、弯弯的、粗粗的、细细的、绿绿的、圆圆的、长长的、黑黑的、厚厚的、薄薄的、宽宽的、白白的

我_____明白了。　河水_____流着。　他_____睡着了。
船_____向前走。　两条_____辫子。　两道_____眉毛。
一片_____小草。　写了封_____信。　一条_____布带。
一块_____月饼。　一条_____小狗。　两件_____衣服。
两本_____字典。　一条_____大街。　一条_____小河。
一片_____月光。

三、根據課文寫出答案

1. 描寫三峽美麗景色的是哪一段？
   描写三峡美丽景色的是哪一段？
   _____。

2. 描寫三峽危險的是哪一段？
   描写三峡危险的是哪一段？

3. 第五段講的是甚麼？
   第五段讲的是什么？
   _____。

4. 第六段講的是甚麼？
   第六段讲的是什么？
   _____。

5. 大壩修好以後，再也看不到甚麼樣的景色了？
   大坝修好以后，再也看不到什么样的景色了？
   _____。

四、翻譯

1. The cloud and rain of Mt. Wu in the Three Gorges is so miraculous. No wonder people want to see it. Several years ago, my girlfriend and I went to the Three Gorges once, and we just wanted to see the beautiful and fantastic Goddess Peak.

   _____
   _____
   _____。

2. It's such a pity that it kept raining heavily in those days. In the rain, in the cloud and mists, we didn't even see the shadow of the Goddess Peak. At that time, quite a number of people on the boat were so upset that they burst into tears.

   _____
   _____
   _____。

3. I said to my girlfriend: It's because the Goddess was so moved that she

burst into tears. Don't be upset, we can come again in a few years' time. Besides, making a tour in the Three Gorges in this heavy rain has a special feeling as well.

_____

_____

_____ 。

五、根據課文回答問題

1. 長江三峽在甚麼地方？
   长江三峡在什么地方？
   _____

   _____ 。

2. 坐船過三峽的人害怕甚麼？
   坐船过三峡的人害怕什么？
   _____

   _____ 。

3. 為甚麼說三峽像一個畫廊？
   为什么说三峡像一个画廊？
   _____

   _____ 。

4. 甚麼是一線天？
   什么是一线天？
   _____

   _____ 。

5. 船路過神女峰時，常常會出現甚麼樣的情形？
   船路过神女峰时，常常会出现什么样的情形？
   _____

   _____ 。

22. 長江三峽　　　　　　　　　　　　　　　　417

6. 建三峽大壩為甚麼要說很可惜？
   建三峡大坝为什么要说很可惜？
   _____
   _____。

7. 你能想像出大壩建好以後三峽的情形嗎？
   你能想像出大坝建好以后三峡的情形吗？
   _____
   _____。

六、課堂討論

1. 建造水壩和保護自然之間的關係。
   建造水坝和保护自然之间的关系。
   _____
   _____
   _____。

2. 建水壩的好處和壞處。
   建水坝的好处和坏处。
   _____
   _____
   _____。

七、小作文

1. 描寫你去過的一條河或者一座山的風景。
   描写你去过的一条河或者一座山的风景。
   _____
   _____
   _____
   _____

_____

_____。

2. 描寫你們家周圍的風景。
   描写你们家周围的风景。

_____

_____

_____

_____

_____

_____。

閱讀

黃河

　　黃河是中國的第二大河流，她發源於青藏高原，經過四川、湖北、陝西、山西、河南等地，最後由山東流入大海。

　　黃河流域是中華民族的發源地。遠古時期，黃河中下游一帶土地肥沃，氣候溫暖，中華民族就是在這裏生長、繁衍、壯大的。

　　早在八十萬年前，中國人的祖先——藍田中國猿人就生活在黃河邊上的陝西藍田。五六千年前，母系社會的氏族部落也居住在離那兒不遠的西安半坡。

　　我們常說中國歷史五千年，就是從原始部落的領袖炎帝、黃帝算起的。從炎帝黃帝到秦漢唐宋，黃河流域一直都是中國政治、經濟和文化的中心。在漫長的歷史中，朝代雖然在不斷地變化，但是相當多的國都都建在黃河流域的河南、陝西一帶。

　　陝西曾經是周、秦、漢、唐等十三個朝代的首都。現在你去西安，不僅能看到唐代的大雁塔、漢代的皇家陵墓，還可以看到被稱作世界第八大奇蹟的秦始皇的兵馬俑。

　　可惜的是，秦阿房宮、漢未央宮、唐大明宮那些雄偉的宮殿，早已經在過去的戰火中燒毀，人們再也見不到那些偉大的建築了。但是它們那種古老的建築風格不但一直保留到今天，而且還流傳到了日本、韓國以及東南亞。

　　在河南和陝西出土的三千多年前的甲骨文和金文，是中國最早的文字。我們今天使用的漢字就是從甲骨文、金文、大篆、小篆、隸書、楷書逐漸發展來的。漢字是目前世界上唯一的一個，已經使用了幾千年，現在仍然在使用的文字。

　　最近，在長江流域發現了若干早期文明的遺蹟，有些人說黃河流域將不再是中華民族唯一的發源地。其實，從中國五千年的文明史來看，中華民族的成長、繁衍、壯大，從來都離不開黃河。

　　中華民族是喝黃河水長大的，中國人把黃河稱作母親河。黃河是如此的偉大，如此的光榮。幾千年來，黃河哺育了偉大的中華民族；中華民族創造出了燦爛的中華文化！

阅 读

黄河

  黄河是中国的第二大河流,她发源于青藏高原,经过四川、湖北、陕西、山西、河南等地,最后由山东流入大海。

  黄河流域是中华民族的发源地。远古时期,黄河中下游一带土地肥沃,气候温暖,中华民族就是在这里生长、繁衍、壮大的。

  早在八十万年前,中国人的祖先——蓝田中国猿人就生活在黄河边上的陕西蓝田。五六千年前,母系社会的氏族部落也居住在离那儿不远的西安半坡。

  我们常说中国历史五千年,就是从原始部落的领袖炎帝、黄帝算起的。从炎帝黄帝到秦汉唐宋,黄河流域一直都是中国政治、经济和文化的中心。在漫长的历史中,朝代虽然在不断地变化,但是相当多的国都都建在黄河流域的河南、陕西一带。

  陕西曾经是周、秦、汉、唐等十三个朝代的首都。现在你去西安,不仅能看到唐代的大雁塔、汉代的皇家陵墓,还可以看到被称作世界第八大奇迹的秦始皇的兵马俑。

  可惜的是,秦阿房宫、汉未央宫、唐大明宫那些雄伟的宫殿,早已经在过去的战火中烧毁,人们再也见不到那些伟大的建筑了。但是它们那种古老的建筑风格不但一直保留到今天,而且还流传到了日本、韩国以及东南亚。

  在河南和陕西出土的三千多年前的甲骨文和金文,是中国最早的文字。我们今天使用的汉字就是从甲骨文、金文、大篆、小篆、隶书、楷书逐渐发展来的。汉字是目前世界上唯一的一个,已经使用了几千年,现在仍然在使用的文字。

  最近,在长江流域发现了若干早期文明的遗迹,有些人说黄河流域将不再是中华民族唯一的发源地。其实,从中国五千年的文明史来看,中华民族的成长、繁衍、壮大,从来都离不开黄河。

  中华民族是喝黄河水长大的,中国人把黄河称作母亲河。黄河是如此的伟大,如此的光荣。几千年来,黄河哺育了伟大的中华民族;中华民族创造出了灿烂的中华文化!

生詞

發源	发源	fāyuán	v.	originate from
河南	河南	Hé'nán		name of a province in China
流域	流域	liúyù	n.	river basin, drainage area
遠古	远古	yuǎngǔ	n.	remote antiquity
肥沃	肥沃	féiwò	adj.	fertile
氣候	气候	qìhòu	n.	climate
適宜	适宜	shìyí	adj.	suitable
繁衍	繁衍	fányán	v.	multiply
壯大	壮大	zhuàngdà	v.	grow in strength
藍田	蓝田	Lántián		place name
猿人	猿人	yuánrén	n.	ape-man
母系社會	母系社会	mǔxìshèhuì	n.	matriarchal society
氏族	氏族	shìzú	n.	clan
領袖	领袖	lǐngxiù	n.	leader
算	算	suàn	v.	count
漫長	漫长	màncháng	adj.	very long
曾經	曾经	céngjīng	adv.	at one time; ever
皇家陵墓	皇家陵墓	huángjiā língmù	n.	emperor's tomb
奇蹟	奇迹	qíjì	n.	miracle
阿房宮	阿房宫	Ēfáng Gōng		Efang Palace
未央宮	未央宫	Wèiyāng Gōng		Weiyang Palace
大明宮	大明宫	Dàmíng Gōng		Daming Palace
雄偉	雄伟	xióngwěi	adj.	majestic
宮殿	宫殿	gōngdiàn	n.	palace

戰火	战火	zhànhuǒ	n.	flames of war
燒毀	烧毁	shāohuǐ	v.	burn down
建築	建筑	jiànzhù	n.	building
風格	风格	fēnggé	n.	style
保留	保留	bǎoliú	v.	keep; preserve
韓國	韩国	Hánguó		Korea
東南亞	东南亚	Dōngnányà		Southeast Asia
出土	出土	chūtǔ	v.	be unearthed
金文	金文	jīnwén	n.	inscriptions on ancient bronzes
大篆	大篆	dàzhuàn	n.	an ancient style of calligraphy current in the Zhou dynasty (1122–221 B.C.)
小篆	小篆	xiǎozhuàn	n.	an ancient style of calligraphy adopted in the Qin dynasty (221–206 B.C.)
隸書	隶书	lìshū	n.	an ancient style of calligraphy current in the Han dynasty (206 B.C.–A.D. 220)
楷書	楷书	kǎishū	n.	regular script
目前	目前	mùqián	n.	at present; now
唯一	唯一	wéiyī	adj.	only; unique
遺蹟	遗迹	yíjì	n.	relic
光榮	光荣	guāngróng	adj.	glorious
哺育	哺育	bǔyù	v.	nurture
創造	创造	chuàngzào	v.	create
燦爛	灿烂	cànlàn	adj.	splendid

問 題

1. 為甚麼說黃河是中華民族的母親河？
   为什么说黄河是中华民族的母亲河？
   _____
   _____ 。

2. 黃河流域作為中國政治、文化、經濟的中心大致在甚麼時候？
   黄河流域作为中国政治、文化、经济的中心大致在什么时候？
   _____
   _____ 。

3. 秦阿房宮、漢未央宮、唐大明宮現在還在嗎？
   秦阿房宫、汉未央宫、唐大明宫现在还在吗？
   _____
   _____ 。

4. 甲骨文、金文是甚麼時候的文字？
   甲骨文、金文是什么时候的文字？
   _____
   _____ 。

5. 為甚麼說黃河流域可能不是中華民族的唯一發源地？
   为什么说黄河流域可能不是中华民族的唯一发源地？
   _____
   _____ 。

詞彙索引
Vocabulary Index

(號碼表示課號,"r"表示閱讀課文)

A

àiqíng	愛情	爱情	love	5
ànzhào	按照	按照	according to	19
àomàn	傲慢	傲慢	arrogant; haughty	10

B

bá	拔	拔	pull out/up	12
báitáng	白糖	白糖	white sugar	15
báitóudàolǎo	白頭到老	白头到老	live to old age in conjugal bliss	12r
bǎi	擺	摆	put	11r
bǎifēnzhī	百分之……	百分之……	... percent	2
bài nián	拜年	拜年	give new year's greetings	11
bānzǒu	搬走	搬走	take away	17
bànbiāntiān	半邊天	半边天	half of the sky	13
Bànpōcūn	半坡村	半坡村	the Banpo village in Xi'an	16
bànfǎ	辦法	办法	way; method	8
bāo	包	包	wrap	15
bāohán	包含	包含	contain; embody	20
báo	薄	薄	thin	9
bǎocún	保存	保存	preserve; conserve	12r
bǎohù	保護	保护	safeguard; protect	11r
bǎoliú	保留	保留	keep; preserve	22r
bǎoyòu	保佑	保佑	bless	21
bào	抱	抱	hold; carry	8
bàokǎo	報考	报考	enter oneself for an examination	7
bàozhà	爆炸	爆炸	explode	8
bàozhǐ	報紙	报纸	newspaper	1
bēi	杯	杯	cup	4r
bēi	揹	背	carry on the back	11
bēiāi	悲哀	悲哀	sad	17r
bēihuān-líhé	悲歡離合	悲欢离合	joy and sorrows, separations and reunions	18r
bēi jù	悲劇	悲剧	tragedy	8r
bēishāng	悲傷	悲伤	sad	18r
bèi	背	背	recite	18r
bèipò	被迫	被迫	be compelled to	9
běnlái	本來	本来	originally	8
běnlǐng	本領	本领	skill; ability	11r

běnsè	本色	本色	natural color	19
běnshì	本事	本事	ability	17r
bèn	笨	笨	stupid; foolish	5
bízi	鼻子	鼻子	nose	5r
bǐ	比	比	compare with; than	9
bǐfāngshuō	比方說	比方说	suppose; for example	1r
bǐyìniǎo	比翼鳥	比翼鸟	a pair of lovebirds—a devoted couple	17r
bǐyì qífēi	比翼齊飛	比翼齐飞	to fly side by side	17r
bǐyù	比喻	比喻	use as a metaphor	19r
bǐzuò	比做	比做	be likened to	19r
bǐcǐ	彼此	彼此	each other	12r
bǐhuà	筆劃	笔划	strokes of a Chinese character	2r
bǐhuàshì	筆劃式	笔划式	strokes of a Chinese character	9r
bì xié	避邪	避邪	ward off evil	11
bì yùn	避孕	避孕	contraception	8
bìxū	必須	必须	must	9r
bìyèshēng	畢業生	毕业生	graduate	7
biān	邊	边	rim; edge	19
biānjiè	邊界	边界	boundary; border	3
biānzào	編造	编造	make up	17
biānfú	蝙蝠	蝙蝠	bat	6
biàn	便	便	then	10
biànchéng	變成	变成	change into	2r
biàndòng	變動	变动	change and move	18
biànhuà	變化	变化	change	1
biànzi	辮子	辫子	braid	13r
biāo yīn	標音	标音	indicating the sound by using phonetic symbols	9r
biǎo	表	表	table; form	9
biǎo	表	表	the relationship between the children or grandchildren of a brother and a sister or sisters	20r
biǎodá	表達	表达	express	18
biǎogē biǎodì	表哥、表弟	表哥、表弟	male cousins from father's sister or mother's brother or sister	20r
biǎojiě biǎomèi	表姐、表妹	表姐、表妹	female cousins from father's sister or mother's brother or sister	20r
biǎomiàn	表面	表面	surface	20
biǎoshì	表示	表示	express; indicate	2
Bīngmǎyǒng	兵馬俑	兵马俑	clay figures of warriors and horses buried with the dead; terra-cotta soldiers and horses	16
bīngtiān-xuědì	冰天雪地	冰天雪地	a world of ice and snow	15
bīngxuě	冰雪	冰雪	ice and snow	6r
bìng(+neg.)	並(+neg.)	并(+neg.)	actually (not); (not) at all	21
bìngpái	並排	并排	be side by side	21
bìngqiě	並且	并且	and; furthermore	3

bóbo	伯伯	伯伯	father's elder brother; address for men of an age approx. that of father, but older	20r
bǒ	跛	跛	lame; cripple	5r
bǔxíbān	補習班	补习班	preparation class	7
bǔyù	哺育	哺育	nurture	22r
bù	部	部	ministry	2r
bùfen	部分	部分	part	1r
bùshǒu	部首	部首	radicals (or other character components) used in dictionaries for indexing purposes	2
bùdàn ... érqiě	不但……而且	不但……而且	not only ... but also	1
bùfáng	不妨	不妨	may (as well); might (as well)	16
bùguǎn ... dōu	不管……都	不管……都	no matter what	3
bùguò	不過	不过	but; however	6
bùguò ... bàle	不過…… 罷了	不过…… 罢了	only	10
bùjǐn ... hái	不僅…… 還	不仅…… 还	not only ... but also	11
bùlǎo sōng	不老松	不老松	evergreen pine	19r
bùrú	不如	不如	not as good as	17
bùshì ... jiùshì	不是……就是	不是……就是	either ... or; if not A ... then B ...	7
bùtíng de	不停地	不停地	ceaselessly; continuously	1r
bùxìng	不幸	不幸	unfortunate; unhappy	5
bùzàihu	不在乎	不在乎	not mind; not care about	14r
bùdài	布帶	布带	a strip of cloth	13r

C

cāshì	擦拭	擦拭	wipe	22
cāi	猜	猜	guess	15
cái	才	才	not until; only then	4
cáifeng	裁縫	裁缝	tailor; dressmaker	13
cáishén	財神	财神	the god of wealth	21r
cǎixiá	彩霞	彩霞	rosy clouds	6r
cǎixié	採擷	采撷	pick	18r
cǎiyòng	採用	采用	adopt	8
càixì	菜系	菜系	culinary systems	15r
cānguān	參觀	参观	visit; look around	16
cànlàn	燦爛	灿烂	splendid	22r
cǎo	草	草	grass	19
cè zì	測字	测字	fortune-telling by analyzing a Chinese character	21r
céngjīng	曾經	曾经	at one time; ever	22r
chàbuduō	差不多	差不多	almost; about	1
chá	察	察	sharp	20
cháhú	茶壺	茶壶	tea pot	4r
chá zìdiǎn	查字典	查字典	look up ... in the dictionary	1

chán	饞	馋	greedy	15r
chán	纏	缠	twine; bind	13r
chánjuān	嬋娟	婵娟	used in ancient texts referring to a lovely woman, here it refers to the moon	18r
Chángchéng	長城	长城	the Great Wall	3
cháng jiǔ	長久	长久	for a long time	18r
chángmìng fùguì	長命富貴	长命富贵	live long and be successful	11
chángshēng bùsǐ	長生不死	长生不死	live forever and never die	21
chángshòu	長壽	长寿	long life	19r
chángyòng	常用	常用	often used	1
cháodài	朝代	朝代	dynasty	3
chǎo	炒	炒	stir fry	15r
chèxiāo	撤銷	撤销	dismiss	8
chén	塵	尘	dust	19r
chén	沉	沉	sink	6
chèn	趁	趁	while	12
chēnghu	稱呼	称呼	form of address	20r
chéng	成	成	accomplish; succeed	5
chénggōng	成功	成功	succeed	18
chéngnián	成年	成年	grow up; be of age	12r
chéngqiān-shàngwàn	成千上萬	成千上万	thousands upon thousands	6r
chéngshuāng-chéngduì	成雙成對	成双成对	in pairs	12r
chéngwéi	成為	成为	turn into; become	4
chéngyǔ	成語	成语	proverb; idiom; set phrase	18
chéng	盛	盛	fill (a bowl)	4r
chéngqiáng	城牆	城墙	(city) wall	3
chéngshì	城市	城市	city	13
chéngrèn	承認	承认	admit; recognize	9
chéngxīn-chéngyì	誠心誠意	诚心诚意	sincerely; faithfully	21r
chī kǔ	吃苦	吃苦	suffer	13r
chī kuī	吃虧	吃亏	suffer losses	20
chīkuī shì fú	吃虧是福	吃亏是福	to suffer losses is good fortune	20
chīxīn de	癡心地	痴心地	infatuatedly	12
chóngfù	重複	重复	repeat	17
chóngxīn	重新	重新	again	9
chōu qiān	抽籤	抽签	draw lots	21r
chōuxiàng	抽象	抽象	abstract	10r
chóubù	綢布	绸布	silk	11r
chǒu	醜	丑	ugly	5
chòuwèi	臭味	臭味	offensive odor	7r
chū	初	初	the beginning of	9
chū hàn	出汗	出汗	sweat	14r
chū jiā	出家	出家	become a monk or nun	21
chūshēng	出生	出生	be born	8r

詞彙索引   429

chūtǔ	出土	出土	be unearthed	22r
chū wūní ér bùrǎn	出污泥而不染	出污泥而不染	emerge unstained from the filth	19r
chūxiàn	出現	出现	appear; emerge	13
chúfēi ... cái	除非……才	除非……才	only if	21
chúle ... yǐwài	除了……以外	除了……以外	apart from	7
chúxī	除夕	除夕	the Chinese New Year's Eve	11
chúshī	廚師	厨师	cook; chef	13
Chǔ guó	楚國	楚国	the states of Chu	15
chuān	穿	穿	pierce through	18
chuānxíng	穿行	穿行	pass through	22
chuānzhuó dǎbàn	穿着打扮	穿着打扮	way of dressing; style	4
chuán	傳	传	pass on; transmit; convey	4r
chuán	船	船	boat; ship	3r
chuándì	傳遞	传递	transmit; convey	18
chuánrǎn	傳染	传染	infect	16r
chuánshòu	傳授	传授	pass on (knowledge)	20
chuánshuō	傳說	传说	legend	5r
chuántǒng	傳統	传统	tradition	8
chuànglì	創立	创立	found; institute	21
chuàngzào	創造	创造	create	22r
chuīxū	吹嘘	吹嘘	boast; crow about	21r
chūn jié	春節	春节	Spring Festival	11
chūnjuǎn	春卷	春卷	spring roll	15r
chūnlián	春聯	春联	Spring Festival couplets	11
Chūnqiū shíqī	春秋時期	春秋时期	Spring and Autumn period	3r
chún jié	純潔	纯洁	pure; clean and honest	18r
cí	雌	雌	female	12r
cíqì	瓷器	瓷器	china	4r
Cí Xǐ	慈禧	慈禧	empress dowager of the Qing dynasty	13
cíxù	詞序	词序	word order	18
cízǔ	詞組	词组	expression; phrase	18
cōngming	聰明	聪明	intelligent; smart	1r
cóng	從	从	from	1
cónglái	從來	从来	at all times; always	5
cū	粗	粗	thick	13r
cūxīn dàyì	粗心大意	粗心大意	careless	5r
cù	醋	醋	vinegar	15r
cúnzài	存在	存在	exist	9
cùn	寸	寸	inch	13r
cuòzì	錯字	错字	wrongly written characters	2r

D

dāchéng	搭成	搭成	put up (temporary structure)	12
dǎdòng	打動	打动	(of emotions) move; touch	18r
dǎ gōng	打工	打工	work	7

dǎmà	打罵	打骂	beat and scold	8r
dǎ pái	打牌	打牌	play cards	14
dǎ quán	打拳	打拳	practice (Chinese) boxing	14r
dǎ zhàng	打仗	打仗	go to war	3
dàdì	大地	大地	world; earth	4
dàdōu	大都	大都	mostly	7
dàduōshù	大多數	大多数	majority	6r
dàfāng	大方	大方	natural and poised	19r
dàgūniang	大姑娘	大姑娘	young woman	5r
dàhóng	大紅	大红	bright red	11
dà jiē-xiǎoxiàng	大街小巷	大街小巷	all streets	15
dàlìshì	大力士	大力士	a man of unusual strength	17
dàliàng	大量	大量	in great quantities	4r
Dàmíng Gōng	大明宮	大明宫	Daming Palace	22r
dànǎo	大腦	大脑	cerebrum	14r
dà niánchūyī	大年初一	大年初一	the first day of the lunar year	11
dà-xiǎobiàn	大小便	大小便	stool and urine	16r
Dàyàn Tǎ	大雁塔	大雁塔	Big Wild Goose Pagoda	16
dàyuē	大約	大约	approximately; about	9r
Dàyùnhé	大運河	大运河	the Grand Canal	3r
dàzhì	大致	大致	generally; roughly	18
dàzhuàn	大篆	大篆	an ancient style of calligraphy current in the Zhou dynasty (1122–221 B.C.)	22r
dàzìrán	大自然	大自然	nature	16
dāi	呆	呆	stay	2r
dài	戴	戴	wear; put on	19
dàibiǎo	代表	代表	represent	12r
dàimàn	怠慢	怠慢	neglect; slight	10
dàizi	帶子	带子	band; belt	12r
dān	單	单	single	6r
dāncí	單詞	单词	word	1
dāng bīng	當兵	当兵	be a soldier	7r
dāngchū	當初	当初	originally; at the beginning	12r
dāng ... shíhou	當......時候	当......时候	when	3
dāngxīn	當心	当心	be careful	2r
dǎng	擋	挡	block	17
dàochù	到處	到处	all over; everywhere	21r
dàodǐ	到底	到底	exactly; after all	9
dàodé	道德	道德	ethics	21
dàogū	道姑	道姑	Taoist nun	21
dàoguàn	道觀	道观	Taoist temple	21
Dào jiào	道教	道教	Taoism	21
dào jīng	道經	道经	Taoist scriptures	21
dàolǐ	道理	道理	argument; principle	14r
dàoshì	道士	道士	Taoist priest	21

dàotuì	倒退	倒退	reverse; retrogress	9
dàoyìng	倒映	倒映	inverted reflection in water	16
déyì	得意	得意	proud of oneself	10
dé-zhì-tǐ	德智體	德智体	virtue, intellectual capability and physical fitness	7
dēng	登	登	step on; ascend; climb	16
dēnglong	燈籠	灯笼	lantern	15
děngděng	等等	等等	et cetera	8r
dī	滴	滴	drip down; weep	18
dīluò	滴落	滴落	drip down	18
dī tóu	低頭	低头	lower one's head	18r
dí	笛	笛	flute; pipe	6r
dísīkē	迪斯科	迪斯科	disco	14r
dǐxia	底下	底下	under	3
dìwèi	地位	地位	position; status	13
dìyù	地獄	地狱	hell	21
diāndǎo	顛倒	颠倒	reverse	2r
diǎn	點	点	dot stroke in Chinese characters	2r
diǎn tóu	點頭	点头	nod	1r
diǎnxīn	點心	点心	pastry	21r
diànnǎo	電腦	电脑	computer	1
diāolíng	凋零	凋零	wither	19r
diàohuàn	調換	调换	exchange; swap	2r
dīng	叮	叮	sting; bite	2r
dǐng	頂	顶	support from below; hold up	13
Dōngnányà	東南亞	东南亚	Southeast Asia	22r
Dōngyà	東亞	东亚	East Asia	4r
dòng	棟	栋	measure word for house	20r
dòngfáng	洞房	洞房	bridal chamber	5r
dòng nǎozi	動腦子	动脑子	use one's brains	14r
dòngwù	動物	动物	animal	6r
dòngxué	洞穴	洞穴	cave; cavern	16
dòu jiāng	豆漿	豆浆	soy-bean milk	15r
dòushā	豆沙	豆沙	sweetened bean paste	15
dòuzhēng	鬥爭	斗争	struggle; fight	17
dú rú	讀如	读如	be pronounced as	9r
dú ruò	讀若	读若	be pronounced as	9r
dú shū gāo	讀書高	读书高	being literate is superior	7r
dútè	獨特	独特	unique	15r
dùzi	肚子	肚子	stomach	15r
duǎn	短	短	short	18r
duàn	段	段	section	3
duàn	斷	断	break	16r
duànliú	斷流	断流	stop flowing	3r
duànliàn	鍛煉	锻炼	exercising for health	14r
duìdài	對待	对待	treat; approach	14

duìmén	對門	对门	the house opposite	17
duìxiàng	對象	对象	marriage partner	5r
duìyú	對於	对于	for; to; with regard to	8
dūnzi	墩子	墩子	block	4r
dùn	頓	顿	measure word for beatings	8r
duōme	多麼	多么	how; what	18
duō zǐ duō fú	多子多福	多子多福	the more children one has, the more happiness	8
duǒ	朵	朵	measure wood for flowers	19
duǒ	躲	躲	hide; dodge	12
duò tāi	墮胎	堕胎	induced abortion	16r

E

Ēfáng Gōng	阿房宮	阿房宫	Efang Palace	22r
èshēng'èqì	惡聲惡氣	恶声恶气	speak in a nasty way	14
ér	而	而	but	11
érsūn	兒孫	儿孙	children and grandchildren	17
értóng	兒童	儿童	child(ren)	9r

F

fā	發	发	generate	6r
fā	發	发	grow; put forth	18r
fā cái	發財	发财	get rich	6
fādá	發達	发达	developed; flourishing	14
fāmíng	發明	发明	invent	4r
fā shāo	發燒	发烧	have a temperature	16r
fāshēng	發生	发生	happen; take place	8r
fāxiàn	發現	发现	find, discover	5r
fāyīn	發音	发音	pronunciation	1
fāyuán	發源	发源	originate from	22r
fāzhǎn	發展	发展	develop	7
fá kuǎn	罰款	罚款	fine; punish by levying fine	8
fān	翻	翻	turn over; capsize	6
fánhuá	繁華	繁华	bustling; flourishing	16
fánróng	繁榮	繁荣	prosperous	4
fánróng-chāngshèng	繁榮昌盛	繁荣昌盛	thriving and prosperous	19r
fányǎn-	繁衍	繁衍	multiply	22r
fánshì	凡是	凡是	every; all; any	13
fǎndào	反倒	反倒	on the contrary, same as "反而"	14
fǎnduì	反對	反对	object; oppose	9
fǎn'ér	反而	反而	on the contrary; instead	13
fǎnqiè	反切	反切	a method of representing the pronunciation of Chinese characters	9r
fǎnzhèng	反正	反正	anyway; anyhow	13
fàn zuì	犯罪	犯罪	commit a crime	8r
fāng	__方	__方	__side	5

fāngbiàn	方便	方便	convenient	3r
fāngfǎ	方法	方法	way; method	8
fáng bìng	防病	防病	prevent disease	14r
fángzhǐ	防止	防止	prevent; avoid	3
fàng biānpào	放鞭炮	放鞭炮	let off firecrackers	11
fàngshèkē	放射科	放射科	X-ray department	16r
fēi … bùkě	非……不可	非……不可	insist on; must; have to	8
fēiqín-zǒushòu	飛禽走獸	飞禽走兽	birds and beasts	22
féiwò	肥沃	肥沃	fertile	22r
fèichú	廢除	废除	abolish	9
fēn	分	分	divide	6
fēnkāi	分開	分开	divide	17r
fēnlí	分離	分离	separate; sever	6
fēnliè	分裂	分裂	split; divide	3
fénmù	墳墓	坟墓	tomb	17r
fèn	份	份	measure word for confidence	17
fēng	封	封	measure word for letters	17r
fēnggé	風格	风格	style	22r
fēngguāng	風光	风光	sight; scene	16
fēng jǐngqū	風景區	风景区	scenic spot	22
fēngqì	風氣	风气	common practice	10
fēngwèi	風味	风味	special flavor; characteristic of a particular place	15r
fēngshōu	豐收	丰收	good harvest	11
fèng	鳳	凤	phoenix	6r
Fó jiào	佛教	佛教	Buddhism	21
fó jīng	佛經	佛经	Buddhist sutra	21
fǒuzé	否則	否则	otherwise	21
fūqī	夫妻	夫妻	husband and wife	6
fú	幅	幅	measure word for paintings	2
fúhào	符號	符号	symbol	9r
fúqì	福氣	福气	good luck	6
fǔdǎo	輔導	辅导	assist; tutor	7
fù	付	付	pay	7
fùdān	負擔	负担	burden	7
fùguì	富貴	富贵	riches and honor	19
fùmǔ	父母	父母	parents	1r
fù-mǔqīn	父母親	父母亲	parents	20r
fùnǚ	婦女	妇女	woman	13

G

gǎi	改	改	change	4
gǎibiàn	改變	改变	change	5
gānhé	乾涸	干涸	dry up; run dry	3r
gānsǐ	乾死	干死	dying of drought	11r
gānyán	肝炎	肝炎	hepatitis	16r

gǎndào	感到	感到	feel	8r
gǎndòng	感動	感动	move	17
gǎn jī	感激	感激	appreciate	5
gǎn jué	感覺	感觉	feeling	10r
gǎnmào	感冒	感冒	catch a cold	16r
gǎnshòu	感受	感受	feel	17
gǎn jǐn	趕緊	赶紧	hastily; in a hurry	12
gāng	剛	刚	just	12r
gāng	缸	缸	big ceramic storage jar	4r
gāotái	高臺	高台	high platform	17r
gāoyuán	高原	高原	plateau	22
gǎo	搞	搞	do; be engaged in	10
gē	割	割	cut	16r
gēda	疙瘩	疙瘩	pimple; spots	16r
gébì	隔壁	隔壁	next door	17
gèrén	個人	个人	individual (person)	8
gèzhǒng gèyàng	各種各樣	各种各样	various kinds; all sorts of	7r
gèzì	各自	各自	each; by oneself; respective	12r
gēn	跟	跟	with	2
gēn	根	根	root of a tree	17r
gēnběn	根本	根本	entirely; at all	10
gēn jù	根據	根据	according to	11
gōngbù	公佈	公布	promulgate; publish	9
gōnggòng chǎnghé	公共場合	公共场合	public place	8
gōngsī	公司	公司	company	5
gōngyuán	公園	公园	park	14r
gōngzhí	公職	公职	public employment	8
gōngdiàn	宮殿	宫殿	palace	22r
gōng jiàn	弓箭	弓箭	bow and arrow	8r
gōng jù	工具	工具	means	3r
gōngláo	功勞	功劳	contribution; credit	11r
gòng	供	供	make offerings	21r
gòng	共	共	share ... together	18r
gòngtóng	共同	共同	common	9r
Gǒubùlǐ bāozi	狗不理包子	狗不理包子	Goubuli stuffed steam bun	15r
gòu wù	購物	购物	shopping	16
gūdú	孤獨	孤独	lonely	14
gūgu	姑姑	姑姑	aunt; father's sister	20r
gǔ	股	股	measure word for strength	17
gǔdài	古代	古代	ancient times	2
gǔlǎo	古老	古老	ancient	17
gǔkē	骨科	骨科	(department of) orthopedics	16r
gùdìng	固定	固定	fixed	18
Gùgōng	故宮	故宫	Forbidden City; Palace Museum	16
gùxiāng	故鄉	故乡	hometown	18r
guǎfu	寡婦	寡妇	widow	17

guà	掛	挂	hang; put up	11
guà hào	掛號	挂号	register	16r
guài	怪	怪	blame	5r
guāncái	棺材	棺材	coffin	19
guānfāng	官方	官方	official	9
guānzhí	官職	官职	official position	8
guānguǎ	鰥寡	鳏寡	widowers and widows	14
guānniàn	觀念	观念	idea; concept	8
guānxì	關係	关系	relationship; link	2
guānxīn	關心	关心	care (about)	14
guānyú	關於	关于	regarding; about	18
guānyīn púsà	觀音菩薩	观音菩萨	Bodhisattva; Goddess of Mercy	21r
guǎn jiào	管教	管教	subject sb. to discipline	8r
guāngróng	光榮	光荣	glorious	22r
guǎngchǎng	廣場	广场	public square	14r
guàng	逛	逛	stroll	16
guīdìng	規定	规定	define; stipulate	7
guǐshén	鬼神	鬼神	ghosts and gods	21
Guìlín	桂林	桂林	name of a city in China	15r
guódū	國都	国都	capital city	3r
guóhuā	國花	国花	national flower	19r
guó jì	國際	国际	international	9r
guówáng	國王	国王	king	15
guǒ	裹	裹	wrap	13r
guòchéng	過程	过程	process	13r
guòlùrén	過路人	过路人	passerby	17r

H

háishì	還是	还是	still	2
háishì	還是	还是	or	6
hǎi	海	海	sea	3r
hǎikū shílàn bù biàn xīn	海枯石爛不變心	海枯石烂不变心	the sea may run dry and the rocks may crumble, but our hearts will always remain loyal	12r
hǎiwài	海外	海外	overseas	9
hǎiyáng	海洋	海洋	sea	16
hài rén	害人	害人	harm people	11
hàisǐ	害死	害死	kill; cause someone's death	3
hán	含	含	keep in the mouth	9r
hányì	含義	含义	implication	18
hánfēng-cìgǔ	寒風刺骨	寒风刺骨	the cold wind chills one to the bone	15
Hánguó	韓國	韩国	Korea	22r
Hán Píng	韓憑	韩凭	name of a person	17r
Hàn cháo	漢朝	汉朝	the Han dynasty	4
Hànyǔ Pīnyīn Fāng'àn	漢語拼音方案	汉语拼音方案	the Scheme for the Chinese Phonetic Alphabet	9r
háng	行	行	line	18r

hǎoxiàng	好像	好像	seem (to be)	2r
hàomǎ	號碼	号码	number	6
hào sè	好色	好色	lustful	17r
hé	禾	禾	standing grain	11
hé	合	合	join; combine	17r
héhuā	荷花	荷花	lotus	19r
Hé'nán	河南	河南	name of a province in China	22r
héshang	和尚	和尚	bonze; monk	21
hétao	核桃	核桃	walnuts	15
hēi	嘿	嘿	hey	1r
héng	橫	横	horizontal stroke in Chinese characters	2r
Héng Shān	恆山	恒山	Mt. Heng	21
héngxīn	恆心	恒心	perseverance	18
hóngdòu	紅豆	红豆	love pea; red bean	17r
hóngniáng	紅娘	红娘	female matchmaker	5
hóngzǎo	紅棗	红枣	red jujube	15
hòu	厚	厚	thick	9
hòuhuǐ	後悔	后悔	regret	5r
hòunǎosháo	後腦杓	后脑勺	the back of the head	13r
hòutuì	後退	后退	lag behind; retrogress	8r
hòuyì	後裔	后裔	descendants	4
hū	乎	乎	classical Chinese particle	2r
hú	胡	胡	a family name	2
húshuō	胡說	胡说	nonsense	21r
hú	湖	湖	lake	2
Húběi	湖北	湖北	name of a province in China	22
Hú'nán	湖南	湖南	name of a province in China	15r
húdié	蝴蝶	蝴蝶	butterfly	2
húlihútu	糊裏糊塗	糊里糊涂	confused; muddled	20
hútu	糊塗	糊涂	confused; bewildered	2
hùxiāng	互相	互相	mutual; each other	10r
huāduǒ	花朵	花朵	flower	19r
Huā Mùlán	花木蘭	花木兰	name of a person	13
huāniǎohuà	花鳥畫	花鸟画	traditional Chinese paintings of flowers and birds	20
huāpíng	花瓶	花瓶	vase	4r
huāshēng	花生	花生	peanut	15
huāyán qiǎoyǔ	花言巧語	花言巧语	honeyed and deceiving words	5
huá	劃	划	draw; scratch	12
huáqiáo	華僑	华侨	overseas Chinese	4
Huáxià	華夏	华夏	an ancient name for China	4
huà	畫	画	draw	2
huàláng	畫廊	画廊	art gallery	22
huàxiàng	畫像	画像	portrait	10r
huà	劃	划	strokes of a Chinese character	2r

huà jiàchù	劃價處	划价处	pricing department	16r
huà	化	化	-ize; -ify	19
huàyàn	化驗	化验	laboratory test	16r
huáibào	懷抱	怀抱	embrace	16
huáiniàn	懷念	怀念	cherish the memory of	15
huái yùn	懷孕	怀孕	pregnant	16r
huàidàn	壞蛋	坏蛋	wicked person	17r
huàihuà	壞話	坏话	vicious talk	15
huānyíng	歡迎	欢迎	welcome	14r
huán jìng	環境	环境	environment	19
huángdì	皇帝	皇帝	emperor	3r
huánggōng	皇宮	皇宫	palace	16
huáng jiā língmù	皇家陵墓	皇家陵墓	emperor's tomb	22r
Huánghé	黃河	黄河	the Yellow River	2
huáng jīn	黃金	黄金	gold	7r
hūnyīn	婚姻	婚姻	marriage	5
húnshēn	渾身	浑身	all over one's body	14r
húntun	餛飩	馄饨	wonton	15r
huódòng	活動	活动	activity	11
huózhe	活著	活着	be alive	17r
huǒguō	火鍋	火锅	chafing dish	15r
huǒtuǐ	火腿	火腿	ham	15
huǒyào	火藥	火药	gunpowder	20
huòzhě	或者	或者	or	6

J

jī	雞	鸡	chicken	11r
Jīdū jiào	基督教	基督教	Christianity	21
jīhū	幾乎	几乎	almost	12
jí	急	急	rapid	22
jí bìng	急病	急病	acute disease	16r
jízhěnshì	急診室	急诊室	emergency treatment room	16r
jídù	嫉妒	嫉妒	be jealous of	15
jílì	吉利	吉利	luck; lucky; propitious	19
jíshǐ	即使	即使	even if	7
jíshǒu	棘手	棘手	thorny; troublesome	10r
jì	季	季	season	19r
jìbài	祭拜	祭拜	sacrifice to; worship	11r
jìdiàn	祭奠	祭奠	hold a memorial ceremony for	15
jìhuà	計劃	计划	plan	8r
jìhuà shēngyù	計劃生育	计划生育	birth control	8
jìniàn	紀念	纪念	memorialize; commemorate	15
jìrán	既然	既然	now that; since	19
jì ... yòu	既……又	既……又	both ... and; as well as	6
jìtuō	寄托	寄托	place (one's hope) in	6r
jiāzhòng	加重	加重	aggravate	13
jiāzú	家族	家族	family; clan	20r

jiǎ	甲	甲	first; shell	2r
jiǎgǔwén	甲骨文	甲骨文	inscriptions on bones or tortoise shells from the Shang dynasty; oracle-bone script	11
jiǎ	假	假	fake	11
jià	嫁	嫁	(of a woman) marry	5
jiàqián	價錢	价钱	price	9
jiān	煎	煎	fry	15r
jiānchí	堅持	坚持	uphold	18
jiānqiáng	堅強	坚强	staunch	19r
jiǎn	剪	剪	cut (hair etc.) with scissors	12r
jiǎndiào	剪掉	剪掉	cut off	13r
jiǎndān	簡單	简单	simple	1
jiǎnliàn	簡練	简练	concise	18
jiǎnqīng	減輕	减轻	lighten; alleviate	7
jiǎnyànkē	檢驗科	检验科	laboratory	16r
jiàn	件	件	measure word: piece, articles, etc.	17
jiàn jiàn de	漸漸地	渐渐地	gradually	11r
jiànkāng	健康	健康	healthy	18r
jiànzhù	建築	建筑	building	22r
jiāng	將	将	will	22
jiāngcuò jiùcuò	將錯就錯	将错就错	leave a mistake uncorrected and make the best of it	10r
jiānglái	將來	将来	future	6r
jiāngmiàn	江面	江面	river surface	22
jiǎng jiū	講究	讲究	stress; value	14
jiàng	醬	酱	soy sauce	15r
jiāo	交	交	pay	16r
jiāocuò	交錯	交错	interlock	17r
jiāotōng	交通	交通	transportation; traffic; communications	3r
jiāowǎng	交往	交往	associate with	20
jiāo'ào	驕傲	骄傲	pride	3
jiāoshí-xiǎntān	礁石險灘	礁石险滩	reefs and dangerous shoals	22
jiǎogǔ	腳骨	脚骨	foot bone	13r
jiǎozi	餃子	饺子	dumplings	11
jiàotáng	教堂	教堂	church	21
jiàoxué	教學	教学	teaching	9r
Jiàoyùbù	教育部	教育部	Ministry of Education	9
jiàozǔ	教祖	教祖	the founder of a religion	21
jiàozi	轎子	轿子	sedan chair	19
jiàozuò	叫做	叫做	to be addressed as	2
jiē	皆	皆	all; each; every	7r
jiēxiàlái	接下來	接下来	follow; go on (with)	16
jié fà	結髮	结发	weave hair	12r
jiéguǒ	結果	结果	(as a) result	10
jiégòu	結構	结构	structure	18

jiéhūn	結婚	结婚	marry	1r
jié jiāo	結交	结交	associate with	19r
jiézā	結紮	结扎	tie together	12r
jiéyú	節餘	节余	surplus	11
jié yù	節育	节育	birth control	8
jiě jué	解決	解决	solve	9
jiěshì	解釋	解释	explain	9r
jièshào	介紹	介绍	introduce; introduction	2
jīnhòu	今後	今后	later; in future	8r
jīn jīn jì jiào	斤斤計較	斤斤计较	excessively mean and small-minded	20
jīnqián	金錢	金钱	money	7r
jīnwén	金文	金文	inscriptions on ancient bronzes	22r
jīnzi	金子	金子	gold	19
jǐn'āi	緊挨	紧挨	be next to	12
jǐn jǐn de	緊緊的	紧紧的	tightly	13r
jǐnguǎn ... háishì	儘管……還是	尽管……还是	although; despite	15
jǐn kě'néng	盡可能	尽可能	try one's best	20
jǐnliàng	盡量	尽量	to the best of one's abilities	20
jìnbù	進步	进步	advance; progress	15r
Jìn cháo	晉朝	晋朝	the Jin dynasty (265–420)	13
jìnzhǐ	禁止	禁止	prohibit	13r
jīng jí	荊棘	荆棘	brambles; thorns	10r
jīng jì	經濟	经济	economy	14
jīngshén	精神	精神	spirit	14
jīngtiān-dòngdì	驚天動地	惊天动地	world-shaking	17
jǐngsè	景色	景色	scenery	18
jìng	敬	敬	piously worship	21r
jìnghuà	淨化	净化	purify	19r
jìng jìng de	靜靜地	静静地	quietly	3r
jìngrán	竟然	竟然	actually; unexpectedly	17r
jìngzhēng	競爭	竞争	compete	7
jìngzi	鏡子	镜子	mirror	16
jiū jìng	究竟	究竟	exactly; after all	9
jiǔ	久	久	for a long time	5
jiǔròu péngyǒu	酒肉朋友	酒肉朋友	fair-weather friends	19r
jiù jiu	舅舅	舅舅	mother' brother	20r
jiùxīng	救星	救星	liberator; emancipator	11r
jūzhù	居住	居住	live; reside	4
jǔ tóu	舉頭	举头	raise one's head	18r
jǔxíng	舉行	举行	hold (ceremony, celebration)	11
jù jí	聚集	聚集	gather; assemble	14r
jùshuō	據說	据说	it is said	11
jùtǐ	具體	具体	specific; concrete	10r
juànshǔ	眷屬	眷属	family dependents	17r
juéde	覺得	觉得	feel; think	1
juéwù	覺悟	觉悟	become aware of	13r

juéduì	絕對	绝对	absolute	16r
jūn	君	君	you; gentleman	18r

K

kāibàn	開辦	开办	set up; start	14
kāichú	開除	开除	fire; discharge from	8
kǎishū	楷書	楷书	regular script	22r
kāndēng	刊登	刊登	publish	19
kān	看	看	look after; take care of	13
kàn xiàng	看相	看相	practice physiognomy	21r
kànbùqǐ	看不起	看不起	look down upon	7r
kǎoyā	烤鴨	烤鸭	roast duck	15r
kào	靠	靠	depend on	8
kàolǒng	靠攏	靠拢	close up	17r
kē	科	科	section	16r
kēxué	科學	科学	science	21r
kē tóu	磕頭	磕头	kowtow	21
kèzǐ miànxiàn	蚵仔麵線	蚵仔面线	noodles with oyster	15r
késou	咳嗽	咳嗽	cough	16r
kělián	可憐	可怜	pitiful	12
kěxī	可惜	可惜	it's a pity; it's too bad	22
kōng	空	空	empty	19r
kōngzhōng	空中	空中	in the air	6r
Kǒngmiào	孔廟	孔庙	Confucian temple	21
Kǒngzǐ	孔子	孔子	Confucius	21
kòngdì	空地	空地	open space/area	14r
kòngzhì	控制	控制	control	8
kǒufú	口服	口服	take orally	16r
kǒuqiāngkē	口腔科	口腔科	(department of) stomatology	16r
kǒutóu	口頭	口头	oral	18
kǔkǔ de	苦苦地	苦苦地	bitterly	12
kǔmèn	苦悶	苦闷	dejected; feeling low	14
kuài	塊	块	a piece of	19
kuàilè	快樂	快乐	happy	10
kuān	寬	宽	wide	12
kuānkuò	寬闊	宽阔	wide	22
kuàngqiě	況且	况且	besides; in addition	22
Kuí	夔	夔	name of a person	10

L

Lādīng zìmǔ	拉丁字母	拉丁字母	Latin alphabet; the Roman alphabet	9r
lā dùzi	拉肚子	拉肚子	have loose bowels; diarrhea	16r
lā guānxi	拉關係	拉关系	try to establish connections with important people	20
là	辣	辣	spicy; hot	10r
là jiāo	辣椒	辣椒	hot pepper	10r

Lántián	藍田	蓝田	place name	22r
lángtou	榔頭	榔头	hammer	8r
lǎngsòng	朗誦	朗诵	declaim	18r
làngfèi	浪費	浪费	waste	9
lǎohǔ	老虎	老虎	tiger	6r
lǎoniánxìng chīdāizhèng	老年性癡呆症	老年性痴呆症	senile dementia	14r
lǎoshì	老是	老是	always; at all times	6
Lǎozǐ	老子	老子	Lao Zi (philosopher in the Spring and Autumn period)	21
lěi	壘	垒	build by piling up bricks	3r
lèi	累	累	tire	3
lèizhū	淚珠	泪珠	teardrop	22
lěngdàn	冷淡	冷淡	indifferent; cold	10
lí	梨	梨	pear	6
lí hūn	離婚	离婚	divorce	12r
Lí Jiāng	灕江	漓江	the Li River	16
lǐ	里	里	Chinese unit of length	3
Lǐ Bái	李白	李白	name of a poet	18r
lǐ jiě	理解	理解	understand	10
lǐmào	禮貌	礼貌	courtesy; politeness	20r
lìhai	厲害	厉害	intense	7
lì ji	痢疾	痢疾	dysentery	16r
lìliang	力量	力量	strength	17
lìrú	例如	例如	for example	2
lìshǐxuéjiā	歷史學家	历史学家	historian	11
lìshū	隸書	隶书	an ancient style of calligraphy current in the Han dynasty (206 B.C.–A.D. 220)	22r
lián	連	连	connect; link	3
lián ... yě	連……也	连……也	even	4
liánlǐzhī	連理枝	连理枝	trees whose branches interlock or join together	17r
liánróng	蓮蓉	莲蓉	lotus bean paste	15
liàn	練	练	practice	11r
liángshi	糧食	粮食	grain	3r
liáo tiān	聊天	聊天	chat	14
liǎo jiě	了解	了解	understand	18r
liǎobùqǐ	了不起	了不起	amazing; impressive	7r
lièchū	列出	列出	list	10r
lín jū	鄰居	邻居	neighbor	20r
línlì	林立	林立	stand in great number (like trees in a forest)	16
línsǐ	臨死	临死	on one's deathbed	17r
líng	鈴	铃	bell	6r
lǐngxiù	領袖	领袖	leader	22r
lǐngzhe	領著	领着	bring(ing)	12

lìng	令	令	order	2r
lìng	另	另	another	9r
liú	留	留	keep	13r
liúxià	留下	留下	leave	17r
liúchuán	流傳	流传	hand down	15
liúfàng	流放	流放	exile	15
liú kǒushuǐ	流口水	流口水	dribble; drool; salivate	15r
liúshuǐ	流水	流水	running water	2
liútǎng	流淌	流淌	flow	3r
liúxíng	流行	流行	prevalent; popular	13
liúyù	流域	流域	river basin; drainage area	22r
liǔ	綹	绺	lock; tuft; skein	12r
lóng	龍	龙	dragon	6r
lóng de chuánrén	龍的傳人	龙的传人	dragon's descendants	11r
lúwěiyè	蘆葦葉	芦苇叶	reed leaves	15
lùqǔ	錄取	录取	admit; enroll	7
lùxù	陸續	陆续	in succession	9
lǜcōngcōng	綠葱葱	绿葱葱	green	19r
lǚyóu	旅遊	旅游	travel	16
luòhòu	落後	落后	lagging behind; backward	21r

M

má	麻	麻	numbing to the mouth	15r
máfan	麻煩	麻烦	troublesome; problematic	6
má jiàng	麻將	麻将	mahjong	14r
mǎ	馬	马	horse	11r
mǎchē	馬車	马车	carriage; cart	3r
mǎlù biān	馬路邊	马路边	roadside	14r
mà	罵	骂	abuse; curse	14
mái	埋	埋	bury	3
mái tóu	埋頭	埋头	immerse oneself in	7r
mài yín	賣淫	卖淫	prostitute oneself	19
mǎnyì	滿意	满意	satisfied	5
màncháng	漫長	漫长	very long	22r
mànhuà	漫畫	漫画	cartoon	16r
màozi	帽子	帽子	cap; hat	19
méi guānxì	沒關係	没关系	does not matter	2r
méihuā	梅花	梅花	plum blossom	19r
méilái-yǎnqù	眉來眼去	眉来眼去	exchange love glances with sb.; make eyes at each other	18
méimao	眉毛	眉毛	eyebrow	18
méipó	媒婆	媒婆	female matchmaker	5
měihuà	美化	美化	beautify	19
měilì-dòngrén	美麗動人	美丽动人	lovely and affecting	12
měimǎn	美滿	美满	happy; satisfactory	19r
měimiào	美妙	美妙	splendid; wonderful	18r

ménshén	門神	门神	door-god	21r
méntóu	門頭	门头	over the door	19
ménzhěnbù	門診部	门诊部	out-patient department	16r
Mèng jiāngnǚ	孟姜女	孟姜女	name of a person	3
míxìn	迷信	迷信	superstition	6
míyǔ	謎語	谜语	riddle	15
mǐfěn	米粉	米粉	rice flour	15
miànxiàng	面相	面相	face	21r
miáoxiě	描寫	描写	describe	13r
mièwáng	滅亡	灭亡	perish; die out	13r
mín jiān gùshi	民間故事	民间故事	folktale	3
mínzú	民族	民族	nation; nationality	4
míngchēng	名稱	名称	name	4
míng'é	名額	名额	quota of people	7
míngshēng	名聲	名声	reputation	5
míngshèng-gǔ jì	名勝古跡	名胜古迹	famous historic and cultural sites	16
Míng cháo	明朝	明朝	the Ming dynasty	3
míngmíng	明明	明明	obviously; plainly	17
mìng	命	命	destiny; fate	21r
mìnglǐzhùdìng	命裏注定	命里注定	decreed by fate; predestined	21r
mìngyùn	命運	命运	destiny; fate	21r
mō	摸	摸	touch	22
móguài	魔怪	魔怪	monster	11
mònián	末年	末年	the last years	7r
mǒu	某	某	some (unspecified); (a) certain	9
mǔdan	牡丹	牡丹	peony	19r
mǔxìshèhuì	母系社會	母系社会	matriarchal society	22r
mù	目	目	eye (classical)	2r
mùqián	目前	目前	at present; now	22r
mùshī	牧師	牧师	minister (in a church)	21

N

nà	捺	捺	right-falling stroke in Chinese characters	2r
nán bàn	難辦	难办	hard to do	10r
nándé	難得	难得	seldom; rarely	20
nándé hútu	難得糊塗	难得糊涂	where ignorance is bliss, 'tis folly to be wise	20
nánguài	難怪	难怪	no wonder	22
nánguò	難過	难过	feel bad	5r
Nánběicháo	南北朝	南北朝	the Northern and Southern Dynasties (420–581)	13
nánfāng	南方	南方	the south	3r
nánguó	南國	南国	the southern land	18r
Nán jīng Lù	南京路	南京路	Nanjing Road	16
nèikē	內科	内科	(department of) internal medicine	16r
nèn	嫩	嫩	delicate; tender	13r

nènlǜ	嫩綠	嫩绿	light green	19
nígū	尼姑	尼姑	nun; priestess	21
níhóngdēng	霓虹燈	霓虹灯	neon light	16
niángāo	年糕	年糕	sweet rice cake	11
niánlíng	年齡	年龄	age	5r
niǎo	鳥	鸟	bird	6r
nìngkě ... yě	寧可……也	宁可……也	would rather; had better	17
niú	牛	牛	ox	6r
Niúláng	牛郎	牛郎	Herd-boy	12
niǔlái niǔqù	扭來扭去	扭来扭去	swing; roll	14r
nónglì	農曆	农历	lunar calendar	11
nòng	弄	弄	make; do	10
nǚbànnánzhuāng	女扮男裝	女扮男装	a woman disguised as a man	13
nǚ'ér	女兒	女儿	daughter	20r
nüèdài	虐待	虐待	ill-treat	14

O

ōu	鷗	鸥	sea-gull	6r

P

pāi piàn	拍片	拍片	take X-ray	16r
páiliè	排列	排列	put ... in order	1
páiliè zǔhé	排列組合	排列组合	arrange and assemble	14r
páizhào	牌照	牌照	license plate; license tag	6
páizi	牌子	牌子	sign	7
pài	派	派	send	17
pán	盤	盘	plate	4r
pànwàng	盼望	盼望	expect; look forward to	14
pànzhe	盼着	盼着	look forward to	12
péi	陪	陪	accompany	2r
péiyǎng	培養	培养	foster; train; develop	8r
pēngrèn	烹飪	烹饪	cuisine; cooking	15r
pēngtiáo	烹調	烹调	cook	15r
pèngdào	碰到	碰到	meet	6r
pīpíng	批評	批评	scold; blame; criticize	8r
pīsan	披散	披散	(of hair) hang down loosely	12r
pífū	皮膚	皮肤	skin	16r
pípò-ròulàn	皮破肉爛	皮破肉烂	skin broken and flesh rotting	13r
pǐ	匹	匹	measure word for horse	5r
piānpáng	偏旁	偏旁	radicals (of characters)	1
piányi	便宜	便宜	cheap	15r
piàn	騙	骗	deceive	5r
piāo	飄	飘	float	22
piāodài	飄帶	飘带	ribbon; streamer	22
piāosǎ	飄灑	飘洒	float and drip	22
piáo chāng	嫖娼	嫖娼	go whoring	19

piàoliang	漂亮	漂亮	pretty	1r
piě	撇	撇	left-falling stroke in Chinese characters	2r
pīndú	拼讀	拼读	spell	9r
pīnmìng de	拼命地	拼命地	exerting the utmost strength	12
pīnxiě	拼寫	拼写	spell	1
pǐndé	品德	品德	moral character	19r
píng	憑	凭	depend on; lean on	17
píngděng	平等	平等	equal	13
pínghuǎn	平緩	平缓	flat and slow	22
píngpíng-ān'ān	平平安安	平平安安	safe and sound	6r
pó jiā	婆家	婆家	husband's family	5r
pò	破	破	break	16r
pūkè	撲克	扑克	poker	14r
pútáo jià	葡萄架	葡萄架	grape arbor	12
pǔbiàn	普遍	普遍	common	14r
pùbù	瀑布	瀑布	waterfall	22

Q

qīmò	期末	期末	end of term	8r
qīzhōng	期中	期中	mid-term	8r
Qīxiānnǚ	七仙女	七仙女	the 7th Fairy	12
qí	騎	骑	ride	5r
qíguài	奇怪	奇怪	strange	8
qíjì	奇跡	奇迹	miracle	22r
qímiào	奇妙	奇妙	marvelous	22
qíshí	其實	其实	in fact; actually	1
qǐ	起 (名字)	起 (名字)	give (name)	6r
qìhòu	氣候	气候	climate	22r
qiàqiǎo	恰巧	恰巧	by chance; happen to	7
qiānwàn	千萬	千万	must; be sure to	20
qiānxū	謙虛	谦虚	humble	19r
qiáncái	錢財	钱财	wealth; money	20
qián'é	前額	前额	forehead	13r
qiǎnzé	譴責	谴责	denounce; condemn	14
qiáng	強	强	strong	8r
qiángdà	強大	强大	strong and powerful	4
qiǎng	搶	抢	take away by force	17r
qiāoqiāohuà	悄悄話	悄悄话	whispered sweet talk	12
qiáo	橋	桥	bridge	12
qièjì	切忌	切忌	avoid by all means	16r
qīnfàn	侵犯	侵犯	violate; invasion	8
qīnlüè	侵略	侵略	invade; invasion	3
qīnqī	親戚	亲戚	relatives	12r
qīnshēn	親身	亲身	personally; by oneself	21r
qīnshǔ	親屬	亲属	relatives	20r

qīnyǎn	親眼	亲眼	see with one's eyes	21
qín	琴	琴	a general name for certain musical instruments	6r
Qín cháo	秦朝	秦朝	the Qin dynasty	3
Qínshǐhuáng	秦始皇	秦始皇	the First Emperor of the Qin dynasty	3
qínshòu	禽獸	禽兽	birds and beasts	17r
qīngshān-lǜshuǐ	青山綠水	青山绿水	blue hills and green rivers	16
qīngtái	青苔	青苔	moss	22
Qīng-Zàng	青藏	青藏	Qinghai and Xizang (Tibet)	22
qīng	清	清	clear	20
Qīng cháo	清朝	清朝	the Qing dynasty	7r
qīngchè	清澈	清澈	limpid	16
qíng	晴	晴	fine; clear	18r
qínglǎnglang	晴朗朗	晴朗朗	clear; sunny	22
qíngkuàng	情況	情况	situation	8
qíngrén jié	情人節	情人节	Valentine's Day	12
qìngzhù	慶祝	庆祝	celebrate	11
qióng	窮	穷	poor	12
qiú	求	求	seek (help); beg	5r
qū guǐ	驅鬼	驱鬼	drive out evil spirits	21r
Qútáng Xiá	瞿塘峽	瞿塘峡	the Qutang Gorge	22
Qū Yuán	屈原	屈原	name of a person	15
qǔ	娶	娶	(of a man) marry	5
qǔbùqǐ	娶不起	娶不起	cannot afford to marry	12
qǔdì	取締	取缔	clamp down	19
qǔxiāo	取消	取消	abolish	7r
qùshì	去世	去世	die; pass away	19
quān	圈	圈	circle; round	13r
quán	全	全	completely; entirely	7
quánmiàn	全面	全面	whole; overall	7
quánshì	權勢	权势	power and influence	7r
quánwēi	權威	权威	authority	11r
quàn	勸	劝	advise; persuade	18r
quē	缺	缺	waning	18r
quēdiǎn	缺點	缺点	defect	9r
quēxiàn	缺陷	缺陷	defect	5r
què	卻	却	but	7

R

rǎn	染	染	contaminate	19r
ràng	讓	让	let; make	5
ràng	讓	让	yield; give ground	20
rǎo	繞	绕	go around	22
rè'nào	熱鬧	热闹	lively	16
rètēngtēng	熱騰騰	热腾腾	steaming hot	15
réngōng liúchǎn	人工流產	人工流产	induced abortion	16r

rénjiā	人家	人家	other people	20
rénjiā	人家	人家	family	21r
rénkǒu	人口	人口	population	8
rénquán	人權	人权	human rights	8
rénshēng	人生	人生	life	18r
rénwù	人物	人物	figure; character	10r
rènhé	任何	任何	any	1
rènwéi	認為	认为	think; consider	4
rènzhēn	認真	认真	conscientious; serious	5r
réngrán	仍然	仍然	still; yet	20
rìcháng	日常	日常	daily; day-to-day	4r
rónghuá-fùguì	榮華富貴	荣华富贵	high position and great wealth	19r
róngyì	容易	容易	easy	1
rúcǐ	如此	如此	such; like that	22
rúshī-rúhuà	如詩如畫	如诗如画	as beautiful as a poem or a painting	16
Rú jiā	儒家	儒家	the Confucian school	21
rù	入	入	enter	2r
ruǎn jiàn	軟件	软件	software	1
ruògān	若干	若干	some; several	22

S

sāncùn jīnlián	三寸金蓮	三寸金莲	three-inch "golden lotuses": describes a woman's beautiful bound feet	13r
sānxīn-èryì	三心二意	三心二意	half-hearted; change one's mind constantly	18
sàn	散	散	break up; disperse	6
sàn xīn	散心	散心	relieve boredom; relax	14
sǎo huáng	掃黃	扫黄	crack down on pornography	19
sèqíng	色情	色情	pornography	19
sè-wèi-xiāng	色味香	色味香	color, taste and smell	15r
shāhài	殺害	杀害	kill	8r
shā tóu	殺頭	杀头	behead; decapitate	13r
shǎ	傻	傻	stupid; foolish	17
shǎguā	傻瓜	傻瓜	fool	21r
Shāndōng	山東	山东	name of a province in China	15r
shānshuǐhuà	山水畫	山水画	landscape painting	20
shǎndiàn	閃電	闪电	lightning	11r
shǎnliàng	閃亮	闪亮	sparkling; shining	12
shāng	商	商	commerce; trade	7r
shāngdiàn	商店	商店	store	16
shāngrén	商人	商人	merchant; businessman	4r
shānghài	傷害	伤害	harm	13r
shāngxīn	傷心	伤心	sad; grieved	3
shàng dàng	上當	上当	be tricked; be fooled	5r
Shàngdì	上帝	上帝	God	17

shàng diào	上吊	上吊	hang oneself	17r
shàng shìjì	上世紀	上世纪	last century	9
shàng-xiàwén	上下文	上下文	context	10
shāobǐng	燒餅	烧饼	sesame seed cake	15r
shāohú	燒煳	烧煳	be burnt	2
shāohuǐ	燒毀	烧毁	burn down	22r
shāo xiāng	燒香	烧香	burn joss-sticks	21
sháo	杓	勺	spoon; ladle	4r
shǎoshù mínzú	少數民族	少数民族	ethnic minority	3
shàonán shàonǚ	少男少女	少男少女	young boy and young girl	18r
shé	蛇	蛇	snake	11r
shèhuì	社會	社会	society	15r
shèhuì huódòng	社會活動	社会活动	social activities	7
shèlì	設立	设立	set up	14
shēn	伸	伸	stretch out	22
shēnkè	深刻	深刻	profound; deep	18
shénhuà	神話	神话	myth; fairy tale	17
Shénnǚ Fēng	神女峰	神女峰	Mt. Goddess; Goddess Peak	22
shénqí	神奇	神奇	magical; miraculous	22
shénxiān	神仙	神仙	immortal; supernatural being	21
shénxiàng	神像	神像	the picture or statue of a god	21r
shènzhì	甚至	甚至	even; (go) so far as to ...	5
shēngcún	生存	生存	survive; live	15r
shēng'ér-yù'nǚ	生兒育女	生儿育女	give birth to children and raise them	21r
shēnghuó	生活	生活	live	12
shēngmǐ zhǔ chéng shúfàn	生米煮成熟飯	生米煮成熟饭	the rice is already cooked—what's done can't be undone	5r
shēngmìng	生命	生命	life	14r
shēngpáng	聲旁	声旁	phonetic element of a character	2
shēngyīn	聲音	声音	sound	1
shěng	省	省	leave out; omit	9
Shèng jīng	聖經	圣经	Bible	21
shèngkāi	盛開	盛开	be in full blossom	19r
shīcí	詩詞	诗词	poems	18
shīzi	獅子	狮子	lion	11r
shí	石	石	stone	18
shífēng	石峰	石峰	rock peaks	16
shífèng	石縫	石缝	crack; crevice	22
shídài	時代	时代	times; age; era	10
shímáo	時髦	时髦	fashionable	7r
shíjì	實際	实际	real(ly); actual(ly)	13
shíxiàn	實現	实现	realize; come true	21r
shípǐn	食品	食品	foodstuff	15
shízì jià	十字架	十字架	crucifix; cross	21
shǐde	使得	使得	make; cause; render	16
shǐyòng	使用	使用	use	3r

shǐzhōng	始終	始终	from beginning to end	21
shì	士	士	scholar	2r
shì	試	试	try	21r
Shìjiāmóuní	釋迦牟尼	释迦牟尼	Sakyamuni	21
shìjiè	世界	世界	world	4r
shìyí	適宜	适宜	suitable	22r
shìzú	氏族	氏族	clan	22r
shōufèichù	收費處	收费处	cashier	16r
shōurù	收入	收入	income; revenue	11
shǒu	守	守	keep watch	12
shǒu	首	首	measure word for poems	18r
shǒushù	手術	手术	surgery	16r
shǒuwén	手紋	手纹	lines of the hand	21r
shòudào	受到	受到	get; receive	9
shòu zuì	受罪	受罪	suffering; hardship	13r
shòumìng	壽命	寿命	life-span; longevity	19r
shū	梳	梳	comb	13r
shūfǎ	書法	书法	calligraphy	14
shūjí	書籍	书籍	books	9
shūmiànyǔ	書面語	书面语	written language	16r
shūrù	輸入	输入	input	1
shūshu	叔叔	叔叔	father's younger brother; address for men of an age approx. that of father	20r
shūyuǎn	疏遠	疏远	become estranged; stand off	15
shúxī	熟悉	熟悉	be familiar with	9r
shǔbùqīng	數不清	数不清	incalculable; numerous	16
shǔyú	屬於	属于	be part of; belong to	16r
shù	束	束	a bunch of	5r
shù	束	束	bundle	13r
shù	樹	树	tree	2
shùgàn	樹幹	树干	trunk (of a tree)	17r
shùzhī	樹枝	树枝	branch	17r
shù	豎	竖	vertical stroke in Chinese characters	2r
shù	豎	竖	erect; set upright	21
shuāi	摔	摔	fall; lose one's balance	16r
shuāiluò	衰落	衰落	be on the wane; decline	15
shuāng	霜	霜	frost	18r
shuāng	雙	双	two; double	6r
shuāngfāng	雙方	双方	both sides	5
shuāngyīnjié	雙音節	双音节	two-syllable	18
shuǐbà	水壩	水坝	dam	22
shuǐdī-shíchuān	水滴石穿	水滴石穿	dripping water wears through a stone—little strokes fell great oaks	18
shuǐguǒ	水果	水果	fruit	21r

shuǐmiàn	水面	水面	water surface	19r
shuǐpíng	水平	水平	level; standard	11
Shùn	舜	舜	the name of a legendary monarch in ancient China around 2200 B.C.	10
shùnkǒu	順口	顺口	easy to read	18
shùnshun liūliu	順順溜溜	顺顺溜溜	smoothly	6
shuōfa	說法	说法	statement; version; argument	4r
shuōmíng	說明	说明	illustrate; show	8r
sīkǎo	思考	思考	ponder	14r
sīniàn	思念	思念	miss	17r
sīwéi	思維	思维	thinking	14r
Sìchuān	四川	四川	name of a province in China	15r
sìhū	似乎	似乎	seem; as if	22
sìmiào	寺廟	寺庙	temple	21
sìzhōu	四周	四周	all around	4
sōnghè-yánnián	松鶴延年	松鹤延年	live as long as the pine and crane	19r
sōngshù	松樹	松树	pine	19r
Sòng cháo	宋朝	宋朝	the Song dynasty	4r
Sòng guó	宋國	宋国	the state of Song	17r
sòng zhōng	送終	送终	attend upon a dying parent or other senior member of one's family	6
Sū Shì	蘇軾	苏轼	name of a poet	18r
sútǐzì	俗體字	俗体字	popular or simplified form of Chinese characters	9
súyǔ	俗語	俗语	common saying; fold adage	18
sùdù dī	速度低	速度低	low speed	10
sùdù gāo	速度高	速度高	high speed	10
sùxiàng	塑像	塑像	statue	10r
suān	酸	酸	sour	15r
suàn	算	算	count	22r
suàn guà	算卦	算卦	divination	21r
suàn mìng	算命	算命	fortune-telling	21r
suīrán ... dànshì	雖然……但是	虽然……但是	(although) ... but	1
Suí cháo	隋朝	隋朝	the Sui dynasty	3r
suíbiàn	隨便	随便	do as one pleases; casual(ly)	2r
suíshí	隨時	随时	at any time	16r
suí yì	隨意	随意	as one pleases	18
suízhe	隨着	随着	along with	21
suìhán-sānyǒu	歲寒三友	岁寒三友	the three companions of winter	19r
sūnnǚ	孫女	孙女	son's daughter; granddaughter	20r
sūnzi	孫子	孙子	grandson	14
suǒ	所	所	place; "agency"	5
suǒ	所	所	(see grammar notes)	18
suǒwèi	所謂	所谓	what is called; so-called	20
suǒyǐn	索引	索引	index	2

T

tā	它	它	it	1
tā	牠	它	it (used when the antecedent is an animal)	11r
tái	抬	抬	lift up; (of two or more persons) carry	11r
tàidu	態度	态度	attitude	10
tāntú	貪圖	贪图	covet; hanker after	19r
tàn	探	探	stretch forward; stick out	22
tāng	湯	汤	soup	4r
Tāngmu	湯姆	汤姆	name of a person: Tom	1r
tāngyuán	湯圓	汤圆	sweet dumplings made of glutinous rice flour	11
táng	堂	堂	relatives born of the same grandfather; hall	20r
tánggē tángdì	堂哥、堂弟	堂哥、堂弟	male cousins from father's brother	20r
táng jiě tángmèi	堂姐、堂妹	堂姐、堂妹	female cousins from father's brother	20r
Táng cháo	唐朝	唐朝	the Tang dynasty	4
Tángrén jiē	唐人街	唐人街	Chinatown	4
tángguǒ	糖果	糖果	candy	8r
táozuì	陶醉	陶醉	be intoxicated with	18r
tǎoyàn	討厭	讨厌	loathe; be sick of	6
tào	套	套	a suit of; a series of	9r
tèbié	特別	特别	especially	1
tèdìng	特定	特定	special	21r
tèshū	特殊	特殊	special; unusual	8
téng'ài	疼愛	疼爱	be very fond of; love dearly	14
tíchū	提出	提出	put forward; advance	9r
tígāo	提高	提高	raise; heighten	9
tíxǐng	提醒	提醒	remind	20
tǐyù	體育	体育	physical education	7
tì	剃	剃	shave	13r
tì	替	替	take the place of	13
tìdài	替代	替代	substitute for; replace	9r
tiān hàn	天旱	天旱	drought	11r
Tiān jīn	天津	天津	name of a city in China	15r
tiānrán	天然	天然	natural	22
tiāntáng	天堂	天堂	heaven	16
tián	田	田	field	2r
tiáo	條	条	measure word for rivers	3r
tiào wǔ	跳舞	跳舞	dancing	14
tiē	貼	贴	paste	11
tīng huà	聽話	听话	obedient	8r
tīng shuō	聽說	听说	hear (of); be told (of)	1r
tíngzhù	停住	停住	stop; anchor	6
tōngcháng	通常	通常	generally; often	14
tōngguò	通過	通过	by way of; by means of	18

tōngyòng	通用	通用	commonly used	9r
tōngyòng	通用	通用	use interchangeably	10r
tóng	銅	铜	bronze	11r
tóngqíng	同情	同情	sympathize with	17r
tóngyàng	同樣	同样	same	1
tóngyì	同意	同意	agree	1r
tóngyīnzì	同音字	同音字	homonym; homophone	6
tǒngjì	統計	统计	statistics	12r
tǒngyī	統一	统一	unify	3
tòngkǔ	痛苦	痛苦	suffering; agony	13r
tōutīng	偷聽	偷听	eavesdrop	12
tōutōu de	偷偷地	偷偷地	by stealth; secretly	12
tóu	投	投	throw	15
tóudǐng	頭頂	头顶	the top of head	13r
tòushì	透視	透视	X-ray	16r
tú	徒	徒	companion; friend	20
tuánjù	團聚	团聚	reunite	18r
tuántuán-yuányuán	團團圓圓	团团圆圆	a reunion of the whole family	11
tuīguǎng	推廣	推广	extend; spread	8
tuījiàn	推薦	推荐	recommend	10
tuīlái tuīqù	推來推去	推来推去	push responsibility onto others	14
tuīxíng	推行	推行	carry out; pursue	8
tuǐ	腿	腿	leg	5r
tuìxiū	退休	退休	retire	14r

W

wā	挖	挖	dig	3r
wáwa	娃娃	娃娃	baby; child (colloquial)	8
wāi	歪	歪	askew	2r
wǎi	崴	崴	sprain	16r
wàigōng	外公	外公	mother's father; grandfather	20r
wàikē	外科	外科	surgical department	16r
wàipó	外婆	外婆	mother's mother; grandmother	20r
wàirén	外人	外人	outsider; stranger	20r
wàisheng	外甥	外甥	sister's son; nephew	20r
wàishēngnǚ	外甥女	外甥女	sister's daughter; niece	20r
wàisūn	外孫	外孙	daughter's son; grandson	20r
wàisūnnǚ	外孫女	外孙女	daughter's daughter; granddaughter	20r
wàiyòng	外用	外用	external use	16r
wàiyù	外遇	外遇	adulterer; paramour	19
wàizǔfù	外祖父	外祖父	mother's father; grandfather	20r
wàizǔmǔ	外祖母	外祖母	mother's mother; grandmother	20r
wān'gōu	彎鉤	弯勾	turn-hook	2r
wānqū	彎曲	弯曲	bend; curve	17r
wánjù	玩具	玩具	toy	8r
wánquán	完全	完全	entirely; totally	1r

wǎn	碗	碗	bowl	4r
wǎnlián	輓聯	挽联	elegiac couplet	19
wǎnnián	晚年	晚年	old age	14
wàn	萬	万	ten thousand	1
wànbān	萬般	万般	all the different kinds	7r
wànbān jiē xiàpǐn, wéiyǒu dú shū gāo	萬般皆下品，唯有讀書高	万般皆下品，唯有读书高	to be a scholar is to be at the top of society	7r
Wángmǔniángniang	王母娘娘	王母娘娘	Queen of Heaven	12
Wáng Wéi	王維	王维	name of a poet	18r
wǎng	往	往	toward	12
wǎngwǎng	往往	往往	often; frequently	18
wàngzǐchénglóng	望子成龍	望子成龙	hope one's child will have a bright future; have great ambitions for one's child	8r
wēixiǎn	危險	危险	dangerous	16r
wēiyī	偎依	偎依	snuggle up to; lean close to	17r
wéiyī	唯一	唯一	only; unique	22r
wéiyǒu	唯有	唯有	only	7r
wěi	偉	伟	great	6r
wěiqu	委屈	委屈	(suffer) injustice; be wronged	20
wèidào	味道	味道	taste; flavor	15r
Wèiyāng Gōng	未央宮	未央宫	Weiyang Palace	22r
wèizhi	位置	位置	place; position	2r
wénjiàn	文件	文件	document	9
wénmíng	文明	文明	civilization	20
wénzhāng	文章	文章	essay	1
wénmíng	聞名	闻名	well-known	16
wěn	穩	稳	steady	13r
wèntí	問題	问题	problem	8
wūní	污泥	污泥	dirt	19r
Wū Shān	巫山	巫山	Mt. Wu	22
Wū Xiá	巫峽	巫峡	the Wu Gorge	22
wūyā	烏鴉	乌鸦	crow	6
wú	無	无	do not have; without	14
wúbǐ	無比	无比	unparalleled	22
wúfēi	無非	无非	nothing but; no more than	21
wúlùn	無論	无论	no matter what	6
wúqióng	無窮	无穷	infinite	14r
wúqióng jìn	無窮盡	无穷尽	endless; inexhaustible	17
wǔgōng	武功	武功	martial arts	11r
Wǔ Zétiān	武則天	武则天	name of an empress	13
wǔ lóng	舞龍	舞龙	dragon dance (a team of men dancing with a cloth dragon at Chinese festivals)	11r
wǔ shīzi	舞獅子	舞狮子	lion dance (a two-man team dancing inside a cloth lion at Chinese festivals)	11r

wǔtīng	舞廳	舞厅	ballroom	14r
wù	物	物	thing; object	18r
wùpǐn	物品	物品	products; goods	3r
wùtǐ	物體	物体	object	2
wùzhì	物質	物质	material goods, etc.	20
wù jiě	誤解	误解	misunderstand	10

X

Xī'ān	西安	西安	name of a city in China	3r
xīfāng	西方	西方	Western	1r
Xīlíng Xiá	西陵峽	西陵峡	the Xiling Gorge	22
xīfàn	稀飯	稀饭	rice porridge; gruel	15r
xīwàng	希望	希望	wish; hope	6r
xífu	媳婦	媳妇	wife	5
xísú	習俗	习俗	custom	8r
xǐhuān	喜歡	喜欢	like	1r
xǐlián	喜聯	喜联	wedding couplet	19
xǐqìng	喜慶	喜庆	auspicious or happy occasions (such as weddings, births, promotions, etc.)	19
xǐquè	喜鵲	喜鹊	magpie	6
xì	細	细	thin	6r
xìlián	繫聯	系联	relate to	20r
xiágǔ	峽谷	峡谷	gorge	22
xià bān	下班	下班	come or go off work	13
xià hǎi	下海	下海	plunge into the (business) sea	7r
xiàpǐn	下品	下品	low-grade	7r
xià qí	下棋	下棋	play chess	14
xiān	鍁	锨	shovel	3r
xiānhè	仙鶴	仙鹤	red-crowned crane	19r
xiānhuā	鮮花	鲜花	fresh flowers	5r
xián	鹹	咸	salted	15
xiàn	餡	馅	stuffing; filling	15
xiànshí	現實	现实	real; actual	17
xiànxiàng	現象	现象	phenomenon	9
xiāng'ài	相愛	相爱	love each other	12
xiāngchǔ	相處	相处	get along with (each other)	20
xiāngdāng	相當	相当	quite	22
xiānggé	相隔	相隔	be at a distance of; be apart	18r
xiānghuì	相會	相会	meet each other	12
xiāng jìn	相近	相近	close; near	6
xiāng jù	相聚	相聚	get together	12
xiāngqīn-xiāng'ài	相親相愛	相亲相爱	love each other	12r
xiāngsī	相思	相思	yearning for each other (of lovers)	17r
xiāngsībìng	相思病	相思病	lovesickness	17r
xiāngxìn	相信	相信	believe	4r

xiāngyīwéibàn	相依為伴	相依为伴	stick together and help each other in difficulties	19r
xiāngpēnpēn	香噴噴	香喷喷	deliciously scented; appetizing	15
xiāngxià	鄉下	乡下	countryside	13
xiǎngshēng	響聲	响声	sound; noise	11
xiǎngshòu	享受	享受	enjoyment; pleasure	15r
xiǎngxiàng	想像	想象	imagine	17
xiàng	項	项	measure word for policies	8
xiàng	像	像	be like	2
xiàng	向	向	toward	18
xiànglái	向來	向来	always; all along	19
xiàngmào	相貌	相貌	appearance	10r
xiàngpiān	相片	相片	picture; photograph	10r
xiàngqí	象棋	象棋	(Chinese) chess	14r
xiàngzhēng	象徵	象征	symbol	11r
xiāomó	消磨	消磨	while away	14r
xiāo zāi	消災	消灾	prevent calamities	11
xiǎohuǒzi	小伙子	小伙子	young man	5r
xiǎozhuàn	小篆	小篆	an ancient style of calligraphy adopted in the Qin dynasty (221–206 B.C.)	22r
xiàohuà	笑話	笑话	ridicule; laugh at	13r
xiàohuà	笑話	笑话	joke	19
xiàoshùn	孝順	孝顺	show filial obedience	14
xīnláng	新郎	新郎	bridegroom	5
xīnniáng	新娘	新娘	bride	5
xīnshǎng	欣賞	欣赏	enjoy; admire	16
xìnxī	信息	信息	message; news	19
xìnxīn	信心	信心	confidence	17
xìnyǎng	信仰	信仰	believe in	21
xīng	興	兴	become popular	19
xíngchéng	形成	形成	form; take shape	18
xíngpáng	形旁	形旁	semantic element of a character	2
xíngróng	形容	形容	describe	10r
xíngxiàng	形象	形象	image	10r
xíngzhuàng	形狀	形状	form; shape	2
xíngdòng	行動	行动	movement; action	14
xíngzǒu	行走	行走	run; move	18
xìng	杏	杏	apricot	2r
xìngfú	幸福	幸福	happy	5
xìnggé	性格	性格	temperament	19r
xìngqù	興趣	兴趣	interest	7
xiōngdì jiěmèi	兄弟姐妹	兄弟姐妹	brothers and sisters	20r
xiōng'è	兇惡	凶恶	ferocious	11r
xióng	雄	雄	male	12r
xióngwěi	雄偉	雄伟	majestic	22r

xiū jiàn	修建	修建	construct; build	3
xiù	繡	绣	embroider	12r
xiùlì	秀麗	秀丽	delicate; graceful	16
xiùtào	袖套	袖套	armband	19
xūyào	需要	需要	be in need of	14
xǔ yuàn	許願	许愿	make a vow to a god	21r
xùshù	敘述	叙述	narrate	18r
xuānchuán	宣傳	宣传	publicity; public information; propaganda	8
Xuánkōng Sì	懸空寺	悬空寺	Hanging Temple	21
xuányá-qiàobì	懸崖峭壁	悬崖峭壁	sheer precipice and overhanging rocks	21
xuǎndìng	選定	选定	decide	7
xuànyào	炫耀	炫耀	show off	11r
xuéfèi	學費	学费	tuition	7
xuékē	學科	学科	branch of learning	15r
xuézhě	學者	学者	scholar	9
xuèyè	血液	血液	blood	16r
xuèyuán	血緣	血缘	blood relationship	20r

Y

yāshèngqián	壓勝錢	压胜钱	money to bring luck and ward off evil	11
yāsuìqián	壓歲錢	压岁钱	money given to children as New Year's gift	11
yá	芽	芽	sprout; bud	18r
yānmò	淹沒	淹没	submerge; flood	22
yānsǐ	淹死	淹死	drown	11r
yán	嚴	严	strict	8r
yán	妍	妍	beautiful	9r
yán	鹽	盐	salt	15r
yán'àn	沿岸	沿岸	along the bank	22
yáncháng	延長	延长	extend; lengthen	2r
yánxù	延續	延续	continue; go on	20
Yándì Huángdì	炎帝黃帝	炎帝黄帝	Emperor Yan and Yellow Emperor	4
yán jiūsuǒ	研究所	研究所	graduate school	7r
yán rú yù	顏如玉	颜如玉	a face as beautiful as jade—a beautiful woman	7r
yánsè	顏色	颜色	color	19
yǎnbiàn	演變	演变	evolve	18
yǎnbō	眼波	眼波	(of a woman's eyes) a fluid glance	18
yǎn jīng	眼睛	眼睛	eye	16r
yǎnkàn	眼看	眼看	soon; in a moment	12
yǎnlèi	眼淚	眼泪	tears	2
yàn	燕	燕	swallow	1r
yāngge	秧歌	秧歌	name of a type of popular rural folk dance	14r

yánglì	陽曆	阳历	the Gregorian calendar	11
yángròu pàomó	羊肉泡饃	羊肉泡馍	pancakes cooked in lamb soup	15r
yǎng	癢	痒	itch; tickle	16r
yǎng ér fáng lǎo	養兒防老	养儿防老	raise sons to provide against (for) old age	8
yǎnglǎoyuàn	養老院	养老院	home for the elderly	14
yǎngwàng	仰望	仰望	look up	22
yāo	夭	夭	die young	2r
yāoqiú	要求	要求	require; request	7
yáo tóu	搖頭	摇头	shake one's head	1r
yǎo	舀	舀	dip; ladle; scoop	4r
yàoburán	要不然	要不然	otherwise	19
yàofāng	藥方	药方	prescription	16r
yàofáng	藥房	药房	pharmacy	16r
yàopíng	藥瓶	药瓶	drug bottle	16r
yě	也	也	(here) classical Chinese word	10
yěhuā	野花	野花	wild flower	22
yèshì	夜市	夜市	night fair; night market	16
yèyá	葉芽	叶芽	a tender leaf	19
yībān	一般	一般	usually; commonly	1
yībèizi	一輩子	一辈子	all one's life	6r
yīchénbùrǎn	一塵不染	一尘不染	not soiled by even a speck of dust	19r
yīdàzǎo	一大早	一大早	early morning	14r
yīdài	一帶	一带	area	4
yīdiǎnr dōu (bū/méiyǒu)	一點兒都 (不/沒有)	一点儿都 (不/没有)	not ... at all	6
yī duì	一對	一对	pair	12
yīgān-èr jìng	一乾二淨	一干二净	thorough(ly); complete(ly)	18
yī jiàn zhōngqíng	一見鍾情	一见钟情	fall in love at first sight	5r
yī ... jiù	一……就	一……就	as soon as...; once	10
yīshí	一時	一时	temporarily; momentarily	8r
yī zì duō yì	一字多義	一字多义	one character with two or more different meanings	10
yīkào	依靠	依靠	rely on; depend on	7
yīrán	依然	依然	still; as before	19r
yí	疑	疑	doubt	18r
Yíhé Yuán	頤和園	颐和园	the Summer Palace	16
yí jì	遺蹟	遗迹	relic	22r
yíshū	遺書	遗书	a letter or note left by someone immediately before death	17r
yízhǐ	遺址	遗址	ruins; relics	16
yíyi	姨姨	姨姨	mother's sister	20r
yǐ jí	以及	以及	as well as; along with	9
yǐwéi	以為	以为	think; consider	4
yǐzhì	以至	以至	as a result; so ... that ...	10
yì	億	亿	a hundred million	6r

yìshù	藝術	艺术	art	15r
yìtǐzì	異體字	异体字	a variant form of a Chinese character	9
yīn	陰	阴	cloudy	18r
yīnguǒ bàoyìng	因果報應	因果报应	as a man sows, so let him reap; retributive justice	21
yīnwèi ... (suǒyǐ)	因為……(所以)	因为……(所以)	because ... (therefore)	1
Yínhé	銀河	银河	the Milky Way	12
Yìndù	印度	印度	India	21
yìnshuāshù	印刷術	印刷术	printing; typography	20
yīng	鶯	莺	warbler; oriole	6r
yīnggāi	應該	应该	should; ought to	8r
yīngjùn	英俊	英俊	handsome	5r
yíngyǎng	營養	营养	nourishment	15r
yǐngxiǎng	影響	影响	influence; affect	19r
yǒnggǎn	勇敢	勇敢	brave	17
yǒngyuǎn	永遠	永远	forever	12r
yònggōng	用功	用功	diligent	7
yòngxīn	用心	用心	do sth. diligently and attentively	6r
yōuměi	優美	优美	graceful; exquisite	18r
yóu	由	由	from; by	2
yóuyú ... yīncǐ	由於……因此	由于……因此	because, due to ..., therefore	6
yóu	油	油	oil	15r
yóutiáo	油條	油条	deep-fried dough sticks	15r
yóuqí	尤其	尤其	especially	8
yóurénrúcháo	遊人如潮	游人如潮	many visitors like a tide	16
yóuwán	遊玩	游玩	go sight-seeing	15
yǒu chūxī	有出息	有出息	successful	6r
yǒumíng	有名	有名	famous; well-known	3
yǒuqíngrén zhōngchéng juànshǔ	有情人終成眷屬	有情人终成眷属	lovers will finally get married	17r
yú	于	于	classical Chinese particle	2r
yú	於	于	from; in	12
yúshì	於是	于是	and then; hence	4
Yú	虞	虞	dynasty founded by Shun	10
Yúgōng-yíshān	愚公移山	愚公移山	the Foolish Old Man removed the mountains	17
yúkuài	愉快	愉快	happy	10
yúlè	娛樂	娱乐	amusement; entertainment	11r
yúlín	魚鱗	鱼鳞	scale	11r
yǔ	與	与	with	20
yǔ cǐ tóngshí	與此同時	与此同时	at the same time	20
yǔqí ... bùrú	與其……不如	与其……不如	rather ... than ...	21
yù	玉	玉	jade	6r
yùdào	遇到	遇到	encounter	18r

yùyán	寓言	寓言	allegory; fable	18
yuānyāng	鴛鴦	鸳鸯	mandarin duck	12r
yuándàn	元旦	元旦	New Year's day	11
yuángù	緣故	缘故	cause; reason	13
yuánliàng	原諒	原谅	excuse; forgive	20
yuánmǎn	圓滿	圆满	satisfactory; complete	15
yuánrén	猿人	猿人	ape-man	22r
yuánshǐ bùluò	原始部落	原始部落	primitive tribe	4
yuánxiān	原先	原先	originally	15
yuánxiāo	元宵	元宵	sweet dumplings made of glutinous rice flour	15
yuǎngǔ	遠古	远古	remote antiquity	22r
yuàn	願	愿	wish	17r
yuànhèn	怨恨	怨恨	resent; hate	5r
yuèbǐng	月餅	月饼	moon cake	15
yuèguāng	月光	月光	moonlight	18r
yuèláiyuè	越來越	越来越	the more ..., the more ...	5
yuèqì	樂器	乐器	musical instrument	6r
yuèqǔ	樂曲	乐曲	music	10
yúnwù	雲霧	云雾	cloud and mist	22
yùn	運	运	transport	3r
yùndòng	運動	运动	exercise; sports	14r
yùnqi	運氣	运气	fate; fortune	21r
yùnshū	運輸	运输	transportation	3r

Z

zā	紮	扎	bind	12r
zázhì	雜誌	杂志	magazine	9
zāihuò	災禍	灾祸	disaster	21r
zāinàn	災難	灾难	calamity	11r
zài ... yě	再……也	再……也	even if; even though	13
zānzi	簪子	簪子	hair clasp	12
zànměi	讚美	赞美	praise; eulogize	18r
zàochéng	造成	造成	create	5
zé	則	则	then	15
zēnggāo	增高	增高	heighten; raise	17
zěnmebàn	怎麼辦	怎么办	What's to be done? What can one do?	1r
zhā shǒu	扎手	扎手	prick the hand	10r
zhá	炸	炸	deep fry	15r
zhǎi	窄	窄	narrow	22
zhǎnxiàn	展現	展现	unfold before one's eyes	22
Zhànguó shíqī	戰國時期	战国时期	Warring States period	3
zhànhuǒ	戰火	战火	flames of war	22r
zhàn piányi	佔便宜	占便宜	profit at other people's expense	20
zhǎngguǎn	掌管	掌管	control; take charge of	11r
zhàngfu	丈夫	丈夫	husband	3

zhào xiàng	照相	照相	take a picture	10r
Zhào Xiǎoyàn	趙小燕	赵小燕	name of a person	1r
zhàozhe	照着	照着	according to	2
zhéduàn	折斷	折断	break	13r
zhě	者	者	(see grammar notes)	19
zhème	這麼	这么	such; so	12
zhèyàng yī lái	這樣一來	这样一来	in this case	8
zhēn	真	真	real; genuine	11
zhēnqí	珍奇	珍奇	rare and valuable	22
zhēnxiàn	針線	针线	needle and thread	8r
zhěntóu	枕頭	枕头	pillow	4r
zhēng	蒸	蒸	steam	15r
zhěnglǐ	整理	整理	put in order; sort out	9
zhěngtiān	整天	整天	all day	7r
zhèng (qián)	掙(錢)	挣(钱)	earn (money)	7r
Zhèng Bǎnqiáo	鄭板橋	郑板桥	name of a person	20
zhèngcè	政策	政策	policy	8
zhèngshì	正式	正式	formal; official	4
zhèngtǐzì	正體字	正体字	standardized form of Chinese characters	9
zhèngzhí	正直	正直	honest	19r
zhī bù	織布	织布	weave	12
zhīchí	支持	支持	support	19r
zhīma	芝麻	芝麻	sesame	15
zhī qián	之前	之前	before	16
zhīsuǒyǐ	之所以	之所以	the reason why	19
zhīxīn péngyǒu	知心朋友	知心朋友	intimate friends	19r
zhīzhū	蜘蛛	蜘蛛	spider	6
zhí	直	直	straight	19r
zhí jiē	直接	直接	directly	16r
zhíyīnfǎ	直音法	直音法	a method of representing the pronunciation of Chinese characters	9r
zhínǚ	侄女	侄女	brother's daughter; niece	20r
zhízi	侄子	侄子	brother's son; nephew	20r
zhǐ	指	指	refer to; mean	11
zhǐnánzhēn	指南針	指南针	compass	20
zhǐzé	指責	指责	criticize; censure	8
zhǐhǎo	只好	只好	have to	7
zhǐyào ... jiù	只要……就	只要……就	if only; as long as	3
zhǐyǒu ... cái	只有……才	只有……才	only when; not until	5
zhǐzhāng	紙張	纸张	paper	9
zhì	至	至	extremely	20
zhìyú	至於	至于	as to; as for	5
zhìcái	制裁	制裁	play sanctions on; punish	8
zhìdù	制度	制度	system	7r
zhìzuò	製作	制作	manufacture	4r

zhìlǐ	治理	治理	administer; manage	15
Zhìsǒu	智叟	智叟	the Wise Old Man	17
zhōng	終	终	in the end; eventually; finally	17r
Zhōnghuá Mínguó	中華民國	中华民国	the Republic of China	4
zhōng-xiàyóu	中下游	中下游	middle and lower reaches (of a river)	4
zhōngxīn	中心	中心	center	4
zhōngrǔshí	鐘乳石	钟乳石	stalactite	16
zhǒng	種	种	kind	1
zhòng dì	種地	种地	cultivate land	7r
zhòngnán-qīngnǚ	重男輕女	重男轻女	favor the male and regard the female as less important	13
Zhōu	周	周	the Zhou dynasty (1122–221 B.C.)	16
zhōusuì	周歲	周岁	one full year (of age)	8r
zhúyè	竹葉	竹叶	bamboo leaves	15
zhúzi	竹子	竹子	bamboo	19r
zhǔ	主	主	preside over	13
zhǔ	煮	煮	boil	15r
zhùmíng	注明	注明	make a footnote; annotate	9r
zhùyì	注意	注意	pay attention to	1
zhùyìlì	注意力	注意力	attention	14r
Zhùyīn fúhào	注音符號	注音符号	the National Phonetic Script (for Mandarin)	9r
Zhù Yīngtái	祝英台	祝英台	name of a person	13
zhùyuàn	祝願	祝愿	wish (someone something)	12r
zhuā	抓	抓	grab; seize; catch	2
zhuā zhōu	抓周	抓周	a traditional custom in China	8r
zhuǎ	爪	爪	claw	11r
zhuān	磚	砖	brick	3r
zhuānmén	專門	专门	specialize in; specially	5
zhuānyè	專業	专业	major; concentration	7
zhuānyòngyǔ	專用語	专用语	special-purpose word	17r
zhuàn qián	賺錢	赚钱	make money	6
zhuāng	裝	装	pretend	20
zhuāngbàn	裝扮	装扮	disguise; masquerade	13
zhuāngjia	莊稼	庄稼	crops	11r
zhuàngdà	壯大	壮大	grow in strength	22r
zhuī	追	追	chase	12
zhǔn	準	准	accurate	21r
zǐsūn	子孫	子孙	descendants	4
zǐxì	仔細	仔细	careful	5r
zì	自	自	from	18
zìcóng	自從	自从	since	9
zìfèi	自費	自费	at one's own expense	7
zìshā	自殺	自杀	commit suicide	15
zìyǒu	自有	自有	naturally have	7r

zì	字	字	calligraphy; writing	20
zìhuà	字畫	字画	calligraphy; painting	20
zìmǔ	字母	字母	letters of an alphabet	1
zìyīn	字音	字音	pronunciation of a character	1
zōngjiào	宗教	宗教	religion	21
zǒngshì	總是	总是	always	12r
zòngzi	粽子	粽子	a pyramid-shaped dumpling made of glutinous rice wrapped in bamboo or reed leaves	15
zǒu hòumén	走後門	走后门	secure advantages through pull or influence (lit.,"go through the back door")	20
zǒumǎ-guānhuā	走馬觀花	走马观花	look at flowers while riding on horseback—gain a superficial understanding through cursory observation	5r
zúgòu	足夠	足够	enough	10
zǔchéng	組成	组成	form; be made of	2
zǔhé	組合	组合	constitute; make up	10r
zǔdǎng	阻擋	阻挡	stop; block	3
zǔlán	阻攔	阻拦	block the way; stop	17r
zǔfù	祖父	祖父	father's father; grandfather	20r
zǔmǔ	祖母	祖母	father's mother; grandmother	20r
zǔxiān	祖先	祖先	ancestors	4
zuò bì	作弊	作弊	practice fraud	10r
zuò huà	作畫	作画	paint	10r
zuò jiǎ	作假	作假	falsify; counterfeit	10r
zuòpǐn	作品	作品	works (of literature and art)	10r
zuò qǔ	作曲	作曲	compose music	10r
zuòwéi	作為	作为	(be) used as; (be) regarded as	2
zuòyòng	作用	作用	function	3r
zuòzhě	作者	作者	author; writer	10r
zuò zhèng	作證	作证	bear witness	10r
zuò cāo	做操	做操	doing calisthenics	14r
zuòfǎ	做法	做法	way of doing or making a thing; method of work	8
zuò gōng	做工	做工	do manual work	7r
zuò guān	做官	做官	to be an official	7r
zuò kè	做客	做客	be a guest	10r
zuò lǐbài	做禮拜	做礼拜	go to church	10r
zuò mǎimài	做買賣	做买卖	do business	7r
zuò méi	做媒	做媒	be a matchmaker	5
zuò mèng	做夢	做梦	have a dream	10r
zuò shī	做詩	做诗	write a poem	10r
zuò shēngyi	做生意	做生意	do business	6
zuò xuéwen	做學問	做学问	do research	7r
zuò láo	坐牢	坐牢	go to jail	14

語法和詞語註釋索引
Grammar and Terms Index

(號碼表示課號)

A

A gēn B yǒu guānxì	A跟B有關係	A跟B有关系	A is related to B; A has something to do with B	2
Adj qǐlái	Adj起來	Adj起来		14
ànzhào	按照	按照	according to	19

B

bǎ ... V zài ... shàng	把……V在……上	把……V在……上	V ... on	14
bǎifēnzhī X	百分之X	百分之X	X percent	2
bāngmáng/bāngzhù	幫忙/幫助	帮忙/帮助	help	5
bǐ	比	比	compared with; than	9
biàn	便	便	then	10
bìng(bù/méiyǒu)	並(不/沒有)	并(不/没有)	actually (not); (not) at all	21
bìngqiě	並且	并且	and; moreover; furthermore	3
bùdàn ... érqiě/yě/hái	不但……而且/也/還	不但……而且/也/还	not only ... but also	1
bùfáng	不妨	不妨	may (as well); might (as well); no harm in V-ing	16
bùguò	不過	不过	but; however	6
bùguò ... bàle	不過……罷了	不过……罢了	only; just	10
bùguǎn ... dōu	不管……都	不管……都	no matter what/how/who	3
bù jǐn ... érqiě/yě/hái	不僅……而且/也/還	不仅……而且/也/还	not only ..., but also	11
bùrú	不如	不如	not as good as	17
bùshì ... jiùshì	不是……就是	不是……就是	either ... or; if not A ... then B ...	7
bùyàoshuō ..., jiùshì ... yě	不要說……就是……也	不要说……就是……也	even if ... still, not to mention	16
bùzài ... le	不再……了	不再……了	not any more; no longer	14

C

cái	才	才	(not) until	4
cái	才	才	intensifier	17
chàbuduō	差不多	差不多	almost	1
chàbùduō/jīhū	差不多/幾乎	差不多/几乎	almost	12
chèn	趁	趁	while	12
chúfēi ... cái	除非……才	除非……才	only if	21
chúle...yǐwài	除了……以外	除了……以外	besides; apart from	7
xíngróngcí chóngdié	形容詞重疊	形容词重叠	adjective reduplication	11
cóng	從	从	from	1

cónglái/yīzhí	從來/一直	从来/一直	always	13
cóngqián/yǐqián	從前/以前	从前/以前	before; previously	9

D

dàdōu/dàduōshù	大都/大多數	大都/大多数	most of; mostly	7
dàzhì	大致	大致	generally; roughly; approximately	18
dānyīn jié xíngróngcí	單音節形容詞	单音节形容词	single syllable adjectives	15
dāng ... shíhou	當……時候	当……时候	when	3
dàodǐ/ jiūjìng	到底/究竟	到底/究竟	exactly; after all	9
de V yě V bù Adj	得 V 也 V 不 Adj	得 V 也 V 不 Adj	degree complement	16
dòngcí chóngdié	動詞重疊	动词重迭	verb reduplication	14
duìyú/duì	對於/對	对于/对	for; to; with regard to	8

E

ér	而	而	but	11

F

fánshì	凡是	凡是	every; all; any	13
fǎn'ér	反而	反而	on the contrary; instead	13
fǎnzhèng	反正	反正	anyway; anyhow	13
fāng	__方	__方	__side	5
fēi ... bùkě/ bùchéng/bùxíng	非……不可/不成/不行	非……不可/不成/不行	insist on; must; have to	8
fǒuzé	否則	否则	otherwise	21

G

gǎi V	改 V	改 V	change; instead of	4
gēnběn	根本	根本	at all; simply	10
gēn jù	根據	根据	according to	11
guānyú	關於	关于	regarding; about	18

H

háishì	還是	还是	still	2
húlihútu	糊裏糊塗	糊里糊涂	in disorderly fashion; act stupidly	20
huà	化	化	-ize; -ify	19
huòzhě	或者	或者	or	6

J

jíshǐ ... yě/háishì	即使……也/還是	即使……也/还是	even if	7
jìrán ..., jiù	既然……，就	既然……，就	since ..., (then) ...	19
jì ... yòu	既……又	既……又	both ... and; as well as	6
jiāng	將	将	will	22
jiéguǒ	結果	结果	as a result; in the end; finally	10
jǐnguǎn ... háishì	儘管……還是	尽管……还是	although; despite	15

jǐnliàng/ jǐn kěnéng	盡量/盡可能	尽量/尽可能	to the best of one's ability	20
jùshuō/tīngshuō	據説/聽説	据说/听说	it is said	11

K

kān	看	看	look after; take care of	13
kěxī	可惜	可惜	it's a pity; it is too bad	22
kuàngqiě	況且	况且	besides; in addition	22

L

lǎoshì	老是	老是	always	6
lián qǐlái	連起來	连起来	connect; link (together)	3
lián ... dōu/yě/hái	連……都/也/還	连……都/也/还	even	4
liàngcí chóngdié	量詞重疊	量词重叠	measure word reduplication	14

M

měidāng	每當	每当	when; whenever; every time	11
míngmíng	明明	明明	it is obvious that	17
mǒu	某	某	some (unspecified); (a) certain	9

N

nǎlǐhái ... ne?	哪裏還……呢?	哪里还……呢?	how could it be ...?	8
nándé	難得	难得	seldom; rarely	20
nánguài	難怪	难怪	no wonder	22
nìngkě ... yě	寧可……也	宁可……也	would rather; had better	17
nòng/gǎo	弄/搞	弄/搞	do; make	10

P

píng	憑	凭	depend on; lean on	17

Q

qíshí	其實	其实	in fact; actually	1
qiānwàn	千萬	千万	must; be sure to	20
qiàqiǎo	恰巧	恰巧	by chance; happen to	7
qīn	親	亲	with one's own	21
què	卻	却	but	7

R

ràng	讓	让	let; make	5
réngrán	仍然	仍然	still	20
rènwéi/yǐwéi	認為/以為	认为/以为	think; consider	4
rúcǐ	如此	如此	such; like that	22
rúguǒ/yàoshì ... nàme	如果/要是……那麼	如果/要是……那么	if ... then	2
ruògān	若干	若干	some; several	22

S

(shí jiān) lái	(時間) 來	(时间) 来	time indication	5
shǐde	使得	使得	make; cause; render	16
shǐzhōng	始終	始终	from beginning to end	21
shòu (dào)	受 (到)	受 (到)	get; receive	9
shéi, nǎr, shěnme, jǐ	誰、哪兒、甚麼、幾	谁、哪儿、什么、几	who, where, what, when	14
suīrán ... dànshì/ kěshì	雖然……但是/可是	虽然……但是/可是	although ... (but)	1
suízhe	隨着	随着	along with	21
suǒ	所	所	that; which; what	18
suǒwèi	所謂	所谓	what is called; so-called	20

T

tōngguò	通過	通过	by way of; by means of	18
tóu	頭	头	first	11

V

V bùqǐ, V déqǐ	V 不起, V 得起	V 不起, V 得起	cannot V, can V	12
V hǎo	V 好	V 好	verb complement	15
V lái V qù	V 來 V 去	V 来 V 去	an action occurring repeatedly	14
V xiàlái/xiàqù	V 下來/下去	V 下来/下去	directional complement	15
V yú	V 於	V 于	from; in	12

W

wǎng	往	往	toward	12
wǎngwǎng	往往	往往	often; frequently	18
wèile	為了	为了	for the purpose of; in order to	3
wúfēi	無非	无非	nothing but; no more than	21
wúlùn ... háishì ... dōu	無論……還是……都	无论……还是……都	no matter how/ whether, etc.	6

X

xiāng V	相 V	相 V	V each other	12
xiāngdāng	相當	相当	quite	22
xiàng	向	向	toward	18
xiànglái	向來	向来	always (up to the present)	19

Y

yánzhe	沿着	沿着	along	16
yǎnkàn	眼看	眼看	soon; in a moment	12
yàoburán	要不然	要不然	otherwise	19
yìdiǎnr dōu/yě (bù/méiyǒu)	一點兒都/也 (不/沒有)	一点儿都/也 (不/没有)	not ... at all; not at all ...	6
yī...jiù	一……就	一……就	once; as soon as	10

yǐběi, yǐnán	以北、以南	以北、以南	(to the) north of, (to the) south of	16
yǐjí	以及	以及	along with; as well as	9
yǐshàng, yǐxià	以上、以下	以上、以下	more than; above / less than; below	10
yǐzhì	以至	以至	so ... that ...; as a result	10
yīnwèi ... (suǒyǐ)	因為……(所以)	因为……(所以)	because ... (therefore)	1
yòng ... V	用V	用V	use/using/with ... V	1
yóuqí	尤其	尤其	especially; particularly	8
yóuyú ... yīncǐ/suǒyǐ	由於…… 因此/所以	由于…… 因此/所以	by reason of; therefore; as a result	6
yóuyú ... yuángù	由於……緣故	由于……缘故	due to; as a result of	13
yóu ... zǔchéng	由……組成	由……组成	be made of; consists of	2
yòu ... ne?	又……呢?	又……呢?	could it be ...?	8
yúshì	於是	于是	and then; hence	4
yǔ	與	与	with	20
yǔqí ... bùrú	與其……不如	与其……不如	rather ..., than	21
yuánlái/běnlái	原來/本來	原来/本来	originally; essentially	8
yuánxiān ... hòulái	原先……後來	原先……后来	formerly ... later; originally ... after	15
yuèláiyuè	越來越	越来越	the more ..., the more ...	5
yuè ... yuè	越……越	越……越	the more ..., the more ...	17

Z

zài ... yě	再……也	再……也	even if; even though	13
zé	則	则	then	15
zěnme/wèishénme	怎麼/為甚麼	怎么/为什么	why; how come	17
zhàozhe	照着	照着	according to; in accordance with	2
zhě	者	者	-er; -ist	19
zhème	這麼	这么	such; so	12
zhèyàng yīlái/ nàyàng yīlái	這樣一來/ 那樣一來	这样一来/ 那样一来	in this case; thus	8
zhīqián, zhīhòu, zhīzhōng	之前、之後、之中	之前、之后、之中	before, after, within	16
zhīsuǒyǐ ... shì yīnwèi	之所以…… 是因為	之所以…… 是因为	the reason why	19
zhǐ	指	指	refer to; be meant for	11
zhǐhǎo	只好	只好	have to	7
zhǐyào ... jiù	只要……就	只要……就	if only; as long as; provided that	3
zhǐyǒu ... cái	只有……才	只有……才	only when; not until	5
zhìyú	至於	至于	as to; as for	5
zhù/jūzhù	住/居住	住/居住	live; reside	4
zì	自	自	from	18
zìcóng	自從	自从	since	9
zuòwéi	作為	作为	be used as; be regarded as	2

主要參考書目
References

中國社會科學院語言研究所編：《現代漢語詞典》。北京：商務印書館，1985。

中國青年出版社編輯部編：《中國古代史常識》。北京：中國青年出版社，1981。

文史知識編輯部編：《古代禮制風俗漫談》。北京：中華書局，1986。

王自強：《現代漢語虛詞用法小詞典》。上海：上海辭書出版社，1984。

北京大學中文系1955、1957級語言班編：《現代漢語虛詞例釋》。北京：商務印書館，1982。

吳光華主編：《漢英大字典》。上海：上海交通大學出版社，1995。

呂叔湘主編：《漢語八百詞》。北京：商務印書館，1996。

李學英、舒彤編：《中國傳統圖案賞析》。石家莊：河北美術出版社，1992。

曹先擢、蘇培成主編：《漢字形音義分析字典》。北京：北京大學出版社，1999。

盛文瀾：《從語句結構談標點符號用法》。福州：福建教育出版社，1987。

符懷青：《現代漢語詞彙》。北京：北京大學出版社，1985。

陸谷孫主編：《英漢大詞典》。上海：上海譯文出版社，1993。

湖北大學語言研究室編：《成語大詞典》。鄭州：河南人民出版社，1985。

楊弘：《地下星空》。廣州：花城出版社，1981。

楊殿奎等編：《古代文化常識》。濟南：山東教育出版社，1984。

語文出版社編：《語言文字規範手冊》。北京：語文出版社，1991。

劉秋霖等編：《中華吉祥物大圖典》。北京：國際文化出版公司，1994。

駱新、姚莽：《衣冠滄桑》。北京：農村讀物出版社，1991。

韓廣澤、李岩齡：《中國古代詩歌與節日習俗》。天津：天津人民出版社，1992。